FORENSIC EVIDENCE: SCIENCE AND THE CRIMINAL LAW

Terrence F. Kiely

CRC Press
Boca Raton   London   New York   Washington, D.C.

Library of Congress Cataloging-in-Publication Data

Kiely, Terrence F.
   Forensic evidence : science and the criminal law / Terrence F. Kiely
      p. cm.
   Includes bibliographical references and index.
   ISBN 0-8493-1896-3 (alk. paper)
   1. Evidence, Expert--United States. 2. Forensic sciences--United States. I. Title.

KF8961 .K54 2000
345.73′067—dc21
                                             00-037856

If any Man be delighted in History, let him read the Books of Law, which are nothing else but Annals and Chronicles of Things done and acted upon from year to year, in which each Case presents you with a petit history; and if Variety of Matter doth most delight the reader, doubtless, the reading of those Cases, (which differ like Men's Faces), tho like the Stars in Number, is the most pleasant reading in the World.

—Giles Duncombe
Trials per Pais, or the Law of England Concerning Juries by Nisi Prius (1725)

. . .

For without Victory at the Trial, to what Purpose is the Science of the Law? The Judge can give no Sentence, no decision without it, and must give Judgement for that Side the Trial goes; therefore I may well say, tis the chief Part of the Practice of the Law. And if so, to whom shall I offer this Treatise, but to you the Practisers?

—Giles Duncombe
Trials per Pais, or the Law of England Concerning Juries by Nisi Prius (1725)

Preface

Forensic Evidence: Science and the Criminal Law is intended to serve as an introduction and guide to the appreciation and understanding of the significant historical,
contemporary, and future relationship between the world of the forensic sciences
and the criminal justice system. This book is not intended to be a close study of
forensic science, nor was it ever conceived as becoming one. It is devoted to a study
of the judicial response to uses of forensic science in the investigation, prosecution,
and defense of a crime. The audience to which this study is directed are those
intimately or potentially involved in that relationship: police, forensic scientists,
prosecutors, defense lawyers, and professors and students of the criminal law. It is
meant to stand on its own but also to complement the growing number of excellent
treatises and studies in the forensic sciences proper, many of which are published
in the CRC Press series in the area of forensic sciences.

The book focuses on those cases questioning the legal acceptability under a
Frye or *Daubert* standard of the methodological basis of the forensic science at
issue. However, equally, if not more importantly, the focus is on the discussions of
the numerous cases where the courts, assuming the acceptability of the underlying
methodology, have scrutinized and accepted or rejected a wide variety of *investigative uses* of the science under discussion, offered as proof of one or more material
facts in a criminal prosecution. This latter area of study is of equal, if not more
central, importance in understanding the place of forensic science in the criminal
justice system of the 21st century. It is time for another close look at both the body
of claims and the actual expert opinions supplied to the criminal justice system as
we enter the new century. The totally justified attention given rapid DNA developments should not overshadow the ongoing judicial acceptance and use of the more
traditional body of forensic sciences, such as hair, fiber, ballistics, and fingerprints,
some of which have never been fully challenged. The contributions of forensic
science to the criminal justice system have been, and remain, significant.

This book is divided into 12 chapters, most of which, with the exceptions of
Chapters 1, Science, Forensic Science, and Evidence, Chapter 2, Science and the
Criminal Law, and Chapter 12, Epilogue, address the legal profile of a specific
forensic science.

Chapter 1, Science, Forensic Science, and Evidence, briefly analyzes the historical and contemporary context in which legal arguments directed to the adequacy
of the findings of forensic science are conducted. This is a necessary precursor to
the more criminally focused discussion that constitutes the bulk of this book. The
framework of the *Frye* and *Daubert* standards for the introduction of scientific
opinion are discussed here, as well as the significant differences that exist when the
legal challenge comes in a civil law forum as opposed to a criminal one.

Chapter 2, Science and the Criminal Law, provides an overview of the entire subject of the uses of forensic sciences in the investigation, prosecution, and defense of criminal cases in U.S. courts. Central topics addressed are the historical and contemporary relationship between forensic science and proof of crime, the fundamentals of the application of forensic science disciplines to the investigation and prosecution of a criminal case, the function of probabilistic analysis to that process, and an extended discussion of the legal aspects of the modern crime scene.

Each of the next nine chapters discusses a specific forensic science discipline: Chapter 3, Hair Analysis, discusses the court's response to both class and individual expert opinions in respect to attempts to connect one or more hairs found at a crime scene to an individual suspect. This controversial subject sets the analytical framework for the discussions that follow on a wide range of forensic science applications. Chapter 4, Fiber Analysis, discusses the identification and use of a wide variety of fiber materials from crime scenes and the processes used to link such materials to a suspect. Chapter 5, Ballistics and Tool Marks, addresses the subjects of firearms and projectile identification, the matching of bullets to a weapon, gunshot residue, tool mark identification, and attempts to match crime scene striations to a tool associated with a suspect. Chapter 6, Soil, Glass, and Paint, discusses the nature of soil and glass-shard particle identification and the attempt to connect such materials with an individual suspect. Chapter 7, Footprints and Tire Impressions, addresses the identification, photographing, and/or casting of footwear and tire impressions found at a crime scene, and their association with a suspect. The chapter ends with a listing of bite mark cases. Chapter 8, Fingerprints, discusses the subject of fingerprint identification procedures and the recent Automated Fingerprint Identification System (AFIS). Chapter 9, Blood Spatter Analysis, analyzes cases involving the subject of presumptive testing for blood products as well as the subject of bloodstain pattern analysis and its importance in many key aspects of crime scene reconstruction efforts. Chapter 10, DNA Analysis, analyzes the court's scientific conditions for the acceptance of identification testimony arising from RFLP, PCR, mitochondrial DNA, and STR DNA analyses, in addition to the small but growing number of cases and articles addressing nonhuman DNA testing, in particular, dog, cat, and plant DNA testimony. Chapter 11, Forensic Anthropology and Entomology, briefly examines those decisions that utilize the methodologies and findings of these fields as aides to the investigation and identification of human remains and providing time-of-death estimates. And, finally, Chapter 12, Epilogue, provides a brief summary note on the subjects not covered in this book and the major points sought to be made in the entire work. The book ends with an appendix containing an extensive primer on how to conduct forensic science and forensic evidence research.

Acknowledgment

I wish to thank Dean Terri Foster of the DePaul University College of Law, for her gracious and ongoing support during the research and writing of this book. I also owe a great debt to friend and colleague James J. Ayres, Adjunct Professor of Computer Law and my cocreator and codirector of the Center for Law and Science at DePaul University College of Law. I also wish to express my gratitude to DePaul students Richard Battle, David Becker, and most recently, Maria Vathes and Laura Pieper, for their research skills, friendship, and untold hours at the final stages of this book. Many thanks to Harvey Kane and Becky McEldowney of CRC Press. Harvey had the faith in the project and Becky has gotten me through it with consistent friendliness, patience, and good humor. Special thanks must go to my editor, Michele Berman, for her great help in smoothing out the rough edges of this book.

My greatest debt is to my students in Forensic Evidence over these past 5 years, for their interest and patience as I developed the content and structure of this book.

It goes without saying that my true reason for accomplishing anything is, as always, my wife Sidni. Thanks again for everything, not the least of which was keeping our Newfoundland Beau and our pitbull Buster from trashing my office and consuming the final draft of this work.

Dedication

This book is dedicated to the loving memory of my mother Elizabeth Wolfe and my step-father John Wolfe

Table of Contents

1 Science, Forensic Science, and Evidence

> A discarded theory remains a theory. There are good theories and bad theories-theories currently regarded as true by everyone and theories that no one any longer believes to be true. However, when we reject a matter of fact, we take away its entitlement to the description: it never was a matter of fact at all.
>
> — Steven Shaplin and Simon Schaffer
> *Leviathan and the Air Pump (1985)*

I. SCIENCE AND THE LEGAL PROCESS

The desire to develop a model for the validation of scientific discoveries and methodology has been a constant struggle since the very early period of modern scientific thinking, in 17th-century England. Sir Francis Bacon, Lord Chancellor and one of the fathers of modern scientific thinking, composed a work called the *New Atlantis,* wherein he created a mythical institution called Saloman's House or the College of the Six Days Work. There, inhabitants were devoted to a serious and widespread search for the identification of scientific discoveries and to developing rigorous standards for testing their credibility. A complex system of experts was described by Bacon whose duties were focused on strict examination of practical results to serve as the basis for more generally applicable scientific principles.[1]

Robert Hooke, the early-17th-century inventor of the microscope and an associate of the great experimentalist Sir Robert Boyle, along with Francis Bacon also recognized the difficulty of finding adequate standards for the testing of scientific validity, especially in cases of attempts to fashion one uniform set of constructs for any such task:

> [F]or the limits to which our thoughts are confined, are small in respect of the vast extent of Nature itself; some parts of it are too large to be comprehended, and some too little to be perceived, and from thence it must follow that not having a full sensation of the object, we must be very lame and imperfect in our conceptions about it, and in all the propositions which we build upon it; hence we often take the shadow of things for the substance, small appearances for good similitudes, similitudes for definitions; and even many of those, which we think to be the most solid definitions are rather expressions of our misguided apprehension then of the true nature of the things themselves.[2]

This concern was at the forefront of efforts by early proponents of observational science and has remained the core issue in modern science-based civil and criminal litigation. As noted by authors Steven Shaplin and Simon Schaffer in their excellent study of the origins of modern scientific thinking, *Leviathan and the Air Pump:*

Hobbes, Boyle, and the Experimental Life,[3] English experimentalists of the mid-17th century and afterward rapidly took the position that all that could be expected of physical knowledge was "probability," thereby removing the radical distinction between "knowledge" and "opinion." Physical hypotheses were provisional and revisable; assent to them was not obligatory, as it was to mathematical demonstrations; and physical science was, to varying degrees, removed from the realm of the demonstrative:

> The probabilistic conception of physical knowledge was not regarded by its proponents as a regrettable retreat from more ambitious goals; it was celebrated as a wise rejection of a failed project. By the adoption of a probabilistic view of knowledge, one could attain to an approximate certainty and aim to secure legitimate assent to knowledge-claims. The quest for necessary and universal assent to physical propositions was seen as inappropriate and illegitimate. It belonged to a "dogmatic" enterprise, and dogmatism was seen not only as a failure but as dangerous to genuine knowledge.[4]

Historically then, a central concern in such cases is how the courts fashion a set of observational and linguistic guidelines to gauge the adequacy of a scientific opinion that is offered to establish a material fact in a trial.

This old debate has come full circle in the search by modern courts for a one-size-fits-all definition of legally sound scientific methodology that will serve justice in the increasing and predictably complex product liability and criminal cases of the next century.

The basic inference-based argument used in modern trials, whether aimed toward a proffered scientific result or a more routine establishment of an important fact, has served the law as the primary historical method since the earliest days of legal systems. The method of persuasion used by the great Roman lawyer and scholar Cicero remains the primary method of convincing a jury to reach one version of history rather than another. An argument by Cicero in a murder-patricide case in the year 80 B.C. could be made today, centered in differing opinions of what the facts were and how they are to be interpreted:

> Sextus Roscius, you say, killed his father. Well, what sort of a person is he then? Obviously he must be some degenerate youth, who has been corrupted by men of evil character. On the contrary: he is over forty years old. Well, then, he must be a veteran cut-throat, a ferocious individual throughly accustomed to committing murders. But the prosecutor has never even begun to suggest anything of the kind. So I suppose he must have been driven to his criminal act by extravagant habits, or huge debts, or ungovernable passions. As regards extravagant living, Erucius himself has already cleared him of that when he indicated that Sextus hardly ever even attended a party. Debts? He never had any. Passions? Not much scope for these in a man who, as the prosecutor himself critically remarked, has always lived in the country, devoting his time to the cultivation of his lands.[5]

This will become important here as we discuss the current theory setting forth the propriety of an expert witnesses opinion and its foundation and the utilization of a wide variety of forensic sciences in the criminal justice system.

As noted by the famous historian, Carl Becker:

> Let us admit that there are two histories: the actual series of events that once occurred; and the ideal series that we affirm and hold in memory. The first is absolute and unchanged—it was what it was whatever we do or say about it; the second is relative, always changing in response to the increase or refinement of knowledge. The two series correspond more or less; it is our aim to make the correspondence as exact as possible; but the actual series of events exists for us only in terms of the ideal series we affirm and hold in memory. This is why I am forced to identify history with knowledge of history. For all practical purposes history is, for us and for the time being, what we know it to be.[6]

Becker's observation could equally apply to any factual search in litigation, not the least of which are efforts to establish scientific facts that will be determinative of the central issues in contemporary environmental, product liability, medical malpractice, and criminal prosecutions. The subject of inference-, probabilistics-, statistics-, and extrapolation-based testimony will be discussed in depth later in this book. Suffice to say here, that in the extensive area of causation theory and forensic science and forensic evidence, the history question continues to be a major component in any analysis of proof of scientific fact.

The ultimate goal of the legal process is not to find absolute truth. Any system that allows a jury to reach a verdict of *guilty* or *not guilty* in such important matters would appear to have something else in mind. The goal of the U.S. litigation system is to provide the best context, the fairest context, the optimal context, for a jury to find the truth. This goal of providing the best opportunity for a jury to find its version of the truth is especially important to understand before entering into extended discussion of the current preoccupation of the nation's courts with the science question.

What is generally acceptable or reliable methodology in various fields that would justify any opinion, such as the cancer-causing potential of a certain commercial product? Who determines the answers to this question? What is the scientific standard to utilize in this inquiry? At what point in the history of a product or a disputed event and its alleged victim are we to focus? Are civil and criminal cases sufficiently different in terms of their goals and processes to require different analyses? Is every opinion that is grounded in some aspect of science subject to pretrial scrutiny to test the adequacy of the methodology used and the opinion based upon such use?

Litigation involving questions of science or the nature of the validity of modes of scientific inquiry has been part and parcel of our legal life since the start of our national life, beginning in and primarily residing in cases brought up in the nation's patent system. In examining the U.S. background to the current preoccupation of legal scholars and courts in respect to the meaning and application of the term *science* in civil and criminal cases, one is struck by the absence of argument on that point over most of our national life. It is also important to note that the patent laws were among the earliest laws promulgated by the new U.S. Congress. Thomas Jefferson was not only a fervent amateur scientist, as was Benjamin Franklin and a host of the founding fathers, but he was also a vocal and strong supporter of patent legislation. In fact, Jefferson served as the first official patent examiner.[7]

"Science" and technology drove the economic development of the U.S. in rapid and explosive ways, not the least of which was the filing of thousands of patent applications and early litigation alleging infringement. Case law from the first 50 years of our national life is replete with discussions of the uniqueness of cotton and wool cards, cutting and heading nails, pumping machinery, banknote plates, carpet weaving machinery, stock-quoting machines, glass knobs, and a host of other products produced by the rapid commercial expansion of the 19th-century commercial world. The first edition of the *Scientific American*, published in 1845, listed the patents issued in that year, which included a large number of patentees for improvements in the areas of beehives, churns, corn shellers, cultivators, fruit-gatherers, harrows, hulling machines, mowers, plows, and a wide variety of advances in agricultural implements. Favorable grants were also made for fabrics made with India rubber (Goodyear), ship anchors, cooking stoves, pianofortes, truss pads, furnaces, turtle-shell bugles, typecasters, door locks, and washing machines.[8]

The term *science* is noted and discussed primarily in patent cases in the sense of *arts and sciences,* a keystone idea in the first and subsequent patent legislation. The term *science* was also used routinely as referring to some general expertise or extraordinary knowledge of some matter or subject. Courts in the late-18th and entire 19th century often praise the "science" of legislation, international law, modern contracts, navigation, morality, writing, military affairs, engineering, political economy, and the like. Questions addressed to the appropriate standards for determining the admissibility of expert opinion based on a relevant scientific methodology were simply not asked.

Before we can understand the tremendous impact of contemporary judicial answers to the question of what is good science, we must discuss the defining influence that both the legal method and the structure of modern litigation will exercise in the effort to have a successful and efficacious resolution to this central issue in our legal future. This, in turn, will necessitate an overview of the various rules of civil and criminal procedure, trial evidence rules, and, most precisely, the strictures surrounding the proffer of expert testimony.

II. LITIGATION AS HISTORY

Any trial, in any area of law, from the simplest to the most complex, is in essence an exercise in establishing a version of history. If a case has proceeded to an actual trial, then some material facts are in question and thus must be determined by the trier of fact. Once the jury has determined the basic facts, then the court can instruct it regarding the law on any facts as found by it to have occurred. The history of Anglo-American common law trials is testimony to the great and ongoing difficulty in determining the basic factual basis of a case. The O. J. Simpson murder prosecution may serve as a recent example of this inherent difficulty in the functioning of the U.S. justice system. Both sides to the case have their respective versions of "what happened that day." The rules of evidence that channel the information flow in a trial, as we know and use them, are primarily exclusionary rules, which determine what historical facts—or, on occasion, opinions—the jury will get to hear. In its simplest terms, evidence is legally approved information for jury consumption.

The search for past fact by a court or jury is a form of historical research, but with significant differences. Initially, the facts are presented by interested parties in an adversary encounter, unaccompanied by the objective search allegedly utilized by academic historians. Second, the rules of evidence do not open the inquiry to any facts that may appear logically relevant to the search, but, rather, hedge the presentation of facts in a context ruled by numerous areas of policy unknown to historians.

Historians do not have as strong a prejudice against hearsay as does the law, nor do they require the rigorous foundations for admission as are needed in common law trials. Historians have few time constraints as to when their task is completed, whereas civil and, especially, criminal litigants are under a number of time constraints, such as statutes of limitations, 120 days within which to try an arrested person, discovery deadlines, and the disfavor that long trials receive from today's judiciary. Finally, although historians have set high standards to determine the validity of historical conclusions,[9] they are not formally operating under a "beyond a reasonable doubt" or "preponderance of the evidence" mandate as lawyers are in criminal and civil cases. The historian's standard is necessarily more fluid.[10]

The history-seeking function of common law trials suffers from the same infirmity that efforts by historians to reproduce a past event suffer. Arguments for either side of a version of history have always been at the center of legal disputes.

III. LAW AND SCIENCE

The key modern decisions addressing the science question have shifted focus as a result of the growth of biological, chemical, and engineering-based issues arising in modern product liability and criminal prosecutions. Science-based disputes also abound in contract actions and regulatory proceedings—those of the Food and Drug Administration (FDA), the Occupational Safety and Health Administration (OSHA), the Consumer Product Safety Administration (CPSA), and a bevy of other science-based government organizations. Modern case law increasingly references a wide variety of science-based matters, which are becoming challenged in pretrial hearings in ever-greater numbers. Modern civil procedure codes require that each party, within a certain number of days after the filing of a complaint, file the names of its expert witnesses plus a summary of any such opinion and the bases upon which it was reached, as well as a list of authoritative books or articles that went into the process. These provisions play a key role in the now-routine pretrial challenge of expert witness testimony.

State and federal courts in both civil and criminal cases are increasingly occupied with cases centered on the need for an encompassing and practice-oriented definition of science and scientific method as an essential precursor to the admissibility of opinions of experts based upon that science. Indeed, in the past decade, the whole subject of the propriety and extent of expert testimony in civil and criminal cases has been attacked from both sides in an ongoing battle over what is a legally acceptable scientific foundation for the proffering of expert opinion in a wide variety of environmental, product liability, and criminal cases. This introductory chapter will briefly examine the issues involved and the considerable differences that exist between civil and criminal cases as regards the ongoing use of science-based expert opinion in modern U.S. litigation.

The question "what is science?" has been one of the most vigorously contested legal questions in the closing years of the 20th century. It will continue to dominate discussions in the area of product liability, toxic tort, and a wide variety of criminal prosecutions in the approaching new millennium. This book will be devoted to the identification and analysis of how the factual findings of the forensic sciences are accepted and interpreted in modern criminal trials. Prior to that analysis, however, it is necessary to set forth the historical and contemporary context within which the offerings of the forensic sciences are and will be viewed in the 21st century.

For the greater part of the functioning of our state and federal judicial systems, the question of what was or was not proper scientific method was not viewed as a prerequisite to the discussion or resolution of a science-related fact question. The focus for most of the 19th and 20th centuries has been on the qualifications of the proffered expert witness which, if deemed adequate, usually resulted in an acceptance of the propriety of the scientific materials and processes that served as a basis for the expert's opinion. Until very recent times in our legal history, most courts routinely expressed appreciation for the contribution of expert witnesses for assisting them in the difficult science-based fact-finding process.[10]

From the founding of the U.S. nation, up until the year 1923, the question of the adequacy of scientific methodology and/or opinion simply was not asked. Any general inquiry into what was adequate scientific methodology as a precursor to the utilization of expert testimony in the case is a relatively recent phenomenon in U.S. law. The impression one receives after a close examination of judicial materials from 1798 until the late 1800s is that the question of what was or was not "science" or a creditable development in the world of science was of concern only to those who were actually engaged in scientific projects of a wide variety of subjects. There was no felt necessity on the part of the legal system, with respect to litigation, to utilize or forge an overarching theory of what was or was not acceptable science.

It is important to note that the term *science* in the discussions to follow has little or no connection to the utilization and understanding of that term as it is uniformly thought of by the international scientific community. John Horgan, the former *Scientific American* editor, in his excellent book *The End of Science: Facing the Limits of Knowledge in the Twilight of the Scientific Age*,[11] sought out the world's leading philosophers of science, theoretical physicists, evolutionary biologists, mathematicians, astronomers, and chaos theorists to get their perspective on whether "science" was at a close, with nothing significant left to be discovered. That book is a superb survey of modern scientific thinking across varied fields. The present legal question, regarding the adequacy of a scientific methodology to support expert opinion, is light years away from the type of scientific inquiry posited by the scholars interviewed by Horgan. Horgan notes the criticism of Nobel prize–winning chemist Professor Stanley Miller of scientific papers culled from other published papers where there has been no hard-won finding resulting from extensive laboratory work. Professor Miller referred to such works as "paper chemistry." In the hard-fought science-based civil cases such as the breast implant actions or polychlorinated biphenyls (PCBs) and cancer litigation, we may borrow the idea and refer to the use of previously published articles by way of extrapolation in such cases to claim or deny causation, as "paper science" such a charge may not be made *in toto* about forensic science-based testimony in criminal cases.[12]

The attempts to formulate an overarching answer to the question of "what is science?" in the civil and criminal arenas are entirely distinct in terms of overall goals, methodology, and practical applications. The issue of whether long-term exposure to PCBs can cause cancer in a product liability lawsuit is quite different from the forensic issue of whether hair or fiber expert testimony may be used to link a defendant to a crime scene in a homicide prosecution. It is also of central importance to understand the differences between civil and criminal cases in respect to the performance of actual laboratory work performed to answer key factual issues in the cases. Forensic scientists "in white lab coats" are routinely involved in forensic evidence–centered criminal prosecutions. Their work is utilized to shed light on the physical dynamics that created the crime scene and, it is hoped, to add significant linking information to the identity of the perpetrator. They are rarely involved in answering the essential "scientific" causation issues at the center of modern product liability litigation, such as the breast implant controversy, issues which are the focus of recent and ongoing U.S. Supreme Court decisions seeking to finalize a "one size fits all" definition of *science*.

Examining a set of rhetorical questions revolving around our core inquiry "what is science?" can help to set the parameters of the discussions to follow. In the legal contexts of tort or criminal law, the questions may be more precisely stated as: is this proffered expert opinion based upon a *generally accepted* and/or *reliable* scientific methodology? What is the context in which the question is asked? What types of information are routinely used by court and counsel in the process of answering such cases? Is any concrete scientific work actually engaged in to answer the question posed in the case at hand? Who wants to know? Is the questioner a peer-reviewed journal making a publication decision? Is it a company-employed biochemist struggling with government product approval processes? Is it a forensic pathologist fighting to support a finding of homicide in a hotly contested murder trial centered on an initial sudden infant death syndrome (SIDS) determination? Is it a prosecutor attempting to save his expert witness's opinion on hair, fiber, or glass particles that arguably link a defendant to the scene of a violent crime? Is it a patent lawyer trying to protect her client's valuable property? Is it a product liability plaintiff or defense lawyer trying to determine the time frame in a product's development history wherein an alleged "defect" issue is focused?

There are two quite distinct areas of legal practice involved here. On the civil side, "science"-related issues are involved primarily in the area of product liability and its subset of chemical-based injuries often referred to as "toxic torts." There are, of course, a whole range of business-related legal issues that may involve scientific matters, from contract, patent-infringement, antitrust cases, and the like. On the criminal law side, the science-based issues cover considerable ground, ranging from proof offerings in the areas of hair and fiber analyses, soil, glass, and paint identification, and a host of facts related to forensic pathology, toxicology, blood products, and the whole area of ballistics and tool marks. In these criminal cases, some degree of science is actually and routinely conducted in forensic laboratories for purposes of generating material facts in the case at hand, such as DNA identifications or bullet or shell casing matching. This is quite different from civil, product liability-type cases centered in issues of causation, where not only is no science done for the immediate case, but published scientific articles, usually not precisely descriptive of the science at issue, are often utilized inferentially by way of extrapolation analyses.[13] Other than demonstrative tests prepared by one or both litigants in a product liability case, there is no science done to resolve the causation issue. This is definitely so in pharmaceutical failure-to-warn cases where each side stacks up the published literature and seeks to tip it to its side of the warnings issue.

True "science" questions are rarely central issues even in the most complex of tort product liability cases. In fact, outside of a clear cause-in-fact or causal relation problem, rarely the central issue in these cases, the questions revolve much more, if not exclusively, around the issue of "science as business." The bulk of product liability cases do not deal with "science," understood in the sense discussed in the world of international science, at least in any sense of that term understood by research scientists. More often, they focus on one of the ways a manufacturing corporation has utilized complex but practical science to develop and market products or publishes communications regarding the risks involved in utilizing such products by their customers.

Failure to warn of risks associated with the intended use of the product, or the providing of inadequate instructions, is the basis for a very large number of product liability cases. The true-cause case, such as the breast implant controversy, is a rarity. It is this limited tort, civil law, context that has provided the source of the contemporary legal stimulus to fashion a one-size-fits-all definition of science and scientific methodology. A representative list of individuals or entities involved in resolving what is or is not adequate scientific method, as that question relates to tort litigation or criminal prosecutions, will rarely include scientists in universities or laboratories engaged in what is traditionally considered pure science. There is a major distinction to be made between and among pure scientists, and corporate research scientists, advertising executives, research physicians and practicing physicians. By the time lawyers arrive on the scene, the injured party has come into contact on a short-term or long-term basis with a product that has a trade name, packaging, advertising, and a whole series of other marketing devices employed to encourage the consumer toward eventual purchase. In this context it is readily seen that the involvement of the science involved in the creation of the product is long past its involvement in respect to the injury suffered by the party. So, among science-based product liability or environmental cases, there is typically no science involved per se, but, rather, questions of ethical business practice regarding packaging, warnings, and instruction issues.[14]

In its simplest and most practical terms, the question of what is or is not "science," typically revolves around the issue of whether an expert witness chosen by one of the sides in civil or criminal litigation may testify at all, or render a particular opinion, assuming he or she is qualified to give any opinion. In cases involving a wide variety of commercially produced chemical compounds, pharmaceuticals, medical devices, and engineered goods, court resources in both the state and federal system are being increasingly taxed in pre-trial hearings seeking to determine the scientific validity of the methodologies or opinions of an amazingly disparate number of expert witnesses. The recent decision by the U.S. Supreme Court in *Kumho Tire v. Carmichael*,[15] holding that the *Daubert* criterion is available to challenge all expert witness testimony, will significantly heighten this pressure in the upcoming century.

This introductory chapter will briefly address the key components in the developing legal doctrine that attempt to provide answers to such questions, the precise issues involved,and the considerable differences that exist between civil and criminal cases regarding the extensive use of science, particularly forensic science, in modern U.S. trials.

IV. SCIENCE AND THE SUPREME COURT

The real-life context out of which the science-based questions addressed in this book arise is based in the proffer of expert testimony in civil or criminal cases, where one side, at a pretrial hearing, seeks to challenge the propriety of the other side's experts testifying at all, or, as is more frequently the case, to challenge the reliability or general acceptability of the methodology used by the expert in forming an opinion. For example, a lawyer in a civil product liability case wants his expert to testify that long-term exposure to PCBs caused cancer in his client, or that migrating silicone from defective breast implants or silicone-coated cerebral shunts caused a range of autoimmune disorders. The company lawyers have their own experts, who will deny the carcinogenic potential of PCBs or the risk to the autoimmune system from silicone. In a criminal prosecution for sexual assault and murder, the state may wish to present complex DNA, hair, and fiber testimony to place the defendant at the crime scene.

According to tried-and-true evidence law theory, any such witness may be challenged on several grounds. Initially, the case may simply not call for expertise at all and the jury may decide the disputed fact without the need for lengthy (and typically highly prejudicial) testimony. Second, a particular expert witness may be challenged on her basic qualifications to give any opinion in the field at issue since she has insufficient background in education or experience to have anything of value to offer on the fact at hand. Third, either the methodology utilized by the expert to support her opinion is not in fact scientifically sound, thereby not capable of supporting the proffered opinion, or the methodology is sufficiently scientifically sound to support an opinion, but this witness's opinion based on such method is not sufficiently derived from such scientific methodology. These third, process-based objections are the key objections at the center of the current state and federal controversy over the utilization of scientific opinion in U.S. courts.

Civil cases with central science-based issues are typically product liability or toxic tort litigation, where the essential science questions often revolve around whether the defendant's product "caused" the death or injury allegedly suffered by the plaintiff. In such cases the defense routinely argues that there is no causative link between its product and the injury to the plaintiff. These defenses focus on the single issue of whether the defendant caused the actual injury alleged, without the need to determine the contribution of the defendant's business practices as a major contributor to any injuries suffered. The evidentiary basis for such arguments is generally grounded in the findings of published peer-reviewed studies, or proprietary in-house, internally generated scientific studies obtained through discovery. These studies, known as state-of-the-art literature, rarely directly address the precise scientific issues that are at the center of the argument. It is from these types of data that an expert opinion is extrapolated. This process, in turn, has and will continue to foment science debates in current and future litigation.

In these civil injury cases the scientific questions of cause are considered in the context of the legal doctrines of *cause-in-fact* or *proximate cause*, which concepts are far removed from questions of causal relation addressed in nonlegal, science-driven inquiries. In these drug-, chemistry-, and engineering-based cases, the major issue is typically who has the most persuasive interpretation of what the literature actually says, to the extent that it does, respecting the physical connection between the plaintiff's injury and the components of the defendant's product with which the plaintiff was in contact.[16] It is important to recall that, aside from some case-specific comparative scientific testing, typically done in attempts to replicate the dynamics of the death-or injury-producing event, there is no actual, long-term science engaged in to answer the causation-related issues involved. Experts in a variety of products cases typically give extensive narrative testimony regarding the scientific background or context of the instant litigation or a case-specific opinion, and it all looks and sounds "scientific." However, the fact remains that these exercises and the growing number of pretrial *Frye* or *Daubert* hearings primarily involve talking about the scientific work of others as to how, utilizing the principles of extrapolation theory, such studies may shed light on one or more of the causation-centered issues involved in the case.[17]

The areas where science per se, as opposed to product-related business practices, is the focus of the litigation are those rare cases actually centered on the existence or nonexistence of physical causation: does silicone released in a breast implant patient's body cause autoimmune damage? Does long-term exposure to certain chemical substances cause cancer? Did the ingestion by pregnant mothers of Bendectin cause birth defects? Even here, opinions based upon preexisting scientific literature are used by hired experts to answer the question. As noted, this is typically accomplished without any actual laboratory studies as case-specific data.[18]

An examination of judicial materials from 1798 until the late 1800s teaches that the question of what was or was not "science" or reputable developments in science was of concern only to those who were indeed engaged in scientific endeavors. There was no pressure or perceived need on the part of the legal system, with respect to court activity, to utilize or forge an overarching theory of what was or was not science. The key factor was the solidity of the foundation for the expertise of the witness herself, not directly the reliability of general acceptability of any methodology utilized. In fact, it was not until 1923 in the case of *Frye v. United States*,[19] that the question was formally addressed by the courts. Even after the *Frye* decision, it was not until 70 years later that the U.S. Supreme Court returned to the issue.

A. SUPREME COURT CASES

1. *Frye v. United States*

The *Frye* test had its origin in *Frye v. United States*,[20] a short and citation-free 1923 U.S. Supreme Court decision concerning the admissibility of evidence derived from a systolic blood pressure deception test, a crude precursor to the polygraph machine. In *Frye*, the defendant was convicted of the crime of murder in the second degree. In the course of the trial, defense counsel proffered an expert to testify to the results of a "deception test" made upon the defendant. The test was characterized as a "systolic blood pressure deception test." It was claimed that changes in blood pressure would be caused by changes in the emotions of the witness, and systolic blood pressure rises were brought about by nervous impulses sent to the autonomic nervous system. Scientific experiments, the defense asserted, confirmed that fear, rage, and pain routinely produced an elevation of systolic blood pressure, and that conscious deception or falsehood, concealment of facts, or guilt of crime, accompanied by fear of detection when the person is under examination, "raised the systolic blood pressure in a curve, which corresponds exactly to the struggle going on in the subject's mind, between fear and attempted control of that fear, as the examination touches the vital points in respect of which he was attempting to deceive the examiner."[21]

The proffer was objected to by the government, and the court sustained the objection. Counsel for the defendant then offered to have the proffered witness conduct a test in the presence of the jury, which was also denied.

The defendant's counsel agreed that no cases directly on point had been found. The broad ground, however, upon which they based their case was the rule that the opinions of experts or skilled witnesses were routinely admissible in cases in which the matter of inquiry is such that inexperienced persons were likely to be incapable of forming a correct judgment upon the matter, due to its subject being a matter of art or science with which they would be unfamiliar. When the question involved did not lie within the range of common experience or knowledge, but required special experience or knowledge, then the opinions of witnesses skilled in that particular science, art, or trade to which the question related were admissible in evidence.[22]

Here, rather than questioning the expertise of the defendant's expert, the government challenged the basic foundation for the methodology of any such machine. Thus, the court was required to construct a rule that would assist it and future courts in determining the sufficient level of confidence that should be reposed in a scientific methodology supporting any proffered opinion based upon it. Such analysis was to be had as a precursor to the admissibility of an opinion based upon it.

The court, speaking through Judge Van Orsdel, noted that the issue of just when a scientific principle or discovery crosses the line between the experimental and demonstrable stages was difficult to define:

> Somewhere in this twilight zone, the court continued, the evidential force of the principle must be recognized, and while courts will go a long way in admitting expert testimony deduced from a well-recognized scientific principle or discovery, the thing from which

the deduction is made must be sufficiently established to have gained general acceptance in the particular field in which it belongs. We think the systolic blood pressure deception test has not yet gained such standing and scientific recognition among physiological and psychological authorities as would justify the courts in admitting expert testimony deduced from the discovery, development, and experiments thus far made.[23]

Thus the court, realizing that legal doctrine had nothing to supplant the views of the scientists, took the position that if the methodology at issue was *generally accepted* by the relevant scientific community, that would be acceptable to the law. The *general acceptability* rule was thus born and continued to be the rule for the next 70 years, until the decision by the U.S. Supreme Court in the famous case of *Daubert v. Merrell Dow Pharmaceuticals*,[24] in 1993. It is of great interest to note that the period of 1923 to 1993 saw the gradual development of and eventual explosion of product liability law in the 1960s and 1970s. The major work of the nation's courts in the products field was the creation and refinement of the mass of principles involved in forming the law of strict liability for products.[25] It was not until 1993 when defendant Merrell Dow Pharmaceuticals challenged the methodology of the plaintiff's expert, which, according to his unique methodology, determined that the interpretation of a body of epidemiological studies opined that the ingestion of the drug Bendectin was the cause of fetal malformations.

2. *Daubert v. Merrell Dow Pharmaceuticals*

In the *Daubert* decision, petitioners were minor children born with serious birth defects, alleged to have been caused by their mothers' ingestion of Bendectin, a prescription antinausea drug marketed by defendant Merrell Dow Pharmaceuticals. After considerable discovery, Merrell Dow moved for summary judgment, contending that Bendectin does not cause birth defects in humans and that petitioners would be unable to come forward with any admissible evidence that it did. In support of its motion, Dow filed the affidavit of Dr. Steven H. Lamm, a physician and epidemiologist, who was an experienced and solidly supported expert on the risks from exposure to various chemical substances. Lamm said that he had reviewed all the 30 published studies on both Bendectin and human birth defects, involving over 130,000 patients and stated that none had found Bendectin to be a substance capable of causing malformed fetuses. Doctor Lamm concluded that maternal use of Bendectin during the first trimester of pregnancy had not been proven to be a risk factor for human birth defects.[26]

Plaintiffs did not contest this portrayal of the literature regarding Bendectin, but countered with the testimony of 8 experts of their own, each of whom concluded that Bendectin can cause birth defects. Their conclusions were based upon *in vitro* (test tube) and *in vivo* (live) animal studies that found a link between Bendectin and malformations; pharmacological studies of the chemical structure of Bendectin that purported to show similarities between the structure of the drug and that of other substances known to cause birth defects; and the "reanalysis" of previously published epidemiological (human statistical) studies.[27]

The district court granted the respondent's motion for summary judgment, where, citing *Frye*, the court stated that scientific evidence was admissible only if the principle upon which it is based was sufficiently established to have general acceptance in the field to which it belonged, concluding that petitioners' evidence did not meet this standard. The court held that expert opinion which was not based on epidemiological evidence was not admissible to establish causation.[28] The animal-cell studies, live-animal studies, and chemical-structure analyses on which petitioners had relied could not, alone, establish a "reasonably disputable jury issue" regarding causation. Petitioners' epidemiological analyses, based as they were on recalculations of data in previously published studies that had found no causal link between the drug and birth defects, were ruled to be inadmissible because they had not been published or subjected to peer review.[29]

The U.S. Court of Appeals for the Ninth Circuit affirmed,[30] holding that expert opinion based on a scientific technique was unacceptable unless the technique was "generally accepted" as reliable in the relevant scientific community. The court held that expert opinion based on a methodology that significantly deviated from the procedures accepted by recognized authorities in the field could not be established to be "generally accepted as a reliable technique."[31] The court stressed that other courts of appeals that had addressed the alleged dangers of Bendectin had declined to accept reanalyses of epidemiological studies that had not been published or subjected to peer review.[32] Those courts had indeed adjudged unpublished reanalyses exceptionally problematic in light of the great import of the original published studies supporting Merrell Dow, all of which studies had been subject to close review by the scientific community.

The U.S. Supreme Court, speaking through Justice Blackmun, noted that in the 70 years since its formulation in the *Frye* case, the "general acceptance" test has been the dominant standard for determining the admissibility of novel scientific evidence at trial, and, that while under increasing criticism, it nonetheless continued to be followed by a majority of courts,[33] including the ninth circuit. Justice Blackmun observed that the merits of the *Frye* test had been much debated, and that the scholarship on its proper scope had continued to grow at an ever-increasing pace.[34] Here the court agreed with Merrell Dow that the proper focus of such discussions should henceforth be the provisions of the Federal Rules of Evidence, not the 70-year-old *Frye* decision. The court noted that they were required to interpret the legislatively enacted Federal Rules of Evidence as they would any statute, and that Rule 401 and 402 provided the baseline theory.[35] These two rules of relevancy were to be utilized in these cases in conjunction with Rule 702, setting forth the basic principle regarding the admissibility of expert testimony.[36] The court observed that nothing in the language of Rule 702 or the rules as a whole mandate general acceptance as an absolute prerequisite to admissibility and, indeed, any such interpretation would be at odds with the liberal thrust of the Federal Rules of Evidence.

Having concluded that the *Frye* test was replaced by the Rules of Evidence, however, did not mean that there were no checks on the admissibility of purportedly scientific evidence. Nor was a trial judge disabled from screening such evidence. Under the Federal Rules of Evidence, the trial judge was required to warrant that any and all scientific testimony or evidence admitted was not only relevant, but reliable.[37] The primary locus for this obligation was Federal Rule of Evidence 702. When presented an offer of expert scientific testimony, a trial judge must determine at the outset whether the expert was proposing to testify to scientific knowledge that would assist the trier of fact to understand or determine a fact in issue. If so, then a preliminary assessment was required of whether the reasoning or methodology underlying the testimony was scientifically valid and of whether that reasoning or methodology properly could be applied to the facts in issue.[38]

Several observations are in order as respects the ruling in *Daubert*. Initially it will be convenient to set out a summary of the requirements for the admissibility of scientific expert witness opinion under *Frye* and *Daubert*. Under either, and regardless of what facts or factors get the nod in a particular case, there are only a limited number of questions that the courts *could* examine:

1. Are there any published peer-reviewed books or articles?
2. Is this methodology taught in universities or discussed in professional scientific meetings or colloquia?
3. Can this methodology be tested for accuracy? Does it have a known error rate?
4. Is this methodology generally accepted in the relevant scientific community where similar concepts are studied and used?

It is important to realize that there really are not any other significant questions that can be asked and that the same questions are basically asked under either *Frye* or *Daubert*. In *Daubert*, by rejecting the *Frye* rule, the court essentially wrapped the above balancing criteria in a Federal Rules of Evidence package, with a stated preference to treat general acceptability as only one, but not the essential, factor to receive attention. Hence, the relevant and reliable standard of *Daubert* as opposed to general acceptability rule of *Frye* is functionally the same as far as its implementation is concerned. The *Daubert* relevancy standard simply means that the scientific information that a party seeks to introduce into evidence has the ability to make some fact that is of consequence to the action more probable or less probable than it would be without it.[39]

The *Daubert* decision has yet to be formally accepted by all of state courts, many of which retain their adherence to a *Frye* standard. However, the greatest number of those states have accepted *Daubert's* more liberal, open analysis approach, making the real differences between the two models increasingly difficult to see. The *Daubert* case prompted another 4 years of decisions applying what was perceived as its requirements in an extensive variety of scientific methodologies.[40] The important question of the extent to which the *Daubert* gatekeeper could make a pretrial judgment regarding *the opinion* of an expert arguably based on relevant and reliable methods was not addressed in *Daubert*. This important point was resolved in the affirmative in the 1997 decision of the U.S. Supreme Court in the case of *General Electric v. Joiner*,[41] involving the question of whether long-term exposure to PCBs could cause cancer. The case also provides an extended discussion of the *Daubert* criterion, especially with regard to the importance of the presence or absence of peer-reviewed scientific articles on the questioned methodology.

3. *General Electric v. Joiner*

Robert Joiner began work as an electrician in the Water & Light Department of Thomasville, Georgia (City) in 1973. Joiner's job required him to work with and around the city's electrical transformers, which used a mineral-based dielectric fluid as a coolant. Joiner often had to stick his hands and arms into the fluid to make repairs, and the fluid would sometimes splash onto him, occasionally getting into his eyes and mouth. In 1983 the city discovered that the fluid in some of the transformers was contaminated with PCBs. PCBs are widely considered to be hazardous to human health. Congress, with limited exceptions, banned the production and sale of PCBs in 1978.[42]

Joiner's theory of liability was that his exposure to PCBs and their derivatives "promoted" the cultivation of his lung cancer. In support of that theory he proffered the deposition testimony of a number of expert witnesses. Defendants argued that Joiner's expert testimony regarding causation was nothing more than unscientific speculation, stressing the absence of any peer-reviewed epidemiological studies and was based exclusively on disconnected studies of laboratory animals. The trial court agreed with petitioners that the animal studies did not support Joiner's position that exposure to PCBs had caused or significantly contributed to his cancer. The trial court also ruled that the four epidemiological studies on which Joiner's experts had relied were not a sufficient basis for their opinions on causation.[43]

In an important concurring opinion, Justice Breyer addressed the perceived problem of the difficulty of the district court "gatekeepers" getting high-level, objective expert support for its pretrial function in these cases. He noted that the trial judges would sometimes be required to make "subtle and sophisticated determinations about scientific methodology and its relation to the conclusions an expert witness sought to offer."[44] This would be particularly so in cases where the involved area of science was tentative or uncertain, or where epidemiological or laboratory testing was offered to prove individual causation. *Amici* had reminded the court of the dangers existent due to judges' lack of scientific expertise and lack of opportunities for meaningful training.[45] Justice Breyer was particularly impressed with the *Amici* brief filed by *The New England Journal of Medicine* and its editor-in-chief, Marcia Angell, M.D., in which the *Journal* writes:

> [A] judge could better fulfill this gatekeeper function if he or she had help from scientists. Judges should be strongly encouraged to make greater use of their inherent authority . . . to appoint experts . . . Reputable experts could be recommended to courts by established scientific organizations, such as the National Academy of Sciences or the American Association for the Advancement of Science.[46]

Justice Breyer concluded by stating his view that given this kind of offer of cooperative effort, from the scientific to the legal community, and given the various Rules-authorized methods for facilitating the courts' task, *Daubert's* gatekeeping function would not prove overly arduous to achieve.[47]

The *Joiner* decision thus expands the perogative of the trial court gatekeeper to include rejecting an expert's opinion, although admittedly based on acceptable or reliable methodology, if the court is of the view that such opinion was not rationally supported by such methodology.[48]

The most recent major Supreme Court decision in the *Frye–Daubert* line, decided on March 23, 1999, is *Kumho Tire v. Carmichael*,[49] addressing the important question of whether the *Daubert* guidelines apply to all expert witness or exclude experts in applied technology or other forms of experience-based expertise, thus depriving corporate defendants of a pretrial opportunity to challenge an expert witness.

4. *Kumho Tire v. Carmichael*

The case, *Kumho Tire*, arose from the explosion of a minivan tire resulting in death and injuries. Plaintiff expert Carlson concluded that the tire at issue was defective in design, which defect led to the fatal explosion. Carlson's conclusion was based upon a number of factors, including his personal examination of the tire carcass. Carlson concluded that the tire did not bear at least two of the four "overdeflection symptoms," nor was there any less obvious cause of separation; and since neither overdeflection nor the punctures caused the blowout, he surmised that either a manufacturing or design defect caused the separation.[51]

Defendant Kumho Tire moved the district court to bar Carlson's testimony on the basis that his methodology for defect analysis was not reliable under a Daubert standard. Justice Breyer, speaking for the Court, held that the primary preliminary issue here was whether the gatekeeping obligation imposed on federal trial courts applied only to scientific testimony or to expert testimony of all types, cutting edge or familiar. Justice Bryer and the Court ruled that the *Daubert* factors analysis was available to test all manner and forms of expert testimony, not just opinions arising out of cutting-edge science. The Court stated that it would prove "difficult, if not impossible" for judges to administer evidentiary rules under which a gatekeeping obligation depended upon a distinction between "scientific" knowledge and "technical" or "other specialized" knowledge. There was no bright line that divides one discipline from another. Engineering rested solidly on scientific knowledge, and so-called pure scientific theory itself often hinged for its emergence and evolution upon observation and properly engineered machinery. The court observed that conceptual efforts to distinguish the two were unlikely to produce clear legal lines capable of application in any particular case.[52]

In addition, Justice Breyer continued, there was no perceived need to carve out any such demarcations between *science* and *engineering*:

> Neither is there a convincing need to make such distinctions. Experts of all kinds tie observations to conclusions through the use of what Judge Learned Hand called "general truths derived from . . . specialized experience." [Citations omitted.] And whether the specific expert testimony focuses upon specialized observations, the specialized translation of those observations into theory, a specialized theory itself, or the application of such a theory in a particular case, the expert's testimony often will rest "upon an experience confessedly foreign in kind to [the jury's] own." . . . The trial judge's effort to assure that the specialized testimony is reliable and relevant can help the jury

evaluate that foreign experience, whether the testimony reflects scientific, technical, or other specialized knowledge.[53]

The Court answered in the affirmative when asked by the petitioners if trial courts may consider the several specific reliability factors that *Daubert* said could bear on a gatekeeping determination:

> The petitioners asked specifically whether a trial judge determining the admissibility of an engineering expert's testimony may consider several more specific factors that *Daubert* said might "bear on" a judge's gate-keeping determination. Those factors include:
>
> —Whether a theory or technique can be (and has been) tested;
> —Whether it has been subjected to peer review and publication;
> —Whether, in respect to a particular technique, there is a high known or potential rate of error and whether there are standards controlling the technique's operation;
> —Whether the theory or technique enjoys general acceptance within a relevant scientific community.[54]

The Court, after emphasizing the elastic nature of the *Daubert* Rule 702 criterion, observed that those factors did not all necessarily apply in a particular case and that one or more could serve as the deciding factor or factors in a particular instance.

The Court concluded that expert Carlson's testimony here was not reliable under the Daubert criteria, and would be barred. There was no indication in the record that other experts in the industry used Carlson's two-factor test or that tire experts such as he generally made the very fragile distinctions about the symmetry of shoulder tread wear that were necessary, if based upon Carlson's own theory, to support his conclusions. The Court also emphasized that there was an absence of any peer-reviewed articles or papers that confirmed the reliability of Carlson's method.[55] Indeed, Justice Breyer continued, no one had argued that Carlson himself, were he still working for Michelin, would have concluded in a report to his employer that a similar tire was similarly defective on grounds identical to those upon which he rested his conclusion here.

In sum, the Court concluded, Rule 702 grants the district judge the discretionary authority, reviewable for its abuse, to determine reliability in light of the particular facts and circumstances of the particular case.

B. SCIENCE ADVISORY BOARDS

Following the decision in *General Electric v. Joiner*,[56] considerable interest was exhibited by Justice Breyer, the American Association for the Advancement of Science (AAAS), and the American Bar Association in trying to develop experimental programs whereby independent scientists would serve as an advisory board for trial judges in scientifically complex mass tort cases such as the breast implant litigation. The October 1999 *ABA Journal* reports the new existence of funding for the Court Appointed Scientific Experts (CASE Project), a 5-year experiment of the American Association for the Advancement of Science, that will supply allegedly objective scientific expertise to federal trial courts in science-intensive litigation. The CASE project is a direct outgrowth of Justice Breyer's efforts following the *Joiner* decision. In fact, the AAAS has agreed in principle to establish such a pilot program. The first of such panel experiments was established in one of the block of breast implant decisions set up pursuant to the federal Manual of Complex Litigation.

In the case of *In re: Silicone Gel Breast Implant Products Liability Litigation*,[57] the Honorable Sam C. Pointer, Jr., Coordinating Judge for the Federal Breast Implant Multi-District Litigation, appointed a panel of four scientific experts in the fields of immunology, epidemiology, toxicology, and rheumatology to serve on a National Science Panel.[58] The panel was instructed to review and critique the scientific literature pertaining to the possibility of a causal association between silicone breast implants and connective tissue diseases, related signs and symptoms, and immune system dysfunction. The panel met, received instructions from the judge, and heard testimony from experts selected by the counsels for the plaintiffs and for the defendants in October 1996. Additional hearings were held in July 1997, when experts identified by the parties provided testimony, and in November 1997, when the panel's invited experts presented their research material.[59]

In spring 1997, over 2,000 documents were submitted to the panelists from the legal counsels for both parties. Subsequently, the counsels pared these numbers down to the approximately 40 most important documents from each side for each panel member. The source of references, whether counsel for the plaintiffs or counsel for the defendants, was not identified to the panelists. The panel members also used their own literature search strategies, and were neither limited to nor obligated to use those submitted by the respective legal counsels. The panel found no reliable evidence of a link between migrating silicone and autoimmune disorders. The case will proceed to its slow conclusion, with both plaintiff and defendant experts contributing to the extensive pretrial activities.

There will be at least a year of depositions and considerable scrambling by plaintiff lawyers before this question comes to rest in these cases. The negative findings by this court-appointed panel of experts cast a considerable shadow over the thousands of breast implant cases. While not determinative of any issues in these cases, it is there and must somehow be countered by another bevy of experts interpreting the same body of literature. The independent panel idea is alive and well. It remains to be seen if it is a help or a major hindrance in resolving the central and perplexing issue of scientifically reliable proof of causation.

V. CONCLUSION

The material in this first chapter is meant to provide a context for the rest of the chapters in this book, which is devoted to an analysis of the relationship between the worlds of law and the forensic sciences. The judicial debate over setting usable reliability standards to assess the admissibility of science-generated fact has not been driven by criminal cases. Corporations with serious money at stake have set the terms of the inquiry over the past decade, with the decision in *Kumho Tire* being the latest word on the subject. It remains to be seen what form the issue will take in increasingly sophisticated genetics-driven products cases in the new millennium. It is important to note at this point in our study that the *Daubert* or *Frye* standards apply with full force to the law and science questions routinely addressed in criminal prosecutions. The bulk of the currently utilized forensic science disciplines—as well as their relatively unchallenged legal acceptability—was perfected prior to heightened focus on these matters in the mid to late 1990s. Some aspects of forensic science routinely involved in modern criminal trials, such as nonhuman DNA, laser technology, and video enhancement techniques, which involve very sophisticated theoretical underpinnings, are yet to be fully tested in U.S. courts.

The chapters to follow will be devoted to a close study of the interaction between the forensic sciences and the criminal justice system. This collaboration of law and science here, is of a quite different nature in type, methods, and goals from those encountered in civil law cases such as product liability or toxic tort litigation. The *Daubert* "one-size-fits-all" reliability standard, developed in hard-fought tort cases involving the existence of causal relation, is the same standard used to challenge the underlying basis or a specific application of one of the forensic sciences. This is not a comfortable fit when seeking to challenge the very foundations of a forensic discipline in daily use for decades. What is of equal, if not more important, significance is the uses made of the various forensic sciences by prosecutors and the powerful fact inferences that are offered to juries as a result of them. Chapter 2, Science and the Criminal Law, discusses these issues in considerable detail, a discussion that will continue throughout the book as discussions are presented of a wide variety of cases involving forensic evidence.

RESEARCH NOTE

The Journal of Forensic Sciences is the official publication of the American Academy of Forensic Sciences. By visiting the Academy's Web site at *http://www.aafs.org* and clicking on the "Journal of Forensic Sciences" link, one can get to a searchable index of the journal from 1981 to the present that uses common search terms. The site also provides tables of contents for more recent issues of the journal, and, for a modest fee, one can download individual articles from issues published after January 1, 1999. The index, content, and article availability site is maintained by the publisher of the journal, The American Society for Testing and Materials (ASTM). There are current plans to move towards the Web-based publication of the journal, although the paper copy will still be available for some time. Individual subscriptions to this essential journal are also available from ASTM for those interested.

Visiting this important Web site on a regular basis and viewing the available abstracts are essential to the early stages of forensic science/forensic evidence research.

ENDNOTES

1. See Brian Vickers, (ed.): *Francis Bacon: A Critical Edition of The Major Works* (The Oxford Authors Series, New York, 1996).
2. Robert Hooke: *Micrographia, or Some Physiological Descriptions of Minute Bodies Made by Magnifying Glasses with Observations and Inquiries Thereon* (London, 1667), at preface, 2.
3. Steven Shaplin and Simon Schaffer: *Leviathan and the Air Pump: Hobbes, Boyle, and the Experimental Life* (Princeton, 1985).
4. *Id.* at 24.
5. Cicero: *"In Defense of Sextus Roscius of Ameria"* (80 B.C.), *Cicero Murder Trials*, trans. by Michael Grant (Penguin Books, New York, 1975).
6. Carl L. Becker: "Every Man His Own Historian," *American Historical Review*, Vol. 37, January, 1932, at 221.
7. For the year 1776, until an official patent system and staff were established, a part of Jefferson's duties as Secretary of State in the Washington administration was the examination of patent applications and witnessing the applicant's demonstrations, at times, performed on his desk. The first patent issued by him was to Samuel Hopkins on July 31, 1790 for making pot and pearl ashes. See Dumas Malone: *Jefferson and the Rights of Man* (Boston, 1951) at 282. Also see Brooke Hindle: *The Pursuit of Science in Revolutionary America 1735–1789* (Chapel Hill, 1956); A. Hunter Dupree: *Science in the Federal Government: A History of Policies and Activities to 1940* (Cambridge, 1957); Ralph S. Bates: *Scientific Societies in the United States* (Cambridge, 1945).
8. See *Scientific American*, Vol. 1, No. 1, August 28, 1845 (*Scientific American*, facsimile), listing on its first page a "Catalogue of American Patents issued in 1844."
9. On this subject, see, generally, David Hackett Fischer: *Historians Fallacies: Toward a Logic of Historical Thought* (Harper Torchbooks, New York, 1970); E. H. Carr: *What is History?* (New York, 1962); Robin W. Winks (ed.): *The Historian as Detective: Essays on Evidence* (Harper Torchbooks, New York, 1968).
10. As noted by historian Robin Weeks, "Evidence means different things to different people, of course. The historian tends to think mainly in terms of documents. A lawyer will mean something rather different by the word, as will a sociologist, or a physicist, or a geologist, or a police officer at the moment of making an arrest. For certain problems evidence must be 'hard,' while for others it may be 'soft.' Even if no acceptable or agreed-upon definitions of evidence may be given, most of us recognize intuitively what we mean when we use the word. Winks, *supra,* note a, at xv.
11. John Horgan: *The End of Science: Facing the Limits of Knowledge in the Twilight of the Scientific Age* (Addison-Wesley, New York, 1996). See also John Maddox: *What Remains to Be Discovered: Mapping the Secrets of the Universe the Origins of Life and the Future of the Human Race* (Free Press, New York, 1998).
12. Horgan, *supra,* at note 11, 139.
13. See, e.g., Duran v. Cullinan, 286 Ill. App. 3d 1005, 677 N.E.2d 999 (1997), at 1013: "Taking as true the plaintiffs' expert's affidavit asserting that the extrapolation method is commonly used by the scientific community as well as various federal agencies, taken along with the similarity between some of the defects described in the scientific literature and those exhibited by Lindsay, we find that the trial court abused its discretion in finding that the plaintiffs' extrapolation from the studies was not a technique sufficiently established to have gained general acceptance in this particular scientific field. Thus, we conclude that the plaintiffs' experts may give their opinion

as to causation and the weight to be afforded those opinions are matters for the jury to resolve. Under the circumstances of the case at bar, the fact that plaintiffs' experts had to 'extrapolate' from various studies in arriving at their opinion rather than rely on a specific epidemiological study affects the weight of the testimony and not its admissibility."

14. If we examine a number of product liability cases from the past 5 years one thing becomes apparent: the concern, the central issue, the debate, is pretty much restricted to the marketing aspects of the corporation who has developed, approved, received government approval, and packaged a commercial good. The only time that science in the sense of recent Supreme Court cases is involved is in pure physical-cause cases. Such cases will in the next century be increasingly less rare as the result of recent understanding of genetic damage. Thus, in most product liability cases, we are talking about the business repercussions of applied science, often completed many decades before the death or injury involved in a current case.

15. Kumho Tire Company, Ltd. v. Carmichael et al., 526 U.S. 137, 119 S.Ct. 1167 (1999). Daubert's "gatekeeping" obligation, requiring an inquiry into both relevance and reliability of proferred expert opinion, applies not only to "scientific" testimony, but to all types and disciplines involving expert testimony. Federal "rules of Evidence Rule 702, 28 U.S.C.A.

16. In most instances these civil products cases actually center on "science" in the context of science as reasonable business practice: Were the product warnings adequate? Was the warning sufficient? Were the instructions clear?

17. See General Electric v. Joiner, 118 S.Ct. 512, 522 U.S. 136 (1997), where the parties argued the applicability of 6 published articles about the cancer-causing potential for long-term exposure to PCBs.

18. It should also be noted at this point that the legal standard of proof of "facts" in criminal cases is "beyond a reasonable doubt", whereas civil tort cases only require that a "fact" be proved by "a preponderance of evidence."

19. Frye v. United States, 54 App.D.C. 46 293 F. 1013 (1923).

20. Id.

21. Id. at 47, 1014.

22. Id.

23. Id.

24. Daubert v. Merrell Dow Pharmaceuticals, 509 U.S. 579, 113 S.Ct. 2786 (1993).

25. See, generally, David G. Owen: *Products Liability and Safety* (3rd ed. Foundation Press, 1996); David Owen: "Products Liability Restated," 49 *S.C. L. Rev.* 273 (1998).

26. Daubert, *supra*, note 24, at 582.

27. Id., at 2792.

28. Daubert v. Richardson Merrell Pharmaceutical [trial court], 727 F.Supp., at 575.

29. Id.

30. Id., 951 F.2d 1128 (1991).

31. Id., at 1130, quoting United States v. Solomon, 753 F.2d 1522, 1526 (Ca.9 1985).

32. Id., at 1130–1131.

33. Daubert, *supra*, note 24, at 2793. For a comprehensive listing of the many cases on either side of this controversy, see P. Giannelli and E. Imwinkelried: *Scientific Evidence* (2nd ed. Charlottesville, VA, 1998), Supp. Vol. I §§ 1-10–1-10(H).

34. Justice Blackmun cited as examples, Green: "Expert Witnesses and Sufficiency of Evidence in Toxic Substances Litigation: The Legacy of Agent Orange and Bendectin Litigation," 86 Nw.U.L.Rev. 643 (1992); Becker and Orenstein: The Federal Rules of Evidence after Sixteen Years—the Effect of "Plain Meaning" Jurisprudence, the

Need for an Advisory Committee on the Rules of Evidence, and Suggestions for Selective Revision of the Rules," 60 *Geo.Wash.I.Rev.* 857, 876–885 (1992); James Alphonzo Hanson: "Frye is Sixty-Five Years Old; Should He Retire?" 16 *West.St.U.L.Rev.* 357 (1989); Black: "A Unified Theory of Scientific Evidence," 56 *Ford.L.Rev.* 595 (1988); Imwinkelried: "The 'Bases' of Expert Testimony: The Syllogistic Structure of Scientific Testimony," 67 *N.C.L.Rev.* 1 (1988); "Proposals for a Model Rule on the Admissibility of Scientific Evidence," 26 *Jurimetrics J.* 235 (1986); Giannelli: "The Admissibility of Novel Scientific Evidence: Frye v. United States, a Half-Century Later," 80 *Colum.L.Rev.* 1197 (1980); "The Supreme Court, 1986 Term," 101 *Harv.L.Rev.* 7, 119, 125–127 (1987).

35. Rule 402 provides: "All relevant evidence is admissible, except as otherwise provided by the Constitution of the United States, by Act of Congress, by these rules, or by other rules prescribed by the Supreme Court pursuant to statutory authority. Evidence which is not relevant is not admissible." Rule 401 provides: "Relevant evidence is defined as that which has any tendency to make the existence of any fact that is of consequence to the determination of the action more probable or less probable than it would be without the evidence."

36. Rule 702, provides: "If scientific, technical, or other specialized knowledge will assist the trier of fact to understand the evidence or to determine a fact in issue, a witness qualified as an expert by knowledge, skill, experience, training, or education, may testify thereto in the form of an opinion or otherwise."

37. Daubert, *supra*, note 24, at 2795.

38. 509 U.S. at 593.

39. Federal Rules of Evidence Rule 401.

40. For an excellent discussion of Daubert and its considerable progeny, see Michael H. Graham: "The Daubert Dilemma: At Last a Viable Solution," 179 *F.R.D.* 1 (1998).

41. General Electric v. Joiner, 118 S.Ct. 512 (1997).

42. See 90 Stat. 2020, 15 U.S.C. 2605(e)(2)(A).

43. In concluding, the court held that abuse of discretion was the proper standard by which to review a district court's decision to admit or exclude scientific evidence, and because it was within the District Court's discretion to conclude that the studies upon which the experts relied were not sufficient, whether individually or in combination, to support their conclusions that Joiner's exposure to PCBs contributed to his cancer, the district court did not abuse its discretion in excluding their testimony. Joiner, *supra*, note 41, at 519.

44. *Id.*, at 520.

45. See, e.g., Brief for Trial Lawyers for Public Justice as *Amicus Curiae* 15; Brief for *The New England Journal of Medicine* et al. as *Amici Curiae* 2 ("Judges . . . are generally not trained scientists").

46. Brief for *The New England Journal of Medicine* 18–19; cf. Federal Rules of Evidendce 706. The Joiner case drew an extraordinary number of *amicus* briefs from business interests seeking to support the decision to bar the testimony of plaintiff's experts. The one that made the most impression was that supplied by Marcia Angell, editor-in-chief of *The New England Journal of Medicine*.

47. Justice Breyer has followed through on his enthusiasm for the idea of cooperation of scientists and courts in the legal task of analyzing the solidity of scientific methodology and opinions based on them. See Breyer: "The Interdependence of Science and Law," 1998 AAAS Meeting, February 16, 1998, advocating the now-implemented program whereby the American Association for the Advancement of Science would

facilitate the cooperation of members with federal trial courts in a selection of cases involving complex gatekeeper pretrial hearings. This experimental program is called Court Appointed Scientific Experts (CASE).

48. See Hall v. Baxter Healthcare Corp., 947 F.Supp. 1387, 1392 (D.Or. 1996), stating that "in an effort to effectively discharge my role as 'gatekeeper' under Daubert I invoked my inherent authority as a federal district court judge to appoint independent advisors to the court." Based upon a subsequent report by his experts, the district court dismissed a large block of breast implant cases.

49. Kumho Tire v. Carmichael, 119 S.Ct. 1167 (1999).

50. *Id.*

51. *Id.* at 1172.

52. *Id.* at 1174.

53. *Id.* at 1175.

54. *Id.*

55. *Id.* at 1178.

56. *Supra*, note 41.

57. MDL 926, Master File No. CV- 92-10000-S, N.D. Ala.

58. Members of the panel include: Betty A. Diamond, M.D., an immunologist from Albert Einstein College of Medicine in the Bronx, N.Y.; Barbara Sorenson Hulka, M.D., an epidemiologist from the University of North Carolina, Chapel Hill; Nancy I. Kerkvliet, Ph.D., a toxicologist with Oregon State University; and Peter Tugwell, M.D., a rheumatologist with the University of Ottawa. The experts participating in Washington, D.C. included Harry Spiera, M.D., clinical professor of medicine at Mt. Sinai Medical School in New York, N.Y.; Janet Daling, Ph.D., professor of epidemiology with the University of Washington, Seattle; Dori Germolec, Ph.D., head of the environmental immunology laboratory with the National Institute of Environmental Health Science in Research Triangle Park, N.C.; Noel Rose, M.D., Ph.D., professor of pathology, molecular biology, and immunology at Johns Hopkins Hospital in Baltimore, MD; Britta Ostermeyer Shoaib, M.D., with the Health Science Consultant Group, Lasker Biomedical Research Building, Columbia University Medical Center in New York, N.Y.; and Charles Janeway, Ph.D., professor of immunology at Yale Medical School in New Haven, CT.

59. See Breast Implant Panel: Executive Summary, at *http://www.fjc.gov/BREIMLIT/SCIENCE/report.htm* (1998). Also see the MDL926 Breast Implant Litigation Home Page, at *http://www.fjc.goc/BREIMLIT/mdl926.htm*.

2 Science and the Criminal Law

We have also houses of deceits of the senses, where we represent all manner of feats of juggling, false apparitions, impostures and illusions, and their fallacies. And surely you will easily believe that we, that have so many things truly natural which induce admiration, could in a world of particulars deceive the senses if we would disguise those things, and labor to make them more miraculous. But we do hate all impostures and lies, insomuch as we have severely forbidden it to all our fellows, under pain of ignominy and fines, that they do not show any natural work or thing adorned or swelling, but only pure as it is, and without all affectation of strangeness.

—Francis Bacon
The New Atlantis (1626)

I. INTRODUCTION

In the 1997 science fiction film *Gattaca*, directed by New Zealand director Andrew M. Nicol, a genetically engineered society of the very near future has perfected its use of DNA and hair analysis to the point where they serve as common identification methods as we would use a driver's license or social security number today. The plot elements, involving forensic science, mixed identities, and murder are chillingly close to the 21st-century world of forensic science we will soon experience. In a recent editorial in the British forensic science journal *Science and Justice*, entitled "Where Will All the Forensic Scientists Go?,"[1] Professor Brian Caddy ponders the possibility of police authorities having forensic scientists as part of the initial police response to a crime, noting the current ability to do an online computer search of a fingerprint from the crime scene. He observes that recent improvements in DNA profiling by the gradual elimination of gel-based DNA profiling in favor of microchip as a medium for DNA strand analyses will facilitate a major change in crime scene processing:

> From these small beginnings we shall see hand held micro-chip based devices placed in the hands of the crime scene officer which will have the capability of relaying the scene DNA profile to the data bank for comparison purpose. The data bank then becomes a primary function of the forensic science laboratory but as robotization advances this role will be managed by a small number of technicians.[2]

Similar advances, already used today relative to digitized collections of fingerprint and footwear impressions, such as the Automated Fingerprint Identification System (AFIS) or the recently created and rapidly expanding CODIS system, linking U.S. state and federal DNA data banks, prove the point.[3] It is essential to make a clear distinction between 21st-century methods for recognizing, storing, and testing potentially important crime scene data and the conceptual apparatus used to interpret it in a court of law. As we enter the new century it is time to take a detailed look back on the relationship between the law and the world of forensic science that has developed up to this point. This chapter attempts to provide just such an analytical retrospective, by discussing the legal context within which the claims and offerings of the forensic sciences are articulated as we depart the century where both forensic science and forensic evidence were born and developed.

The quotation that precedes this chapter may serve as a signpost for the discussion of forensic evidence to follow. Both Sir Francis Bacon and Thomas Hobbes warn of the dangers inherent in exaggerated, misleading, or simply absurd claims made about the results of scientific theory and experimentation.[4] The historian Carl Becker, in a related observation, points out the elusive nature of the proof of historical events and the near impossibility of recreating them in later times. This, of course, is the central problem encountered in ligation, especially in the U.S criminal justice system, where, more often than not, proof statements are couched in terms of probabilities. The economist John Maynard Keynes, among a host of others, alerts us to the continuing problem of society, again, especially in litigation, of carelessly accepting a certain level of proof of a probability that certain facts are true as proof that they are true:

> It has been pointed out already that no knowledge of probabilities, less in degree than certainty, helps us to know what conclusions are true, and that there is no direct relation between the truth of a proposition and its probability. Probability begins and ends with probability.[5]

Probability, as will be noted throughout this chapter, is the central and controlling idea in the utilization of forensic science in the modern criminal trial.[6]

Proof of fact in significant late-20th-century litigation is increasingly focused on inferences flowing from the application of the findings of one or more of the natural sciences. The methodologies change as science progresses. The legal system has survived many such changes and will survive yet more as the 21st century rushes into our national life. The important aspect of this increasing dependence on scientific method as a basis for determining dispositive facts, as far as the litigants are concerned, is the fact generated, not the method used to do it. The existence or nonexistence of a matter of fact depends in large part on the theory of fact-finding being used by the fact seekers.

Discussions of the use of science in the criminal law typically revolve around the subject of forensic evidence. Forensic evidence refers to facts or opinions proffered in a criminal case that have been generated or supported by the use of one, typically by more than one, of the corpus of forensic sciences routinely used in criminal prosecutions. There is an extensive list of such disciplines, the legal ramifications of which will receive extended attention in this chapter. The more important among the body of forensic sciences are set out below:

- Hair Analysis.
- Fiber Analysis.

- Glass Fragments and Paint Chips Analyses.
- Soil Analysis.
- Ballistics and Tool Marks.
- Fingerprints.
- Footwear.
- Tire Impressions.
- Blood Spatter Analysis.
- DNA Analysis.
- Forensic Anthropology.
- Forensic Archaeology.
- Forensic Pathology.
- Forensic Odontology.
- Questioned Document Analysis.
- Forensic Psychiatry and Psychology.

The central concept in the utilization of the findings of forensic science is the crime scene. While a crime scene can consist of the basement of a counterfeiter or the broken door lock of a supermarket, typically the term refers to the scene of a violent crime such as a sexual assault or a homicide. The use of the crime scene paradigm is not only a familiar focus for the training of forensic scientists, it is also the central source and reference point for analysis of the many legal issues that are involved directly or indirectly in the field of forensic evidence. What types of materials are typically or often found at a crime scene that may, through close examination by forensic scientists yield valuable information leading to an arrest and successful prosecution of the perpetrator or the equally important elimination or exclusion of a putative suspect?

The listing that follows enumerates the physical or the data source for the forensic science and legal discussions that comprise the bulk of the materials in this book. A brief listing of the data and the accompanying forensic sciences follows:

- Blood, semen, and saliva (DNA matching and typing; blood spatter analysis).
- Nonhuman DNA (dog, cat, deer, whales).
- Drugs (drug identification, forensic pathology).
- Explosives (bomb and arson identifications and source traces).
- Fibers (fiber typing, source identification and matching).
- Hair (hair typing and matching).
- Fingerprints (fingerprint matching, AFIS, etc.).
- Bones (gender and age typing; identification of remains, weapon identification).
- Wound analysis (weapons typing, physical movement patterning).
- Firearms and ammunition (ballistics and tool mark identification).
- Powder residues (shootings, suicides).
- Glass (glass typing and matching).
- Foot, tire, and fabric impressions (impression typing and matching).
- Paint (paint typing and matching in automobile collisions, hit and run).

- Petroleum products (product typing and matching).
- Plastic bags (typing and matching, garbage bags as suffocation devices or used in transports).
- Soils and minerals (mineral typing and matching, forensic geology).
- Tool marks (tool identification and matching, homicides, burglary, home invasions, etc.).
- Wood and vegetative matter (plant typing and matching, plant DNA RAPD matching, limnology, Forest Service laboratory).
- Insects, larvae, maggots (forensic entomology, time of death, location analyses).
- Dentition and bite marks (identification of victim, matching bite marks to defendant).
- Tobacco and related smoking materials.[7]
- Documents (typewriter, printers and handwriting analyses).

Forensic evidence—information generated by one or more of the forensic sciences—comes to the law in one or both of two forms. The first is referred to as a *class characteristic* statement that speaks generally to some aspect of the crime scene under examination. Testimony that the pubic hairs found on a rape-homicide victim came from a Caucasian male or that shell casings found at the scene came from a certain make and model of firearm are two typical examples of such type of statement. The second type of potential testimony generated by a forensic science is known as individual or *matching* statements, i.e., that serve to link some data found at the crime scene to a particular defendant. Testimony finding that court-ordered pubic hair exemplars obtained from the defendant are consistent in all respects to the hair located on the victim, or that fibers found on the victims clothing are consistent with fibers from the defendant's jacket will serve as examples.[8]

This idea of class characteristic statements references the reality that many confident general statements may be made under the auspices of an individual forensic discipline.[9] Several brief examples may be noted:

- A hair at the crime scene came from a Caucasian, African, or Asian male, or came from a dog or cat.
- A fiber found at the crime scene was silk or rayon or wool, or is of the type typically used in sleeping bag liners, or T-shirts, or automobile upholstery, or outdoor carpeting, etc.
- A shoe print was made by a certain type of athletic shoe sized 12 and thus the wearer was a male approximately 5'11 to 6'0, etc.
- The leafy material found on the corpse was not native to the area of the crime scene but was of a nearby area or the soil found on the victim's clothing was not native to the crime scene or the insects on the body of the victim indicate the approximate time of death.
- There are two sets of fingerprints on the knife or gun used to kill the victim, neither of which match those of the victim.
- The shell casings indicate the type of handgun used or not used, etc.

- The bones found in the grave were those of a female approximately 10 years of age, who had at one time suffered a broken collarbone.
- The blood spatter locations indicate a nondefensive series of encounters between the victim and the perpetrator.

Whether the importance of the testimony of a particular forensic scientist lies in general or class statements about units of crime scene data or an opinion linking the defendant to the crime scene through an individual or "match" opinion, the scientific foundation or basis for any such testimony, as in civil cases, is of the utmost concern to the law.

The term *forensic evidence* encompasses two distinct ideas and processes. The forensic part refers to the processes utilized in the forensic science at issue through which facts are generated. The manner in which DNA is extracted, tested, and subjected to population analyses serves as a major example. The methodologies of hair, fiber, and fingerprint examination are other illustrations. The area of forensic science encompasses a fairly discrete number of well-known disciplines, whereas the "science" addressed in product liability and environmental civil cases does not lend itself to such finite boundaries. Although there are repetitive areas of scientific focus in civil cases, such as chemistry and pharmaceuticals or biological, mechanical, or electrical engineering, there is much less of an opportunity to discuss the general outlines of acceptable methodology in such cases. The forensic sciences, traditionally associated with the prosecution of crime, do allow for such broad methodological reviews and, accordingly, are required to varying degrees by criminal courts. Nonetheless, the legal concerns are basically the same.

Initially, it is important to recall the fundamentally different reasons for the introduction of scientifically generated information in the civil and criminal litigation systems. The use of the term *litigation* is important here since it is in the process of litigation that the issues discussed here come to the fore. This is quite distinct from other contexts where the nature or acceptability of scientific methodologies or opinions are at the center of the inquiry, such as grant requests, patents, contractual disputes, or publication in a scientific peer-reviewed publication. The legal issues most involved in the science debates of the past decade are questions of the relation between scientific and legal standards to determine causation. As the century closes, similar questions are being directed to the information claims of the forensic sciences.

The evidence part of the concept of forensic evidence refers to a distinct set of procedures unique to the litigation process, separate and distinct from the processes of any forensic science or sciences that are the basis for the proffer of facts in criminal cases. At this point a discussion of the basic components of what may be referred to as the forensic science process, across individual disciplines, is necessary, as a means of furthering an understanding of the broad judicial support given the evidentiary contributions made to the criminal justice system in the form of factual assertions and/or opinions from the forensic community.

In the civil as well as criminal cases, the parties are seeking to prove or disprove a sufficiently strong connection between the defendant's act or omission and the death or injury in a suit. However, the science at issue usually consists of studies only be probative of any such connection by way of extrapolation, without individualizing expert testimony typically provided by forensic scientists.[10] Forensic evidence deals with scenarios far different from civil law tort cases, where in the latter type of case no real science is done to serve the theoretical need to prove causation. In the criminal case the use of forensic science means that some form of laboratory work is performed to resolve factual matters in the case itself. In both civil and criminal cases the information provided from scientific sources must be relevant to one of the issues in the case. In civil cases this typically involves the question of whether some commercial application of some scientific formulation "caused" the plaintiff's death or injury.

The value of forensic evidence for police and prosecutors lies in its ability to interpret multiple physiological aspects of a crime scene and, it is hoped, to link a particular suspect to it. In this respect it is of central importance to recognize that in any criminal case there are actually four crime scenes involved, each with its own set of rules and guiding principles:

- The physical crime scene created and left by the perpetrator.
- The crime scene material collected by the crime scene personnel.
- The crime scene material capable of being tested by the crime laboratory and the results of any such tests.
- The crime scene information allowed into evidence by the trial court according to the case issues and the rules of evidence.

The relative importance and focus of each of these successive crime scenes depend upon a solid understanding of four major factors, which are the bases for all aspects of the forensic sciences:

Recognition—The ability to understand what could be present at the scene.
Collection procedures—Understanding and utilizing the most current thinking on the subject of collection procedures.
Testing prodedures—Understanding and utilizing the most current thinking on the subject of forensic laboratory testing protocols.
Trial evidence requirements—Witness and exhibit foundation requirements and the applicability of relevancy under the rules of evidence.

The value of information generated by the techniques and methods of forensic science, as far as the law is concerned, initially rests upon the police authorities at the scene of a crime recognizing an item as having potential value, and properly collecting and storing it prior to laboratory analysis. If the material is not seen and collected, the forensic evidence analysis is nullified. This reality underscores the need for increased training, especially in smaller communities across America in the basic and advanced procedures for crime scene analysis.[11] In a post-O. J. Simpson legal environment, the collection process itself has become fair game for defense lawyers eager to stop the forensic evidence process from reaching its evidentiary conclusion.[12]

In many ways the O. J. Simpson trial was a timely catalyst for the current renewed focus by trial counsel and judges on the rights and wrongs of crime scene investigation and testing, from alleged failure to conduct an adequate crime scene investigation, contamination of samples, deficient testing processes, and a host of other crime scene–related issues. Law school and postgraduate legal training has recently begun reemphasizing the importance of forensic evidence instruction as well as the more familiar tools of criminal law, such as constitutional criminal procedure, criminal law theory, and the law of evidence. The importance of forensic science to criminal law lies in its potential to supply vital information about how a crime was committed and who committed it, which information may survive the screening function of the rules of evidence and be accepted as evidence of a material fact in the ensuing trial.

The basic legal antagonism between forensic scientists and the courts can be encapsulated in a single question: how far do forensic scientists say they can go in making a definitive statement about a crime scene and/or the linking of a suspect to it because they have a microscope, and how far do we let them go because we have a constitution? The importance of this question lies in the recognition of just how far and on what empirical basis any such statements can be made at all, and the impact that any such statements may have on a jury in causing any such match testimony, albeit given in a qualified manner, to be taken as true by a jury. The concern has always been that a criminalist's testimony that a hair or fiber obtained from a suspect was consistent in all respects or not dissimilar will be internalized by jurors as a statement of a definite match. It is important in this respect to realize that with the possible exception of fingerprint and ballistics testimony, the opinions of most forensic experts are typically only permitted to be couched in such qualified terms.[13]

In broadest terms the "matching" process utilized by forensic scientists involves demonstrating the manner in which a physical item from a crime scene or other data may be analyzed to provide a purported link between the defendant and the crime scene involved in the prosecution.[14] Each of the datum recovered from a crime scene, whether hair, fiber, soil, glass particles, blood products, foot or tire prints, or firearms, may be broken down into a series of subcomponents for purposes of analysis and comparison. These analytical processes and the response of the criminal justice system to them will be discussed in the chapters to follow.

It is most important to recall that the greatest number of the forensic sciences routinely used in criminal cases are basically observational, experience-based disciplines, centered in the employment of the latest microscope technology such as the comparison microscope. In today's judicial climate, especially as seen in the string of recent U.S. Supreme Court "science" cases, the designation of forensic science as science has come under pretrial scrutiny as respects the relevant methodologies that a forensic scientist routinely relies upon.

There are a series of questions that courts, prosecutors, and defense counsel need to address:

- What is the relevant scientific world I need to know?
- Where can I locate the scientific literature that I must master to use forensic science effectively to generate evidence to prosecute or defend a crime or to counter any such evidence presented?
- What are the key scientific treatises on the general subjects of criminalistics and discrete forensic sciences?

- What are the key texts regarding the theoretical and practical application of each of the discrete forensic disciplines, such as forensic anthropology, DNA analysis, or crime scene bloodstain interpretation?
- What are the basics of the forensic science involved?
- What are the leading forensic science journals that will reflect both the tried-and-true as well as the cutting-edge thinking about forensic science theory and applications?
- Who are the leading experts in each field? (We saw many of today's best in the O. J. Simpson case—i.e., Dr. Henry Lee, Dr. Michael Baden, Dr. Cyril Wecht, Dr. Robin Cotton, and William Bodziak.)
- What are the emerging theories in the world of forensic science? Where are the upcoming conferences to be held, what papers will be presented, and how are they accessible?
- Who are the emerging scholars/practitioners in the world of forensic science?
- What are the relevant professional associations for each area of forensic science, in particular, crime laboratory accreditation? What are their individual accreditation standards and procedures and how do I access them?
- Where are the leading forensic science degree programs located? How can I access their curricula and associated faculty information?[15]

II. SCIENCE AND THE CRIMINAL LAW: OVERVIEW

Shakespeare's Sir John Falstaff's impassioned narrative in *Henry IV, Part I*, of the circumstances of his skirmish with a group of vicious highway men, actually the very friends to whom he was relating the tale, has been declaimed for almost 500 years:

> I am a rogue if I were not at half sword with a dozen of them two hours together. I have scaped by miracle. I am eight times thrust through the doublet, four through the hose, my buckler cut-through and through, my sword hacked like a handsaw-ecce signum! [Behold the proof!][16]

As has also been known for almost half a century, Falstaff's spirited request to Prince Hal and companions to simply *behold the proof*, as observationally convincing as it might have been, fell on deaf ears in Mistress Quickly's Inn. Alas, the inferences were there, but the truth was known to be otherwise. Police, lawyers, and judges unfortunately do not have the benefit of knowledge of truth like Shakespeare's boon companions having a great time at Falstaff's expense. Appearances are often all they have. Often, those appearances are only there as a result of hard-won advances in the theoretical bases and laboratory tools of modern forensic science.

The gradual development of legal protections against the so-called coerced confessions and illegally seized evidence by way of 4th and 5th Amendment case law sanctions[17] has increased the simple need to prove a crime by way of circumstantial evidence. This typically involves inference "packaging" from physical data retrieved from a crime scene, analyzed in a forensic laboratory and presented to a court and jury to meet one or more of the essential facts required by criminal law theory. While the development of federal criminal procedural rights has indeed thrown prosecutorial units back onto the more traditional proof processes, it has always been the case, throughout the history of common law trials, to center proof in inferences generated from a wide variety of circumstantial evidence.

Increasingly, in the late-20th-century criminal trial, this circumstantial proof often comes in the form of forensic evidence. While this book concentrates on the subject of contemporary forensic evidence, it is important to note that the long history of proof of crime has always depended more on the experience of jurors' lives than any startling analysis developed in a laboratory. Logic and common sense have always had and will continue to have as great, if not greater, force as proba-bilistically based forensic facts. The famous French mathematician Pierre Laplace observed in 1820 that "[t]he theory of probabilities is at bottom nothing but common sense reduced to calculus."[18]

In 81 B.C., the famous orator Marcus Tullius Cicero, then the leading defense lawyer in Rome, represented Sextius Roscius of Ameria, accused of murdering his father to get possession of the patrimonial estates in the country. In the absence of forensic aid, Cicero relied on the jurors' sense of community mores, experience, common sense, and history. In response to an assertion that the defendant may have hired paid assassins, Cicero countered:

> I won't even ask you why Sextus Roscius killed his father. I only ask how he killed him . . . . How did he kill his father then? Did he strike the blow himself, or get others to do the job? If you are trying to maintain that he did it himself, let me remind you that he wasn't even in Rome. If you say he got others to do it, then who were they? Were they slaves or free men? If they were free men, identify them. Did they come from Ameria, or were they some of our Roman assassins? . . . If they were from Rome, on the other hand, how had Roscius got to know them? For after all he himself had not been to Rome for many years, and had never on any occasion stayed there for more than three days at a time. So where did he meet them? How did he get into conversation with them? What methods did he use to persuade them? He gave them a bribe. Who did he give it to? Who was his intermediary? Where did he get the money from, and how much was it?[20]

Common sense and shared experience have always had more to do with proof of fact than science. The marshaling of facts that comport with the life experience of triers of fact remains the bedrock of any criminal justice system. Indeed, a history of forensic proof might as well be referred to as a history of close observation or paying attention. For example, both Shakespeare and Sherlock Holmes knew their soil analysis.

In *Henry IV, Part I*, King Henry marked the arrival of his ally Sir Walter Blunt:

> Here is a dear, a true industrious friend,
> Sir Walter Blunt, new lighted from his horse,
> Stained with the variation of each soil
> Betwixt that Holmedon and this seat of ours,
> And he hath brought us smooth and welcome news.[21]

Dr. Watson observed of Holmes:

> Tells at a glance different soils from each other. After walks has shown me splashes upon his trousers, and told me by their colour and consistence in what part of London he had received them.[22]

Indeed, a considerable number of the forensic sciences were presaged in the first Sherlock Holmes story, *A Study in Scarlet*, where Holmes, to the amazement of Dr. Watson, arrives at important clues by rudimentary deductions utilizing blood, soil, anatomical, and footwear analyses. Holmes' observation in that famous case that the most mysterious crime scene is the most common one, still rings true as we cross the edge of the 21st century:

> It is a mistake to confound strangeness with mystery. The most commonplace crime is often the most mysterious, because it presents no new or special features from which deductions may be drawn.[23]

Inspector Lestrade's caution to the world's greatest detective that "[i]t's all very well for you to laugh, Mr. Sherlock Holmes. You may be very smart and clever, but the old hound is the best, when all is said and done,"[24] is a long-standing concern that lies at the heart of many modern arguments about the validity of forensic pronouncements in modern trials.[25]

The history of the forensic sciences is a fascinating study,[26] primarily centered around the work of individual scientific pioneers, rather than any truly systematized, publicly funded entities designed and intended to aid government prosecutors as at present.[27] The aspect of the forensic sciences that is of interest to practitioners in the criminal justice system is its potential for the production of forensic evidence, that is, facts, which, when typically combined with probability assessments geared toward a defendant's participation in a crime, aid in establishing one or more essential elements of the crime, such as intent.

How does forensic evidence differ from other evidence? Well it does and it doesn't. Forensic science involves the application of scientific theory accompanied by laboratory techniques encompassing a wide variety of the natural sciences (many of which are centered in the use of the comparison microscope and other developments in the field of microscopy) to the investigation and prosecution of crime. The sciences referred to here are often designated the *hard sciences* as opposed to the so-called *soft sciences*, based in psychiatry or psychologically centered disciplines such as criminal profiling or credibility assessments. It is important to remember that the reason for using the forensic sciences is to generate forensic evidence. That is the forensic part. The whole point is to get to the evidence part. All of this carefully gathered information is to accomplish the goal of establishing a material fact or facts at or before trial, not to demonstrate the latest technological advance or the most recent forensic science methodology.[28] The very extensive DNA testimony in the O. J. Simpson case was offered to prove his presence at the crime scene when the murders were committed.

Police and prosecutors can use all sorts of things as investigative tools, including experience, hunches, and informers, but their later use of physical data recovered from a crime scene is determined by the "evidentiary" care shown toward the entire crime scene investigation process, not the least of which is the seizing, collecting, and protection of the physical evidence before and after laboratory analysis. If the authorities do not recognize it at all or do not collect, store, and transfer it properly, it may very well be useless information. Forensic evidence, along with all other evidence, is used to reconstruct the historical event that encompasses the crime being prosecuted. Given speedy trial rules and other constitutional protections, not the least of which are the rules of evidence, such re-creations are often a formidable task for prosecutors and defense counsel.

The historian Carl Becker's observation on writing history applies with equal force to the investigation and prosecution of a crime:

> I ought first of all to explain what I mean when I use the term history. I mean knowledge of history. No doubt throughout all past time there actually occurred a series of events which, whether we know what it was or not, constitutes history in some ultimate sense. Nevertheless, much the greater part of these events we can know nothing about, not even that they occurred; many of them we can know only imperfectly; and even the few events that we think we know for sure we can never be absolutely certain of, since we can never revive them, never observe or test them directly. The event itself once occurred, but as an actual event it has disappeared; so that in dealing with it the only objective reality we can observe or test is some material trace which the event has left.[29]

Any trial, in any area of law, from the simplest to the most complex, is in essence an exercise in establishing a version of history. If a case has proceeded to trial, then one or more material facts are in question and thus must be determined by the trier of fact. Once the jury has determined the basic facts, then the court can instruct it on the law on any facts as found by it to have occurred. The history of Anglo-American common law trials is testimony to the great and ongoing difficulty in determining the basic factual basis of a case. The O. J. Simpson and JonBenet Ramsey murder cases may serve as recent modern example of this inherent difficulty in the functioning of the U.S. justice system. Both sides to the investigation of a case have their respective versions of "what happened that day." The rules of evidence that channel the information flow in a trial, as we know and use them, are primarily *exclusionary* rules, which determine what historical facts—or, on occasion, opinions—the jury will get to hear. In its simplest terms, evidence is legally approved information.

The search for past fact by a court or jury is a form of historical research, but with significant differences. Initially, the facts presented are presented by interested parties in an adversary encounter, unaccompanied by the objective search allegedly utilized by academic historians. Second, the rules of evidence do not open the inquiry to any facts that may appear logically relevant to the search, but, rather, hedge the presentation of facts in a context ruled by numerous areas of policy unknown to historians.

Historians do not have as strong a prejudice against hearsay as does the law, nor do they require the rigorous foundations for admission as are needed in common law trials. Historians have few time constraints regarding when their task is completed, whereas civil and, especially, criminal litigants are under a number of time constraints, such as statutes of limitations, 120-day speedy trial rules within which the state must try an arrestee, discovery deadlines, and the disfavor that long trials receive from today's judiciary. Finally, although historians have set high standards to determine the validity of historical conclusions,[30] they are not formally operating under a "beyond a reasonable doubt" or "preponderance of the evidence" standard as are lawyers in criminal and civil cases. The historian's standard is necessarily more fluid.[31]

Nonetheless, the history-seeking function of common law trials suffers from the same infirmity as efforts by historians to reproduce the past event.[32]

Arguments for either side of a version of history have always been at the center of legal disputes. The basic inference-based argument set out by the Roman orator Cicero still remains the primary method of convincing a jury to reach one version of history rather than another. This reality is of considerable importance in the discussion of contemporary concerns over the propriety of an expert witness's opinion and its foundation and the utilization of a wide variety of forensic sciences in the criminal justice system.

Becker's observation[32] could equally apply to any factual search in litigation, not the least of which are efforts to establish scientific facts that will be determinative of the central issues in contemporary environmental, product liability, medical malpractice, and criminal prosecutions. In the important areas of causation theory and forensic science and forensic evidence, the history question continues to be a major component in any analysis of proof of scientific fact.[33]

III. FORENSIC SCIENCE AND LEGAL HISTORY

Examining a set of rhetorical questions revolving around our core inquiry regarding the nature and value of forensic science can help to clarify the discussion to follow.

What facts, assumptions, or surmises may be obtained from the examination of one or more physical items gathered at a crime scene? What could serve as the basis for any such assumptions or projection or, simply, guesses? What value should be assigned to any such factual estimations in a criminal justice system where life, liberty, and essential justice to a victim are all in play? What does it mean to say that one or more physical items, such as hair or fiber, are or are not consistent or not dissimilar or substantially similar with another physical specimen? What would be the basis for any such statements and what value should be allocated to them if one set of exemplars was taken from a crime scene and the others from a suspected perpetrator? What does it mean in terms of long-held requirements that the elements of a crime must be proved beyond a reasonable doubt? How does circumstantial evidence fit in prosecutorial efforts designed to meet such a high bar of proof in a case partially supported by physical forensically generated evidence? How much does physical evidence depend for its force upon the other more traditional observations by eyewitnesses? How much does of all of this in the area of crime scene data comparison testimony have to do with scientific theory or recognized scientific methodology? What science, if any, has been traditionally associated with the analysis of crime scene data and how has that changed as we enter the 21st century? Is forensic analysis really sound science because of known theoretical underpinnings of the various disciplines, or because of its use of microscopy and other processes that aid its essentially observational nature?

Should it make any difference if forensic crime scene testimony is simply a combination of experience and modern microscopy? What else, from a forensic scientist's standpoint, is there to say about physical matter and its examination and the factual assumptions that follow? On the criminal law side the science-based issues cover considerable ground, ranging from proof offerings in the areas of hair and fiber analyses, soil, glass, and paint identification, and a host of facts related to forensic pathology, toxicology, blood products, and the whole area of ballistics and tool marks. In these kinds of criminal cases, some degree of science is actually being accomplished for purposes of generating material facts in the case at hand, such as DNA identifications or bullet or shell casing matching. This is quite distinct from civil, product liability–type cases centered in issues of causation, where not only is no science done for the immediate case.[34]

As noted in Chapter 1, forensic scientists are routinely involved in laboratory exercises forensic evidence-focused in criminal prosecutions. Their work is utilized to shed light on the physical dynamics that created the crime scene and, it is hoped, to add significant linking information as to the identity of the perpetrator. They are rarely involved in answering the dispositive "scientific" causation issues at the center of modern product liability litigation, the types of issues that are the focus of recent and ongoing U.S. Supreme Court decisions seeking to finalize a definitive definition of "science."[35]

The bulk of product liability cases do not deal with "science," understood in the sense discussed in the world of international science, at least in any sense of that term understood by research scientists. Rather, they focus on one of the ways a manufacturing corporation that has utilized complex but practical science to develop and market products actually designs it, or more often, publishes communications regarding the risks involved in utilizing such products by their customers.[36] Adverse drug reactions cases may serve as an illustration.

The historical hallmark of crime scene investigation has always been close observation, paying attention, and the application of common sense and logic to solving the crime being observed. This was well before the current preoccupation of the courts and legal scholars with the precise relationship of law and science, especially in areas of tort causation in the civil law and the forensic sciences in the criminal. In fact, the law has never really had anything to bring to the table regarding developing acceptable scientific methodologies, theories, and opinions.

Recourse has always been for the scientific community involved to give guidance. This was seen, however reluctantly, as an inevitable necessity in some form, from the earliest days of the common law. In *Spencer Cowper's Trial*,[37] held in England in 1699, the ongoing skirmish between courts and expert witnesses can be seen in the following exchange:

Dr. Crell: Now, my lord, I will give you the opinion of several ancient authors.

Baron Hatsell: Pray, doctor, tell us your own observations.

Dr. Crell: My lord, it must be reading, as well as a man's own experience, that will make anyone a physician, for without the reading of books of that art, the art itself cannot be attained to. Besides, my lord, I conceive that in such a difficult case as this we ought to have a great deference for the reports and opinions of learned men. Neither do I see why I should not quote the fathers of my profession in this case as well as you gentlemen of the long robe quote Coke upon Littleton in others.[38]

Baron Hatsell's understandable reluctance to allow "testimony" of authors not subject to cross-examination notwithstanding, the common law dependence on the world of science and its experts remains.

Modern criminal courts, post-*Daubert*, are feeling the increasing need to comply with defense demands to delve into the scientific bases of the whole corpus of the forensic sciences, not the least of which are the trace evidence staples of hair, fiber, soil, and finger and footwear impressions. What is coming to the surface in these recent challenges are basic observational disciplines aided by modern microscopy, without the existence of the minimal type of comparative statistical databases available in more science-based disciplines such as DNA typing and population predictability. In a legal milieu that has praised itself for its constitutionally responsible attitude regarding the imposition of scientific incursions into the factual foundation of legal theory, the basic observational base of a significant amount of the contribution of forensic sciences to the criminal law may seem alarming, but it has always been the case. This reality does not detract from the increasingly modern scientific environment in which so much forensic work is done and its factual offerings input into modern criminal trials.[39]

IV. FORENSIC SCIENCE AND CIRCUMSTANTIAL EVIDENCE

The next discussion revolves around the central topics of circumstantial evidence, specifically, traditional modes of observation and forensic practices and probability analyses. These subjects are separate but intimately related aspects of historical and contemporary attempts at truth-seeking and truth-finding in the criminal trial process. Contemporary forensic evidence conferences and the forensic literature exhibit considerable enthusiasm for the power and potential of 21st-century scientific advances for the investigation and solution of crimes, such as DNA research and developments in laser-based technology. It is often forgotten or overlooked, however, that the greater number of the traditionally employed forensic sciences are in effect based, and centered on, close observation aided by the use of modern microscopy, and do not employ any additional statistics-based projections of the potential accuracy of any proffered laboratory "match."[40] It must be remembered that the term *forensic* is a very old one. It has always been cast in terms of the presentation of arguments in public forums.[41] In fact, in the face of ongoing criticism that forensic or rhetorical arguments merely taught methods for embellishing the truth, the rejoinder, from

Plato's day, has been, on the contrary, that forensic argument is designed to "make the truth sound like the truth."[42]

An examination of U.S. criminal cases from the earliest days of the republic reveals several interesting observations in respect to expert assistance in establishing material facts in a prosecution for crime. Initially, it is of value to note just how few such cases there are that address the issue in any significant way. It is clear—as in the many more numerous science-based patent cases—that courts were generally willing to listen, even gratefully, to qualified experts, but given the basic observational and logical base for forensic-based testimony, were generally much more skeptical and, at times, demanding in such cases. Given the centrality and importance of the observational core of much of modern forensic sciences, it will be of value to examine a small selection of criminal cases from the 19th century, to mark the traditional judicial approach to premicroscopic offers of forensic assistance. The practical application of the principles of modern microscopy utilized in well-funded, professionally staffed and equipped public laboratories is a creature of the second half of the 20th century. The beginnings of the legal response to information based on studied observation, logic, and common sense are to be found in both the late 18th and second half of the 19th centuries. The real history of forensics in the law does not begin with the increasingly impressive applications of science until the 1920s and 1930s. If the assumption that forensic science is basically and historically centered in observation and extrapolation is accurate, its history runs much deeper than currently considered.[43]

A. 18TH AND 19TH CENTURY CASE ANALYSES

On a day of heavy rain on June 10, 1792 in the city of Philadelphia, Jane M'Glaughlin lost her life as the result of being pushed down a set of stairs at the entrance to her home by Margaret Biron, her landlady, and striking her head on a wall. According to Biron, she had refused M'Glaughlin admittance due to her intoxication and obstreperous behavior. Witnesses testified that the two had argued in the past without any blows being struck. Margaret Biron was indicted for murder and put to trial. At her hearing, a Doctor Hutchinson, a medical doctor, testified that he had examined the deceased's body and found "considerable" injury to the bone on one side of the head, but that the wound was not necessarily mortal. He also testified that the deceased appeared to be intoxicated at the time of her contact with the wall. Based on his testimony and that of neighbors who recalled no previous encounters between the two involving other than verbal blows, the court failed to find the mental state for murder and reduced the charge to "atrocious manslaughter."[44]

This brief report of the contribution of a medical doctor's simple observations and its obvious effect upon the court determination respecting the legal element of intent, is a very early example of the importance of the use of scientific observation as an aid to supplying material facts necessary to secure a fair decision. Three cases selected from the late 19th century are discussed next, because of their comprehensive and perceptive analyses of the nature of the idea of circumstantial evidence arising in forensic science–type settings.

'eople v. Smith,[45] decided in Ohio in 1853, the prosecuting witness, one ~lcomb, was fired at at about half-past ten o'clock at night, while standing in the parlor of a saloon near a window constructed of common window glass. Since the window sash was down, it was imperative to look through the glass to see an object on the outside. The shooter stood on the outside, not over a few feet from the window. To prove the shooter's identity, the only testimony was that of the victim, Holcomb. Holcomb testified that while leaning over to pick up his books from a table he happened to look out the window, and saw a man whom he identified as the defendant, within one or two feet of the window. The man he observed had his arm extended, and a pistol in his hand pointing toward Holcomb, and discharged it in his direction. Holcomb claimed that due to the flash of the discharge, he distinctly saw and recognized the defendant, and that he "saw his eyes, nose, and white teeth, and that he was as certain of that as he was of anything under heaven." He further testified to being in fear of the defendant for some time.

The state presented several witnesses, who were not present at the shooting, to prove by way of experiments and observations subsequently made by them at the tavern, under circumstances as to light, position, firing with a pistol, etc., like those that existed when Holcomb was shot at. This was done "for the purpose of proving by inferences, from such experiments and observations, of the light within, the darkness without, the firing of a pistol, etc., that the said Holcomb might or could have seen and known the said defendant under these circumstances and in the manner related by him."[46]

The defendant offered to prove that the state's witnesses had, at another place than that where the crime was committed, tried experiments as near as possible to those stated above, under the same circumstances of light, distance, etc., wherein the party standing inside was unable to identify the outside shooter. The state objected and argued that the witness, as an expert, was permitted to state whether he was acquainted with the laws of light and vision, and, if so acquainted, to state his opinion of the effect of a sudden light on one's vision, like that made by the firing of a gun or pistol and whether it would or would not aid one looking at a person or object in the night and darkness, in distinguishing or seeing more clearly the person or object looked at.

The court was of the unanimous opinion that the trial court erred in rejecting the defendant's offered testimony. The court noted that the victim Holcomb had sworn that he distinctly recognized the prisoner by the flash made by the discharge of the pistol:

> This was a most material statement. Without it, there was no pretense of sufficient evidence to convict. Now, it was certainly lawful to disprove this statement, by showing the impossibility, or natural improbability, of its being true. This is not denied, but it is said that it could not be done by proof of experiments. If not, how could the proof be made? No one but Holcomb was looking through the window when the crime was committed. No one but he saw the pistol fired, or the person who fired it. Direct contradiction, by eye-witnesses of the transaction, was therefore impossible and would perhaps be equally impossible in a large majority of like cases. Unless, then, proof of experiments is receivable, a man is very much at the mercy of another, who swears

against him, and perjury or mistake, however great, instead of incurring punishment, or being rectified, may answer to produce conviction. But it is said that the proper rebutting proof would be the opinions of "experts," to use the language of the bill of exceptions. Now, I apprehend, that the firing of a pistol in a man's face, at the distance of a few feet, is not quite so common an occurrence as to have raised up a class of "experts," whose acquaintance "with the laws of light and vision" makes their opinion, in a case like the present, the only competent testimony, or gives to such opinions any preference over the proof of facts. It requires no scientific witness to tell a jury whether he saw the eyes, and nose, and white of the teeth, of a man who shot at him, by the flash of the pistol that he fired.[47]

The value of common sense observations by ordinary citizens was deemed the equal, if not the more profitable basis for proof of identity here:

And proof that a number of men, of ordinary powers of vision, have tried the experiment, and found themselves unable thus to distinguish countenances—found that their vision was not thereby aided at all—is evidence entitled to as much, if not more, weight, than the opinions of scientific men can be; for the question whether a face can be thus told, is merely one of fact, and not one of science; and any man, whether learned or unlearned, after hearing the proofs, can decide with reasonable certainty upon its probability. If a man were to swear that he distinguished the color of another's eyes, at the distance of a hundred yards, could his statement be disproved only by the opinion of some one skilled in the "laws of vision?" Or, if he should testify that, with a lever of a given length, he moved a certain weight, would it be necessary, in order to contradict him, to call a witness able to talk learnedly of the vis inertiae of matter and the laws of mechanical forces? Might not experiments made by unlearned men, with such an instrument, be quite satisfactory?[48]

The state had also argued that the defendant's experiments were not made by looking through the same window-pane that Holcomb looked through. The court equally rejected that contention:

But does that deprive them of all value? Is there such a difference, in common window-glass, that the judgment could not, in any degree, be aided by an experiment made with another pane? Suppose that scientific men had been called to give their opinions, as the court ruled was proper, would all of them have been set aside who had not experimented at that identical window? Or, suppose that particular pane had been wholly destroyed by the shot, would it follow that no experiments could be made at all?[49]

In another 19th-century case, *People v. Deacons*,[50] decided by the New York Court of Appeals in 1888, the defendant, an itinerant tramp, was accused of the murder of a Mrs. Stone. The *corpus delecti* was conclusively proved by the finding of her dead body with the unambiguous evidence of a murder having been committed. The defendant confessed in a rambling and contradictory nature, claiming that he struck her in anger and panicked, trying to hide the comatose body in the victim's basement.[51]

The court moved to the single error it felt was worth discussing, a blood spot identification introduced to support the deliberate nature of defendant's actions.

Witnesses Raines and Atwood had identified certain spots which they had observed as characterized as *blood* at the top and bottom of the entrance to the victim's cellar. Raines testified that within 3 days of the killing he discovered a spot of blood on the surface of the trapdoor of the deceased's home. He proceeded to cut it out, and gave it to Mr. Atwood, and he then examined the spots on the cellar bottom. He opined that these spots were indeed blood. He testified that he inspected them under a microscope, and after comparing the spots with blood from his own finger, concluded that their appearances were *similar*. The defendant objected to the testimony as being a nonscientific offer and, accordingly, inadmissible. The court dismissed that contention, ruling that there was an important distinction between testimony that what was observed was blood as opposed to human blood:

> He thus stated simply facts, giving no opinion, and expressly admitted that he could not determine whether the spots were human blood. Mr. Atwood described himself as engaged in the business of fire insurance, but as having done a little in chemistry, and something more in microscopy. He examined the splinter under the microscope, and swears that he ascertained the stain upon it to be blood. He swears to this not as an opinion, but a fact directly founded upon his own observation. In each instance the evidence was objected to as incompetent, and the objection is defended here upon the ground that the witnesses were not experts. It was not needed that they should be. That a spot or stain is blood may be proved by any person who has observed it, and is able from such observation to state the fact . . . . If the effort had been to distinguish between human blood and that of some animal the question would have been one of science, and have required the application of very great skill and knowledge. No such effort was made.[52]

In *People v. Justus*,[53] decided by the Oregon Supreme Court in 1883, the defendant was accused of the murder of his father, by shooting him at close range while the father sat on the family front porch. The defendant testified that the discharge was accidental, occurring as a result of his having tripped in the process of putting the gun away and the gun discharging. The defendant stated that he was about 6 feet from the door when the gun went off, which he felt was about the same distance to where his father was sitting in the chair when the gun discharged, killing him. At the coroner's jury the defendant had testified that he had taken the gun at the suggestion of his father, and had gone out and shot a squirrel the dogs had treed.[54]

The defendant objected to the testimony of state witnesses that based on simulated experiments with cardboard cutouts, they concluded that the father victim was shot at a closer range than testified by the defendant, indicating a purposeful shooting. State witness, James Birdseye, at the request of the coroner and in full sight of the coroner's jury, performed several *experiments* with the defendant's gun, by firing it at targets made out of pasteboard, at different distances. During the testimony of the coroner, the state showed him the three pasteboard targets which he identified. He then testified that he saw the defendant's gun tested at different distances, and that the distances were marked, respectively, on the targets; that he saw the gun loaded when the experiments were made; that the loads of powder were a charger full; and that the charger was the one on the pouch used by the defendant. James

Birdseye testified that he loaded the gun and used the powder-flask that the defendant said he used to load the gun and filled the charger full each time and that the distances on the targets were all accurate.[55]

The court recognized that the purpose of the test and the testimony related to them were proffered to rebut by inference the defense of accidental killing by showing that the statements of the prisoner (i.e., the defendant) upon which this defense was based were inconsistent with the inferences arguably flowing from the target experiments, which would prove to be the true circumstances of the case:

> As no one was present except the prisoner when the deceased was killed, they ruled, and that his statements were inconsistent with the theory of a "near" gunshot wound, which the prosecution claimed was the cause of the death, the object of the experiments made on the pasteboard targets which were offered in evidence was to prove by inference that the deceased came to his death by a near gunshot wound at the hands of the defendant.[56]

The court noted that the witnesses who made the experiments were not experts, and thus incapable of expressing an opinion as to whether the pattern indicated by near gunshot wounds upon the human body sufficiently corresponded in appearance with that observed as the result of their experiments to connect the similitude of the fact offered to be proved with the fact in issue. The state had argued that it was offered to show only the effect engendered by near gunshots on the pasteboard targets. The state argued that the jury was undoubtedly qualified and permitted to infer that similar results would be effected by near gunshot wounds on the human body. Such inferences would suffice to illustrate that the gunshot wound from which the deceased died was the result of a near gunshot wound, arguably establishing a murderous intent.[57] The court challenged this assertion, expressing concern over the apparent lack of expertise in medical matters on the part of the witnesses:

> Is the evidence of such experiments admissible for the purposes claimed? Gunshot wounds belong to a branch of medical science, and often gave rise to many questions of a difficult nature, although, generally, a gunshot wound is easily distinguished. And among the questions frequently rising is, was the ball fired near the deceased or from a distance? Observation and study, however, in this department of science have noted and described with much exactness the appearance and character of gunshot wounds. In "near" wounds, as they are termed, when the muzzle is placed near the surface of the body of the deceased when fired, the characteristics of the wound is thus described: (1) A superficial bluish color of the skin from the contusion caused by the explosion. (2) Particles of charcoal and ignited powder imbedded in the skin. (3) Slight burning. (4) Coagulation of blood mixed with powder on the lips of the wound. If the muzzle is placed in direct contact when exploded, the wound is large and circular, the skin denuded, blackened, and burned, and the point at which the ball entered is livid and depressed.[58]

Continuing, the court observed:

> Now, it must be manifest that there are here noted so many marked characteristics of near gunshot wounds which could by no possibility be reproduced, or represented by

experiments upon pasteboard, yet upon which the fact of a near wound is made to depend, and often to be determined, that it would be utterly unsafe to apply the inferences sought to be deduced from such experiments to the fact in dispute, unless there can be found in such experiments, and the subject-matter which it is their object to explain or illustrate, some point of similitude or ground of common resemblance, always present, as a result induced by a similarity of conditions or circumstances. It may be suggested that some identity of resemblance may be traced in the powder burns exhibited by the experiments as the result of near shots, and in the wounds of the deceased which the medical authorities indicate are usually if not always present in "near" wounds. But when, as here, the case is not susceptible of direct proof, and the fact in issue—whether the ball was fired near or from a distance—depends of necessity for a correct determination upon the appearance of the wound, the fact, and its experienced consequences, does not belong to the ordinary information of men, but lies within the limits of a particular branch of medical science, and requires to be proved by persons skilled in it, the better to enable the jury to reach a safe conclusion.[59]

It would seem very questionable, the court continued, to allow nonprofessional witnesses to prove, through the instrumentality of experiments, matters not within the scope of their personal observation and experience. In addition, when it is was calculated the extent to which other aspects of near wounds aided in determining the fact of near wounds, some seemingly minor factors along with a host of other factors, the courts should clearly pause to admit such experiments as evidence, unless supported by solid reasoning or sanctioned by prior cases. Hence, the results of the pasteboard experiments were not admitted and the judgment was reversed and a new trial ordered.[60]

V. FORENSIC SCIENCE AND FORENSIC EVIDENCE

Forensic evidence for trial purposes cannot be separated from the testimony of forensic experts. Based upon this reality, many legal issues follow, not the least of which is a minimal understanding of the rules of criminal discovery and the overarching rules of evidence themselves, which control the entirety of the information flow in any trial, not just one for the prosecution of a criminal act.

Many important and dispositive issues arise from the necessary presence of forensic experts in criminal trials: what is science? Who qualifies as an expert? Who must pay for them? How does criminal discovery provide for the exchange of scientific information between the prosecution and defense? The first big subject involves the question of what the appropriate standards of "forensic" science are that can support a proffer of fact that can be used to establish a material fact in a case. It cannot be overlooked that the term *forensic science* implies the use of a scientific theory or methodology to generate facts in the investigation and prosecution of a crime. The *Daubert* question is a preliminary question as to whether it is a reliable and fair way to generate a material fact, let alone a particular fact that may be used in any particular prosecution.

VI. FORENSIC SCIENCE, PROBABILITY, AND THE LAW

The foregoing brief review of several selected cases from the 19th century are instructive as we begin the 21st, especially in regard to the look that inference and probability may have in our near and distant future. These are the kernel and *raison d'etre* of circumstantial evidence, the engines of forensic evidence and the criminal prosecutorial process itself.

Robert Hooke, the early-17th-century inventor of the microscope and an associate of the great experimentalist Sir Robert Boyle, along with Francis Bacon, recognized the difficulty of finding adequate systems for the testing of scientific claims and productions, especially in cases of attempts to fashion one uniform set of constructs for any such task:

> For the limits to which our thoughts are confined, are small in respect of the vast extent of Nature itself; some parts of it are too large to be comprehended, and some too little to be perceived, and from thence it must follow that not having a full sensation of the object, we must be very lame and imperfect in our conceptions about it, and in all the propositions which we build upon it; hence we often take the shadow of things for the substance, small appearances for good similitudes, similitudes for definitions; and even many of those, which we think to be the most solid definitions are rather expressions of our misguided apprehension than of the true nature of the things themselves.[61]

The danger of seeing more than there is to see in the results of experimental processes continues to be a focus of attention in countless criminal appeals involving forensic evidence issues. It is an old worry that has been with us since the birth of modern scientific method.

Professors Steven Shaplin and Simon Schaffer in their book *Leviathan and the Air Pump* provide a fascinating study of the struggle between theorists and those who considered themselves experimentalist pioneers in the study of nature. They observe:

> The English experimentalists of the mid-seventeenth century and afterwards increasingly took the view that all that could be expected of physical knowledge was "probability," thus breaking down the radical distinction between "knowledge" and "opinion." Physical hypotheses were provisional and revisable; assent to them was not obligatory, as it was to mathematical demonstrations; and physical science was, to varying degrees, removed from the realm of the demonstrative. The probabilistic conception of physical knowledge was not regarded by its proponents as a regrettable retreat from more ambitious goals; it was celebrated as a wise rejection of a failed project. By the adoption of a probabilistic view of knowledge, one could attain to an approximate certainty and aim to secure legitimate assent to knowledge-claims. The quest for necessary and universal assent to physical propositions was seen as inappropriate and illegitimate. It belonged to a "dogmatic" enterprise, and dogmatism was seen not only as a failure but as dangerous to genuine knowledge.[62]

This perceptive observation applies with equal force to contemporary discussions of the place of probability in the forensic sciences and the use of their contributions to the investigation and trial of criminal cases.

Beginning with the famous decision by the California Supreme Court in *People v. Collins*[63] in 1968, there has been a steady stream of law review articles and symposia, that come and go, arguing for or against the development of a mathematically centered system for the weighing of evidence in criminal cases and the devising of a juror system for both weighing and compounding such values into a verdict.

The rapid disintegration of all such proposals into mathematical symbols that would befuddle the most conscientious judge and jury has considerably diminished the attractiveness of the ideas for the practicing forensic scientists and trial lawyers. Nonetheless, there is still considerable respectable academic interest in and support for such systems of evidence evaluation.[64]

In a recent article in the *Jurimetrics Journal* entitled "Forerunners of Bayesianism in Early Forensic Science,"[65] authors F. Taroni, C. Champod, and P. Margot observe that in many areas of forensic science, such as those involving hair, fiber, fingerprints, tool marks, shoe prints, paint, and document examination, the Bayesian approach remains ignored or untrusted. The article argues that it is time for Bayesian methods of evaluating evidence to be generalized to all transfer traces including shoe prints and fingerprints. Such a broad use of the Bayesian perspective, the authors contend, not only follows from the recent achievements of statistical argument in forensic science, but also from the history of its earlier and productive use, at the turn of the 19th century, in a number of disparate trace evidence cases and contexts.[66]

As noted by Taroni, Champod, and Margot:

> Scientific evidence, though used in court for centuries, did not achieve real prominence until the end of the 19th century, when new scientific techniques (such as anthropometry and fingerprinting) became increasingly common in police inquiries. Alphonse Bertillon provided solutions to the problem of identification of habitual offenders. His most famous innovation was the application of anthropometry in the context of criminal law, following the techniques employed at the time by Quetelet, Topinard, or Broca. Bertillon proposed to use somatic measurements (nine, and later twelve, measures taken with utmost precision at particularly invariable adult body locations) as discriminating characteristics for the identification of habitual offenders.[67]

Edmond Locard was perhaps the most famous forensic scientist of the 19th century, renowned for his "Locard Principle," i.e. all close physical contacts result in an exchange of trace amounts of matter, typically hairs, fibers, soils, and other trace evidence physical specimens. He taught that the physical certainty provided by scientific evidence rested upon evidential values of different orders, which were measurable and could be expressed numerically:

> Hence the expert knows and argues that he knows the truth, but only within the limits of the risks of error inherent to the technique. This numbering of adverse probabilities should be explicitly indicated by the expert. The expert is not the judge: he should not be influenced by facts of a moral sort. His duty is to ignore the trial. It is the judge's duty to evaluate whether or not a single negative evidence, against a sextillion of probabilities, can prevent him from acting. And finally it is the duty of the judge to decide if the evidence is in that case, proof of guilt . . . . These guidelines remain pertinent to scientists or lawyers even today, eighty years later.[68]

Taroni, Champod, and Margot indicate in their footnote materials a somewhat blasé acceptance of the reality that, to date, there are no statistics available for the greatest number of forensic sciences involving fields such as hair, fiber, soil, footprints, tire impressions, etc.:

Currently, probabilities of error are not provided with most scientific evidence. While DNA evidence is necessarily accompanied by some statistics, other forensic fields, such as those involving fingerprints, shoe prints, tool marks, or document examinations, do not appear to lend themselves to a statistical approach . . . . Moreover, even if probabilities are common in biological evidence, a large span of error estimations (in laboratory errors, for example) is systematically ignored.[69]

An editorial in *Science and Justice*, the leading British forensic journal, entitled, "Does Justice Require Less Precision Than Chemistry?"[70] takes issue with the latest and perhaps most successful brief for a Bayesian approach to the evaluation of criminal evidence, "Interpreting Evidence,"[71] by Robertson and Vignaux. The editorial cites recent DNA rulings in England holding that the use of statistics based on Bayes theory by a jury trespassed on an area particularly within the province of the jury's traditional perogatives. The English Appeal Court has held that the use of defense-sponsored mathematical formulas for the weighing of evidence was inappropriate and might be impractical should different jurors apply different values to particular items of evidence, commenting that jurors evaluate evidence by the joint application of their individual common sense and knowledge of the world to the material before them.[72] The editorial writer, Alistair R. Brownie, concludes:

This appears to signal a fairly comprehensive rejection of the use of probability calculations in English criminal law and a dashing of the hope expressed by Robertson and Vignaux that logic, probability and inference would provide the language of which lawyers and scientists would communicate with each other . . . . [J]ustice in the United Kingdom does not require or welcome the precision of the chemist. Or at least at present it does not encourage the amateur to dabble.[73]

The combination of logic, experience, and common sense remains the tool of judges, prosecutors, defense lawyers, and jurors, as it has since the earliest days of English and American criminal jurisprudence. The use of probability analysis in nonforensic criminal settings illustrates its ongoing validity, if not necessity, in a criminal justice system centered in the balancing of conflicting bodies of circumstantial evidence. Indeed, given the historical necessity for the gathering and arguing of inferences from circumstantial evidence and the concomitant use of formal or informal probability analyses, we must always remind ourselves that our system of criminal justice resides in a world of probability.

Indeed, the use of inferences is at the center of many, if not most, of our factfinding experience. As observed by the historian Robin Winks:

We all make inferences daily, and we all collect, sift, evaluate, and then act upon evidence. Our alarm clocks, the toothpaste tube without a cap, warm milk on the breakfast table, and the bus that is ten minutes late provide us with evidence from which we infer certain unforeseen actions. The historian must reconstruct events often hundreds of years in the past, on the basis of equally homely although presumably more significant data, when the full evidence will never be recoverable and, for that portion of it recovered, when it may have meanings other than we would attach to similar evidence today. Thus the historian has evolved his standards of inquiry, of thoroughness, and of judgment to provide him with a modus operandi.[74]

Given the fragility of contemporary litigation's version of reconstructing an historical event—due to the consistent absence of direct proof on central issues—how do we accept and shape our uses of probability and what does its centrality say about our theoretical insistence on proof beyond a reasonable doubt?

In the 1998 case of *Wynn v. State*,[75] the defendant was charged with housebreaking and thefts, based upon his being found in possession of the stolen items. The state sought to introduce evidence of his having been charged with similar activity in the past. The Court of Appeals held that evidence that the defendant committed housebreaking and theft other than the case for which he was on trial was not admissible under the "absence of mistake" exception to the "other crimes" rule.[76] Justice Raker, dissenting, agreed with both the trial court and the Court of Special Appeals that the admission of the evidence in question was fitted properly under the "absence of mistake or accident" exception to the general rule of exclusion of other crimes evidence set out in Maryland Rule 5-404(b). Wynn's possession of the goods stolen from the Quigley home, the home in question, explained throughout his trial defense as the result of an innocent and unknowing purchase at a flea market, might otherwise be characterized as "unintentional," "mistaken," or even "accidental." It was for the purpose of dispelling Wynn's express claim, and its various possible characterizations, that the trial court rightfully permitted the prosecution to present evidence of Wynn's possession of goods stolen from the other residences. Justice Raker's analyzed the problem from the standpoint of probability analyses under the aegis of the *doctrine of chances:*

> The theory of relevance underlying the admission of the other crimes evidence in this case is perhaps better, and more intuitively, explained by the doctrine of chances, also known as the "doctrine of objective improbability," a doctrine first articulated by Professor Wigmore, and now recognized generally by courts and commentators. In actuality, the doctrine was recognized by the trial judge, although not articulated as such . . . . The doctrine of chances is based on probabilities, and is premised on the proposition that mere coincidence is less probable as the recurrence of similar events increases.[77]

Professor Wigmore articulates this doctrine as follows:

> The argument here is purely from the point of view of the doctrine of chances—the instinctive recognition of that logical process which eliminates the element of innocent intent by multiplying instances of the same result until it is perceived that this element cannot explain them all. Without formulating any accurate test, and without attempting by numerous instances to secure absolute certainty of inference, the mind applies this rough and instinctive process of reasoning, namely, that an unusual and abnormal element might perhaps be present in one instance, but that the oftener similar instances occur with similar results, the less likely is the abnormal element likely to be the true explanation of them.[78]

Professor Edward Imwinkelried, one of the best American evidence scholars, has commented that the fortuitous coincidence may become too abnormal, bizarre, implausible, unusual, or objectively improbable to be believed. The coincidence becomes telling evidence of *mens rea*.[79] Dean Wigmore observed, in short, that similar results do not usually occur through abnormal causes.[80] The U.S. Court of Appeals for the Seventh Circuit, in the case of *United States v. York*, has recently characterized the basis of the doctrine in noting that "the man who wins the lottery once is envied; the one who wins it twice is investigated."[81] In this example, the *Wynn* dissent noted, the probative value of the legally permissible inference can be drawn independently of the prohibited inference: the subjective character of the two-time lottery winner. It is the objective implausibility of the occurrence, *sans* nefarious activity, which, according to the dissent, rebuts the claim of an innocent occurrence.[82]

The dissent in *Wynn* observed that the doctrine of chances rests on the trial court's assessment of the improbability that someone would be innocently involved in similar activity. In determining whether other crimes evidence is sufficiently probative, even one act may be sufficient. The proper focus was not necessarily quantitative; instead, the proper focus was the qualitative value of the evidence within the particular context of an individual case. Similarly, the question of how many similar events are enough depends on the complexity and relative frequency of the event rather than on the total number of occurrences. The unlikely coincidence that *Wynn* purchased the items at a flea market triggered the court's appropriate, albeit unspecified, application of the doctrine of chances.[83]

The standing of probability analyses in our criminal justice system is still of the greatest concern in respect to achieving basic justice. This is especially the case in the area of forensic science and its outgrowth in the form of forensic evidence. Not the least of the probability analyses question marks is the absence of a statistical base in most of the forensic sciences, with which to determine the chances of any proffered "match" occurring in the general population.[84]

VII. FORENSIC SCIENCE, FORENSIC EVIDENCE, AND THE MODERN CRIME SCENE

The basic methodologies of the majority of the forensic sciences have received guarded acceptance in most state courts. Many, however, have never really been subjected to a close *Frye* or *Daubert* preliminary scrutiny. Until very recent years, forensic sciences such as hair and fiber analysis have simply been routinely accepted without objection.

A good recent example is the Indiana Supreme Court 1997 opinion in *McGrew v. State*,[85] a rape case involving testimony "matching" a pubic hair found in the car where the victim was allegedly attacked and a pubic hair exemplar from the defendant. Prior to releasing the state's expert hair analyst, the court directed a telling series of questions to him:

COURT: [I]n regard to the examination. It is simply a physical, visual examination of the hair?

ANALYST: Yes, sir.

COURT: You simply say that one hair looks like another one or it doesn't look like another one?

ANALYST: I say its sufficiently similar to have come from that person or it is dissimilar.

COURT: And if you say that it . . . [is] similar to come from that person . . . that doesn't mean that it comes from that person.

ANALYST: It just simply means that it could have come from that person.

COURT: And you do not know the statistical percentages of how many people would have similar hair?

ANALYST: There are no statistics. It's hard to say.[86]

Modern case reports are increasingly filled with lengthy discussions of forensic expertise.[87] Whether under claims of incompetency of counsel or the trial court's failure to supply indigents with adequate funding with which to hire their own experts, courts are increasingly engaging in wide-ranging forensic science discussions. A striking fact about such recent cases is that in most states before the post-*Daubert* era, the bulk of the contemporary claims of scientific inadequacy were either not raised at all or given short shrift by the courts. Today, prosecutors, citing the years-long use by police of these sciences, argue for their unchallenged acceptance. Defense counsels are increasingly seeking to challenge the bases for forensic science, especially in the trace evidence area. However, a recent examination of cases seems to indicate that a serious post-*Daubert* challenge to the scientific validity of the corpus of forensic sciences may be a day late and a dollar short. A very recent discussion of this type is found in cases analyzing the *Frye* standard's general scientific acceptability or the *Daubert*'s relevant and reliable standards on the subject of Luminol or phenolphthalein testing as presumptive tests for the presence of blood at a crime scene.

Luminol and phenolphthalein are used as presumptive tests in the field to identify potential bloodstains. However, the two tests can generate false-positive reactions.[88] The tests can react to metal surfaces, cleansers containing iron-based substances, horseradish, and rust. Neither test can distinguish between animal blood and human blood, nor can they determine how long the substance has been at the scene. When a positive reaction occurs, a criminalist must do a confirmatory test to determine conclusively that the test sample is human blood. For these reasons, courts have been very wary of accepting the scientific validity of blood findings. It is important, however, to realize that Luminol and phenolphthalein have been and continue to be routinely used by police as investigative tools and as a basis for obtaining a search warrant. There is a noticeable movement toward acceptance of these chemical tests as presumptive proof of the presence of human blood at a crime scene. Luminol analyses are often used in conjunction with blood-spatter pattern analysis, central to many crime scene reconstruction efforts.[89]

Courts since the late 19th century have been willing to accept testimony from both lay and expert witnesses that they observed what appeared to be human blood.[90] This issue has been recently revisited in a 1998 Arkansas murder case.

In *Ayers v. State*,[91] a 1998 Arkansas Supreme Court decision, the defendant was convicted a of capital murder and theft of property in excess of $2,500.00.

Sometime between 12 o'clock midnight, February 24, 1995, and 1:00 A.M., February 25, 1995, in the parking lot of the Whisperwood Apartments on Baseline Road in Little Rock, appellant Antonio Ayers and William Hall were involved in an argument. As the argument intensified, Ayers drew a gun and shot Hall once in the chest and once in the back, as Hall tried to run away. Hall continued running from Ayers, but Ayers caught up with Hall and began kicking him and beating him until Hall was left lying on the parking lot. Ayers then left but returned in Hall's vehicle and drove over Hall's body. Ayers then fled the scene in Hall's vehicle, leaving Hall for dead.[92]

At trial, the state presented evidence showing that after appellant shot the victim he got into Hall's vehicle and drove over him. During the state's direct examination of Annette Tracy, a Little Rock Police Department crime scene specialist, Tracy described an exhibit as a photograph of the underside of Hall's vehicle with what appeared to her to be possible blood on the oil pan. The state then moved to admit the photograph. Defendant objected to the admission of the exhibit, claiming that it was not relevant and was unduly prejudicial because Tracy had described only "possible blood." The state responded that subsequent evidence would establish that samples collected from the underside of the car were identified as human blood of the victim's blood type. On that basis, the trial court admitted the photograph.

At trial, Scott Sherill, a forensic serologist with the state crime laboratory, testified that the substance shown in the state's Exhibit 25 was indeed human blood but that he was unable to determine the blood type. The defendant relied on *Brenk v. State*,[93] a 1993 Arkansas opinion, and the court here noted that the Brenk case confronted the issue of whether or not evidence of Luminol testing should be allowed in light of the fact that Luminol does not distinguish among certain metals, vegetable matter, human blood, and animal blood. There, the court had held that evidence about the use of Luminol would not be admissible unless additional tests showed that the substance tested was human blood related to the alleged crime. *Brenk* clearly did not apply to the facts of the instant case because Luminol was not used and because serological testing showed that the substance found underneath Hall's car was, in fact, human blood.[95]

In the instant case, the state having presented unchallenged evidence that the appellant drove over Hall in Hall's vehicle after shooting him, the court found that the state proved that Hall had, in fact, been underneath the car, where the blood was found, at a time when he was bleeding profusely from newly inflicted gunshot wounds. This, the court found, presented very convincing circumstantial evidence connecting the blood found underneath the victim's vehicle with this crime.[95]

In *State v. Canaan*,[96] a 1998 Kansas Supreme Court case involving presumptive tests for the presence of blood, the defendant was convicted of premeditated murder, aggravated robbery, and aggravated burglary. Sometime in the morning hours of October 20, 1994, Michael Kirkpatrick was murdered. The evening before, he was observed at a bar with Canaan. During the investigation, a neighbor of the deceased, one Jerry Staley, informed police that the defendant had been at the victim's house the evening before and had been driving a maroon Oldsmobile. Because the victim had been with Canaan, police went to the defendant's home to ask what he knew of the homicide. The officers observed a maroon Oldsmobile at Canaan's home.

The defendant was soon after injured in a crash following a high-speed car chase while attempting to evade arrest. During the investigation, the police requested John Wilson of the Regional Crime Laboratory to conduct Luminol tests. During the course of the investigation, John Wilson also performed a Luminol test on the Oldsmobile Canaan was driving the night of the murder, which indicated the possible presence of blood on the left corner of the driver's seat and door panel. An additional Luminol test of Canaan's home showed the presence of bloody footprints on the front porch and step and down the main hallway into the master bedroom. The footprints turned at the edge of the bed as if someone had turned and sat down on the bed. The Luminol also reacted when it was placed on a watch found in a bedroom. Further presumptive tests validated the reaction to blood on the Oldsmobile seat.[97]

Canaan then filed a motion asserting that the Luminol testing failed to meet the general acceptability requirement of *Frye*, but the trial court found that Luminol testing had achieved widespread acceptance, was not really novel or new, and, once the State laid its foundation for use in the instant case, no *Frye* hearing was warranted.

At trial, Canaan renewed his objection to the introduction of Luminol evidence, asserting Luminol is only a presumptive test for blood. In other words, it may indicate the presence of blood, but also reacts similarly with other materials, including common household cleansers. The district court ruled that the fact that the Luminol test was a presumptive test goes only to the weight, rather than the admissibility, of the evidence. On appeal, Canaan argued the district judge should have conducted a *Frye* hearing because Kansas had never determined the reliability of Luminol evidence.[98] Additionally, Canaan argued, there was no evidence that state expert John Wilson was qualified to testify as an expert in the field of Luminol testing techniques or as to the validity and reliability of the exact techniques he used in this case.

At trial, John Wilson testified that he had been the chief chemist at the Regional Crime Laboratory in Kansas City since 1978, where he supervised other chemists, analyzed various categories of trace evidence (such as blood), and went to crime scenes when requested. He also taught 2 crime scene classes a year for local law enforcement in Kansas and Missouri to train people how to conduct a proper crime scene investigation. He had also earned a degree in biology and chemistry and had worked at the Johnson County Crime Laboratory 2 years prior to becoming the chief chemist for the Regional Crime Laboratory. He attended a number of seminars in blood analysis presented at the FBI academy in Quantico, Virginia, some classes presented by the American Association of Forensic Sciences,[99] some at the University of California, and others. His total forensic chemistry career had spanned 23 years.[100] Wilson further testified that he had received training in Luminol testing. He had completed a number of classes at the FBI academy, including a crime scene investigation course, and had attended various seminars sponsored by the Midwest Association of Forensic Scientists.[100] The court accepted expert Wilson's careful description of the process of presumptive blood testing using Luminol:

> Wilson testified that Luminol testing has been used by forensic scientists for about 60 years. It has been available for approximately 80 years and scientific papers on Luminol were published in the 1920's. He testified that he had conducted Luminol testing hundreds of times and has testified as an expert witness in other criminal cases over

the years regarding the results of Luminol testing . . . . Wilson explained how Luminol testing works: Luminol is a chemical that reacts with blood and undergoes a chemical reaction that gives off light (chemiluminescence). When blood and Luminol come into contact, it essentially causes a very faint blue glow that one can see in the dark. Luminol testing works by placing a Luminol reagent in very small concentrations in a sodium hydroxide water solution and then placing it in a spray mister, which creates a very fine mist. The forensic chemist makes the area as dark as possible because the actual spraying needs to occur in total darkness. The forensic chemist then begins spraying the very fine mist in the area to be searched for blood stains. If blood is present, a chemical reaction causes a blue glow. The chemiluminescence of the blood and Luminol mixture occurs if it is dark enough and there is enough blood present. Luminol testing is extremely sensitive, depending on what one is looking for and what surface is being sprayed. It is sensitive to 1:1,000,000 to 1:10,000,000 parts per million.[101]

Responding to defendant's claims of the reaction of Luminol to a number of common non-blood substances, Wilson testified that Luminol is actually fairly specific for blood and that there are few things other than blood that cause it to react. Forensic scientists, he continued, use it on a regular basis as an investigative tool to locate crime scenes that have been cleaned and are able on occasion to reconstruct what occurred at the crime scene, such as the sequence of events, where the blood was, perhaps how it was cleaned up, and maybe even tracks made by footprints that have blood on them. Luminol could reveal tire tracks, shoe prints, and handprints that were made in blood. The duration of the luminescent results of a positive test before fading would vary from a few seconds to several minutes, and, ideally, it would last long enough to photograph.[102]

The time it remains luminescent depends upon the material the blood is on and how the spray that is being used affects it. In his years of experience, Wilson had had occasion to have positive Luminol results for footprints 20 to 50 times. There was one occasion where he was able to follow a person outdoors across a public park for over a quarter of a mile. Wilson stated that the Luminol test is generally accepted as a presumptive test for blood in the scientific community of forensic science and is recognized as reliable within the scientific community of forensic scientists.

The court in *Canaan* ruled that only when there was a doubt about the scientific reliability of evidence must the state prove its reliability and acceptance of the science, and held that Luminol testing was universally accepted. The trial court did require the state to lay a foundation as to Wilson's qualifications to administer the test, and a review of Wilson's testimony shows he was clearly qualified to administer the Luminol tests and that the underlying science was reliable and accepted.[103]

Luminol also withstood challenge in the recent case of *State v. Maynard*,[104] where defendant was convicted of second-degree murder and armed criminal action. The court of appeals also held that a testifying police detective was qualified as expert witness in Luminol testing.

Wendell Maynard lived with his girlfriend, Rewa Walker, in Kansas City, Missouri. Ms. Walker spent the evening of March 10, 1993, with Lashawn Hollingshed, Mr. Maynard's cousin. According to Ms. Hollingshed, Ms. Walker called Mr. Maynard from a pay phone between 10:00 and 11:00 P.M. to tell him that she was on her way home and that she loved him. Ms. Walker's body was found over a year later. She had been murdered. Mr. Maynard was charged with first-degree murder and armed criminal action.

The detective assigned to the case, Detective Owings, found blood droplets on a living room mirror and similar specimen scrapings on the fish tank in the living room. The detective noticed visible blood spatters on the living room walls, ceiling, and door molding and noticed a large bloodstain on a carpet remnant. Detective Owings found a steamer carpet cleaner on the defendant's porch which had blood in its internal chamber, a checkered comforter with blood on it in the dining room, a table in the kitchen with blood on it, and two pieces of a gold-colored chain, a gold-colored lion pendant, and a broken gold-colored ring in the bedroom, all with blood on them.[105]

Police performed Luminol tests on the stairs leading up to the front door of defendant's apartment, the dining room carpet, and the trunk of the deceased's automobile. The tests displayed a blue glowing color, which is a positive indication of blood. Frank Booth, a forensic chemist with the Regional Crime Laboratory, also testified that the positive tests indicated the presence of blood. Mr. Booth agreed, however, that the presence of rust, dust particles, or some cleaning agents could also cause a positive response.[106]

The police determined that the 24-inch bloodstain on the carpet remnant was consistent with having resulted from a gunshot wound to the head. Although the blood spatters found throughout the house were not consistent with gunshot wounds, they could have been caused by two persons fighting or by moving a bloody object around. The bloodstains on the stairway leading up to Mr. Maynard's apartment were likely caused by someone's having dragged a bloody object up or down the stairs. The bloodstains in the trunk of Ms. Walker's Saab were likely caused by a large bloody object being placed in the trunk. The examination of the defendant's coveralls showed that they contained bloodstains on the left hip area, across the lap area, the back left shoulder, and the right sleeve.[107]

The court ruled that Detective Owings was sufficiently qualified to testify as an expert about Luminol testing, since he received training at the Regional Crime Laboratory from the chief chemist, John Wilson, respecting Luminol tests at crime scenes and had conducted Luminol tests on multiple occasions.[108]

The extensive nature of the modern crime scene investigation and prosecution becomes apparent each year as defense counsels raise an increased number and variety of challenges to the claims of modern forensic science. Recent cases in a wide range of crimes, but especially in homicide and sexual assault charges, may serve as indicators of the complexity of modern crime scenes and the extensive knowledge of forensic matters with which lawyers are charged with knowing. A single crime scene can involve a multiple of forensic science and concomitant legal issues.

VIII. FORENSIC SCIENCE AND THE CRIMINAL LAW: A CASE STUDY

This chapter concludes with a case study arising out of the rape-murder of a 10-year-old child in a rural Illinois community. The purpose of this exercise is to demonstrate the complexity of the modern crime scene from a forensic science and forensic evidence standpoint. This is especially the case in instances of sexual assault and homicide.

In *People v. Sutherland,*[109] decided by the Illinois Supreme Court in 1993, the defendant was convicted of aggravated kidnaping, aggravated criminal sexual assault, and murder. An oil field worker discovered the nude body of 10-year-old Amy Schultz. Her clothes—her shirt, shorts, underpants, shoes, and socks—were found strewn along the oil lease road. Due to the lack of any eyewitnesses, the trial was centered in the presentation of forensic evidence in the areas of forensic pathology, hair and fiber analysis, and tire tread casting impression comparisons. The Sutherland case study serves as a clear example of the ongoing interrelationship between the world of forensic science and the investigation and proof of crime.

Significant questions about justice are at the heart of this and all other similar prosecutions. Let's return to some critical questions set forth earlier in this chapter. What facts or assumptions or surmises may be obtained from the examination of one or more hairs or fibers gathered at a crime scene? What could serve as the basis for any assumptions or projections or, simply, guesses? What value should be assigned to any such factual estimations in our criminal justice system where life and liberty and justice to a victim are all in play? What does it mean to say that one or more hairs or fibers or tire tracks are or are not "consistent or not dissimilar or substantially similar" with another? What would be the basis for any such statements and what value should be allocated to them if one set of exemplars was taken from a crime scene and the others from a suspected perpetrator?

What does it mean in terms of long-held requirements that the elements of a crime must be proved beyond a reasonable doubt? How does forensically generated circumstantial fact fit in with prosecutorial efforts designed to meet such a high bar of proof in cases partially supported by hair or fiber evidence? How much does hair, fibe, or tire tread evidence depend for its force upon other more traditional observations by eyewitnesses? How much of all of this in the area of hair or fiber analysis and comparison testimony has to do with scientific theory or recognized scientific methodology? What science, if any, has been traditionally associated with hair, fiber, or tire tread analyses and how has that changed as we approach the 21st century? Are hair, fiber, or tire tread comparisons *scientific* in respect to the theoretical underpinnings of those who are devoted to its functioning in a criminal investigation and trial or because of its use of microscopy, business, or other processes that aid its essentially observational nature? Should it make any difference if they are simply a combination of experience and modern microscopy? What else, from a forensic scientist's standpoint, is there to say about hair, fiber, or tire tread analyses and the factual assumptions that follow? Is there more there to give hair, fiber, or tire tread analysis as great or greater claim to belief than fingerprint, impression, ballistics, tool marks, or DNA?[110]

In the "trace areas" of hair, fiber, soil, paint, and glass, the predictive capabilities will vary widely, with something less, *or much less*, than individual identification of a sample exemplar with crime scene data. So, for each separate discipline discussed henceforth, we need to ask what this science *can say* and what it *cannot say*. What are the basic methodologies used in this field in its practitioner's efforts to bring forth "identifying" evidence? How many accepted modes are there to compare hair, fiber, tire casts, soil samples, DNA, bullets, shell casings, etc.? How have the courts responded to these various techniques and their exclusionary or inclusionary claims? It is also very important to note the definitive *exclusionary* capability of these "trace" sciences. The trick here is trying to figure out how strong is the *inclusion*.

What can be determined with a fairly high confidence level as respects hair analysis? Hair is class evidence and thus it is not possible, except in rare instances, to determine that a questioned hair sample came from a particular individual to the exclusion of others. However, as long as a match is not claimed, and there are good class comparisons made, particular transactional facts can pretty much cinch it in the eyes of a jury. The science makes very strong claims in the area of *class characteristic* statements, such as that the examined exemplar is hair, and is human vs. animal hair, male vs. female hair, infant vs. mature adult hair, Caucasian, Negroid, or Asiatic hair, whether the hair was forcibly removed, the body area as source, and an increasing number of other general conclusions.

However, in respect to linking a hair from a crime scene to a hair exemplar obtained from a suspect, the terms allowed by courts to support the "identification" of a crime scene hair with a sample taken from a defendant are much more verbally circumspect. The typical terminology encompasses such conclusory terms as *compatible with, consistent with, not dissimilar, substantially similar,* and *consistent in all respects.*

What can a simple fiber tell us from a class characteristic standpoint? To what degree should police and defense counsel be concerned with weather, temperature, terrain, wildlife, and other nonfiber elements and influences invariably present in many crime scene scenarios? What are possible fiber sources in each crime scene? What are the class characteristics of fiber data? What are the comparison points in attempts to connect fibers found at the crime scene to fibers associated with the defendant in the case at hand? What is there to compare in fiber analyses?[111] Initially, it is important to identify the broadest categories of fibers and then work down to the fiber characteristics actually used in making fiber comparisons and accompanying pronouncements by forensic specialists.

Fibers fall into two categories, natural and synthetic. Both types are used in the manufacture of commercial products of a wide variety, ranging from all types of apparel, automobile seat covers, and home, office, toys, and automobile coverings. All commercial offerings typically provide an immense variety of styles and colors to choose from. To a significant degree, all such fiber and the commercial processes used to produce the fiber itself and its applications are patented and collected in massive proprietary databases maintained by manufacturers. Although not generally available to police authorities or the public at large, these database collections are typically available to forensic experts on a cooperative, case-by-case basis by the international fiber industry.

Fibers come in three basic categories: animal, vegetable, and mineral. Natural fibers thus include animal fibers such as wool, silk, and furs. Vegetable fibers include cotton, linen, jute, hemp, and sisal. Mineral fibers include asbestos, glass, wool, and fiberglass. The number of synthetic fibers is legion, including acetates, acrylics, nylons, polyester, spandex, and a host of others. These are the types of fibers that can be located at a crime scene and subsequently identified as to type and commercial application, if need be.[112]

Tire treads are also quite varied in design and easily traced to a manufacturer, dependent, however, on the quality of the casting and photographic technique used to preserve the tread impression at the crime scene. The comparison of tread impressions is a commonly used tool in crime scene investigations.[113]

Given this brief background on the types of forensic issues involved in the *Sutherland* case, we will now proceed to a close examination of the case study.

A. THE FACTS

At 9 A.M. on July 2, 1987, an oil field worker discovered the nude body of 10-year-old Amy Schultz of Kell, Illinois. The body was found approximately 100 feet from an oil lease access road in rural Jefferson County, lying on its stomach covered with dirt. There were shoe prints on her back and several hairs were found stuck in her rectal area. In addition, a large open wound on the right side of Amy's neck exposed her spinal cord area. A pool of blood around Amy's head indicated that the murderer had killed her where she lay.[114]

Amy Schultz's shirt, shorts, underpants, shoes, and socks were found scattered along the oil lease road. Automobile tire impressions were found 17 feet from the body, and a shoeprint impression was found near the tire impressions similar in design to that on the body. The police took casts of the tire and shoe print impressions.[115]

Dr. Steven Neurenberger performed an autopsy on July 3, 1987. He observed a 14.5-centimeter wound running from the middle of Amy's throat to behind her right ear lobe, which cut through the neck muscles, severing the carotid artery and jugular vein, and cutting into the cartilage between the neck and vertebrae. Amy's right eye had hemorrhaged and there was a small abrasion near her left eyebrow; her ear was torn off the skin at the base of the ear and both her lips were lacerated from being compressed against the underlying teeth. There were also linear abrasions to the outer lips of the vagina which demonstrated that force had been applied to the back, forcing the vagina against the ground.

His search for internal injuries found three hemorrhages inside the skull, a fractured rib, a torn liver, and tearing of the rectal mucosa. Amy's vocal cords were hemorrhaged and her esophagus was bruised. Dr. Neurenberger deduced from these injuries that the killer had "strangled Amy to unconsciousness or death, anally penetrated her, slit her throat, and stepped on her body to force exsanguination." Dr. Neurenberger placed the time of death between 9:30 and 11 P.M. on July 1, 1987, based on the contents of her stomach.[116]

B. THE PROSECUTION'S FORENSIC EVIDENCE: HAIRS AND FIBERS AND TIRE TRACKS

Several months after the discovery of Amy's body, the police at Glacier National Park in Montana notified Illinois authorities about Sutherland's abandoned car, a

1977 Plymouth Fury. At the time of the murder, Sutherland had been living in Dix, Illinois, in Jefferson County, on the county line between Dix and Kell. Illinois police authorities ascertained that defendant's car had a Cooper "Falls Persuader" tire on the right front wheel. Deputies and David Brundage, a criminalist, then traveled to Montana where they made an ink impression of the right front wheel of Sutherland's car. Illinois State Police forensic scientist David Brundage evaluated the plaster casts of the tire print impressions made at the scene of the crime and testified that the tire impressions left at the scene were "consistent in all class characteristics" with only two models of tires manufactured in North America; the Cooper "Falls Persuader," and the Cooper "Dean Polaris."[117] After comparing the plaster casts of the tire impression at the scene with the inked impression of the tire from Sutherland's car, Brundage concluded that "the tire impression at the scene corresponded with Sutherland's tire and could have been made by that tire." Brundage, however, was unable to exclude all other tires as having made the impressions due to the lack of comparative individual characteristics, such as nicks, cuts, or gouges.[118]

Mark Thomas, the manager of mold operations at the Cooper Tire Company, determined "mal" wear similarity, and hence Sutherland's tire "could have made the impression found at the crime scene." Thomas also compared blueprints of Cooper tires with the plaster casts of the tire impressions and determined that the "probability" was "pretty great" that a size P2175/B15 tire—the same size as Sutherland's Falls Persuader tire—had made the impression preserved in the casts. He admitted that there were a great number of such tires on the roads of America.[119]

Criminalist Kenneth Knight compared the two pubic hairs recovered from Amy Schulz's rectal area with Sutherland's pubic hair. He also made comparisons with pubic hairs from members of Amy's family as well as pubic hairs from 24 prior offenders, concluding that the pubic hairs found on Amy did not originate from her family or the 24 suspects, but "could have originated" from Sutherland.

Knight also examined 34 dog hairs found on Amy's clothing and concluded that the dog hairs "were consistent with and could have originated" from Sutherland's black Labrador, Babe. Knight also testified that the dog hairs on Amy's clothes were "dissimilar" from her family's three dogs, her grandparents' dog, and dogs of three neighboring families. Tina Sutherland, Sutherland's sister-in-law, testified that Sutherland usually carried Babe in his car, making it virtually impossible to be in the car without getting covered with dog hair. Multiple dog hairs found in Sutherland's car were found to be consistent with the hairs from Babe.[120]

Knight also examined Amy's clothing for foreign fibers, finding a total of 29 gold fibers in her socks, shoes, underwear, shorts, and shirt. Knight testified that all but one of the gold fibers found on Amy's clothes "could have originated" from the defendant's auto carpet, but could not exclude all other auto carpets as possible sources. He also testified that the one remaining gold fiber found on Amy's clothes "could have originated" from defendant's car upholstery.

Knight also examined and compared 12 cotton and 4 polyester fibers found on the front passenger side floor of Sutherland's automobile with cotton and polyester fibers from Amy's shirt. He concluded that the fibers from the car displayed the same size, shape, and color of the fibers from the shirt and thus "could have originated from the shirt." He also compared three polyester fibers found on the front passenger seat and floor with fibers from Amy's shorts and found them consistent in diameter, color, shape, and optical properties and opined that the fibers from the car "could have originated from the shorts."[121]

The forensic defense expert Richard Bibbing agreed with the state's expert's conclusions on all the comparison evidence except the cotton fibers found in the defendant's car. He did not agree that the cotton fibers were consistent, due to what he determined were differences in size and color.[122]

C. THE COURT'S ANALYSIS: HAIRS AND FIBERS AND TIRE TRACKS

The defendant argued that the prosecution's circumstantial hair, fiber, and tire print comparison evidence was insufficient to prove guilt beyond a reasonable doubt, contending that the probative value of the state's forensic evidence lay merely in establishing that defendant could not be excluded as the possible offender, not that he must be found by a jury actually to be the offender.[123]

The jury ruled that the evidence here, when viewed in the light most favorable to the prosecution, established that the defendant was proved guilty beyond a reasonable doubt. The "overwhelming and overlapping nature of the circumstantial evidence" supported the jury finding that the defendant kidnaped, sexually assaulted, and murdered 10-year-old Amy Schulz.[124]

The court also rejected the defendant's claim that the prosecutor had overstepped his bounds in arguing that the forensic testimony here had established a series of fiber "matches" when the actual testimony was couched in terms of consistency. The state argued in its closing that:

> In every single case the fibers found on Amy's sock shoes and underpants and shorts, shirt were consistent with the fibers from the defendant's car carpeting and dissimilar to all the carpets in her home environment and in her grandparents' house and the vehicles that they drive and in the business where her father works, so there can be no doubt that she got them from there. They came from one place. Those fibers on her clothing came from the defendant's car.

> ". . . The red shorts are a very big part of this case . . . . " Mr. Brisbing [defense expert witness] didn't examine the shorts at all, and we know from Ken Knight's testimony that fibers from the shorts were found in the passenger side of the car.

> . . . This evidence doesn't stand alone. It can be considered together with the carpet fibers on her clothing, the seat fabric fiber on her shirt, the dog hair all over her clothes, the foam rubber on her clothing, the defendant's tire impressions being the, the same as that found near Amy, and the clothing fibers from Amy's shirt and shorts which were deposited in the front passenger side area of the car.

> . . . You know, with regard to the evidence in the car that Amy was in there, you know what's uncontradicted in this case? The evidence that the red polyester fibers from her shorts were found in the passenger side area of the defendant's car. That is fibers just like them—uncontradicted because the defense expert didn't look at them.[125]

The defendant argued that these alleged misstatements constituted reversible error, citing the important case of *People v. Linscott,*[126] decided in 1991. In *Linscott*, the state's evidence established that hairs found in the victim's apartment were "consistent with" the defendant's hairs. As in this case, the state's expert could not conclusively identify the hairs as originating from the defendant. Despite the expert witness's testimony to such effect, the prosecutor argued to the jury that "the rug in the area where Karen was laying [sic] was ripped out sometime later, rolled up and shipped to the laboratory. And that another group of hairs were obtained. The head hairs of Steven Linscott."[127] The Linscott court found such overreaching to be reversible error.

In the Sutherland case the court was also of the opinion that the prosecutor's overstatement of the fiber-comparison evidence was improper. Prosecutorial misconduct in closing argument, the court ruled, warranted reversal and a new trial, however, only if the improper remarks resulted in substantial prejudice to the defendant. In other words, the comments must have constituted a material factor in the conviction, circumstances absent in Sutherland's case:

> We do not find that the remarks in this case substantially prejudiced the defendant. Unlike Linscott . . . the evidence in this case was not closely balanced. The State presented an overwhelming volume of circumstantial evidence: the tire print found by the crime scene was consistent with defendant's car's tire; the dog hair on the victim's clothing was consistent in all respects to the defendant's dog's hair and the dog hair found in his car; the foreign fibers found on the victim's clothing were consistent with the carpeting and upholstery in defendant's car; the clothing fibers found in the defendant's car were consistent with the fibers in the victim's clothing; finally, the pubic hair found on the victim were consistent with the pubic hair standards obtained from the defendant. Given the amount of evidence, it is implausible to think that the prosecutor's remarks could have been a material factor in the conviction. In this case, the jury would not have reached a different result, even if the prosecutor had not made the remarks [citations omitted]. Accordingly, defendant was not denied a fair trial and we will not disturb the conviction.[128]

In a spirited dissent, Justice Clark took aim at the whole question of the weight to be given the large amount of "consistent with" forensic testimony in the trial, in light of the requirement of a finding of guilt beyond a reasonable doubt:

> In my opinion, the sum total of all of this circumstantial evidence leads one to the less than convincing belief that it "could have been" the defendant who committed this brutal crime. Nearly half of the proffered circumstantial evidence has holes in it. With regard to the tire impression evidence, Mark Thomas did not state that the "probability" was "pretty great" that it was defendant's right front tire that made the impression near the crime scene but, rather, that the "probability" was "pretty great" that the same size tire as the defendant's made the impression. This is a distinction with a great deal of difference. Equally important is Thomas' concession that there were a significant number of such tires on the road.
>
> In terms of the 12 cotton fibers found in the defendant's car which the State's expert, Kenneth Knight, stated could have originated from the victim's shirt, the defense expert

Richard Brisbing noticed differences in the size and color of these cotton fibers. Thus, like the tire impression evidence, this evidence is not as convincing as the majority finds . . . . Consequently, because the circumstantial evidence suggesting that the defendant committed this crime was far from overwhelming, and because two prejudicial errors occurred which denied the defendant a fair trial, I would reverse defendant's convictions and remand for a new trial.[129]

IX. CONCLUSION

The Sutherland case study set out above serves as an example of all of the points discussed in this chapter, which has attempted to provide an overview of the field of forensic evidence. A great deal remains to be said about the court's response to forensic testimony admitted in a host of discrete areas such as blood spatter analysis, DNA, forensic anthropology, odontology, entomology, and fingerprint analysis. The new century will bring rapid and amazing new developments in this vital area of criminal law and science. It is more important than ever before for lawyers and courts to increase efforts to both understand and responsibly use the awesome potential of the world of forensic science in our criminal justice system. It is not the absolute truth of the theory being utilized that is the essential goal of the use of forensic science in the trial of crimes, but rather the basic rightness and commonsense nature of the case facts generated with any such theory. Theories come and go. The criminal justice system's need to search fairly and responsibly for facts continues into the 21st century. As noted by author John Horgan, in his insightful study of end of the century science:

Science's success stems in large part from its conservatism, its insistence on high standards of effectiveness. Quantum mechanics and general relativity were as new, as surprising, as anyone could ask for. But they were believed ultimately not because they imparted an intellectual thrill, but because they were effective: they accurately predicted the outcome of experiments. Old theories are old for a good reason. They are robust, flexible. They have an uncanny correspondence to reality. They may even be true.[130]

The rest of this book will be devoted to an examination of the core forensic sciences encountered most frequently in the Anglo-American criminal justice system. The pattern of both acceptance and, equally important, utilizations of the discrete sciences will be closely examined. The discussion will begin with hair analysis, perhaps the most controversial of the often-encountered forensic disciplines.

RESEARCH NOTE

The Journal of Forensic Sciences is the official publication of the American Academy of Forensic Sciences. By visiting the Academy's Web site at *http://www.aafs.org* and clicking on the "Journal of Forensic Sciences" link, one can get to a searchable index of the journal from 1981 to the present that uses common search terms. The site also provides tables of contents for more recent issues of the journal, and, for a modest fee, one can download individual articles from issues published after

January 1, 1999. The index, content, and article availability site is maintained by the publisher of the journal, The American Society for Testing and Materials (ASTM). There are current plans to move toward Web-based publication of the journal, although the paper copy will still be available for some time. Individual subscriptions to this essential journal are also available from ASTM for those interested.

Visiting this important Web site on a regular basis and viewing of available abstracts are essential to the early stages of forensic science/forensic evidence research.

ENDNOTES

1. *Science & Justice*, Vol. 37, No. 4 1997, at 223 (1997).
2. *Id.* The routine use of forensic scientists is not the norm in most countries, especially in civil law legal systems. This underutilization may well be the result of limited resources, but can also be attributed to a lack of sophistication about the advantages of a rigorous forensic science component in routine police crime scene work. See P.R. De Forest: Editorial, "Proactive Forensic Science," *Science & Justice,* Vol. 38, No. 1, at 1 (1998). For the utilization of forensic sciences in civil law systems, see, generally, Pierre Margot: Editorial, "The Role of the Forensic Scientist in an Inquis-itorial System of Justice," *Science & Justice*, Vol. 38, No. 2, at 71 (1998). For an examination of the effort to achieve international standards for the gathering, testing, and use of crime scene data, see generally, Janet Thompson: Editorial, "International Forensic Science," *Science & Justice,* Vol. 38, No. 3, at 141 (1998). For a detailed study of the developments in international forensic science standards and methodol-ogies, see Richard S. Frank and Harold W. Peel (eds.): *Proceedings of the 12th INTERPOL Forensic Science Symposium* (The Forensic Sciences Foundation Press, New York, 1998).
3. Professor Caddy further notes that with the advent of microcolumns being etched onto microchips the miniaturization of gas chromatographic and capiary electro-phoretic systems seem to be assured as crime scene instruments, especially when new detector systems for drugs, fire accelerants, and explosives have been developed. *Supra,* note 1.
4. The desire to develop a paradigm for the validation of scientific discoveries and methodology has been a constant struggle since the very early period of modern scientific thinking in 17th-century England. Sir Francis Bacon, Lord Chancellor and one of the fathers of modern scientific thinking, wrote a work called the *New Atlantis*, where he created a mythical institution called Saloman's House or the College of the Six Days Work, where the inhabitants were devoted to a serious and widespread search for the identification of scientific discoveries and developing rigorous standards for testing their credibility.
5. John Maynard Keynes: *Treatise on Probability* (Macmillan, London, 1948 reprint of 1921 ed.), at 322.
6. The use of probability theory, along with its cousins inferential statistics and extrap-olation theory, is also at the heart of causation debates in product liability, toxic tort, and environmental litigation.
7. Also note that while the greatest amount of the forensic evidence issues arise from a crime scene, there are many crimes involving forensics where there is no crime scene in a traditional sense. Examples would be the movement of a body, forgery,

mail fraud, and other questioned documents settings, and many cases where there simply is only little or no forensic evidence to be had.

8. This division of the information supplied to the criminal justice system into *class* and *individual* is of the utmost importance for both forensic scientists and the criminal bar and will receive extensive examination in each of the chapters to follow that address the legal acceptance or rejection of the specific offerings of the forensic sciences.

9. See, generally, Saferstein: *Criminalistics: An Introduction to Forensic Science* (6th ed. Prentice-Hall, Upper Saddle River, NJ, 1998); Eckert: *Introduction to Forensic Sciences* (2d ed. CRC Press, Boca Raton, FL, 1997); Fisher: *Techniques of Crime Scene Investigation* (5th ed. CRC Press, Boca Raton, FL, 1993); Bodziak: *Footware Impression Evidence* (CRC Press, Boca Raton, FL, 1995); Geberth: *Practical Homicide Investigation* (3d ed. CRC Press, Boca Raton, FL, 1996); DiMaio and DiMaio: *Forensic Pathology* (CRC Press, Boca Raton, FL, 1993); Pickering and Bachman: *The Use of Forensic Anthropology* (CRC Press, Boca Raton, FL, 1997); Janes (ed.): *Scientific and Legal Applications of Bloodstain Pattern Interpretation* (CRC Press, Boca Raton, FL, 1999); Ogle and Fox: *Atlas of Human Hair: Microscopic Characteristics* (CRC Press, Boca Raton, FL, 1999). Also see, Cyril H. Wecht (ed.): *Forensic Sciences* (Matthew Bender Co., New York, 1997) (a five-volume, 90-chapter loose-leaf collection of a wide variety of forensic science subjects, both traditional and contemporary).

10. See Duran v. Cullinan, 286 Ill.App.3d 1005, 677 N.E.2d 999 (1997).

11. See Fisher, *supra,* note 9; Geberth: *Practical Homicide Investigation: Tactics, Procedures and Forensic Techniques* (4th ed., CRC Press, 1998); Eckert, *supra,* note 9; Eckert: *Interpretation of Bloodstain Evidence at Crime Scenes* (CRC Press, Boca Raton, FL, 1989); Saferstein, *supra,* note 9, Brenner: *Forensic Science Glossary,* (CRC Press, Boca Raton, FL, 2000).

12. See, generally, Geberth, *supra,* note 9; Fisher, *supra,* note 9; Saferstein, *supra,* note 9; Eckert, *supra,* note 9. Also see the trial transcript testimony of Dr. Henry Lee in the O. J. Simpson murder trial, available on Westlaw.

13. This is a fact quite distinct from whether these forensic sciences themselves have been sufficiently challenged on their basic assumptions, to justify any opinion being given. See Michael J. Saks: "Merlin and Solomon: Lessons from the Law's Formative Encounters with Forensic Identification Science," 49 *Hastings L.J.* 1069, 1081 (1998), for an analysis of the heretofore unquestioning acceptance by the courts of most forensic sciences, in particular, the much debated discipline of handwriting analysis.

14. *Id.*

15. A host of additional questions will arise when court and counsel are deep into admissibility arguments regarding the factual offspring of the application of a particular forensic science. Questions of that nature for each discipline covered will be isolated and addressed in the remainder of this book.

16. William Shakespeare: *Henry IV,* Part I, Act II, Scene IV.

17. See Decker: *Revolution to the Right: Criminal Procedure Jurisprudence during the Burger-Rehnquist Court Era* (Garland Series, New York, 1992), for a history and concern over retrenchments in this area.

18. Pierre Simon de Laplace: *Theorie Analytique des Probabilities, Introduction* (Paris, 1820).

19. Cicero: *Murder Trials*, Michael Grant, trans. (Penguin Books, New York, 1990), at 50.

20. *Id.* at 67.

21. Shakespeare, *supra,* note 16, Act I, Scene 1.

22. Arthur Conan Doyle, *A Study in Scarlet,* at 13.

23. *Id.* at 64.

24. *Id.* at 30.

25. In 1889, in Chicago, the famous trial of William Coughlin and others for the murder of Dr. Phillip Patrick Cronin, was the longest criminal trial in American history to that point involved no forensic proof. In fact a noteworthy point of contention among expert witnesses was whether a difference could be determined between animal and human blood. See Coughlin v. People, 144 Ill. 140, 33 N.E. 1 Sp. Ct. Ill. (1889).

26. See Colin Wilson: *Clues: A History of Forensic Detection* (Warner Books, New York, 1989). Also see Jurgen Thorvald: *Century of the Detective* (Harcourt, Brace and World, New York, 1965); *Crime and Science* (Harcourt, Brace and World, New York, 1966).

27. See, generally, Saferstein, *supra,* note 9, at 3–7. The Saferstein text is the standard text in the field and should be in the library of anyone interested in the forensic sciences. The following summary is adapted from his introductory pages. Mathieu Orfila (1787–1853), often referred to as the father of forensic toxicology, was a Spaniard who became a famous French professor of medicine and wrote the first major work on the detection of poisons and their effect on animals; Alphonse Bertillon (1853–1914) developed a system of measurement of the facial features of criminals to identify criminals from witness statements. (See discussion *infra,* re Bayesianism); Francis Galton (1822–1911) made the first serious study of the possibility of a fingerprint identification theory and system. His seminal work *Fingerprints* was published in 1892. The statistical study therein serves as the basis for today's system; Leon Lattes (1887–1956) and Dr. Karl Landsteiner (1901) developed blood typing (A, B, AB, O). Lattes developed a system for determining the typing for a dried bloodstain; Calvin Goddard (1891–1955) pioneered ballistics identifications through his work with the comparison microscope, still the basic laboratory tool of contemporary firearms examiners; Albert Osborn (1858-1946) authored the standard text *Questioned Documents,* establishing the discipline of examining questioned documents; Hans Gross (1847–1915) was the author of *Criminal Investigation,* the first book to analyze systematically the many applications of the natural sciences to the investigation of crime. This was the "bible" in the area of criminal investigations for many years and is still quoted, although most recently by feminist legal scholars for his dubious references to women as morally unsuitable witnesses; Edmond Locard (1877–1966) is famous for his theories and experiments regarding what today is referred to as "trace evidence" (fiber, glass shards, soil, metal traces on clothes and tools etc.), and the famous "Locard Principle"—i.e., something is always left and always taken away as a predictable result of close contact of two persons; August Vollmer and Paul Leland Kirk (1920s–1950s) were architects of the first major, professional crime laboratories in California.

28. While proof at trial is the primary purpose of generating forensically based facts, such facts are also routinely used to generate investigative leads and provide search warrants and charging instrument support.

29. Carl Becker: "Everyman His Own Historian," *American Historical Review,* 27 (January, 1932). Also see David Hackett Fischer: *Historians' Fallacies: Toward a Logic of Historical Fault* (Harper Torchbooks, New York, 1970).

30. On this subject, see, generally, Fischer, *supra,* note 29. E. H. Carr: *What is History* (New York, 1962); Robin W. Winks, (ed.): *The Historian as Detective: Essays on Evidence* (Harper Torchbooks, New York, 1968).

31. As noted by historian Robin Winks: "Evidence means different things to different people, of course. The historian tends to think mainly in terms of documents. A

lawyer will mean something rather different by the word, as will a sociologist, or a physicist, or a geologist, or a police officer at the moment of making an arrest. For certain problems evidence must be 'hard,' while for others it may be 'soft.' Even if no acceptable or agreed-upon definitions of evidence may be given, most of us recognize intuitively what we mean when we use the word." *Supra,* note 30, at xv.

32. Carl Becker, *supra,* note 29.
33. TThe history-creating function is the central task of prosecutors and defense lawyers, increasingly effected through the vehicle of the forensic sciences.
34. See the discussion of peer review and the difficulties of determining causal relation in Marcia Angell's comprehensive, if flawed, analysis of the breast implant controversy in *Science on Trial* (Norton, New York, 1997).
35. John Horgan notes the criticism of Nobel prize-winning chemist Professor Stanley Miller of scientific papers culled from other published papers where there has been no hard-won finding resulting from extensive laboratory work. Professor Miller referred to such works as "paper chemistry." In the hard-fought science-based civil cases such as the breast implant actions or PCBs and cancer litigation, we may borrow the idea and refer to the use of previously published articles by way of extrapolation in such cases to claim or deny causation, as "paper science," a charge that may not be made *in toto* about forensic science-based testimony in criminal cases. John Horgan: *The End of Science: Facing the Limits of Knowledge in the Twilight of the Scientific Age* (Addison-Wesley, New York, 1996), at 139.
36. See, generally, Keeton, Dobbs, Keeton, and Owen: *Product Liability* (West Publishing, Minnesota, 1999); Owen, Montgomery, Keeton, and Dobbs: *Products Liability and Safety, Cases and Materials* (3rd ed. West Publishing, 1998); Phillips' *Products Liability in a Nutshell* (4th ed. West Publishing, Minnesota, 1998).
37. *Spencer Cowper's Trial*, 13 How. St. Tr. 1106, 1163 (1699).
38. J. Wigmore: *Evidence*, 1697, at 16. The *Spencer Cowper* case is cited as one of the earliest instances of the legal issues raised by attempts to utilize authoritative treatises to establish a fact or, alternatively, to effect impeachment of an expert under the strictures of the hearsay rule.
39. See Saferstein, *supra,* note 9, at 1–26.
40. This observation would arguably apply to the analysis of hair, fiber, soil, footprints, fingerprints, tire impressions, forensic anthropology and archaeology, entomology, limnology, and bite mark identification techniques.
41. "[F]orensic 1. Pertaining to or used in courts of law or in public debate. 2. Adapted or suited to argumentation." Random House, *Webster's College Dictionary* (New York, 1995). It was applied in ancient times to the law arguments in the Athenian democracy and taught until the late 19th century as a mainstay of the English public school curriculum. It has always been used in tandem or even interchangeably with the idea of classical rhetoric. The term *forensics* is still used today to reference secondary school programs of instruction and competition in speech, dramatic oratory, and legislative argument.
42. See Carol G. Thomas and Edward Kent Webb: "From Orality to Rhetoric: an Intellectual Transformation," in Ian Worthingto (ed.): *Persuasion: Greek Rhetoric in Action* (Routledge, London, 1994).
43. A full-blown history of forensic science and the criminal law awaits to be written. See Saferstein, *Criminalistics, supra,* note 9, Chap. 1, for a general overview. Also see Wilson: *Clues! A History of Forensic Detection* (Warner Books, New York, 1989).
44. Commonwealth v. Biron, 4 Dall. 125, 1 L.Ed. 769 (Sp. Ct. Penn. 1792).
45. People v. Smith, 2 Ohio St. 511 (1853).

46. *Id.* at 516.
47. *Id.* at 518.
48. *Id.*
49. *Id.*
50. People v. Deacons, 109 N.Y. 374, 16 N.E. 676 (1888).
51. *Id.* at 379.
52. *Id.* at 382. See also the statement of the court in People v. Gonzalez, 35 N.Y. 61: "Stains of blood, found upon the person or clothing of the party accused, have always been recognized among the ordinary indicia of homicide. The practice of identifying them by circumstantial evidence, and by the inspection of witnesses and jurors, has the sanction of immemorial usage in all criminal tribunals. Proof of the character and appearance of the stains by those who saw them has always been regarded by the courts as primary and legitimate evidence. It is in its nature original proof, and in no sense secondary in its character. The degree of force to which it is entitled may depend upon a variety of circumstances, to be considered and weighed by the jury in each particular case; but its competency is too well settled to be questioned in a court of law. Science has added new sources of primary evidence, but it has not displaced those which previously existed. The testimony of the chemist who has analyzed blood, and that of the observer who has merely recognized it, belong to the same legal grade of evidence; and though the one may be entitled to much greater weight than the other with the jury, the exclusion of either would be illegal." See also, Greenfield v. People, 85 N.Y. 82.
53. State v. Justus, 11 Or. 178, 8 P. 337 (1883).
54. *Id.* at 182.
55. *Id.*
56. *Id.* at 183.
57. *Id.* 8 P. at 339.
58. Forensics serves to establish the necessary *mens rea*, or mental states, along with all other essential elements of the crime being prosecuted.
59. *Supra*, note 53, at 184.
60. *Id.* at 185. In Rash v. State, 61 Ala. 89 (18), it was held that one not a surgeon or expert, although he had been in war, and seen the range of balls in gunshot wounds, was properly excluded from testifying at a trial for murder by shooting. Also see, People v. Millard, 53 Mich. 63, 18 N.W. 562 (1884) where problems associated with inferences drawn from testimony centered in forensic toxicology are analyzed at length in a case where the defendant was charged with homicide as the result of poisoning his wife. The state alleged that the death was the result of a slow chain of acts of administering arsenic with her medicine and continuing until her death.
61. Robert Hooke: *Micrographia, or Some Physiological Descriptions of Minute Bodies Made by Magnifying Glasses with Observations and Inquiries Thereon* (London, 1667), at Preface, 2.
62. Steven Shaplin and Simon Schaffer: *Leviathan and the Air Pump* (1985), at 24.
63. People v. Collins, 438 P.2d 33 (Cal. 1968).
64. See, e.g., Richard Lempert: "Some Caveats Concerning DNA as Criminal Identification Evidence: With Thanks to the Reverend Bayes," 13 *Cardozo L. Rev.* 303 (1991); Ordway Hilton: "The Relationship of Mathematical Probability to the Handwriting Identification Problem," 1 *Int. J. Forensic Document Examiners* 224 (1995); James McGivney and Robert Barsley: "A Method for Mathematically Documenting Bitemarks," 44 *J. Forensic Sci.*, No. 1, 45 (1999); F. Taroni and C.G.G. Aitken: "Probabilistic Reasoning in the Law: Art I: Assessment of Probabilities and Explanation

of the Value of Trace Evidence Other Than DNA Evidence, 38 *Sci. & Just.*, no. 3, at 179 (1998); J.M. Curran, C.M. Triggs, J.S. Buckelton, K.A.J. Walsh, and T. Hicks, "Assessing Transfer Probabilities in a Bayesian Interpretation of Forensic Glass Evidence," 38 *Sci. & Just.*, No. 1 (1998); Frederick Schauer and Richard Zeckhauser: "On the Degree of Confidence for Adverse Decisions," 25 *J. Legal Stud.* 27 (1996); Richard Lempert: "The New Evidence Scholarship: Analyzing the Process of Proof, *66 B.U. L. Rev.* 439 (1986); Symposium: "Decision and Inference in Litigation," *13 Cardozo L. Rev.* 253 (1991); Frederick Mosteller and Cleo Youtz: "Quantifying Probabilistic Assessments," 5 *Statistical Sci.* 2 (1990); Edward J. Imwinkelried: "The Use of Evidence of an Accused's Uncharged Misconduct to Prove Mens Rea: The Doctrines Which Threaten to Engulf the Character Evidence Prohibition," 51 *Ohio St. L.J.* 575, 586–93 (1990). Also see, generally, Ian Hacking: *The Emergence of Probability* (Cambridge University Press, London, 1975).

65. 38 *Jurimetrics J.* 183 (1998). This is an excellent review of the earliest Bayesian-type applications of probabilities in the investigation of crime. It should be examined by anyone interested in this central problem in criminal justice and legal studies.

66. *Id.* at 188–189.

67. The classification of the anthropometric forms (one per individual) was based on a division of measurements into three classes (small, medium, and large), defined arbitrarily by such fixed intervals as would apportion an average set of measurements into three approximately equal divisions. In practice, data were classified according to the following procedure. When an arrested individual refused to provide his identity after an inquiry, his anthropometric measurements were taken. If a match with previously collected data could be found, taking into account the table of tolerance values established by Bertillon, the identification was completed by the examination of accompanying file photographs and physical marks (such as tattoos, scars, etc.). Faced with the evidence, the suspect generally admitted his identity. *Id.* at 184–185.

68. *Id.* at 187.

69. *Id.* at footnote 13, citing Taroni, Champod, and Margot: "Statistics: A Future in Tool Marks Comparisons?" 28 *J. Assoc. Firearms & Toolmarks Examiners* 222 (1996); Jonathan J. Koehler, Audrey Chia, and Samuel Lindsay: "The Random Match Probability in DNA Evidence: Irrelevant and Prejudicial?" 35 *Jurimetrics J.* 201 (1995); Frederick Schauer and Richard Zeckhauser: "On the Degree of Confidence for Adverse Decisions," 25 *J. Legal Stud.* 27 (1996) for an interesting article quantifying levels of proof in non-criminal processes for allocating guilt.

70. 37 *Sci. & Just.*, No. 2 at 73–74 (1997).

71. B. Robertson and G.A. Vignaux: *Interpreting Evidence: Evaluating Forensic Evidence in the Courtroom* (John Wiley & Sons, 1995).

72. See *Denis Adams* [1996] 2 Cr. App. R. 467.

73. *Supra*, note 70.

74. Winks, *supra*, note 30, at xvi.

75. Wynn v. State, 351 Md. 307, 718 A.2d 588 (1998).

76. See Federal Rule of Evidence 404(b).

77. See, e.g., United States v. Danzey, 594 F.2d 905, 912 (2nd Cir. 1979), cert. denied sub nom. Gore v. United States, 441 U.S. 951, 99 S.Ct. 2179, 60 L.Ed.2d 1056 (1979); State v. Crawford, 458 Mich. 376, 582 N.W.2d 785, 793-95 (1998); State v. Lough, 70 Wash.App. 302, 853 P.2d 920, 930–31 (Div. 1 1993), aff'd, 125 Wash.2d 847, 889 P.2d 487 (1995). Also see Westfield Ins. Co. v. Harris, 134 F.3d 608, 615 (4th Cir. 1998) ("[T]he more often an accidental or infrequent incident occurs, the more likely it is that its subsequent reoccurrence is not accidental or fortuitous").

78. Professor Wigmore's famous example is worthy of repeating here: "[I]f A while hunting with B hears the bullet from B's gun whistling past his head, he is willing to accept B's bad aim . . . as a conceivable explanation; but if shortly afterwards the same thing happens again, and if on the third occasion A receives B's bullet in his body, the immediate inference (i.e., as a probability, perhaps not as a certainty) is that B shot at A deliberately; because the chances of an inadvertent shooting on three successive similar occasions are extremely small; or (to put it another way) because inadvertence or accident is only an abnormal or occasional explanation for the discharge of a gun at a given object, and therefore the recurrence of a similar result (i.e., discharge towards the same object, A) excludes the fair possibility of such an abnormal cause and points out the cause as probably a more natural and usual one, i.e., a deliberate discharge at A. In short, similar results do not usually occur through abnormal causes; and the recurrence of a similar result . . . tends (increasingly with each instance) to negative . . . inadvertence . . . or good faith or other innocent mental state, and tends to establish (provisionally, at least, though not certainly) the presence of the normal, i.e., criminal, intent accompanying such an act; and the force of each additional instance will vary in each kind of offense according to the probability that the act could be repeated, within a limited time and under given circumstances, with an innocent intent. J. Wigmore: *Evidence in Trials at Common Law,* Vol. 2, 302, at 241 (Chadbourn rev. ed., 1979).

79. Edward J. Imwinkelried: *Uncharged Misconduct Evidence,* 5:05, at 11 (1995). Prof. Imwinkelried also has observed that the doctrine of chances may be used to prove the *actus reus* of a crime. Edward J. Imwinkelried: "The Use of Evidence of an Accused's Uncharged Misconduct to Prove *Mens Rea:* The Doctrines Which Threaten to Engulf the Character Evidence Prohibition," 51 *Ohio St. L.J.* 575, 586-93 (1990). See also Eric D. Lansverk: "Comment, Admission of Evidence of Other Misconduct in Washington to Prove Intent or Absence of Mistake or Accident: The Logical Inconsistencies of Evidence Rule 404(b)," 61 *Wash. L.Rev.* 1213, 1225–26 (1986) ("When the evidence reaches such a point, the recurrence of a similar unlawful act tends to negate accident, inadvertence, good faith, or other innocent mental states, and tends to establish by negative inference the presence of criminal intent.").

80. Wigmore, *supra*, note 78, 303 at 241.

81. See, United States v. York, 933 F.2d 1343, 1350 (7th Cir. 1991).

82. Wynn, *supra,* note 75 at 613. For other cases applying or discussing the doctrine of chances, see, e.g., United States v. Queen, 132 F.3d 991, 996 (4th Cir.1997), cert. denied, 118 S.Ct. 1572, 140 L.Ed.2d 805 (1998); United States v. Robbins, 340 F.2d 684, 688 (2nd Cir. 1965); *Lee v. Hodge,* 180 Ariz. 97, 882 P.2d 408, 412 (1994); People v. Erving, 63 Cal.App.4th 652, 661–63, 73 Cal.Rptr.2d 815, 821–22 (1998); State v. Kahey, 436 So.2d 475, 488 (La. 1983); People v. VanderVliet, 444 Mich. 52, 508 N.W.2d 114, 128 n. 35 (1993); State v. Sadowski, 247 Mont. 63, 805 P.2d 537, 542–43 (1991); In re Estate of Brandon, 55 N.Y.2d 206, 448 N.Y.S.2d 436, 433 N.E.2d 501, 504 (1982); Morgan v. State, 692 S.W.2d 877, 881 (Tex.Crim.App. 1985).

83. Prof. Imwinkelried cautions that "in analyzing the applicability of the doctrine of chances, it seems wrong-minded to focus on the absolute number of incidents. Rather, the focus should be on relative frequency." Imwinkelried: *supra*, note 79, at 597–600.

84. See Frederick Schauer and Richard Zeckhauser: "On the Degree of Confidence for Adverse Decisions," 25 *J. Legal Stud.* 27 (1996) for an interesting article quantifying levels of proof in noncriminal processes for allocating guilt.

85. McGrew v. State, 682 N.E.2d 1289 (Indiana Sp. Ct. 1997).

86. *Id.* 682 N.E.2d 1289, 1292. See Chapter 3, Hair Analysis, for an extended discussion of the McGrew appellate and Supreme Court decisions.

87. See e.g., Mealey's Daubert Reports available on Westlaw, Lexis, and in most law school libraries. Also see Gianelli and Imwinkelried: *Scientific Evidence* (2d ed. The Michie Company, 1993, plus supplements).

88. See, generally, Dale L. Laux "Effects of Luminol on the Subsequent Analysis of Bloodstains," *J. of Forensic Sci.* 36, 5, pp. 1512–1520, 1991; Joseph C. Niebauer and Jack B. Booth, Jr.; "Recording Luminol Luminescence in its Context using a Film Overlay Method", B. Lee Brewer: *J. of Forensic Identification* 40:5, p. 278–278 (1990); Fred E. Gimeno; "Fill Flash Color Photography To Photograph Luminol Bloodstain Patterns," *J. of Forensic Identification* 39:5, p. 305–306 (1989).

89. See Bevel and Gardner: *Bloodstain Pattern Analysis* (CRC Press, Boca Raton, FL, 1997); James (ed.): *Scientific and Legal Applications of Bloodstain Pattern Interpretation* (CRC Press, Boca Raton, FL, 1999).

90. See People v. Deacons, *supra,* note 50 and People v. Gonzalez, *supra*, note 52.

91. Ayers v. State, 334 Ark. 258, 975 S.W.2d 88 (1998).

92. *Id.* at 264.

93. Bronk v. State, 311 Ark. 579, 847 S.W.2d 1.

94. Ayers, *supra,* note 91 at 266.

95. The court noted that the tests appellant now complained of had been in existence for many years, were a routine part of criminal investigations, and were frequently admitted. In each of those cases, the evidence of blood identity, i.e., animal or human and blood typing, was introduced without challenge based upon its novelty or reliability.

96. State v. Canaan, 265 Kan. 835, 964 P.2d 681 (Kan. 1998).

97. *Id.* at 686.

98. It is important to realize that Canaan's observation is true for most jurisdictions and could apply equally to post-Daubert continuing acceptance of hair, fiber, footprint, and many of other "widely accepted" forensic sciences.

99. *Id.* at 693.

100. *Supra,* note 96, at 692 .

101. *Id.* at 851.

102. *Id.* at 693.

103. *Id.*

104. State v. Maynard, 954 S.W.2d 624 (Mo. Ct. App. 1997).

105. *Id.* at 628.

106. The police performed DNA tests on the blood stains in the carpet, the overalls, and the carpet cleaner. Utilizing a genetic profile from blood samples obtained from Ms. Walker's parents, it was determined that only 64 out of 100 million couples could have produced the kind of genetic profile found in the blood stains. Additionally, the genetic profile found in the bloodstains would occur only twice in a population of 100 million.

107. *Supra,* note 104 at 629. Ms. Walker's skeletal remains were found over 1 year after her disappearance. Ms. Walker's skull was covered with a pair of shorts and a striped Unitog rental workshirt bearing the name "Wendell" and the numbers "8223760004." The shirt and shorts that covered Ms. Walker's skull were wrapped with duct tape. Four projectiles were within the duct tape. Information obtained from Unitog established that the shirt had been rented by Mr. Maynard. Mr. Maynard admitted the shirt was his but stated that he had 2 to 3 weeks' worth of these shirts and did not realize one was missing. An examination of the skull showed multiple fractures of the left

temporal and parietal areas and a gunshot wound in the left temporal region. Michael Edward Berkland, Deputy Medical Examiner from the Jackson County Medical Examiner's office, testified that Ms. Walker died from multiple gunshot wounds to the head. Mr. Berkland testified that the $^1/_2$ liter of blood found in the apartment carpet remnant was consistent with multiple gunshot wounds to the head.

108. Also see State v. Stenson, 132 Wash.2d 668, 940 P.2d 1239 (1997), where the defendant was convicted of the first-degree premeditated murder of his wife and his business partner. The pants the defendant was wearing at the time of the murders was an important piece of evidence. There were stains on the right leg and smaller stains on the left leg of the pants. The stains were visually identified as blood by the forensic scientist whose specialty was crime scene reconstruction and the interpretation of bloodstain patterns. The stains all reacted positively upon application of phenolphthalein (phenol), which is a catalytic color test that is a presumptive test for blood. The court accepted the reliability of Luminol as a presumptive test for the presence of human blood. The appeals court ruled that the trial court correctly admitted the results of the phenol testing, which were supported by the forensic scientist's testimony that the stains on the pants looked like blood by visual inspection and under a microscope. So long as a jury is clearly told that the phenol test is only a presumptive test and may indicate a substance other than human blood, it is admissible.

However, see, State v. Fukusaku, 85 Hawaii 462, 946 P.2d 32 (1997), where the trial court excluded expert testimony on the Luminol and phenolphthalein test results, ruling that, because of the limitations of the tests, the presumption of the presence of blood was relevant only to the extent that it could be supported by confirmatory tests. Moreover, the trial court ruled that, without confirmatory tests, the prejudicial effect of the evidence was not outweighed by its probative value. Inasmuch as confirmatory tests were not conducted, the trial court excluded the evidence.

109. People v. Sutherland, 155 Ill.2d 1, 610 N.E.2d 1 (1993). The defendant in this case is currently on death row awaiting the results of further appeals in this case.

110. See, generally, Geberth, *supra,* note 9; Fisher, *supra,* note 9; Saferstein, *supra,* note 9; Eckert, *supra,* note 9; Also see the trial transcript testimony of Dr. Henry Lee in the O. J. Simpson murder trial, available on Westlaw.

111. An initial determination has to be made that the crime scene datum is indeed fiber as opposed to hair or other substances.   .

112. See Chap. 3, Hair Analysis. Also see, e.g., Saferstein, supra, note 9, Chap. 8, Hairs, Fibers and Paint; Eckert: *supra,* note 9; Chap. 17, Collection of Evidence. Also see Harold Deadman: "Fiber Evidence and the Wayne Williams Case," *FBI Law Enforcement Bulletin* (March, May, 1984). For a critical assessment of the need for independent crime laboratories, see Paul Giannelli: "The Abuse of Scientific Evidence in Criminal Cases: The Need for Independent Crime Laboratories, 38 *Santa Clara L. Rev.* 1001 (Winter 1997).

113. See, Saferstein, *supra,* note 9, and Chapter 15, Firearms, Tool Marks, and Other Impressions.

114. Sutherland, *supra,* note 109, at 8. Amy had last been seen alive at approximately 9:10 in the evening of July 1, 1987, walking alone on Jefferson Street near 4th Street in the town of Kell, Illinois, in Marion County. Tina Sutherland, the defendant's sister-in-law, testified that on the evening of July 1, 1987, the defendant was visiting his brother and her at their home in Texico, Illinois, in Jefferson County, and often visited since he was living with his mother in Dix, Illinois, a short 5 minutes away. On the

night of Amy's murder, the defendant left Ms. Sutherland's home at approximately 8 to 8:30. She also testified that the ride from her house to Kell took 6 to 7 minutes. A Deputy Sheriff testified that the distance from Kell to the crime scene is 12.1 miles and takes 14 minutes to drive.

115. *Id.* at 8. At the time of the defendant's indictment in connection with Amy Schulz's death, he was serving a 15-year sentence in a federal prison after pleading guilty to shooting at employees of the National Park Service at Glacier National Park, in Montana. Prior to the trial, the defense filed a motion-in-limine to exclude from evidence knives found in his possession at the time of his arrest in Glacier National Park. The trial court denied the motion, ruling that the knives had "some slight probative value" and would not substantially prejudice the defendant by their introduction.

116. *Id.* at 8.

117. *Id.*

118. *Id.* at 9.

119. *Id.* at 10.

120. *Id.*

121. *Id.* at 11.

122. *Id.* at 17.

123. *Id.*

124. *Id.* at 11.

125. *Id.*

126. People v. Linscott, 142 Ill.2d 22, 566 N.E.2d 1355 (1991). Also see People v. Giangrande, 101 Ill.App.3d 397, 56 Ill.Dec. 911, 428 N.E.2d 503 (1981).

127. Linscott, *supra* at 30. The prosecutor also distorted the mathematical probability regarding the hair–comparison evidence. Despite the lack of a solid foundation, the prosecutor argued that the odds of another individual having hair with the same characteristics as defendant's hair were about 1 in 3 million.

128. Sutherland, *supra*, note 109, at 12.

129. *Id.* at 15.

130. Horgan, *supra*, note 35, at 136.

3 Hair Analysis

And all depends on keeping the mind's eye fixed on things themselves, so that their images are received exactly as they are. For God forbid that we should give out a dream of our imagination for a pattern of the world.

—Sir Francis Bacon:
Novum Organum: Aphorisms on the Interpretation of Nature and the Empire of Man (1620)

I. INTRODUCTION

The forensic discipline of hair analysis is largely centered in microscopy—the close examination of a hair sample using modern microscope technology. Although it may be and is used to determine the kind and category of a hair sample, i.e., whether human, animal, or even a hair at all, the principal goal in hair analysis is to try and establish a common origin between known and recovered samples in a criminal case. Recently, in addition to visually oriented examinations, limited work on identification has been investigated using DNA methodology in instances of the presence of adequate hair root cells.[1] More often than not, however, such material is not available, so the new DNA methods are unavailable as a tool. Hair analysis is nonetheless used extensively in criminal prosecutions for purposes of garnering investigative leads and/or material facts for use at trial.

The ongoing general utility of hair analysis was recently noted in the *Proceedings of the 12th INTERPOL Forensic Science Symposium:*

> It is therefore not possible to dispense with the microscopic examination of hairs. Such a situation could only be envisaged if DNA profiling became so simplified that all hairs which were found could be analysed with little effort and with the certainty that the analysis would have evidentiary value.[2]

What is there to compare in hair analyses? The new *Atlas of Human Hair: Microscopic Characteristics*, by Robert Ogle, Jr. and Michelle J. Fox,[3] posits and presents photographic plates referencing 24 microscopic characteristics of human hair. The primary purpose of this new text, according to the authors, is to "present photographic archetypes which will provide a uniform basis for the generation of data on study populations, so that data from different researchers or examiners can be combined to form a larger database of characteristic variate frequencies."[4] This laudable goal is necessary if hair analysis as currently engaged in by criminalists is to gain the respect afforded other observation-based forensic disciplines such as fingerprints and ballistics, or ever rise to the respectability currently afforded to disparate DNA methodologies and population-frequency databases projections.

The early-17th-century concerns of philosophers and nascent experimentalists regarding the validity of factual claims, remain concerns today, especially when transposed into the use of expert opinions regarding identification in a criminal trial. What more can we say about what we cannot see and compare? Quite a lot, according to modern practitioners of the corpus of forensic sciences. A brief look at the two basic contributions of forensic hair analysis follows.

All forensic sciences function in a context of providing information in one of two modes: *class characteristics* or *individual characteristics*. Class characteristics provide a valuable number of facts about a crime scene sample that do not reference any particular suspect. These class characteristics serve to put discussions of individualization efforts in a context. In the area of hair analysis, class characteristic information may include a great amount of exclusory information in this broad contextual analysis. In these areas we can expect very solid evidence of exclusion of a suspect's sample from participation in the crime but cannot achieve unqualified identification as we pretty much can with fingerprints or DNA or the identifications provided by ballistics.

In the area of hair analysis, a number of factual offerings may be confirmed with a fairly high confidence level. Is the examined item actually hair as opposed to a fiber? Is it a human hair as opposed to an animal hair? If it is an animal hair, what kind is it? Is it male or female hair? Is it infant or mature adult hair? Is the hair source a human being of Caucasian, Black, or Asiatic ethnicity? Does the hair appear to have been forcibly removed? If so, is there sufficient root tissue to perform new DNA testing? What part of the body was its apparent source, i.e., was it a head or pubic hair? Does the hair contain traces of drugs or other chemical content such as cocaine, heroin, methamphetamine, alcohol, or prescription drugs? Does is indicate the presence and type of a shampoo product? Is here an indication of some identifiable illness that may be gleaned from hair analysis methods?

This sampling of potential contributions in the form of class characteristic statements garnered from modern hair analyses,[5] illustrates the great value in a criminal investigation of statements drawing the contextual lines for subsequent attempts to link a particular suspect to the crime scene, especially in the exclusion of one or a body of potential suspects.[6] The ultimate goal of all forensic science is the linking of an offender to the crime scene by way of testimony as to individual characteristics, connecting some physical sample obtained from the suspect with datum from the crime scene. A considerable portion of this book will be devoted to the examination of reported decisions where just such linkages have been testified to by forensic experts.

It is essential at this point in our discussion for the reader to understand the very limited number of occasions where an expert is allowed to make any absolute claims of any such match. The bulk of the forensic sciences, including DNA, do not support any such claims and the courts have consistently refused to allow any such testimony or prosecutorial glosses to that effect in closing arguments. Francis Bacon's fear that scientists may "give out a dream of our imagination for a pattern of the world,"[7] is still a major concern of criminal defense lawyers in cases involving some contribution by forensic science experts. Statements of forensic scientists wrapped in impressive

credentials and complex foundational testimony have always put a shine on prosecution witnesses' testimony and glazed the entire case with an aura of certainty that
it may not possess. This is especially the case where needed forensic financial support
for indigents is typically not forthcoming.

Terms allowed by courts to support the "identification" of a crime scene hair,
for example, with a sample taken from defendant, include the following:

- Match [reversible error in most states].
- Compatible with.
- Consistent with.
- Similar in all respects.
- Not dissimilar.
- Same general characteristics.
- Identical characteristics.
- Could have originated from.
- Probability was "pretty great."

These conclusory linkage pronouncements and variations on them are the grit and
gristle of forensic testimony in a wide variety of crimes and forensic disciplines.
That is not to say that such testimony is grossly unfair and a fraud on the court.
Quite the contrary. This "something less than certain"-type of opinion has powerful
effect on a jury. It may essentially be deemed to support the basic common sense
of the jury as to its understanding of the culture and the historical connection
between and among events. It might even be seen as the scientific contribution to
the venerable "who is kidding who" test known to all jurors from their earliest years.
It is of value to repeat the observation of the great 18th-century mathematician
LaPlace that "the theory of probabilities is at bottom nothing but common sense
reduced to calculus."[8]

Hair is class evidence and thus it is not possible to determine that a questioned
hair sample came from a particular individual to the exclusion of all others. However,
as long as a *match* is not claimed, and there are a sufficient number of variants
compared and found consistent, or not dissimilar, etc., such particular transactional
facts can pretty much cinch a factual dispute in the eyes of a jury. The specific case
analyses to follow, especially in the Moore and Williams prosecutions, will illustrate
this central point.

The authors of the 1998 *Proceedings of the 12th INTERPOL Forensic Science
Symposium* section on hair and fiber analysis concluded that for the foreseeable
future, interdisciplinary analysis of hair samples remains the direction to follow to
achieve successful examinations of hair in forensic science.[9] It is important to note
that while macroscopic and microscopic characteristic variates used by the forensic
examiner in the comparison of hairs can be used to distinguish between hairs from
different individuals, there has been no systematic attempt to develop data on the
frequency of those characteristic variates in study populations as there has in DNA
analyses.[10] The lack of such population databases useful in determining the chances
of any such "match" occurring in the general population, here, as in most of the

forensic sciences, is of major concern to students of the criminal justice system. It will be useful at this point—equally applicable to all subsequent chapters in this book—to ask a series of recurrent questions about the benefits of hair analysis, in respect to its designated goal of providing important information in the prosecution of a criminal case in our courts.

Recurring questions:

- What facts or assumptions or surmises may be obtained from the examination of one or more hairs gathered at a crime scene?
- What could serve as the basis for any such assumptions or projections or simply guesses?
- What value should be assigned to any such factual estimations in the criminal justice system where life and liberty and justice to a victim are all in play?
- What does it mean to say that one or more hairs are or are not consistent or not dissimilar or substantially similar with another hair?
- What would be the basis for any such statements and what value should be allocated to them if one set of exemplars was taken from a crime scene and the other from a suspected perpetrator?
- What does it mean in terms of long-held requirements that the elements of a crime must be proved beyond a reasonable doubt? How does circumstantial evidence fit in with prosecutorial efforts designed to meet such a high bar of proof in cases partially supported by hair evidence?
- How much does hair evidence depend for its force upon the other, more traditional observations by eyewitnesses?
- How much does of all of this in the area of hair analysis and comparison testimony have to do with scientific theory or recognized scientific methodology? What science, if any, has been traditionally associated with hair analysis and how has that changed as we enter the 21st century?
- Is hair analysis "scientific" in respect to the theoretical underpinnings of the discipline or because of its use of microscopy and other processes that aid its essentially observational nature?
- Should it make any difference if hair analysis testimony is simply a combination of experience and modern microscopy? What else, from a forensic scientist's standpoint, *is* there to say about hair and its examination and the factual assumptions that follow.
- Is there more there to give hair analysis as great a claim, or greater, to belief as fingerprints, impressions, ballistics, tool marks, or DNA?

II. RECENT CASE DISCUSSIONS

The discussion of the response to the claims of forensic hair analysis by contemporary courts will begin with a detailed examination of two important decisions by Indiana's appellate and supreme court in the case of *McGrew v. State*.[11] These two opinions merit close attention since they address the very foundations of forensic hair analysis, focus on the key concerns of lawyers, and provide a clear example of the potential conflict between the methodology of observation-based forensic sciences and the constitutional requirement of proof beyond a reasonable doubt.

In the *McGrew* case, the defendant was charged with deviate sexual assault. The state alleged that McGrew struck up a conversation with the victim, whom he had met before, in a local tavern. They traveled to several other bars to continue their conversations. On their way to a final destination, they drove in defendant's automobile, until the defendant pulled onto a dead-end road to urinate. The victim testified that when he returned, he entered on the passenger side, instructing her to move behind the steering wheel. After a brief period of talking and kissing, McGrew forced her to perform oral sex on him.[12] McGrew was indicted on a charge of criminal deviate conduct.

Several hairs were recovered 2 weeks after the incident from an area near the center of the front seat, and were compared with head and pubic hair samples obtained from both the victim and the defendant. Upon defense motion, a hearing was held outside the presence of the jury to determine the admissibility of proffered testimony by Carl Sobieralski, a state police DNA analyst who was also trained in hair analysis and did the comparisons of the hairs taken from McGrew's automobile. McGrew moved to exclude Sobieralski's testimony, asserting that microscopic hair analysis had never been empirically tested and that, accordingly, any findings by an expert such as Sobieralski were too uncertain to be scientifically reliable. The trial court denied the motion, observing that expert testimony focused on microscopic hair analysis had been allowed in Indiana courts. Therefore, any issues regarding the reliability of the results went to the weight, and not the admissibility, of Sobieralski's testimony. The trial judge acknowledged that microscopic hair analysis was not a traditional scientific evaluation, but rather, was simply a person's observations under a microscope, much like an expert in handwriting analysis comparing handwriting exemplars.[13]

Sobieralski then testified, over McGrew's objection, that examination of the hairs retrieved from his car revealed a hair "dissimilar" to McGrew's head hair sample, but "sufficiently similar" to the victim's head hair sample to be of common origin, thus evidencing her presence in that area of his car. The reverse result was obtained when Sobieralski compared a pubic hair recovered from the car with McGrew's pubic hair sample. Sobieralski acknowledged that he was not testifying the hairs found in the car were from the victim's head and McGrew's pubic region, only that they were "sufficiently similar" to her head hair and McGrew's pubic hair.[14]

The Indiana Court of Appeals observed that while Indiana had previously used the spirit of the "general acceptability standard" of the *Frye* case, the Indiana Supreme Court had made it clear that expert scientific testimony was no longer admissible unless the court was satisfied that the scientific principles upon which the testimony rests were reliable, a precondition to be imposed on all scientific evidence, regardless of whether the underlying principles were based on novel science or were rooted in established principles.[15] Once the court has determined that the particular scientific technique is capable of producing reliable results, however, any questions regarding the reliability of a specific testing procedure, or the results of a specific test, go to the weight of the scientific testimony and not its admissibility.[16]

In this case, the court noted, the trial court did not expressly take judicial notice of the reliability of the scientific principles supporting microscopic hair analysis. In fact, it was apparent that the trial judge did not consider hair analysis to be a "traditional" type of scientific evaluation *requiring* that the proponent lay a foundation of reliability. The court observed that while a colorable argument could possibly be made to support this view, neither party had argued that microscopic hair analysis was nonscientific testimony exempt from the foundational requirement imposed by Evidence Rule 702(b).[17] It seemed clear that in the *McGrew* case they were dealing with more than just a visual observation of a hair under a microscope. In that sense, the court ruled, there were therefore "scientific principles" intimately and necessarily involved in the process that led to the expert testimony.[18]

The appellate court carefully noted that the "scientific" principles at work in this case were far from sophisticated assurances of reliability and of probative value:

> As noted, the conclusion of microscopic hair comparison is usually couched in terms merely of "similarity," "might be" or "could be." Such testimony does not lend itself to categorization as evidence of meaningful probative value. This deficiency has prompted a good deal of the debate concerning admissibility of hair analysis by comparison microscope. Early on, at least one commentator noted that hair analysis by microscope was primitive even in 1982 and not the best technological device to produce meaningful hair analysis evidence. The author proposed that hair analysis evidence was underemployed because of the valid criticism of less conclusive methods such as by comparison microscope, and that "the modern hair analyst has tools more powerful than the microscope . . . and that the analyst can make many findings more specific than a general conclusion that two hair samples appear similar."[19]

The appellate court made it clear that it was not concerned whether hair analysis could be made more meaningful to a criminal jury or whether it could be made meaningful at all. Assuming that hair analysis could aid the jury in its deliberations and might be relevant, however, its task was simply to determine whether an appropriate and adequate foundation preceded the admission of the expert opinion.[20]

During trial, the expert Sobieralski explained that microscopic hair analysis consisted of visually examining the hair samples side-by-side under a comparison microscope, looking at a number of different physical characteristics such as the cortex, cuticle, root, tip, cortical fusi, ovoid bodies, pigment and pigment dispersal, cuticle thickness, gaping, and whether the hair had been dyed or specially treated. If, upon comparison, the hairs were found to be "sufficiently similar," he would make a determination that they "could have come from" the same person. He defined "sufficiently similar" in the context of microscopic hair analysis with the following example:

> [I]f I took that pubic hair and dropped it into a pile of standards that was pulled from [the victim, J.W.], I'd be able to tell the difference. But when I dropped [the pubic hair recovered from the car] into a pile of standards of [McGrew], I could not tell the difference between them.[21]

The court of appeals, while noting that microscopic hair analysis has been routinely admitted by state and federal courts for many years with little skepticism,[21] nonetheless, found here that the state witnesses bald assertions totally failed to present any evidence to satisfy the first three prongs of *Daubert*:

> Upon questioning by McGrew's counsel and the trial court, Sobieralski acknowledged that he was not aware of any error ratio for the technique, nor was he aware of any articles or journals disputing the methodology. He also admitted that he did not know the statistical percentages of certain hair characteristics in the general population or the probability of a particular hair sample coming from persons other than McGrew or J.W. The court emphasized that expert Sobieralski did make the bald assertion that microscopic hair analysis was accepted in the scientific community, but did not describe which scientific community nor expound upon the degree of acceptance.[23]

Here, the appellate court ruled that the trial court erred in admitting Sobieralski's testimony. The court emphasized that it was not establishing a per se rule of unreliability, and hence inadmissibility, for microscopic hair analysis. It was obvious from the cited sources in the area, that the methodology had been tested and peer-reviewed to a degree that an expert could conceivably come to court loaded down with sufficient information in the form of data, studies, and scholarly articles to meet at least three of the *Daubert* prongs. Here, however, the state mistakenly believed that a *Daubert* reliability foundation was only required for novel scientific techniques, and thus did not even attempt to lay a requisite foundation.[24]

The evidence that hair found in McGrew's car "probably" came from the victim's head was merely cumulative of McGrew's admission that J.W. was in his car. The same could not be said, however, of Sobieralski's testimony that a pubic hair found on the front seat was "substantially similar" to McGrew's. In this case, the court noted, the conviction rested in large part upon the victim's credibility. The pubic hair comparison was the only physical evidence corroborating her claim that McGrew removed his pants. The defendant had not admitted to disrobing in his car and there was no medical evidence that an act of sexual deviate conduct had occurred.[25] The pubic hair testimony would most likely have had a considerable influence upon the mind of the average juror because it was the only evidence implying that McGrew exposed his genitals:

> This impact was heightened by the special aura of trustworthiness surrounding expert testimony, and the fact that, in the case of microscopic hair analysis, jurors do not generally have the opportunity for direct evaluation . . . We conclude that the erroneous admission of the pubic hair evidence constitutes reversible error because, reviewing the record as a whole, there is a substantial likelihood that this evidence contributed to the conviction.[26]

In the Indiana Supreme Courts decision in *McGrew v. State*,[27] the court, with misgivings, reversed the appellate court's decision and reinstated McGrew's conviction. At the trial, the court observed, immediately prior to the hair analyst's testimony during the trial, the defendant challenged the admissibility of the hair comparison analysis under Indiana Evidence Rule 702(b). In a hearing outside the presence of the jury, the defendant called the Indiana State Police analyst to the stand. When asked by the defendant what "scientific principle is used to base the reliability of hair sample technique," the analyst testified, "Scientific principle? It's just simply a physical comparison of one hair directly to another one." He testified that he used a microscope to make a "physical comparison of one hair to another," looking at several "different physical characteristics." Specifically, he testified that he compares the medulla, cortex, cuticle, root, tip, cortical fusi, ovoid bodies, pigment, thickness, gaping, condition of hair, whether the hair had been cut with a razor or scissors, and whether it had been dyed or specially treated. He testified that these character- istics were physically observed through a microscope.[28]

The court observed that when the defendant questioned the analyst about the statistical error ratio for hair comparison as compared with the statistical error ratio for blood/DNA typing, the analyst testified that while blood/DNA typing had sta- tistical error ratios, he was not aware of any statistics with regard to the probability of a hair sample belonging to someone else. This, the expert continued, was simply due to the nature of hair comparison. The defendant asked whether there was another way to determine this scientifically, other than from his own physical observations. The analyst answered "yes" and testified that this was accepted in the scientific community, and that there "were absolutely no articles or journals that [he was] aware of that dispute this method."[29] On cross-examination, the state elicited testi- mony that microscopes were generally accepted in the scientific community, that, as far as he knew, no state disallowed hair comparisons, and that he was an expert in the use of microscopes.[30]

Prior to dismissing the expert, the trial court directed several questions to him:

Court: [I]n regard to the examination. It is simply a physical, visual examination of the hair.

Analyst: Yes sir.

Court: You simply say that one hair looks like another one or it doesn't look like another one.

Analyst: I say it's sufficiently similar to have come from that person or it is dissimilar.

Court: And if you say that it . . . [is] similar to come from that person . . . that doesn't mean that it comes from that person.

Analyst: It just simply means that it could have come from that person.

Court: And you do not know the statistical percentages of how many people would have similar hair?

Analyst: There are no statistics. It's hard to say.[31]

In finding the evidence to be admissible, the trial court had concluded:

> As I see it, what we're talking about is not the traditional scientific evaluation. We are talking about simply a person's observations under a microscope, which is a magnification to compare some hairs to one another, much as an expert in handwriting analysis compares handwriting. They can't tell you how many people out there have the same . . . handwriting. They just say whether it's sufficiently similar. I believe that it has been accepted in the State. Although I don't know of any . . . specific cases. I know that it has been utilized here before . . . . It seems to me as though it goes to the weight of the evidence and it is, of course, highly subject to the questions about [the] statistical comparisons and, apparently, there are none . . . but it can say that this hair looks like the other hair . . . . So what [the analyst] has observed through the microscope will be admissible.[32]

In the present case, the Indiana Supreme Court concluded that the trial court, contrary to the ruling of the court of appeals, had indeed exercised appropriate discretion as to the reliability of the proffered hair comparison analysis:

> The analyst testified that the hair comparison he performed was a comparison of physical characteristics, as seen under a microscope. Inherent in any reliability analysis is the understanding that, as the scientific principles become more advanced and complex, the foundation required to establish reliability will necessarily become more advanced and complex as well. The converse is just as applicable, as demonstrated by the trial court's conclusion that "what we're talking about is not the traditional scientific evaluation. We are talking about simply a person's observations under a microscope." This conclusion is not unlike our recent statement that the evidence at issue was more a "matter of the observations of persons with specialized knowledge" than "a matter of 'scientific principles' governed by Indiana Evidence Rule 702(b)."[33]

The judgment of the trial court against defendant McGrew was affirmed.

The status of hair analysis, as an observational discipline utilizing modern microscopes as opposed to a novel scientific technique requiring an extensive *Daubert* reliability hearing, was raised again in the recent 1999 Montana Supreme Court decision in *State v. Southern*.[34] There, the defendant was convicted of kidnaping, burglary, theft, and sexual intercourse without consent. The victims were all older women who were sexually assaulted in the same limited geographic area—either at their homes in Helena, Montana, at a rural location west of Helena, or both. The perpetrator covered each victim's face with an article of clothing and demanded money. All assaults occurred within a time span of $2^1/_2$ years (April 25, 1994 to November 2, 1996).[35]

Among a host of alleged errors claimed by the defendant, Southern, he cited the denial of his motion in limine regarding the state's proposed offer of microscopic hair analysis. Southern filed a motion in limine to exclude the testimony of a forensic scientist at the Montana State Crime Laboratory, who eventually testified at the trial that she microscopically compared Southern's hair sample with hairs from the rape scenes and that the hair from the rape scenes was either "similar to" or "consistent with" the defendant's sample. Southern objected to this testimony, maintaining that her testimony was inadmissible because it did not satisfy the factors for the reliability of expert testimony which the U.S. Supreme Court set out in *Daubert v. Merrell Dow Pharmaceuticals, Inc.*[36]

The state responded that, since microscopic hair comparison was not considered novel scientific evidence, the defendant's reliance on *Daubert* was misplaced. The Montana Supreme Court took note of the recent U.S. Supreme Court ruling in *Kumho Tire Co. v. Carmichael*,[37] where the trial court's gatekeeping obligation under Federal Rule of Evidence Rule 702 applied not only to testimony based on scientific knowledge but also to testimony based on technical and other specialized knowledge. Regardless of *Kumho Tire*, the Montana Supreme Court emphasized that the test of reliability was flexible and that *Daubert*'s factors neither necessarily nor exclusively apply to all experts or in every case.[38]

In the instant case, the court ruled that microscopic hair comparison was not novel scientific evidence, its research having indicated that the court had considered and so found on least 5 cases since 1978 where a witness had testified on microscopic hair comparison.[39] Moreover, the court noted, here the expert had testified that comparing hair samples with a microscope had been done for decades. Therefore, since microscopic hair comparison was not considered "novel scientific evidence," the district court was not in error in refusing to conduct a *Daubert* reliability hearing to test its reliability.[40]

In the recent case of *State v. Fukusaku*,[41] however, a finding by the Hawaii Supreme Court also placed microscopic hair analysis outside of the *Daubert* reliability requirements. In *Fukusaku*, the defendant was charged with second-degree murder. After responding to a fire at an apartment building, firefighters found the body of a female shooting victim in a bedroom closet and determined that she had been shot through the chest. At about 10:30 P.M. the same night, firefighters were called to the parking lot of a hotel, where they discovered a red sports car on fire, which contained the body of the first victim's son on the front passenger seat, also shot through the chest. The defendant, an acquaintance of the son, was charged with one count of murder in the first degree and two counts of murder in the second degree in connection with the deaths.[42]

In the basement of the apartment house, the police found a love seat with a section of the bottom removed. From the love seat, the police recovered a bullet, blood samples, and some hair and fiber samples. Police criminalist Tracy Tanaka testified that a hair recovered from the sofa bed in apartment 1306, where the defendent resided, was consistent with the female victim's hair. She continued that hair and fiber samples recovered from the love seat in the basement and from the son's body were "consistent with" cat hair and carpet fibers found in apartment 1306.[43]

Prior to trial, the defendant requested a separate hearing on the reliability of the state's hair and fiber evidence, which was denied. In the course of the hearing on the motion, the following exchange occurred:

The Court: Well, counsel, hair is not in the nature of scientific evidence as such, if you look at the case law, it's not subject to, uh, the kind of [*Daubert*] scrutiny that's required of DNA and Luminol.

[Defense Counsel]: . . . I asked the Court for a 104 hearing, it wasn't given, but again I think that one is necessary for the hair.

The Court: I don't think so, and—and the reason is what I've stated, I think that, um, under [*Daubert*], [*Daubert*] applies to scientific evidence and that there is language in [*Daubert*] requiring the Court to conduct, um, a hearing outside the presence of the jury with respect to so-called, uh, scientific evidence. And I do not believe that hair analysis like ballistic analysis is in the nature of scientific evidence.

There are laboratory techniques, uh, I guess that have been developed over the years and I believe that the case law in this area, um, suggests that it is not subject to scientific scrutiny as such. They're laboratory techniques, and they—they operate under different standard and different standard of evidentiary admissibility, so if— . . .

[Defense Counsel]: Your Honor, at some point during the state's presentation of evidence they're going to have to put someone on the stand, qualify them as an expert and have them give an opinion that in their opinion this hair is—this sample is consistent with this known or this piece of evidence that was recovered. I mean, it's much like a fingerprint comparison by Russell Crosson.

The Court: That's right, they're–they're all similar types of evidence, counsel, and they're not treated as scientific evidence, they're–they're different kind of evidence.

. . .

The Court: [T]hey are not, as far as I have determined to be the nature of scientific evidence that requires a pretrial determination of reliability as to this extent.[44]

On appeal, the defendant argued that the trial court should not have allowed expert testimony on the hair and fiber samples without first requiring the prosecution to establish the reliability of the expert's conclusions, based on the requirements of *Daubert*.[45] Furthermore, argued the defendant, the need for a judicial determination of reliability was not limited to novel scientific procedures.[46] The prosecution's response was that hair and fiber evidence was clearly reliable, noting that the overwhelming majority of cases addressing the issue had found such evidence to be reliable and admissible.[47] The trial court's decision, the state argued, was apparently based on the erroneous distinction between scientific evidence and laboratory techniques, the trial court improperly ruling that while scientific evidence was subject to a *Daubert* reliability analysis, laboratory techniques were not.

The Hawaii Supreme Court rejected the state's position, ruling in favor of that crucial distinction:

> We agree with the trial court's approach to this issue. "Scientific knowledge" must be distinguished from "technical knowledge." Expert testimony deals with "scientific knowledge" when it involves the validity of the scientific principles and the reliability of the scientific procedures themselves. In contrast, expert testimony deals with "technical knowledge" when it involves the mere technical application of well-established scientific principles and procedures. In such a situation, because the underlying scientific principles and procedures are of proven validity/reliability, it is unnecessary to subject technical knowledge to the same type of full-scale reliability determination required for scientific knowledge. Thus, although technical knowledge, like all expert testimony, must be both relevant and reliable, its reliability may be presumed.[48]

Because the scientific principles and procedures underlying hair and fiber evidence were well-established and of proven reliability, the evidence in the case under scrutiny could be treated as *technical knowledge*, resulting in a reliability determination being unnecessary. Accordingly, the trial court did not abuse its discretion in refusing to hold such hearing.[49]

The above discussion of the *McGrew*, *Southern*, and *Fukusaku* cases clearly demonstrates the general acceptability or reliability of microscopic hair analysis by recent decisions of U.S. courts. It remains to be seen if this basic pattern of acceptance is substantial enough to place this issue in the legal dead-letter office or if it simply reflects momentary resignation in the face of the ubiquitous use of hair analysis and its unchallenged status over the years.

The next topic to be addressed is the extent to which forensic scientists can make linking statements, given the nature of microscopic hair analysis and the other "trace evidence" disciplines. This question has been the subject of a number of appellate cases and is one of the areas of clear difference between practitioners of the forensic sciences and those of the criminal law. This issue can be examined from the standpoints of investigation of crime and its prosecution. Investigators quite properly are less insistent on the legally precise linking terminology than courts, choosing to take an expert's statement of a "match" for hair, fiber, soils, etc., as solid leads. In the legal world this difference in language can be understood simply by asking two questions: what can the expert legally say? What can the prosecutor say the expert said?

In the 1991 Illinois Supreme Court decision in *People v. Linscott*,[50] the court extensively addressed the pitfalls of statistical evidence in relation to hair analysis as well as the linguistic range of permissable "match" statements by expert witnesses and prosecutors. Karen Ann Phillips, the victim, was found dead in her apartment in Oak Park, Illinois. Police found the victim's body face down and naked except for a nightgown pushed up around her neck and shoulders. An autopsy revealed that her death was caused by several blows to her head and strangulation. Hairs were found clasped in the victim's hands, in her pubic region, and on a carpet on the floor of her apartment. These hairs were removed and tests were conducted on them as part of the investigation.[51]

Three expert witnesses testified on the subject of hair comparisons. Mark Stolorow, the coordinator of serology for the Illinois Department of Law Enforcement, testified for the state concerning the procedures for hair comparison testing that, were employed by the department, explaining that through the employment of a comparison microscope, a simultaneous visual comparison is made of the characteristics of hair samples from two different sources. He testified that this methodology excluded classes of individuals from consideration as suspects in an investigation and was conclusive, if at all, only to negate identity.[52]

A second state expert, Mohammad Tahir, a forensic scientist for the Illinois Department of Law Enforcement, testified regarding hair comparisons he performed on the hair samples taken from the victim and from the defendant, explaining that he looked at approximately 7 to 12 characteristics.[53]

Based upon those comparisons, Tahir concluded that certain of the hairs found in the victim's apartment were "consistent with" the samples provided by defendant. Tahir defined "consistent as no dissimilarity." Tahir testified that defendant's hair samples were consistent with those hairs found in the victim's right hand, hairs found on the carpet, and two pubic hairs that were combed from the victim's pubic region. On cross-examination, however, Tahir conceded that a person cannot be identified by the hairs he leaves behind:

Defense: And you sure can't determine from whose head that hair came from, can you?

Tahir: You cannot positively say.

. . .

Defense: Okay, you couldn't even say that if you had two pieces of hair from the same head, could you?

Tahir: My answer is the same, what I told you that you cannot say that this hair came from this individual, only could say is that it is consistent with [sic].[54]

Despite this testimony, the prosecutor argued that hairs found in the victim's apartment and on the victim's body were in fact defendant's hairs. In closing argument, the prosecutor told the jury that:

... the rug in the area where Karen was laying [sic] was ripped out sometime later, rolled up and shipped to the laboratory. And that another group of hairs were obtained. The head hairs of Steven Linscott.

. . .

. . . he [defendant] left eight to ten hairs of his in that apartment; his [defendant's] pubic hairs [were found] in her crotch; and his [defendant's] hairs are found in the most private parts of the woman's body.[53]

The court ruled that the prosecutor improperly argued, by these statements, that the hairs removed from the victim's apartment were conclusively identified as coming from defendant Linscott's head and pubic region, when there simply was no testimony at trial to support such assertions. In fact, the court continued, both state experts, as well as defendant's had all testified that no such identification was possible. The prosecutor's misrepresentation of the hair-comparison evidence was compounded, the court observed, by his argument that the mathematical probabilities that the hairs found on the victim's body and in her apartment came from anyone other than defendant were minuscule. The prosecutor relied on hair-comparison studies published by the forensic scientist Barry Gaudette for the statistics he used. The only testimony heard on these numerical arguments were elicited from defendant's expert on cross- examination.

Because of the importance of this subject and the scarcity of judicial discussion of it, the entire text of the cross-examination follows:

Prosecutor: You are aware of a forensic scientist by the name of Barry Gaudette, are you not?

Siegesmund: Gaudette is one of the proponents of X-ray analysis.

Q: Mr. Gaudette performed a study in the early to middle 70's, did he not, with regard to the percentages and probabilities of hair comparisons?

A: Absolutely.

Q: And his technique that he used was with a comparison microscope, was it not sir?

A: He used comparison. And he, also, used other microscopes.

Q: But he used a comparison microscope. The one microscope you did not use, is that correct?

A: Yes, he did use that, also.

Q. And his probabilities came to the substance that a match between head hairs is likely in one out of every 4,500 cases, is that correct.

A: Well, can I explain that?

Q: I'll rephrase the question. Did he not come up with a figure that any two individuals, the probability they would have matching head hairs is a likelihood in one out of 4,500?

A: It depends on how many hairs you are talking about.

Q: Would you say, the more hairs you have to compare, the closer to that figure you get?

A: The higher the probability, that is correct.

Q: So in this case if we had but one hair that Mr. Tahir linked to Mr. Linscott, that would have that much meaning, is that correct?

A: Yes. Using the conventional techniques that Gaudette used, yes.

Q: That Gaudette used, that's correct?

A: Yes.

Q: If you have two to three hairs, your information is a little better, is that correct?

A: Yes. Only if you do the forty tests he recommends.

Q: Fine, if you had, approximately, seven or eight hairs, you have more information to base it on?

A: According to Gaudette, that would give you a higher probability. If you did the forty tests.[56]

Based on the evidence at trial, the court ruled that the mathematical probabilities from Gaudette's study should not have been considered by the jury. Siegesmund had made it clear in his testimony that Gaudette's findings in his work were based on the completion of 40 tests, not simply the 7 to 12 comparison tests performed by state expert Tahir. Since there was no evidence that "forty tests" were ever performed in this case, there was no foundation for the thesis that Gaudette's mathematical statistics were applicable here. In addition, the prosecutor in closing argument commented that the defendant's hair had been found at the crime scene. The *Linscott* court found that the prosecutor's comment was improper because the evidence merely showed that the defendant was in a class of possible donors of the hair and not that the hair conclusively belonged to the defendant. Because the evidence in *Linscott* was so closely balanced, this court concluded that the improper comment amounted to plain error.[57]

In most published opinions involving hair evidence, the underlying methodology has gone unchallenged or is deemed reliable by a court due to its allegedly venerable past "acceptance" by courts across the nation. It bears repeating that the existence of adequately founded expert witness testimony has very considerable impact on a jury, who may be unable or unwilling to separate less than certain conclusions from the scientific patina given the testimony by the establishing of the expert's credentials and the description of the laboratory procedures used in the case at hand. Again, this is not to criticize the experts, simply to recognize the cleansing effect that such tentative but microscopically based forensic disciplines may have on the more traditional types of evidence presented in criminal cases, such as eyewitness testimony. In the past several decades there have been over 200 reported decisions making passing reference to the propriety of using microscopic hair analysis in prosecutions. The discussion of the cases to follow will serve to highlight some of the numerous utilizations of microscopic hair analysis testimony made in a wide variety of fact settings.

In the case of *People v. Moore*,[58] the defendant was charged with first-degree murder, home invasion, residential burglary, aggravated criminal sexual assault, robbery, and arson. The defendant had previously worked at the victim, Judy Zeman's, home as a house-painter and the victim was alone at her home when the defendant returned. The victim was bound with duct tape, tied to the back of a car, and set on fire.[59] Having compared hairs found on the floor mat of the defendant's car to known standards, a forensic scientist testified that two hairs were "consistent" with the victim's head hairs, and that one hair was "consistent" with the defendant's head hairs and showed signs of extreme heat damage.[60]

The defendant argued that the prosecutor in rebuttal also overstated the evidence when he said, "Judy Zeman didn't know that that burnt hair was in her car that came off his [defendant's] head," since a forensic scientist had only testified the burned hair was "consistent" with the defendant's hair, not that the burned hair was conclusively his. The defendant argued that the prosecutor's burned hair statement constituted reversible error. Here, as in *Linscott*, the court ruled that the prosecutor's comment that the burned hair in the car came from the defendant's head had indeed overstated the evidence. However, unlike the evidence in *Linscott*, the evidence here was not closely balanced, and the court concluded that the burned hair statement did not deprive the defendant of a fair trial.[61]

Microscopic hair testimony involving the age of the victim was presented in the case of *State v. Williams*,[62] where the defendant was charged with aggravated child abuse. The victim, the defendant's stepdaughter, was 13 months old when she suffered the very serious injuries in question. The defendant claimed that the child had fallen from her crib when he was out of the room.

The left side of the child's head was bruised and swollen to such an extent that her left ear extended perpendicular to her head. X-rays disclosed a hematoma and fracture on the left side and back of the child's head. A child abuse investigator searched the defendant's home and in the process found that the distance between the crib and a twin bed in the same room was $30^1/_2$ inches. The investigator testified if the crib railing was lowered, the distance to the floor was $32^1/_2$ inches, estimating that the distance with the railing raised would be approximately $44^1/_2$ inches. During the course of the search, the investigator noticed a louvered door that was broken and off its track and contained a blonde hair in a broken slat found on the kitchen table. A hair sample of the victim was obtained and subsequently sent to the FBI Crime Laboratory for comparison with the hair found on the broken slat.[63]

Dr. Donald Lewis, a pediatrician at Holston Valley Hospital, testified that his examination of the child victim revealed a hematoma to the left side of the child's head and a fracture to the right back portion of the child's skull. He testified that this was not the type of injury that could conceivably result from a $32^1/_2$ inch fall to a carpeted surface. He also testified that the injuries were the result of more than one impact. Because the skull of a 13-month-old infant is considerably more pliant than that of an adult, it would take significantly more force to cause trauma to a child's skull. In his view, a fall onto a tiled surface would cause less significant injuries than those suffered by the victim, and that these injuries were consistent with the child "being struck with a cornered or edged object," and that swinging the child into a louvered door would be one possible scenario of how these severe injuries occurred.

Clealand Blake, an anatomic pathologist with 28 years' experience, who had examined over 100 children, many of whom were victims of head injuries, examined the child victim here. He observed an enlarged lymph node near the fracture, which was consistent with the body's reaction to injury. The child's left eyelid and left ear still showed some residual bruising and, based upon the pictures taken at the hospital, the injuries seem to be approximately 36 hours old. Dr. Blake was of the opinion that the child's injuries could not conceivably have occurred as a result of falling 2 feet, $2^1/_2$ feet, or 3 feet off of a bed onto a carpeted floor or even a vinyl floor, commenting that it takes above a third-story window fall onto a hard surface for a child to experience such a major head injury. He also opined that there were at least two major injuries to the head of the victim in the case.[64]

Wayne Oakes, a supervisory special agent with the FBI Crime Laboratory, testified that the blonde hair found in the slat had been forcibly removed and "showed no microscopic differences" from the hair taken from the child's head during her examination by Dr. Blake. While conceding that microscopic hair analysis did not provide an absolute personal identification, he stated that, based upon his experience, the hair found on the slat came from a very young child and contained no bleach or dyes.[65]

McCarty v. State,[66] was a first-degree murder and death-penalty case where a forensic scientist testified that an autopsy had revealed a hair linked to the defendant found inside a knife wound suffered by the victim, followed by testimony that established that the defendant was present when the violence occurred. The state used the testimony of a forensic scientist in this regard in an effort to counter the defendant's claim. He claimed that his hair was found in the house because he was a social companion of the residents and had been there on prior occasions. On December 5, 1982, due to marital problems, Dale Coffman moved out of the house that he shared with his wife Melanie Coffman. On that same day, Pam Willis moved into the house with Melanie. The police found the nude body of victim Pam Willis, after receiving a call from Dale Coffman, who had walked to the front porch when his estranged wife failed to answer the door. When he noticed that one of the windows to the side of the front door was broken, he walked to the side of the house and looked into the side windows where he observed a pair of bare legs on the floor between the dining room and the kitchen area.[67]

State forensic chemist Joyce Gilchrist testified that 16 scalp hairs and one pubic hair found at the scene of the homicide were consistent with the appellant's hair and, therefore, could have come from him. She also testified that a single fragment of scalp hair removed from the screen that had been pulled back from the window in the bedroom exhibited similarities to appellant's scalp hairs. In response to a question if she had an opinion, based on her expertise and examination of the forensic evidence, on whether Mr. McCarty was physically present during the time violence was committed on the victim, Gilchrist replied, "he [McCarty] was in fact there." The court ruled that this testimony was clear error:

Ms. Gilchrist did not, and could not, testify that such opinion was based on facts or data "of a type reasonably relied upon by experts in the particular field" in forming such an opinion. Ms. Gilchrist herself testified that forensic science techniques had not advanced to the point where a person could be positively identified through blood types, secretor status, or hair examination. We find it inconceivable why Ms. Gilchrist would give such an improper opinion, which she admitted she was not qualified to give. While defense counsel attempted to demonstrate the impropriety of Gilchrist's opinion through the testimony of John Wilson, we cannot say this was sufficient to overcome the devastating impact of improper identification testimony by a police forensic expert . . . . Whether or not Ms. Gilchrist's opinion constituted an improper personal expression of the appellant's guilt, her opinion that appellant was in fact present when violence was done to the victim was an improper expert opinion, because it was beyond the present state of the art of forensic science.[68]

In addition, the court observed, because Gilchrist's so-called expert opinion was much more like a personal opinion beyond the scope of present scientific capabilities, it should have been barred as its probative value was substantially outweighed by the dangers of unfair prejudice and misleading the jury.

The defendant also alleged error as a result of the trial court permitting Ms. Gilchrist to testify that a scalp hair "consistent with" the appellant was found in one of the victim's chest wounds, in which a knife was embedded. The court agreed, noting that no evidence was introduced that Ms. Gilchrist had personal knowledge of this matter or that such information was contained in the medical examiner's report. On cross-examination, Ms. Gilchrist admitted that she was not present at the autopsy when the scalp hair was collected, and the medical examiner who performed the autopsy did not testify at trial. This clear example of forensic scientist overreaching should serve as an important example and reminder of the ongoing concern over the tremendous impact that well-packaged forensic testimony may have, especially on less well-versed defense counsel.

In the Arkansas Supreme Court decision in *Suggs v. State*,[69] a first-degree murder case, the defendant was accused of murdering his girlfriend, Debbie McKenzie. The defendant challenged the opinion of state criminalist Don Smith, who testified that he was given hair samples from Debbie McKenzie's body and from Suggs, and he compared those samples with hair found on a tennis shoe belonging to the defendant, concluding that the hair found on Suggs's shoe was Debbie's. However, the defendant noted that expert Smith agreed with the statement that the scientific field of microscopic hair analysis cannot prove the hair came from a certain individual to the exclusion of any other person, thus rendering his testimony error.[70]

Here, the appeals court held that the trial court correctly qualified Smith as an expert concerning the field of trace evidence. Smith testified that, as a criminalist, he dealt with scientific evidence and trace evidence or residues recovered at a crime scene, which includes such things as hair. His training included specialized areas of hair analysis, including experience with the FBI Laboratory and St. Louis Metropolitan Police Laboratory. The court observed that after having been qualified as an expert, Smith went into considerable detail concerning the analysis performed on Suggs's and Debbie McKenzie's hair samples and how those samples were analyzed and compared with the hair found on Suggs's tennis shoe. Suggs's counsel then took the opportunity to cross-examine Smith thoroughly concerning his qualifications and whether he could actually prove the hair on Suggs's shoe belonged to Debbie. The court concluded that both sides did a more than adequate job of airing the hair analysis issues and that the weight to be given his testimony was for the jury to determine. In sum, the trial court did not err in allowing Smith's testimony.[71]

There are a number of additional interesting and illustrative cases addressing various aspects of the utilization of microscopic hair analysis in U.S. criminal trials. These cases are deserving of brief attention as we conclude this chapter.

In the case of *Pruitt v. State*,[72] decided by the Georgia Supreme Court in 1999, the defendant was accused of the rape-murder of a 10-year-old female victim who lived in a trailer next door to his ex-wife's trailer, where he was staying the night. The police became suspicious of Pruitt because of the description of his movements during the last few hours before the estimated time of death. The police noticed that he had scratches and cuts on his hands and found bloodstains on the clothes Pruitt had been wearing the previous night. Given the strength of the Locard Principle discussed in Chapter 2, that close physical encounters inevitably result in trace transfers of hair and fiber, and the reality of the considerable physical interaction in rape-homicide settings, it is rare that any such cases will depend solely upon hair analysis. Here, inside the victim's bedroom, hairs "consistent with" Pruitt's head hair were found on the bedroom floor, a bedsheet, a pillow, and the victim's body, panties, socks, and shirt. Hairs "consistent with" Pruitt's pubic hair were also found on the bedsheet and the bedroom floor. Considerable other forensic evidence was found at the scene and testified to at trial.[73]

In the 1999 case of *Commonwealth v. Snell,* the defendant was convicted of murder in the first degree of his wife.[74] Here, the victim had obtained a protective order and an arrest warrant against the defendant. The next day, when the victim's children were unable to reach her, police were called, and they located the victim's body in the family home. The medical examiner concluded that the victim had died as a result of asphyxia due to smothering, and recorded 17 injuries on the victim's body which were inflicted contemporaneously or within minutes of the time of her death.[75]

In attacking the entirety of the crime scene investigation, the defendant argued that the police had not sufficiently investigated the case, in particular, by failing to gather evidence that might have exculpated him. Specifically, the defendant argued that the court erred in failing to continue the case to permit further DNA testing on hairs found on the blanket used to cover the victim's body. Testing had previously determined that some hairs recovered from the blanket were consistent with the victim's hair, and that seminal fluid on the blanket probably came from the defendant. The trial court ruled that the onus was on the defendant to explain the delay and to establish a need for further testing. The court determined that there was no basis seen in the testimony of the defendant's chemist, or elsewhere, to indicate that further testing of hairs found on the blanket might furnish exculpatory evidence. Hence, the trial judge properly ruled that further delay was unwarranted. Obtaining sufficient, or any, funding for purposes of conducting forensic testing for the defense is directly related to the quality of the demonstration regarding what could be potentially exculpatory. The Massachusetts Supreme Court made an interesting observation respecting such requests:

> The defendant's expert removed approximately 300 hairs from the blanket. Some were animal hairs and some were human hairs. The expert testified that examination for trace evidence was important, if there was nothing else. He did not say that failing to look for trace evidence might show something wrong with the investigation. He indicated that it was the decision of the investigators based on what they felt was necessary at the time. The expert testified to the presence of five separate categories of hair found on the blanket, but did not suggest they had come from different people. It may have come from only two people. The defendant lived with the victim in the marital home.[76]

The initial lack of adequate funding in most jurisdictions illustrates the catch-22 nature of any such motions.

In *State v. Ware*,[77] a 1999 Tennessee appellate court decision, the defendant, Paul Ware, was indicted for felony murder and multiple counts of rape of a child. The defendant was staying with the victim's mother and, according to the state, sexually assaulted the child after the mother and friends left the residence to go to a tavern. Significant issues in this case involved certain hairs found on and inside the child's body. During the autopsy, a "reddish hair" was found stuck to the victim's lip, a dark brown body hair was found "partly touching . . . the mucosa of the rectum and partly touching the skin of the anus," and a reddish pubic hair was removed from the victim's pharynx. The defendant had hair coloring that was deemed red or auburn. In a horrifying rendition of the autopsy findings, the pathologist testified that with regard to the dark brown hair, "it would take direct contact and a little pressure applied to get that hair to stick to the mucosal lining in the rectum . . . . Any handling of the body, moving of the body from one place to another, examination of the body by a person or persons could potentially be sources of contamination to supply loose hair . . . . Furthermore, he testified that the pubic hair found in the victim's pharynx was highly unusual. He explained that a normal, breathing, living person would not be expected to tolerate a hair in this location because any intrusion into this area would trigger a cough reflex.[78]

Special Agent Chris Hopkins of the FBI Hair and Fibers Unit characterized the hair that was found in the victim's pharynx as a "red Caucasian pubic hair" which had been "naturally shed." He also discussed "at least ten red Caucasian pubic hairs" which were taken from the sheet on the bed where the defendant admitted he had placed the sleeping victim. Agent Hopkins testified that pubic hairs were naturally shed from putting on and off your underwear, changing clothes, or taking a shower. He also stated that pubic hairs may be naturally shed when one person rubs against another. Agent Hopkins explained that the hairs on the sheet were very significant:

> [W]hen hair or fibers fall on a piece of evidence, they tend not to stay there very long . . . [I]f there is no activity in [a] bed, then you would expect the hairs to stay there

because there is no reason for them to move around, but if someone is using that bed on a regular basis, . . . you wouldn't expect those hairs to stay there.

He also stated, "I would not expect to find that many pubic hairs in [a] bed that has just been slept in."[79]

Hopkins opined that all hairs, the hair from the victim's pharynx and those from the sheet, were "consistent with originating from the [D]efendant." As in all other cases, when pressed, he testified that hair comparison was "not capable of individual identification" and thus he was unable to state conclusively whether the hairs belonged to the defendant. However, he did conclude that Carl Sanders, Danny Gaddis, and Paul Crum, the other men in the home at that period, were each eliminated as being potential sources of the pubic hairs.[81]

Agent Hopkins also concluded that the hair found on the victim's lip was red in color and was likely a chest hair. He stated that the hair removed from the victim's anus was a brown Caucasian body hair and therefore was "not suitable for comparison," explaining:

The only two regions, the only two types of hairs that are suitable for comparison purposes are . . . head hairs and pubic hairs . . . . Hairs, other hairs than head hairs and pubic hairs, these body area hairs or hairs on your arms or your legs, they tend to look like other people's hair, so there's not a significant association that can be made when comparing those hairs.[81]

Despite some evidence suggesting that the defendant may not have committed the crime, there was clearly substantial evidence presented at trial, in addition to the crucial hair testimony, indicating that the defendant did commit the crime. As noted above, sufficiently clear and well presented trace evidence such as microscopic hair analysis can lend significant support to the credibility of nonscientific evidence which typically constitutes the greater part of the state's proof.[82]

In *Manning v. State*,[83] a 1998 Mississippi Supreme Court decision involving numerous aspects of forensic science, the defendant was charged with the double homicide and armed robbery of two college students. The State called Chester Blythe, special agent with the FBI, to testify as an expert in the field of hair analysis. He testified that he could "microscopically determine if the hairs look alike and determine with some degree of certainty, although not absolutely, but with some degree of certainty if hairs, for example, found in vacuum sweepings from an automobile originated from a particularly named individual." Agent Blythe testified that in the two specimens he had, which were collected from victim Tiffany Miller's car, he was able to determine that hairs that were found in these specimens "exhibited characteristics associated with the black race."[84]

Defendant argued that hair analysis was "latter-day voodoo." The court, disagreeing, stated that hair analysis expert testimony was admissible, finding it to be a very useful tool in criminal investigation. Here, the expert did not claim that the hair matched that of the defendant, but only that the hair came from a member of the black race. He also admitted that his expertise could not produce absolute certainty. This did not invade the province of the jury, the court stated, but left it to them to decide if these were Manning's hairs or not.[85]

In another case involving child victims, *State v. Butler*,[86] a 1998 Missouri ruling, the defendant was convicted of one count of sodomy, one count of felonious restraint, and two counts of armed criminal action, arising out of the sexual assaults upon two minor males. The victims described the man as about 5 feet 7- or 8-inches, 170 lb., with brown curly hair that came down from under a dark baseball cap, wearing a dark T-shirt, shorts, and tennis shoes. The defendant, Mr. Butler, who lived in the same mobile home park, became a suspect, and head and pubic hair samples were taken from him. The major point on appeal concerned the state's expert testimony with regard to an unknown head hair recovered from the victim J.L.'s shirt, and the unknown pubic hair recovered from J.L.'s underwear.

The state expert forensic chemist testified the unknown hair came from the same person. She admitted that microscopic hair analysis was unable to positively identify individuals based on hair comparison. She testified that there were not as many distinguishing characteristics in hair as in DNA samples or fingerprints, so that a criminalist could not tell what percent of the population could have contributed that hair, and the opinion would be subjective but based on experience. As to the head hair samples she stated, "I feel there is a very strong probability that those two hairs came from the defendant."[87] Her opinion was based in part on an "unusual spot on a certain part of the hair" found on the victim, which also appeared in the same spot on Butler's hair. The witness testified that she could, within a reasonable degree of certainty, testify that the unknown hairs were in fact from the defendant.

The defendant argued that the circumstantial evidence of the match between his head and pubic hair with those taken from the victim's clothing was insufficient, and without other evidence of the defendant's involvement, the state's case was insufficient and must fail. The court noted that the issue raised here did not depend upon the admissibility of hair testimony, but, rather, on the lack of certainty inherent in the discipline of hair examination and the inability of an expert to quote statistical support as in DNA contexts:

> This court is mindful of Butler's contention the only thing linking him to this crime is the opinion evidence of the state's forensic expert, but, . . . that evidence is sufficient to sustain the verdict reached by the jury. The jury here was free to reject Butler's assertion he had been at the park's swimming pool the afternoon in question and the hairs could have been picked up by the victim during the afternoon when he may have been swimming at the same pool. The expert's testimony was admitted into evidence, and was sufficient to allow the jury to find that the head and pubic hairs found on the victim, which contained the same characteristics and unusual mark as those of Butler, were Butler's hairs, and conclude that Butler was the assailant.[88]

Judge Breckenridge, in an important dissenting opinion, took considerable exception to the unchallenged, accepted value of microscopic hair analysis comparison evidence. In the *Butler* case he observed that the only evidence connecting Mr. Butler to the crime was the fact that he lived in the trailer park where the assault occurred and that two hairs recovered from J.L.'s clothing both "matched"

Mr. Butler's hair samples, according to the state's forensic expert. However, Judge Breckenridge noted, the expert admitted that she could not state that the hair was from Mr. Butler beyond a reasonable doubt. The question then was whether hair evidence alone could ever be sufficient to provide proof beyond a reasonable doubt of the commission of this or any other crime:

> One of the bases for her conclusion that Mr. Butler was the source of the two hairs found on J.L.'s clothing was the fact that both Mr. Butler's pubic hair sample and the pubic hair found in J.L.'s underwear had distinctive black spots which she considered "very unusual." She opined that such spots were unique based upon the infrequency of her own observation of the characteristic. In *State v. Jones*, 777 S.W.2d 639, 641 (Mo.App.1989), the expert witness testified that hair taken from the victim and that of the defendant both contained "big black spots" which were not common, but the expert witness did not testify that the hair found on the victim came from the defendant. In contrast, Ms. Duvenci infers in her testimony that the spots are so unique that they would serve as a basis for a positive identification of Mr. Butler. The State does not demonstrate, and this court is unaware, that the scientific community recognizes an exception to the principle that hair comparisons cannot produce a conclusive positive identification if the hair samples contain specific characteristics, such as black spots.[89]

The only evidence implicating Mr. Butler in the crimes charged was circumstantial evidence of the hair comparison and the fact that he lived in the trailer park. This evidence, at best, argued the dissent, only raised a suspicion or conjecture that he committed these crimes.

III. CONCLUSION

The foregoing discussion of microscopic hair analysis may serve to set the tone for most of the subjects yet to be covered in detail. The reality of the greatest number of the forensic sciences is their grounding in close observations and comparisons of characteristics of the type of crime scene data under review, by use of the latest microscopic aids. Fiber, soil, glass and paint, ballistics, tool marks, footwear, and fingerprint analyses are all observational disciplines whose current and future value hinges in large part on developments in modern microscopy. These investigative disciplines work within a culture of proof guided by probability analyses to provide tremendous assistance in the investigation and trial of criminal cases.

ENDNOTES

1. W. Bruschweiler and M.C. Grieve: "State of the Art in the Field of Hair and Textile Fibre Examinations," *Proceedings of the 12th INTERPOL Forensic Science Symposium* (New York, 1998), at 179–180.
2. *Id.*
3. Ogle and Fox: *Atlas of Human Hair: Microscopic Characteristics* (CRC Press, Boca Raton, FL, 1999) at 5.

4. The authors of this important new study offer a numerical scoring system permitting the hair type to be presented as an array of alphanumeric scores, with the goal of simplifying the development of the database noted above. *Id.*

5. See, generally, Saferstein: *Criminalistics: An Introduction to Forensic Science* (6th ed. Prentice-Hall, Upper Saddle River, NJ, 1998); Eckert: *Introduction to Forensic Sciences* (2d ed. CRC Press, Boca Raton, FL, 1997); Fisher: *Techniques of Crime Scene Investigation* (5th ed. CRC Press, Boca Raton, FL, 1993); Bodziak: *Footwear Impression Evidence* (CRC Press, Boca Raton, FL, 1995); Geberth: *Practical Homicide Investigation* (3d ed. CRC Press, Boca Raton, FL, 1996); DiMaio and DiMaio: *Forensic Pathology* (CRC Press, Boca Raton, FL, 1993); Pickering and Bachman: *The Use of Forensic Anthropology* (CRC Press, Boca Raton, FL, 1997); Janes (ed.): *Scientific and Legal Applications of Bloodstain Pattern Interpretation* (CRC Press, Boca Raton, FL, 1999); Ogle and Fox, *supra,* note 3.

6. See the discussion of the *Sutherland* case study in Chapter 2, Science and the Criminal Law, regarding exclusions of suspects by class characteristic statements.

7. Sir Francis Bacon: *Novum Organum: Aphorisms on the Interpretation of Nature and the Empire of Man,* (1620) (Peter Urbach and John Gibson, trans. Open Court, Chicago, 1994) at 29–30.

8. Pierre Simon de Laplace: *Theorie Analytique des Probabilities,* Introduction (Paris, 1820).

9. *Supra,* note 1.

10. *Id.*

11. McGrew v. State, 673 N.E.2d 787 (Ct.App. Ind. 1997); 682 N.E.2d 1289 (Ind.Sp.Ct. 1997).

12, *Id.* at 791.

13. *Id.* at 796.

14. *Id.*

15. *Id.* at 797. See Harrison v. State, 644 N.E.2d 1243 (Ind. Sp.Ct. 1995).

16. See Hopkins v. State, 579 N.E.2d 1297, 1305 (1991).

17. Under both the Indiana and the federal rules, the general test for the admission of expert testimony regarding "scientific, technical, or other specialized knowledge" was that it must assist the trier of fact to understand the evidence or determine a fact in issue. Rule of Evidence 702 (a). Federal courts are still split, however, as to whether additional requirements imposed by Daubert should apply to nonscientific testimony. See the discussion of Kumho Tire v. Carmichael, in Chapter 1, Science, Forensic Science, and Evidence. Also see United States v. Quinn (1994) 9th Cir., 18 F.3d 1461, 1464–65, cert. denied, 512 U.S. 1242, 114 S.Ct. 2755, 129 L.Ed.2d 871 ("photogrammetry," in which the varying heights of known objects in a photograph are used to calculate the height of other objects in the photograph, does not require analysis under Daubert); United States v. Velasquez (1995) 3d Cir., 64 F.3d 844, 850, reh'g denied (questioning whether Daubert standard should be applied to handwriting analysis); Iacobelli Const. v. County of Monroe (1994) 2d Cir., 32 F.3d 19, 25 (determining that affidavits from geotechnical consultant and underground construction consultant are not the type of "junk science" targeted by Daubert); United States v. Starzecpyzel (1995) S.D.N.Y., 880 F.Supp. 1027, 1040–41 (Daubert not applicable to nonscientific field of forensic document examination). But see Frymire-Brinati v. KPMG Peat-Marwick (1993) 7th Cir., 2 F.3d 183, 186 (Daubert analysis applied to decision to admit accountant's testimony).

18. McGrew, *supra,* note 11, at 798–799.

19. *Id.* at 799. See Edward J. Imwinkelried: "Forensic Hair Analysis: The Case Against the Underemployment of Scientific Evidence" 39 *Wash. & Lee L. Rev.* 41 (1982). Also see Clive A. Stafford Smith and Patrick D. Goodman: "Forensic Hair Comparison Analysis: Nineteenth Century Science or Twentieth Century Snake Oil?" 27 *Colum. Hum. Rts. L. Rev.* 227, 231 (1996).

20. McGrew, *supra* note 11, at 799.

21. *Id.*

22. King v. State (1988) Ind. 531 N.E.2d 1154; Bivins v. State (1982) Ind. 433 N.E.2d 387; Fultz v. State (1976) 265 Ind. 626, 358 N.E.2d 123; see, generally Clive A. Stafford Smith and Patrick D. Goodman, *supra,* note 19. Whether microscopic hair analysis rested upon reliable scientific principles was an issue of first impression for Indiana courts.

23. McGrew, *supra,* note 11, at 787, 800 (Ct. App. Indiana 1997). The court recognized that Daubert reliability assessments did not formally require, although they did permit, precise identification of a relevant scientific community and an explicit finding of a particular degree of acceptance within any such identified community.

24. *Id.* at 802.

25. *Id.* at 803. The court also observed that the state's own medical expert admitted that the defendant suffered from a severe case of Peyronie's disease, making it extremely painful for him to achieve sexual arousal.

26. *Id.* at 803. McGrew also presented several alibi witnesses who testified that he was at various locations in the latter part of the evening which would have made it impossible for him to have been with J.W. on the deserted road during the time frame that the crime occurred. After briefing in the McGrew appellate case was completed, a federal district court in Oklahoma ruled that microscopic hair analysis was inadmissible under Daubert. In Williamson v. Reynolds, E.D.Okla., 904 F.Supp.1529, 1558 (1995), the defendant was convicted of murder in state court and sentenced to death. At his trial, a forensic expert testified that hair samples found at the crime scene were consistent with the defendant's head and pubic hair, and could have come from the same source. The federal district in a subsequent *habeas corpus* proceeding found that microscopic hair analysis failed to pass muster under any of the Daubert prongs. In reaching its determination, the court cited "an apparent scarcity of scientific studies regarding the reliability of hair comparison testing," noting that the few available studies tended to point to the method's unreliability. Nor did the evidence gain admission through the "general acceptance" threshold. The court determined that general acceptance of microscopic hair analysis seemed to be limited to forensic experts testifying for the prosecution, and did not extend to the objective scientific community which in the past had aimed pointed criticism at the technique. On appeal, the U.S. Court of Appeals for the Tenth Circuit affirmed the district court's decision based on petitioner's ineffective assistance of counsel claim. Williamson v. Ward, 110 F.3d 1508, 1510 (10th Cir. 1997). However, the Tenth Circuit specifically reversed the district court's ruling on the admissibility of hair analysis evidence because the district court had applied the wrong standard. *Id.* at 1522–23.

27. McGrew, *supra,* at 11.

28. The expert testified that the microscope used was a "centrical light type microscope that allows various different magnifications," unlike an electron microscope. The court noted that, although the terms used sounded "technical and scientific," the meanings were quite simple, citing, James G. Zimmerly: *Lawyers Medical Cyclopedia* 45.2, LEXIS Law Publishing, Charlottesville, VA, at 768 (3rd ed. 1991). See Ogle and

Fox, *supra,* note 3, listing 24 characteristics for hair analysis. This small but excellent study should be in the library of all prosecution and defense offices.

29. McGrew, *supra,* note 11, at 1291.

30. *Supra,* note 27, at 1290–1291.

31. *Id.* at 1292.

32. *Id.* at 1290–1291.

33. *Id.* See Jervis v. State, 679 N.E.2d 875, 881 n. 9 (Ind.1997).

34. State v. Southern, 980 P.2d 3 (Mont.Sp.Ct. 1999).

35. *Id.* at 10.

36. Daubert v. Merrell Dow Pharmaceutical, Inc., 509 U.S. 579, 113 S.Ct. 2786 (1993). Also see State v. Moore, 268 Mont. 20, 885 P.2d 457 (1994). Also see Chapter 1, Science, Forensic Science, and Evidence, for a discussion of the Daubert case and its progeny.

37. Kumho Tire v. Carmichael, 119 S.Ct. 1167, 1175 (1999).

38. *Id.* at 1175.

39. See State v. Bromgard, 261 Mont. 291, 293-94, 862 P.2d 1140, 1141 (1993); State v. Kordonowy, 251 Mont. 44, 47, 823 P.2d 854, 856 (1991); Coleman v. State, 194 Mont. 428, 447, 633 P.2d 624, 636 (1981); State v. Higley, 190 Mont. 412, 428, 621 P.2d 1043, 1053 (1980); and State v. Coleman, 177 Mont. 1, 26-27, 579 P.2d 732, 747 (1978). See also Gregory G. Sarno: "Annotation, Admissibility and Weight, in Criminal Case, of Expert or Scientific Evidence Respecting Characteristics and Identification of Human Hair," 23 *A.L.R.* 4th 1199 (1983).

40. The court, in this regard, found that a proper foundation for the witness to qualify as an expert was established. She had been working with trace evidence (such as hair, fibers, glass, and paint) for 4¹/₂ years at the Montana State Crime Laboratory, spent about 90% of her time examining trace evidence, had taken several training courses at the FBI Academy that dealt with trace evidence, as well as several other courses on forensic microscopy. She was a member of two forensic scientist groups, was involved with writing guidelines for trace evidence examination for one of the groups, and had been found qualified to testify in other cases regarding her examinations of trace evidence. Southern, supra, note 34, at 17.

41. State v. Fukusaku, 85 Hawaii 462, 946 P.2d 32 (1997).

42. *Id.* at 37, 467.

43. *Id.* at 40, 470.

44. *Id.* at 471.

45. Daubert, *Supra,* note 36.

46. Defendant's position was subsequently adopted by the U.S. Supreme Court in the 1998 decision in Kumho Tire, *supra,* note 37, where the court ruled that the Daubert reliability criteria must be applied to all types of expert testimony. See Chapter 1, Science, Forensic Science, and Evidence.

47. See, e.g., United States v. Hickey, 596 F.2d 1082, 1089 (1st Cir.), cert. denied, 444 U.S. 853, 100 S.Ct. 107, 62 L.Ed.2d 70 (1979); United States v. Brady, 595 F.2d 359, 362–63 (6th Cir.), cert. denied, 444 U.S. 862, 100 S.Ct. 129, 62 L.Ed.2d 84 (1979); United States v. Cyphers, 553 F.2d 1064, 1071-73 (7th Cir.), cert. denied, 434 U.S. 843, 98 S.Ct. 142, 54 L.Ed.2d 107 (1977); Jent v. State, 408 So.2d 1024, 1028–29 (Fla. 1981), cert. denied, 457 U.S. 1111, 102 S.Ct. 2916, 73 L.Ed.2d 1322 (1982); Robinson v. State, 18 Md.App. 678, 308 A.2d 734, 744–45 (1973); Commonwealth v. Tarver, 369 Mass. 302, 345 N.E.2d 671, 676–77 (1975); State v. White, 621 S.W.2d 287, 292–93 (Mo. 1981); People v. Allweiss, 48 N.Y.2d 40, 421 N.Y.S.2d 341, 346,

396 N.E.2d 735 (1979); State v. Green, 305 N.C. 463, 290 S.E.2d 625, 629–30 (1982); State v. Kersting, 50 Or.App. 461, 623 P.2d 1095, 1098–1102 (1981), aff'd, 292 Or. 350, 638 P.2d 1145 (1982); State v. Batten, 17 Wash.App. 428, 563 P.2d 1287, 1292–93, review denied, 89 Wash.2d 1001 (1977).

48. Fukusaku, *supra*, note 41, at 474.

49. The court cited Giannelli and E. Imwinkelried: *Scientific Evidence* § 24-3, at 360–61. See also G. Sarno: "Annotation—Admissibility and Weight, in Criminal Case, of Expert Testimony or Scientific Evidence Respecting Characteristics and Identification of Human Hair," 23 *A.L.R.*4th 1199 (1983).

50. People v. Linscott, 142 Ill.2d 22, 566 N.E.2d 1355 (1991).

51. *Id.* at 26.

52. *Id.*

53. See Ogle and Fox, *supra*, note 3, setting out 24 characteristic capable of comparison.

54. Linscott, *supra*, note 50, at 1359.

55. *Id.*

56. *Id.*

57. *Id.* Similarly, in People v. Giangrande, 101 Ill.App.3d 397, 56 Ill.Dec. 911, 428 N.E.2d 503 (1981), the court held that a prosecutor overstated the evidence arguing that defendant's hair had been found at the crime scene, when the state's expert testified only that hairs from the crime scene could have originated from the defendant. *Id.* at 402–03. The appellate court found such arguments improper and reversed the conviction stating that it could not conclude "that the closing argument comments of the prosecutor did not result in substantial prejudice to defendant." *Id.* at 403.

But see People v. Gomez, 215 Ill.App.3d 208, 574 N.E.2d 822 (1991), where the court reversed a first-degree murder conviction because there was insufficient circumstantial evidence to establish the defendant's guilt beyond a reasonable doubt. There was evidence of the defendant's fingerprint at the murder scene, a place where he paid his monthly rent, as well as samples of blood and paint taken from the murder scene and the defendant's home. The state also introduced, as part of its case in chief, hairs found on the victim's body which shared some similarity with the defendant's hair. The court held that hair samples "do not possess the necessary unique qualities of fingerprints to allow positive identification." *Id.* at 828, 158 Ill.Dec. at 715. "The mere physical probabilities inferred from . . . hair . . . samples alone are insufficient to sustain a conviction beyond a reasonable doubt." *Id.* Also see People v. Brown, 122 Ill.App.3d 452, 77 Ill.Dec. 684, 687, 461 N.E.2d 71, 74 (Ill.App.1984). (Because the court found that the circumstantial evidence was insufficient to prove guilt, the court reversed the defendant's conviction.)

58. People v. Moore, 171 Ill.2d 74, 662 N.E.2d 1215 (1996).

59. A forensic scientist testified that two fingerprints on the adhesive side of the duct tape removed from the victim's hair and one fingerprint on a key tag found in the victim's abandoned car were identified as defendant's. Another forensic scientist testified that seminal material taken from the victim's vaginal swab was consistent with defendant's blood type. See Chapter 8, Fingerprints, and Chapter 10, DNA Analysis.

60. *Supra*, note 58, at 92.

61. *Id.* at 100.

62. State v. Williams, 1995 WL 324021 (Tenn.Crim.App.).

63. *Id.* at *1.

64. *Id.* at *2.

65. *Id.* at *2.

66. McCarty v. State, 765 P.2d 1215 (Ct. App.Okla. 1995). McCarty was retried in September of 1989 and reconvicted. The case was remanded for additional hearings on sentencing issues. See McCarty v. State, 977 P.2d 1116 (1999).

67. Addressing defendant's claim that he was denied a fair trial due to extraordinary delays in responding to his discovery request, the court, while not condoning defense counsel's delay in not naming an independent expert until Monday, March 10, 1986, found that Ms. Gilchrist's delay and neglect in not completing her forensic examination and report until Friday, March 14, 1986, for a trial which was scheduled for and began on Monday, March 17, 1986, was inexcusable, depriving defendant of a fair and adequate opportunity to have critical hair evidence examined by an independent forensic expert. The right to a fair trial would be rendered meaningless unless an accused is afforded a fair and adequate opportunity to make a competent independent pretrial examination of scientific evidence to be used against him. *Id.* at 1218.

68. *Id.* at 1219. The court stated that this view was buttressed "by the fact that on December 14, 1987, Max Courtney, President of the Southwestern Association of Forensic Scientists, Inc., issued a prepared statement of the board of directors concerning allegations of professional misconduct lodged against Ms. Gilchrist. A certified copy of this statement, which was filed with this court on January 4, 1988, concluded that Ms. Gilchrist had violated the ethical code, but, interestingly, she was not disciplined. That statement reads in relevant part: "Our Professional Conduct Committee thoroughly investigated the allegations against Ms. Joyce Gilchrist and . . . communicated with [her] that she should distinguish personal opinion from opinions based upon facts derived from scientific evaluation . . . . We further conclude that, in our system of jurisprudence, undue pressure can be placed upon the forensic scientist to offer personal opinions beyond the scope of scientific capabilities."

69. Suggs v. State, 322 Ark. 40, 907 S.W.2d 124 (1995).

70. *Id.* at 126.

71. *Id.* at 44.

72. Pruitt v. State, 270 Ga. 745, 514 S.E.2d 639 (1999).

73. A broken window screen at the Gottschalk trailer indicated the assailant's entry point, and beneath the window inside the trailer was a vinyl chair containing a partial shoe print. A state expert determined that this shoe print matched Pruitt's Reeboks. Gottschalk testified that Pruitt had never been a guest in her home; the only time she had ever seen him in her trailer was the brief time he felt for the victim's pulse on the morning of April 10, 1992. Semen was discovered in the victim's anus and DNA extracted from the semen matched Pruitt's. The state's DNA expert testified that the frequency of this DNA profile among Caucasians is 1 in 7 billion. Type O blood was found on the jeans and shirt that Pruitt had been wearing the night of the murder, and on the steering wheel cover in his car. At the Gottschalk trailer, type A blood was found on the porch lightbulb, the screen door latch, and near the entry window. Pruitt is type A and the victim was type O. *Id.* at 644.

74. Commonwealth v. Snell, 428 Mass. 766, 705 N.E.2d 236 (1999).

75. *Id.* at 239.

76. *Id.* at 772.

77. State v. Ware, 1999 WL 233592 (Tenn.Crim.App).

78. *Id.* at *6.

79. *Id.* at *8.

80. *Id.*

81. *Id.*
82. Also see State v. Montgomery, 341 N.C. 553, 461 S.E.2d 732, 735 (1995), where defendant was convicted of first-degree murder, for the rape-murder of a college coed after wrongfully entering her apartment. Five pubic hairs, which were consistent with those of defendant, were found in front of and on the sofa and love seat. The police later found the missing butcher knife in a parking lot located between Piccolo's apartment and the house owned by defendant's sister; defendant was staying in this house with his sister at the time of the murder. Blood and fibers consistent with fibers from Piccolo's sweatshirt were on the knife.
83. Manning v. State, 726 So.2d 1152 (Miss.Sp.Ct. 1998).
84. *Id.* at 1180.
85. *Id.* Also see Mason v. State, 1998 WL 96608 (Ala.Crim.App.), where the defendant was convicted of murder committed during the course of a robbery and sentenced to death. (A Negroid pubic hair, "consistent with a known pubic hair from the appellant," was found in the combings from the victim's pubic hair.)
86. State v. Butler, 1998 WL 141993 (Mo.App. W.D.).
87. *Id.* at *1.
88. *Id.* at *2.
89. *Id.* at *5.

4 Fiber Analysis

[F]or the limits to which our thoughts are confined, are small in respect of the vast extent of Nature it self; some parts of it are too large to be comprehended, and some too little to be perceived, and from thence it must follow, that not having a full sensation of the object, we must be very lame and imperfect in our conceptions about it, and in all the propositions which we build upon it; hence we often take the Shadow of things for the substance, small appearances for good similitudes, similitudes for definitions; and even many of those, which we think to be the most solid definitions, are rather expressions of our misguided apprehensions than of the true nature of the things themselves.

—Robert Hooke
Micrographia (1665)

I. INTRODUCTION

Here, as in hair analysis, footwear and tire impressions, glass, paint, and soil analyses, bite marks, and most other forensic science settings, we seek to discover what general non-suspect-related categories of information can be received from the analysis of a datum; here, fiber, obtained at a crime scene. These class statements begin the sketch of the person or persons who were present and are essential investigative links in the chain of circumstantial evidence pointing toward a particular suspect. The success of such efforts, of course, is directly related to the integrity of the crime scene preservation. The sad results in the recent JonBenet Ramsey case testify to that simple fact.

What can a simple fiber tell us from a class characteristic standpoint? To what degree should police and defense counsel be concerned with weather, temperature, terrain, wildlife, and other nonfiber elements invariably present in many crime scene scenarios that may affect the legitimacy of any opinions regarding fiber data?[1] What are potential fiber sources in each crime scene?

What is there to compare in fiber analyses?[2] What are the comparison points to look at in attempts to connect fibers found at the crime scene to fibers associated with the defendant in the case at hand? Initially, it is important to identify the broadest categories of fibers and then work down to the fiber characteristics actually used in making fiber comparisons and accompanying pronouncements by forensic specialists. The FBI has substantially upgraded the offerings on its Web site, one of which is the Forensic Fiber Examination Guidelines, published by the Federal Bureau of Investigation's Scientific Working Group on Materials Analysis (SWGMAT). This is an extensive release of technical papers on the entire issue of fiber analysis, including materials on the general background to this discipline, fiber analysis and modern microscopy, visible spectroscopy, thin-layer chromatography of nonreactive dyes in textile fibers, pyrolysis gas chromatography of textile fibers, infrared analysis of textile fibers and fabrics and cordage.[3] Despite recent criticisms of practices at the FBI Laboratory, the forensic collection practices, trace evidence, impression, and DNA databases and testing protocols and standards remain the bellwether for forensic science. Courts are not likely to dismiss out-of-hand the recommendations of the FBI databases.[4]

Fibers fall into two broad categories: natural and synthetic.[5] Both types are used in the manufacture of commercial products of a wide variety, ranging from all types of apparel, automobile seat covers, and home, office, and automobile coverings. All commercial applications have an immense variety of styles and colors to choose from. To a significant degree, all such fiber and the commercial processes used to produce the fiber itself and its applications are patented and collected in massive proprietary databases maintained by manufacturers.[6]

Natural fibers are divided into the three categories: animal, vegetable, and mineral. Animal fibers used in commercial production, led by wool, are wool, silk, camel hair, and a wide variety of furs such as mink, racoon, chinchilla, and alpaca. The vegetable category contains such fibers as cotton, linen, hemp, sisal, and jute. Cotton is the primary fiber used in commercial applications.[7] Fiber materials classified mineral, include asbestos, glass wool, and fiberglass.

Synthetic fibers are extensive in category and subcategory, but may be readily identified due to the massive commercial and FBI database collections used for proprietary uses and investigative purposes. Synthetic fiber categories include acetates, acrylics, aramid, modacrylic, nylon, olefin, polyester, PBI, PBF, rayon, spandex, sulfar, and vinyon.[8]

Many synthetic fiber categories exist, with an extensive listing of brand names under each heading.[9] For purposes of this chapter it is important to know that there is an excellent chance of identifying the generic type, origin, and a typical commercial source of fibers found at a crime scene. The question remains, of course, how many others in the general population have clothing, carpeting, etc. that would yield similar "consistent in all respects" forensic conclusions. The class characteristic statements in the fiber area are significant aides to getting an investigation focused and moving toward a suspect.

In Chapter 2, Science and the Criminal Law, a discussion on fiber evidence was initiated during the case analysis of *People v. Sutherland*.[10] In that case there were considerable fiber transfers involved, of fibers from the defendant's car to the body of the child victim and from the victim's shorts to the defendant's car. In this chapter we focus on fiber cases only, introducing the considerable problem for defendants, as in hair cases, of an absence of databases used to determine the presence of such fibers in the general population of a similar laboratory "match." Fiber testimony is subject to the same linguistic limitations of all other trace evidence categories, i.e., conclusions may only be couched in less than certain or absolute terms. Fiber cases differ from hair cases in that the initial determination of its basic character is significantly more complex than determining if a human hair was male, female, Caucasian, Negroid, or Asian, and from what portion of the body. These crucial matters will be revisited in the discussions of the Wayne Williams Atlanta murders case discussed below.

II. THE *WAYNE WILLIAMS* CASE

The best-known, if not the best-reasoned, fiber case in U.S. legal history involving fiber evidence issues is the Wayne Williams trial growing out of the infamous Atlanta murders of 12 young African-American males in 1979 to 1980.[11] The *Williams* case involved all of the subjects still in controversy as we enter the world of forensic science and forensic evidence in the 21st century. How do we gain sufficient knowledge of fiber manufacture, dyes, commercial applications, and differences among them to make any intelligent class characteristic or individual-linking statements in a criminal case? What are the primary characteristics of fibers per se or fiber types that allow for a comparative examination? How does the absence of meaningful "fiber match databases" from which to engage in population frequency analyses affect our confidence in the meaningfulness of fiber testimony? How do probability analyses work here: better, worse, or the same as in any other trace evidence exercise attempting to link a suspect to a crime scene?

In *Williams v. State*,[12] the defendant was charged and convicted of two of the twelve murders actually involved. Given the centrality of the *Williams* case in fiber analysis literature and judicial authorities, a detailed recitation of the central facts and forensic analyses is warranted. In a case of such complexity it is essential always to place whatever forensic claims that are made squarely in the midst of the nonforensic context where they arose. Probabilistically based forensic facts originate from real-world contexts that support or deter from belief in the fact for which it is offered. The crime scene facts are the thread weaving all forensic claims and give them meaning and credibility. The central issues raised by Williams on appeal focused on the collection, testing, and testimony regarding certain fibers located in Williams's home and automobiles, and linked by experts to similar fibers found on a number of the murder victims.

Initially, the court set out a recital of facts the jury would have been authorized to find from the evidence presented on the homicides of Jimmy Ray Payne and Nathaniel Cater, the two crimes with which appellant was charged. Over a 22-month period beginning in July 1979, more than 30 African-American children and young men were reported missing in the Atlanta, Georgia area. Williams was charged with the murder of two of the victims, Nathaniel Cater, aged 28, and Jimmy Payne, aged 21. The murders of 10 other victims were linked to Williams in support of the identity element, by way of complex fiber analysis testimony. Some victims were found floating in the Chattahoochee River, while others were discovered on or near rural roads or abandoned buildings in the Atlanta area.[13]

Victim Payne was 21 years of age, unemployed, and had no automobile or driver's license. A product of a broken home, he lived with his mother, sister, and girlfriend. The late morning of April 21, 1981, was the last time Payne was seen by any member of his household. It was then he told his mother he was on his way to the Omni. The following day a witness saw Williams and Payne standing by a taxi which was stopped on Highway 78 approximately 1 mile from the Chattahoochee River. The witness saw Williams and Payne talking to the driver of the taxi, and he also saw a white station wagon parked on the opposite side of the street from the cab.

Payne's body was discovered clad only in red shorts in the Chattahoochee River on April 27, 1981. The medical examination and autopsy resulted in opinion evidence that the cause of death was asphyxia by an undetermined method.[14]

The state presented the testimony of 7 fiber and hair associations between Wayne Williams and Jimmy Ray Payne. Georgia Bureau of Investigation Employee Larry Peterson testified that:

1. Two pale violet acetate fibers removed from Payne were consistent with violet acetate fibers present in the bedspread of Williams, except that they were lighter in color.
2. Three green Wellman-type fibers removed from Payne's shorts were similar to and could have originated from appellant's bedroom carpet, except that, again, they were lighter in color.
3. A blue-green or blue-gray rayon fiber removed from Payne was consistent with the rayon fibers composing the carpet of the 1970 station wagon.
4. Several light yellow rayon fibers and a light yellow acrylic fiber found on Payne were consistent with fibers composing the yellow blanket found in appellant's bedroom, except that they were lighter in color.
5. A blue acrylic fiber removed from Payne was consistent with the blue acrylic fibers that composed the blue throw rug found in appellant's bathroom.

FBI Agent Harold Deadman testified that:

1. A blue rayon fiber removed from Payne was consistent with blue rayon fibers, for which no source was known, found in various fibrous debris removed from the Williams home.
2. The approximately 7 animal hairs removed from Payne could have originated from appellant's German Shepherd dog.

There was evidence that the fibers found on Payne which were lighter in color than their supposed counterparts from the Williams environment were lighter because of their exposure to river water.[15]

Nathaniel Cater was 28 years old, lived at the Falcon Hotel in downtown Atlanta, and did not own an automobile. Robert Henry, a friend of Cater, saw Cater holding hands with Wayne Williams outside the Rialto Theatre about 9:00 to 9:15 P.M. on May 21, 1981. About 3:00 A.M., May 22, 1981, a member of a police surveillance team stationed at the Jackson Parkway Bridge heard a loud splash in the Chattahoochee River and saw a circle of waves form on the water. An automobile was then observed starting up and crossing the bridge. When the car was stopped, it was found to be a white Chevrolet station wagon and Wayne Williams was the driver. Cater's body was discovered in the Chattahoochee River on Sunday, May 24, 1981. It was located about 200 yards downstream from Interstate Highway 285. (The Cater body was found only a short distance from where the Payne body was found.) The medical examination and autopsy of the body revealed Cater weighed about

146 pounds and that his death was caused by asphyxia due to some kind of choke hold formed with a broad, soft surface such as a forearm.

Cater's body was nude; therefore, only his pubic and head hair regions were capable of holding fiber or hair evidence.[16] Even so, several fibers and hairs were recovered. Larry Peterson testified that:

1. Two pale violet acetate fibers removed from the head hair of Cater had the same characteristics as the violet acetate fibers present in Williams's bedspread, except that they were lighter in color.
2. A green nylon fiber removed from Cater's head hair had similar characteristics and properties as the fibers that composed the carpet in appellant's bedroom, except that it was lighter in color.
3. A green polypropylene fiber taken from Cater's pubic hair had the same microscopic and optical characteristics as the fibers that composed the carpet in the workroom in the Williams home.
4. A melted nylon fiber removed from Cater's head hair was consistent with nylon fibers found in the fibrous debris vacuumed from appellant's 1970 station wagon.
5. A yellow rayon fiber removed from Cater's hair was consistent with the properties of the fibers present in the yellow blanket found in appellant's bedroom, except that it was lighter in color.
6. Four animal hairs recovered from Cater were consistent with the characteristics of the hair of Williams's dog.

There was evidence that the fibers found on Cater that were lighter in color than their supposed counterparts in the Williams environment were lighter because of their exposure to river water.[17]

The court next set out the evidence pertaining to connections between Williams and the other 10 murder victims. The circumstantial evidence linking the defendant and each of these 10 other victims was a combination of the range of similarity in the victims lack of a strong family base, some sightings of the victim with Wayne Williams, and most importantly, evidence of fiber found on each that experts testified was linked to his home or automobiles. The fiber testimony was presented for each victim by Agent Harold Deadman of the FBI. The actual comparisons were conducted by 3 state's experts: FBI microanalyst Harold Deadman, Georgia Bureau of Investigation employee Larry Peterson, and Royal Canadian Mounted Police employee Barry Gaudette.[18]

The types of fibers and hairs that Agent Deadman testified were taken from appellant and his environment, along with the items from which they were taken, are as follows:

1. Violet acetate and green cotton fibers representing the composition of a bedspread, found in Williams's bedroom.
2. Green and yellow nylon fibers used to fabricate the carpet, found in Williams's bedroom.

3. Dog hairs removed from Williams's German Shepherd.
4. Yellow rayon and acrylic fibers used to fabricate a yellow blanket, found in Williams's bedroom.
5. Rayon and nylon fibers used to fabricate the carpet of a white 1970 Chevrolet station wagon, to which Williams had access during part of the period over which the crimes occurred.
6. Blue acrylic fibers used to fabricate a blue throw rug, found in the porch or garage area of Williams's home.
7. Polypropylene fibers used to fabricate a carpet, located in a workroom in the back of Williams's home that was adjacent to his bedroom.
8. Yellow nylon, blue rayon, white polyester, and pigmented polypropylene fibers, for which no source from Williams's environment was identified, but which were recovered from vacuum sweepings made by the state of defendant's 1970 station wagon.
9. Fibrous debris removed from a vacuum cleaner, found in Williams's home.
10. White polypropylene fibers used to fabricate the trunk liner of a 1978 Plymouth Fury, to which Williams had access during part of the period over which the crimes in question occurred.
11. White acrylic and secondary acetate fibers used to fabricate the trunk liner, and red trilobal nylon fibers used to fabricate the interior carpet of a burgundy-colored 1979 Ford LTD, to which Williams had access during part of the period over which the crimes in question occurred.
12. Blue secondary acetate fibers representing the composition of a bedspread, taken from the porch or garage area of Williams's home.
13. Brown woolen and rayon fibers which composed the lining of a leather jacket, owned by Williams.
14. Gray acrylic fibers used to fabricate a gray glove, which was found in the glove compartment of Williams's 1970 station wagon.
15. Yellow nylon fibers which were used to fabricate a toilet seat cover, taken from the Williams home and which were found in the fibrous debris vacuumed from the 1970 station wagon.
16. Yellow acrylic fibers used to fabricate a carpet, which was found in the kitchen of Williams home.[19]

Significant amounts of fiber evidence were presented by Agent Deadman and supported by expert Larry Peterson, allegedly linking Wayne Williams to 10 other young victims in addition to the 2 for whose murder he was on trial.

The state offered expert testimony of 4 fiber and hair associations between Williams and victim Alfred Evans, aged 15. FBI Agent Harold Deadman testified that 2 violet acetate fibers removed from Evans exhibited the same microscopic and optical properties as the violet acetate fibers removed from the bedspread of appellant; that a fiber removed from Evans exhibited the same microscopic and optical properties as the Wellman fibers present in the carpet in Williams's bedroom and could have originated from that carpet; that 6 polypropylene fibers found on Evans could have originated from the trunk liner of the Williams's 1978 Plymouth Fury; and that animal hairs removed from Evans could have originated from defendant's dog.[20]

The fiber evidence linking to Eric Middlebrook, aged 14, consisted of testimony by Agent Deadman that 4 violet acetate fibers removed from Middlebrook were consistent with having originated from Williams's bedspread; that 32 red nylon fibers that were found in a clump on one of his shoes could have originated from the interior carpet of the 1979 Ford LTD; that 2 white acrylic and 2 secondary acetate fibers found on Middlebrook could have originated from the trunk liner of the 1979 Ford; that 1 yellow nylon fiber found on Middlebrook could have originated from either the toilet cover in the Williams home or from the same source (unidentified) that produced the loose yellow nylon fibers that were found in the debris vacuumed from the 1970 Chevrolet station wagon; and, finally, that 1 animal hair removed from Middlebrook could have originated fromWilliams's dog.[21]

The body of Charles Stephens, aged 12, was also found to contain similar fiber samples. Agent Deadman testified that it contained 35 violet acetate and a number of green cotton fibers that could have originated from the bedspread found on Williams's bed; that 3 yellow nylon fibers removed from Stephens could have originated from the carpet found in Williams's bedroom; that 2 polypropylene fibers found on Stephens could have originated from the workroom in the back of the Williams home; that about 30 undyed synthetic and about 20 secondary acetate fibers recovered from Stephens were consistent with having originated from the trunk liner of the 1979 Ford LTD; that 9 blue rayon fibers found on Stephens were similar to blue rayon fibers, the source of which was unknown, found in debris vacuumed from the 1970 station wagon, debris removed from the sweeper found in the Williams home, and debris removed from the bedspread found in Williams's bedroom; that 1 yellow nylon fiber taken from Stephens could have originated from the toilet cover found in the Williams home, or from the same source, which was unknown, that produced the yellow nylon fibers found on some of Williams's clothing in the debris removed from the 1970 station wagon; that 5 coarse white polyester fibers removed from Stephens could have originated from the same source (unknown) that produced the white polyester fibers removed from a white rug found in Williams's 1970 station wagon; and, finally, that the approximately 17 animal hairs found on Stephens could have originated from Williams's dog.[22]

Regarding victim Terry Pue, aged 15, Deadman testified that over 100 violet acetate and a number of green cotton fibers found on Pue were all consistent with having originated from the bedspread found in Williams's bedroom; that 3 yellow nylon fibers found on Pue could have originated from the carpet located in Williams's bedroom; that 2 pale green polypropylene fibers removed from Pue could have originated from the carpet located in the workroom in the back of the Williams home; that 1 coarse white polyester fiber recovered from Pue had the same properties as white polyester fibers, the source of which was unknown, vacuumed from the rug and interior of Williams's 1970 station wagon; and that approximately 17 animal hairs found on Pue could have originated from Williams's dog.[23]

Agent Deadman testified regarding victim Lubie Geter, aged 14, that several violet acetate fibers found on Geter were consistent with having originated from the bedspread found in Williams's bedroom; that 5 yellow nylon carpet fibers removed from Geter had the same characteristics as the fibers present in the carpet located in Williams's bedroom; that 1 yellow acrylic fiber discovered on Geter could have originated from a carpet found in the kitchen of the Williams home; that a green rayon fiber found on Geter could have originated from the carpet of Williams's 1970 station wagon; and that 10 animal hairs removed from the body could have come from Williams's dog.[24]

The body of Patrick Baltazar, aged 11, was found by Deadmen to contain violet acetate and green cotton fibers consistent with having originated from Williams's bedspread; that 7 yellow nylon Wellman-type fibers removed from Baltazar exhibited the same characteristics and properties as fibers present in the carpet located in Williams's bedroom and could have originated from that carpet; that 4 yellow rayon fibers removed from Baltazar's jacket could have come from the yellow blanket found in Williams's bedroom; that 4 deteriorated rayon fibers, ranging in color from green to yellow, could have originated from the carpet of Williams's 1970 station wagon; that 2 woolen fibers and 1 rayon fiber found on Baltazar's remains exhibited the same characteristics as woolen and rayon fibers taken from the cloth waistband of Williams's leather jacket; that 13 gray acrylic fibers removed from the T-shirt, jacket, and shirt of Baltazar could have originated from the gray glove that was found in the glove compartment of Williams's 1970 station wagon; that a light yellow nylon fiber, a coarse white polyester fiber, and a pigmented polypropylene fiber had the same properties as fibers present in the debris vacuumed from the 1970 station wagon, and could have originated from the same sources (unknown) that produced the fibers discovered in the debris; that the approximately 20 animal hairs found on the clothing of Baltazar could have come from Williams's dog; and that 2 scalp hairs removed from Baltazar were inconsistent with Baltazar's own scalp hair, but were consistent with scalp hairs taken from Williams, and could have originated from the appellant.[25]

For the body of 18-year-old Larry Rogers, Deadman testified that it was found to contain 13 violet acetate fibers consistent with the violet acetate fibers taken from the Williams bedspread; that 3 yellow-green nylon fibers removed from Rogers were similar to the Wellman fibers found in Williams's bedroom carpet; that 8 yellow rayon fibers discovered on Rogers could have originated from the yellow blanket found in Williams's bedroom; that 1 yellow-brown to green fiber taken from Rogers could have come from the carpet of the 1970 station wagon; that 2 secondary acetate fibers removed from the deceased's shorts could have originated from the bedspread that was found in the Williams garage; and that a light yellow nylon fiber removed from the head hair of Rogers exhibited the same characteristics as yellow nylon fibers removed from the toilet cover found in the Williams home, from the sweepings made of the 1970 station wagon, and from several items of clothing of appellant.[26]

The fully clothed body of 28-year-old John Porter was found by Deadman and the other experts to contain violet acetate and green cotton fibers that could have originated from Williams's bedspread; they found that 1 yellow-green nylon fiber removed from the sheet used to carry Porter exhibited the same characteristics as the Wellman fibers making up Williams's bedroom carpet and could have originated from that carpet; that 3 yellow rayon fibers removed from Porter matched the yellow rayon fibers removed from the blanket found in Williams's bedroom; that several green rayon fibers removed from Porter could have originated from the carpet of the 1970 station wagon; that 2 secondary acetate fibers removed from Porter could have originated from the bedspread found in the carport of the Williams home; that a blue rayon fiber found on Porter could have come from the same source (unknown) that produced the blue rayon fibers found in the debris removed from the 1970 station wagon and in the debris removed from the vacuum cleaner found in the Williams home; and that the approximately 7 animal hairs removed from Porter were consistent with having originated from the Williams's dog.[27]

The remains of Joseph Bell, aged 15, contained 5 blue rayon fibers that were similar to rayon fibers recovered from debris collected from the 1970 station wagon and from debris collected from Williams's bedspread, and 2 pale violet acetate fibers which were consistent with the fibers present in the bedspread of Williams, with the exception that they were considerably lighter in color.[28]

Agent Deadman testified with respect to the body of William Barrett, aged 16, that it contained many violet acetate and green cotton fibers that could have originated from Williams's bedspread; that 5 yellow-green nylon fibers recovered from Barrett could have originated from the Williams' bedroom carpet; that 7 yellow rayon fibers removed from Barrett could have originated from the blanket found under Williams's bed; that a blue rayon fiber recovered from Barrett had the same characteristics as blue rayon fibers recovered from the debris removed from the station wagon, from the vacuum cleaner found in Williams's home, and from his bedspread; that approximately 30 gray acrylic fibers recovered from Barrett could have originated from the glove found in the glove compartment of the defendant's 1970 station wagon; that 3 fibers removed from Barrett could have originated from the carpet of the 1970 station wagon; and that the approximately 13 animal hairs recovered from Barrett could have come from the Williams dog.[29]

Although there was significant fiber evidence, as set forth above, the court recognized that the principal support for the state's fiber evidence case was expert testimony concerning the alleged uniqueness of 2 types of carpet fibers recovered and analyzed by the state's experts: the green nylon carpet in Williams's bedroom and the green-black rayon floorboard carpet of the 1970 Chevrolet station wagon Williams was driving the night he was discovered near the Jackson Parkway Bridge.[30]

The carpet found in Williams's bedroom was central to the forensic fiber testimony in the case, being referenced as "unique" in its textile makeup and in its pattern of commercial manufacture, sale, and subsequent distribution. The director of technical services for Wellman, Inc., a Boston, Massachusetts manufacturer of synthetic textile fibers, testified that he had begun working for Wellman in 1967, and that one of the first things he was asked to do was to assist in the development of a synthetic fiber known as the 181-b. According to him, this fiber had an unusual shape, trilobal with two long lobes and one short lobe, which was designed to avoid infringing upon a patented DuPont equilateral trilobal shape. The witness was shown state's exhibit 616, which was identified as a scanning electron microscope photograph of a fiber from the green carpet in Williams's bedroom, and he said it appeared to be a Wellman 181-b fiber. Gene Baggett, an employee of West Point Pepperell, a Dalton, Georgia carpet manufacturing company, testified that his company had purchased the Wellman fibers in 1970 and 1971 and used the Wellman 181-b fiber to manufacture several lines of carpet, including lines known as Luxaire and Dreamer, both of which, he testified, had been colored with a dye formulation called English Olive. He testified that while he was not a chemist and was not qualified to perform microscopic analysis and identification of single fibers, based upon his visual inspection of such aggregate physical characteristics as height of pile, weight of carpet, and type of backing, the company sample appeared to be similar to a similar fiber taken from defendant's home.[31]

Agent Harold Deadman testified that the FBI had obtained the latter exhibit from West Point Pepperell, which had identified it as a piece of Luxaire, and that, based on his examination of the gross physical characteristics of the two exhibits, he could find no significant differences in their construction, and concluded that "in all probability they were manufactured by the same company. They certainly could have come from the same source."[32]

Deadman relied on Luxaire and Dreamer sales records of West Point Pepperell, information orally supplied him by Baggett, housing statistics provided by the Atlanta Regional Commission, and, according to the dissent, "a number of wholly speculative assumptions (chief of which was that the Williams carpet was in fact a West Point Luxaire or Dreamer English Olive carpet)." Deadman attempted to use the calculus of compound probabilities to perform a series of calculations to establish the rarity of that type of carpet in the Atlanta metropolitan area.[33] He concluded that there was a 1 in 7792 chance of randomly selecting a home in the Atlanta area and finding a room containing carpet similar to the Williams bedroom carpet. Regarding the green-black 1970 Chevrolet carpet, both Deadman and his fellow expert Peterson testified that they had information indicating that in the Atlanta area only 620 out of over 2 million cars had that type of carpet. Deadman explained that this data had been supplied by the General Motors Corporation.[34]

Williams argued that in addition to the substantial error in allowing evidence to 10 murders for which he was never charged, the court erred in permitting Deadman to discuss mathematical probabilities concerning the fiber evidence and in permitting the prosecutor to argue mathematical probabilities to the jury. The majority, in a surprisingly terse ruling, held that neither of those contentions had merit, as experts were permitted to give their opinions based upon their knowledge, including mathematical computations. Counsel are given wide latitude in closing argument, the court opined, and are not prohibited from suggesting to the jury inferences that might be drawn from the evidence. "Such suggestions may include those based upon mathematical probabilities."[35]

The sole dissent, Justice Smith, noted that during closing arguments the district attorney summarized this testimony and then proceeded to "embellish" his summary with his personal attempt to quantify the probative force of the fiber evidence:

> Accordingly, he rounded off the figures for the 181-b bedroom carpet and the green-black floorboard carpet and multiplied them together in order to calculate the chances "that there is another house in Atlanta that has the same kind of carpet as the Williams house and that the people who live in that house have the same type station wagon as the Williamses do, . . . " arriving at a probability of one in forty million. Adjusting this figure to account for an additional assumption of his own, the prosecutor argued that the appropriate figure was actually one in an astounding one hundred fifty million.[36]

Taken at face value, Justice Smith continued, the testimony establishing the rarity of the two fiber types would appear to provide substantial support for the critical opinions of the experts that the fibers of those types found on the bodies were probably transferred from the Williams home or car. Examining the majority opinion's factual review of the Payne and Cater murders, Justice Smith continued, and the 10 uncharged offenses, one was indeed struck by a number of similarities among the 12 crimes. Each of the victims was a low-income black male, slightly built, who was often seen alone in the streets of Atlanta. Payne, Cater, and 5 of the 10 other crimes victims were seen with Williams sometime prior to their deaths. All but 2 of the victims, Porter and Middlebrook, were killed by some form of asphyxiation.[37]

However, those similarities were outweighed by the significant dissimilarities between the 2 charged offenses and the 10 extrinsic crimes:

> Payne and Cater, age 21 and 28, respectively, were adults; the ages of the victims of the uncharged crimes ranged from 11 years to 28 years and averaged only 15.7 years. With the exception of 28-year-old John Porter, the extrinsic offense victims were essentially children. Another striking dissimilarity between the Payne and Cater killings, on the one hand, and the ten extrinsic offenses, on the other, is that while the bodies of Payne and Cater were both apparently thrown into the Chattahoochee River near the I-285 overpass, only one of the ten extrinsic offense victims' bodies, that of Joseph Bell, was found in a river.[38]

Justice Smith observed that victim Bell's body was discovered in the South River near Rockdale County, miles from where Payne and Cater were found and that the remaining 9 were deposited on land. Although there was evidence tending to show that the Cater killing was sexually motivated, there was a total absence of medical evidence showing sexual abuse of any of the other victims:

In addition, it is critical to note that the state's fiber evidence allegedly linking Williams to all twelve victims, while slightly probative on the issue of whether Williams actually perpetrated the ten other crimes, . . . has no relevance to the modus operandi issue, for the simple reason that the fiber evidence in this case provides no information as to the murderer's technique in killing or disposing of his victims. The state's own experts testified that they could not determine the exact mechanism of the alleged transfer of fibers from Williams to the victims. Thus, the sole implication of this type of trace evidence is that each of the victims possibly was in contact with Williams, his house, or his car sometime before his death. Although this inference may be probative of the identity of the killer of the ten extrinsic victims, it does not establish a unique modus operandi, since it would be possible for the murderer to apprehend, kill, and dispose of his twelve victims in dissimilar ways, yet transfer fibers to them in each case . . . . Thus the presence or absence of fiber evidence has no relevance in the case before us to the narrow issue of modus operandi.[39]

The dissent by Justice Smith is well worth reading for its trenchant criticism of the majority's legitimization of microscopic hair analysis, and especially the probabilistic extensions made from such comparisons in this case. Nonetheless, the conviction was affirmed. The *Wayne Williams* case still fascinates the American media and public and efforts to get Williams a new trial continue.[40]

III. OTHER FIBER ANALYSIS CASES

Microscopic fiber evidence is used routinely in police work across the world and continues to be discussed in appellate decisions.[41] The discussion to follow will focus on the utilization of fiber evidence in several of the more important of those cases.

In *People v. Miller*,[42] the defendant was convicted of first-degree murder. In September, 1993, the nude bodies of 3 women were found in rural Peoria County, Illinois. The body of Marcia Logue was found in a drainage ditch in the 500-block of South Cameron Lane on September 18, with a pillowcase stuck in her mouth. The body of Helen Dorrance was found 50 feet from Logue's body on the same date. The body of Sandra Csesznegi was found in a drainage ditch near Christ Church Road on September 26. Csesznegi's body was in a state of advanced decomposition. All three women were known prostitutes in the Peoria area.

On September 29, 1993, the authorities went to the defendant's Peoria apartment to question him about crimes in the Peoria area. A search of the defendant's apartment uncovered two robes, female underwear, a broken miniblind rod, and a brown and white cloth covered with what appeared to be dried blood. The police also recovered pillows and a mattress, which contained reddish-brown stains. Blood spatters were found on a wall of the bedroom and the bed's headboard, as well. A subsequent search uncovered a glove, a throw rug, and more women's underwear. During the second search, the police collected hair and fibers.[43]

Glenn Schubert, a forensic scientist, testified regarding the hair and fibers recovered from the defendant's apartment, Logue's body, and the maroon automobile. He reported that debris from the pillowcase found in Logue's mouth was consistent with the defendant's pubic hair, and that fibers on the pillowcase matched fibers taken from a throw rug located in the defendant's apartment and fibers collected from the defendant's living room floor. Several fibers taken from Logue's body also matched fibers taken from the living room floor of the defendant's apartment. Also, several acrylic-like fibers from the car were consistent with the fibers found on the defendant's floor.[44]

In *Trawick v. State*,[45] the defendant was convicted of murder and kidnaping. On October 10, 1992, the partially nude body of victim Stephanie Gash was found on the side of a road. Her mouth and nose were covered with duct tape and a medical examiner testified that she died as a result of both a 3-inch knife wound that entered her heart and asphyxiation caused by strangulation.

Steven Drexler, of the Alabama Department of Forensic Sciences, testified that two fibers found on the victim's sweater, recovered from the crime scene, were consistent with fibers from the carpet of the defendant's Toyota van. Also, fibers found on the duct tape that covered the victim's mouth were the same as the fibers from the carpet of the Toyota van.

The appellant gave a detailed statement to the police in which he confessed to having murdered Stephanie Gash. The appellant's confession was corroborated by the following facts. The Toyota van was towed to the police station where they discovered a piece of carpet, a tarpaulin, a ball-peen hammer, and a plastic bucket that contained an 11-inch knife. Using Luminol spray, police discovered blood traces on the tarpaulin, the piece of carpet, the ball-peen hammer, the tailgate of the van, and on the knife. A Ford station wagon which the appellant was known to drive was also impounded. A toy gun was found in the passenger's floorboard of that vehicle.

In *State v. Smith*,[46] the defendant was convicted of aggravated kidnaping, rape of a child, and sodomy on a child. Information given by the victim led the authorities to the defendant. Physical evidence consisting of, among others, microscopic fiber analyses findings, confirmed the victim's rendition of her attack.

Fibers on the victim's clothing matched fibers from Smith's shirt and fibers in the carpet of his car.[47] Pubic hair matching the defendant's was found on the victim, and head hairs consistent with the victim's were found in defendant's back seat. Fibers "matching" the fibers in Smith's shirt and in the carpet of his car were found on the victim's clothing.[48]

Broeckel v. State[49] was a case addressing discovery issues in a routine microscopic fiber analysis setting. Here, the defendant was convicted of first-degree sexual assault. The defendant assaulted the adult victim at his home during the course of a social visit. The state submitted a number of items to the state crime laboratory for testing, including the defendant's bathrobe and items of the victim's clothing that had been collected in the investigation. The victim's clothing was examined to see if there were fibers that matched those from Broeckel's robe. The court set out its basic understanding of the fiber examination process:

> Fibers that compose a garment have identifying characteristics such as the color, shape, and origin of the material from which they are made. When one garment comes in contact with another, small fibers can transfer. Fibers can be collected from a garment, as by the lab here, with a tapelift, which is essentially similar to a sizeable piece of adhesive tape that can be applied to successive areas of the garment causing loose fibers to stick to it. The tape is then examined under magnification in an attempt to locate fibers that could have originated from another garment.[50]

In the laboratory's original examination, fibers with the same color, composition, and shape as those from Broeckel's robe were found on the victim's pants, pantyhose, bra, and blouse.

A discovery violation was alleged by the defendant based upon his investigator's subsequent interview with laboratory personnel. Broeckel's investigator spoke to state criminalist Janeice Fair about her report, where she allegedly stated that she had found fibers that matched fibers from Broeckel's bathrobe on every item of A.D.'s clothing, but she did not find any on the inside of A.D.'s pants. Soon after, Fair reexamined the tapelifts originally taken from the victim's clothing and, upon such reexamination, she concluded that some of the fibers that matched fibers from Broeckel's robe on the tapelift originally were taken from inside the victim's pants, having apparently having been overlooked during her original examination. The first the defense knew about this was when Fair testified at trial that she had found fibers that matched fibers from Broeckel's robe inside the pants.

Broeckel argued that his case had been irretrievably prejudiced because his opening statement and his cross-examination of prosecution witnesses had been carried out in the expectation that Fair would testify that no fibers were found inside A.D.'s pants.[51]

In affirming the defendant's conviction, the court ruled the impact of discovery violations based on a mistake in the criminalist's reports as to the absence of fibers on certain clothing of the victim and the expert's subsequent change in testimony did not warrant a reversal; the court concluded that the absence of matching fibers inside the victim's pants would not have ruled out the assault:

> Although Broeckel and his counsel were surprised by the discovery violation, they had not promised the jury that they would present any evidence regarding the presence or absence of fibers. Whether or not Fair originally found fibers on the tapelift taken from the inside of A.D.'s pants that matched fibers from Broeckel's robe, Broeckel knew before trial that Fair had found matching fibers on tapelifts taken from all of the other items of A.D.'s clothing and on the tapelift from the outside of A.D.'s pants. Also, the prosecutor did not argue that the fibers inside the pants had any greater significance than the presence of fibers on A.D.'s other articles of clothing. The absence of matching fibers inside A.D.'s pants would not have ruled out the assault. The matching fiber evidence only supports the conclusion that Broeckel's robe was likely to have come in contact with A.D.'s clothing. Even if there had been no matching fibers on the inside of A.D.'s pants, the absence of those fibers would not have undermined the state's case in the manner argued by Broeckel, because the testing found fibers on every item of A.D.'s clothing including A.D.'s pantyhose.

The matching fiber evidence only supported the conclusion that the defendant's robe was likely to have come in contact with the victim's clothing.[52]

In *Ross v. State*,[53] the defendant was convicted of two counts of rape, two counts of kidnaping, two counts of aggravated sodomy, two counts of armed robbery, violation of the Georgia Controlled Substances Act, and possession of a firearm by a convicted felon. The defendant and a friend stopped two women in a car, entered, demanded their jewelry and money, and then forced the women to disrobe and repeatedly raped them. The women were also threatened throughout the night-long ordeal with guns and were tortured by being burned with cigarette lighters and candle wax.[54]

The defendant alleged ineffective counsel requiring a new trial. While some DNA evidence was used at the trial, fingerprint, fiber, and hair analyses were not because they failed to connect the defendant to the crime. The defendant argued that his counsel was ineffective because of his failure to secure the testimony of an expert in the field of microscopic fiber analysis to testify that none of the fibers taken from the apartment where the victims were held was found on defendant's clothing and that none of the fibers from the defendant's clothing was found at the crime scene. The court noted that the record clearly indicated that the jury was aware that fiber samples were taken and that the tests of the samples did not indicate the defendant as a match, through the testimony of state experts.

The jury was free to make its own decision based upon the information, and the failure of the defendant's counsel to present an expert to speak about the lack of match regarding fiber samples did not likely have an influence on the outcome of the case. Absent a proffer as to what the testimony of this microscopic fiber expert would have been at trial, Ross could not show there was a reasonable probability that, but for trial counsel's failure to call this expert as a witness, the result of the trail would have been different. [55]

In *State v. Blanton*,[56] the defendant, James Blanton, was convicted by a jury of two counts of first-degree premeditated murder, four counts of grand larceny, and three counts of first-degree burglary.

Eight escaped convicts, including the defendant, committed a series of robberies, burglaries, and the murder and home invasion involved in this case. The victims' residence had one entryway which was through a screen door located at the side of the house opposite to the victims' bedrooms. A cloth glove was on the ground by the concrete block. Following the discovery of the victims' bodies at the Vester residence, the sheriff's deputies began checking cabins in the surrounding area, and learned that the Crawford residence, less than a quarter of a mile from the murder victim's home, had been burglarized. One of the gloves found at the Crawfords' trailer matched a glove found outside the Vesters' front bedroom window. A fiber analysis of the two gloves indicated that it was likely that they were originally sold together as a pair.

State v. Higgenbotham,[57] a murder and kidnaping case, established that the defendant sought out a prostitute, "hog-tied," gagged, and killed her, and then dumped the body in a ditch. In affirming the kidnaping conviction, the Kansas

Supreme Court accepted fiber evidence to establish that the defendant had satisfied the elements of the crime of kidnaping. The victim's body was facedown in the dirt. A white sweater and bra were on one side, a pair of panties on the other. Her shirt was pulled down to her waist. Her hands and feet were bound together (hog-tied) behind her back with black plastic pull ties. A yellow rope secured the pull ties. A separate piece of yellow rope was around one of her wrists. Green duct tape was wrapped around her nose and mouth. A bandanna that had been used as a gag was found under the duct tape over her mouth.[58]

The defendant's wife led police to storage rented by her husband's friend, Chuck Peters, who allowed the defendant to use the locker to work on cars. The wife had previously spoken to the deceased who had been sitting in the car. The police began an investigation of the defendant and were led to the storage unit, wherein a search turned up black nylon wire ties, rolls of duct tape, and yellow rope. Wadded-up duct tape was found in the back of a Chevette that was inside the unit and a button was located on the floor as well as a used condom found in a cardboard box. A crime scene investigator collected hairs and fibers from the Chrysler vehicle parked in the locker area. The defendant's friend testified that the black plastic ties that were found in his storage shed did not belong to him.[59]

The FBI Laboratory hair and fiber analysis found evidence of hair transfer between Higgenbotham's items and the deceased's and also reported that red fibers found on Jodi's socks were consistent with a carpet sample from the defendant's Chrysler. Also, blue olefin fibers that were found on all of the items of Jodi's clothing, and on the rope on her body, were consistent with fibers from the deck area of the Chevette, causing the examiner to believe Jodi had been in both of those vehicles. A similar blue fiber was also found in Higgenbotham's Plymouth. The examiner also compared the thread from the button in the shed with the thread in a button from Jodi's shirt and found they were consistent. However, the rope on the body was not the same as the rope from the storage shed. Finally, head hairs on the duct tape in the Chevette, while not consistent with Jodi's, were consistent with Higgenbotham's.[60]

Tests performed by a microanalyst from the Bureau of Criminal Apprehension and a private analytic forensic microscopist were discussed in *State v. Profit*,[61] a 1999 Minnesota homicide case. The defendant was convicted of two counts of first-degree murder and one count of intentional second-degree murder for the May 1996 killing of one Renee Bell, whose nude body was found floating in Basset Creek in Theodore Wirth Park in Golden Valley, Minnesota. An elastic waistband from an article of clothing had been wrapped around Bell's neck and was secured in a knot, and one end looped through Bell's mouth and under her tongue in a gaglike manner. An autopsy report concluded that the victim had been strangled with the ligature and that Bell had been dead from 1 day to 1 week. Police discovered the defendant's wallet a few feet from where Bell's body had been discovered.[62]

Bell's body was just the first of several bodies to be found in or near Theodore Wirth Park during the summer of 1996.[63]

After the defendant's brother-in-law, who had lent a vehicle and clothing to him, stated that the defendant had implicated himself in the murder and burning of Keooudorn Phothisane, a male transvestite, the police executed search warrants for Profit's home and the various vehicles driven by him or his family. While searching a 1990 Pontiac Grand Am known to have been driven by Profit, investigators found threads and fibers "similar to" threads and fibers found on the ligature used to strangle Bell. Tests performed by a microanalyst from the Bureau of Criminal Apprehension and a private analytic forensic microscopist revealed that the threads and fibers from the trunk were "chemically and physically indistinguishable" from the threads and fibers from the ligature.[64]

In *Floudiotis v. State*,[65] a 1999 Delaware case, defendants were convicted in the Superior Court, New Castle County, of second- and third-degree assault and second-degree conspiracy arising from the beating of a couple in the parking lot of a tavern. Both sustained broken jaws, cuts, and bruises, and one victim also sustained a broken collarbone.[66] Police observed the same pickup truck described by witnesses to the assault and followed it on suspicion of drunken driving. Police pulled the pickup truck over and arrested the 4 occupants, one of whom was the defendant Eaton. Subsequent to an interview and photograph session, Detective Johnson seized the footwear of all 4 suspects because he had reason to believe that all 4 were involved in the assault at Deer Park and that the footwear might contain hairs or fibers that would implicate them. Through subsequent forensic tests, the state discovered fibers on defendant Eaton's shoes that were consistent with the same source of the fibers taken from the tank top victim Kimberly Butler wore the night of the incident.[67]

Eaton contends that the trial court erred in admitting evidence recovered from his combat boots. He argues that, because Detective Johnson illegally seized his boots at the police station, they are the fruit of this unlawful warrantless search, and the fibers consistent with Kimberly Butler's tank top that the police found on his boots should not have been admitted by the trial court.[68] The fiber evidence went unchallenged here as is so often the case in recent decisions.

In *State v. Young*,[69] the defendant was convicted of aggravated murder due to the killing of 14-year-old Heidi Bazar, who he had been dating until a breakup occurred. At the conclusion of a dance, a friend accompanied Heidi to the store and overheard her telephoning the defendant to come and pick her up there. The friend heard the deceased arguing with the defendant on the phone. Heidi disappeared and her body was found at the bottom of a remote "lover's lane" location. The police arrested the defendant. The defendant stated that after exiting his truck they began to fight and he pushed Heidi after she slapped him a second time, that she was apparently too close to the cliff's edge, and that she fell backward down the side of the cliff. He claimed that Heidi fell off the cliff after he instinctively pushed her when she slapped him.

The autopsy, however, indicated that the victim suffered over 30 wounds, including a fractured jaw, a broken nose, a liver severed almost in half, a tooth knocked out of her braces, and strangulation, which were clearly indicative of an intentional, not accidental, killing:

> The coroner and pathologist testified that the wounds which caused the death could not have resulted from a thirteen foot fall off of a cliff or from an accident and most likely were caused by multiple blunt force to her face and neck. From the number and severity of the wounds suffered by Heidi, any reasonable trier of fact could find that there existed an intent to kill by Appellant.[70]

Although the appellant testified that he never struck or beat Heidi in any manner or with any object, including his hands, except for pushing at her, the court noted that a large brick, an 18-pound chunk of concrete, and a board were found near the location of Heidi's body and contained Heidi's blood:

> The board contained fibers from Heidi's blue jeans and the chunk of concrete had been thrown away from Heidi's body. Appellant's testimony that he only pushed Heidi and she fell over the cliff to her death is inconsistent with the testimony of the coroner, the pathologist conducting the autopsy and the forensic pathologist. These experts testified that Heidi's fatal injuries resulted from a deliberate and intentional infliction of blunt force impacts to her head and trunk and did not result from a thirteen foot fall or an accident.[71]

From this scientific testimony, the court concluded, the jury could have reasonably inferred that Heidi was beaten to an extent that caused her to bleed and then beaten again on already exposed blood sources. Additionally, the testimony of the coroner and pathologist established that Heidi sustained approximately 35 wounds, many that were inconsistent with a fall, including a severed liver, a fractured jaw, a tooth missing from her braces, a fractured eye socket, and manual strangulation.

In *Woodward v. United States*,[72] the defendant was convicted of second-degree murder. James Butler went out the back door of his house and saw what he believed to be a body lying on top of some brush. After his neighbor and a nearby woman confirmed that it was a body, the police were called. The body was that of a woman wearing dark-colored sweatpants and a blue and gray sweatshirt with no shoes. On November 24, 1992, police officers entered a building at 924 Ingraham Street, the body having been found at the rear of that building. The defendant had recently vacated an apartment in the structure. They discovered blood on the side of a dresser inside the room and found a large light-blue plastic trash can in the basement that had dried blood on it and contained a blanket with a very large bloodstain on one end. The door to the basement opened out of the rear of the house into the Ingraham alley where the victim's body was found.[73]

An FBI special agent assigned to the Hairs and Fibers Unit testified that the carpet fibers found on the deceased's sweatshirt matched those in Woodward's second-floor bedroom. He also testified that the dog hairs found on the victim's sweat pants and transport sheet matched the dog hairs in Woodward's home.

In *State v. Timmendequas*,[74] the defendant was convicted of capital murder. The victim, Megan Kanka, aged 7, lived diagonally across the street from the defendant, who, upon questioning, stated that he had killed the young victim and put her body in a nearby park. In his statement, the defendant said that victim came to his house while his roommates were out, wanting to see the defendant's puppy. He then forced her into his bedroom and attacked and killed her. Testimony by a forensic chemist and a criminalist indicated that the fragments of the victim's shorts found in the garbage of the defendant's home contained fibers chemically and physically consistent with fibers found on the defendant's bedroom rug, his sleeping bag, and in the lint trap of defendant's dryer. Fibers were also found on the defendant's sweatpants that matched those taken from Megan's blouse.[75]

Finally, the famous Locard principle,[76] whereby all close physical contacts are bound to result in hair or fiber transfers, was discussed in the 1999 case of *State v. Goney*,[77] where the defendant was convicted of rape and raised incompetency of counsel in his postconviction filing.[78] A forensic examination of hair and fibers from the couch where the rape was alleged to have occurred was negative when compared with defendant Goney. The defendant argued that Detective Menke, the trace evidence examiner, should have been called to testify. The crime laboratory report indicated that a small envelope labeled "Hair and Fibers from Love Seat" had been tested, showing Caucasian head hairs similar to that of the victim, Caucasian body hair not suitable for comparison, and fibers of various colors. The defendant argued that based on this report, that his lawyer should have called the examiner to proffer an "expert" opinion that a rape could not have taken place on the couch in the absence of such physical evidence.

The court soundly rejected this Locard-type argument, both from an analysis of the relative positions of the defendant and victim on the couch and the simple lack of relevance of the basic argument based on the supposed inevitability of trace material transfers in sexual assault settings:

> [W]e fail to see the relevance of this point. Clearly, sexual intercourse and ejaculation did take place without the Defendant leaving apparent fiber or hair evidence. In fact, the lab technician who testified at trial said she did not perform any hair analysis based on Goney's hair samples because no foreign hairs were obtained from a nightgown Canton was wearing or from the sexual assault kit (which included pubic hair combing). Given the absence of hair in these areas where it could be expected, the lack of hair or fibers on the couch where the rape allegedly occurred is not surprising. Furthermore, we have serious doubt (and Goney has not convinced us otherwise) that a police deputy—or indeed, any "expert"—could competently conclude from the absence of fiber or hair that a rape did not occur.[79]

Specifically, the court ruled, the lack of forensic hair or fiber evidence from the couch did not make the defense version either more or less probable. Since this evidence could have been present under either the defense or the prosecution version of the case, the fact that it was absent was deemed no more helpful to one side than it was to the other.[80]

RESEARCH NOTE

The Journal of Forensic Sciences is the official publication of the American Academy of Forensic Sciences. By visiting the Academy's web site at *http://www.aafs.org* and clicking on the "Journal of Forensic Sciences" link, one can get to a searchable index of the journal from 1981 to the present that uses common search terms. The site also provides tables of contents for more recent issues of the journal, and, for a modest fee, one can download individual articles from issues published after January 1, 1999. The index, content, and article availability site is maintained by the publisher of the journal, The American Society for Testing and Materials (ASTM). There are current plans to move toward the Web-based publication of the journal, though the paper copy will still be available for some time. Individual subscriptions to this essential journal are also available from ASTM for those interested.

Visiting this important Web site on a regular basis and viewing the available abstracts are essential to the early stages of forensic science/forensic evidence research. Also see the recent bibliography prepared by Dr. Walter Bruscweiler and Michael C. Grieve, "State of the Art in the Field of Hair and Textile Examinations," in *Proceedings of the 12th INTERPOL Forensic Science Symposium* (1998), at 187–197.

ENDNOTES

1. See, e.g., Richard Spencer: "Significant Fiber Evidence Recovered from the Clothing of a Homicide Victim after Exposure to the Elements for Twenty-Nine Days," *J. of the Forensic Sci. Soc.*, Vol. 39, No. 3, pp. 854–859.
2. An initial determination has to be made that the crime scene datum is indeed fiber as opposed to a human or nonhuman hair. See Chapter 2, Science and the Criminal Law, for an examination of People v. Sutherland, 155 Ill.2d 1, 610 N.E.2d 1 (1993), an important example of the uses of microscopic fiber, hair, and tire impression analysis, set out as a case study.
3. See *http://www.fbi.gov/programs/lab/fsc/backissu/april1999/houcktoc/htm.*
4. Also see the new extensively revised "FBI Handbook of Forensic Services" available on the FBI Web site. See *http:/www.fbi.gov/programs/lab/handbook/intro.htm.*
5. See, generally, Saferstein: Criminalistics: An Introduction to Forensic Science (6th ed. Prentice–Hall, Upper Saddle River, NJ, 1998), 221239, 81–96; Giannelli and Imwinkelried: *Scientific Evidence* (2d ed. The Michie Company, Charlottesville, VA, 1993), 365–380 and 1998 Cumulative Supplement, 93–95; Fisher: *Techniques of Crime Scene Investigation* (5th ed. CRC Press, Boca Raton, FL, 1993), 178–187; Geberth: *Practical Homicide Investigation* (3rd ed. CRC Press, Boca Raton, FL, 1996), 517–519. There is growing international interest and work in the area of standardizing fiber investigation analysis. In addition to the FBI materials noted above, the European Fibres Group (EFG) maintains a Web site located at *http://www.sol.co.uk/p/pfsld.efg.htm.*
6. As will be seen in the extensive discussion of the Wayne Williams case, while not generally available to police authorities or the public at large, these database collections are typically available to forensic experts on a cooperative, case-by-case basis

by the international fiber industry. There is also a very significant amount of information about the fiber and textile industries available through searches on the Dialog Information service.

7. See "Forensic Fiber Examination Guidelines," *supra,* note 4, at 3.

8. See the categorized listing of fiber types and trade names produced by the American Fiber Manufacturers Association, set forth in Saferstein, *supra,* note 5, at 224–225. Also see, *"Forensic Fiber Examination Guidelines," supra,* note 4.

9. See, e.g., State v. Ritt, 599 N.W.2d 802 (Minn.Sp.Ct. 1999), where defendant was convicted of two counts of first-degree murder, two counts of second-degree murder, one count of third-degree murder, and one count of first-degree arson. The case contains an excellent discussion of acrylic fibers in relation to a faked accidental fire resulting in the death of a 23-month-old victim at the hands of her mother.

10. People v. Sutherland, 155 Ill.2d 1, 610 N.E.2d 1 (1993).

11. See Deadman: "Fiber Evidence and the Wayne Williams Trial," *FBI Law Enforcement Bulletin,* March and May, 1984, for an account by the agent involved. The dissenting judge in Williams strongly criticized Agent Deadman's testimony.

12. Williams v. State, 251 Ga. 749, 312 S.E. 2d 40 (1984). The state introduced evidence of 10 other alleged murders to aid in establishing appellant's identity as the perpetrator of the murders of victims Payne and Cater.

13. See *Id.,* at 759–771, for a detailed listing and description of the individual circumstances of each victim's discovery and attendant circumstances. Also see pages 773–783 for the court's profiles of each murder illustrating the similarities of the victims and their deaths, the logical connection of the homicides, and the evidence that Williams was the perpetrator of each. See text.

14. *Id.* at 759.

15. *Id.* at 772.

16. *Id.* at 760.

17. *Id.*

18. Deadman, a microanalyst, described the microscopes that can be used to compare fibers and were in the case at hand: a stereobinocular microscope, which can magnify a single fiber about 70 times, and which is used to compare fibers visually; a compound microscope, which can magnify a single fiber approximately 400 to 500 times and which, like the stereobinocular microscope, is used to compare fibers visually; a comparison microscope, which can magnify two fibers side by side, and which is used to compare the microscopic and optical properties of the two fibers; a microspectrophotometer; a polarizing light microscope, which is used to examine the optical properties of fibers in a more discriminating fashion than that provided by a comparison microscope; and a fluorescence microscope, which is used to determine the type of light a fiber emits after it has been illuminated with a certain type of light. A scanning electron microscope was also used to a more limited degree by these three experts. *Id.* at 756.

19. *Id.* at 53, 757.

20. *Id.* at 761.

21. *Id.* at 749, 762.

22. *Id.* at 55, 763.

23. *Id.* at 764.

24. *Id.* at 59, 766.

25. *Id.* at 60, 767.

26. *Id.* at 61, 769.

27. *Id.* at 770. The state also attempted to link Porter with Williams through a bloodstain found on the rear car seat of Williams's 1970 station wagon. Forensic serologists from the Georgia Crime Laboratory examined a blood sample from Porter, and determined that his blood type was International Blood Group B and that his blood enzyme type was PGM-1, a combination, a serologist testified, that exists in approximately 7% of the population. Another bloodstain found on the car seat was determined to be blood from International Blood Group B, with an enzyme type PGM-1, and a serologist testified that this bloodstain was not more than 8 weeks old. Moreover, a serologist testified that Williams could not have left this blood stain as his blood type was International Blood Group O. *Id.* at 312 S.E. 2d 40.

28. *Id.* at 40, 63. Deadman attributed this paleness of the two fibers to exposure to river water basing his opinion on an experiment wherein the state had taken fibers from Williams's bedspread and placed them in water from both the Chattahoochee and South Rivers; the water had bleached the fibers, causing their color to fade.

29. *Id.* at 772, 773.

30. In April 1981, the task force staked out bridges over rivers in the metropolitan Atlanta area in an attempt to apprehend whoever was responsible for throwing bodies into rivers in the Atlanta area. On the morning of May 22 a loud splash was heard, which, according to officers present, sounded like a human body hitting the water below the bridge. No lights had been observed up to that point, nor had the characteristic noise of the expansion joint been heard. There was testimony that the vehicular traffic was light at that hour of the day, and that a period of at least 10 minutes elapsed between the time the last car was seen to cross the bridge and the sound of the splash. Shortly after the splash, a car's lights appeared on the bridge directly above where the splash had occurred, and were seen to start moving slowly toward the Fulton end of the bridge. Officers followed the car, stopped it, and determined that was driven by defendant, Wayne Williams. *Id.* at 791.

31. *Id.* at 823.

32. *Id.* at 758.

33. This fact, critical to the state's "uniqueness" argument, stressed by Justice Smith in his dissenting opinion, was never conclusively established and was indeed questionable in light of testimony (based on Wellman sales records) that Wellman fiber was sold to a number of Georgia and southeastern manufacturers during the period in question. *Id.* at 98, 824.

34. *Id.* at 98.

35. *Id.* at 73. Also see Stewart v. State, 246 Ga. 70, 75, 268 S.E.2d 906 (1980); Wisdom v. State, 234 Ga. 650, 655, 217 S.E.2d 244 (1975).

36. Williams, *supra,* at 824. Historically, statistical evidence has not been a prerequisite to the admission of matching samples. Expert testimony about matching carpet fibers has been admitted in the absence of statistical evidence about the probability of the match. State v. Koedatich, 112 N.J. 225, 548 A.2d 939 (1988); State v. Hollander, 201 N.J.Super. 453, 467–68, 493 A.2d 563 (App.Div.1985). In Koedatich, a capital case, the state presented evidence of matching fibers from the defendant's automobile carpet and seat covers. In Koedatich the defense attacked the weight of the evidence by showing that manufacturers produced hundreds of thousands of yards of such fibers in a given year. State v. Koedatich at 939. The court upheld the admission of the evidence of the matching fibers, observing that the quantity of the fibers went to the weight, not the admissibility, of the evidence.

37. Williams, *supra*, at 92, 815.

38. *Id.* at 814.

39. *Id.* at 91, 814.

40. See, e.g., *Dateline, NBC*, Tuesday, June 2, 1998 segment "The Wrong Man?" discussing interesting facts about the deaths of several of the victims that allegedly distort the unity of the forensic evidence presented at the 1984 trial and the nagging doubts of some of the key detectives involved in the investigation. 1998 WL 6098121.

41. In fact, by the beginning of 1997, there had been over 250 cases that have discussed, or much more often, accepted without much or any discussions, evidence based on such forensic discipline. Westlaw search conducted by the author in November, 1999.

42. People v. Miller, 173 Ill.2d 167, 670 N.E.2d 721 (1996).

43. *Id.* at 176.

44. *Id.* at 178. Also see Commonwealth v. McEnany, 667 A.2d 1143 (Sup. Ct. Penn. 1995), a 1995 Pennsylvania case, where defendant was convicted of second-degree murder, burglary, robbery, and conspiracy. Kathryn Bishop, aged 82, was found dead on the floor of her residence, having been stomped to death sometime between 9:00 and 11:30 P.M. on March 3, 1993. Paint chips were found on Mrs. Bishop's hands, and black T-shirt fibers were on her face, neck, and clothing. The deceased's kitchen door window had been smashed, her basement window had been opened, and scuff marks were found on her clothes dryer located under the basement window. As the investigation continued, Trooper Stansfield obtained search warrants for McEnany's van and residence and took the clothes worn by appellant on the date of the murder. Chemist Lee Ann Grayson testified that fibers found on Mrs. Bishop's body "matched" those of the T-shirt appellant wore on the day of the murder.

45. Trawick v. State, 698 So.2d 151 (Ct.Crim.App.Ala. 1995). Also see Ex Parte Jack Harrison Trawick, 698 So.2d 162 (1997), addressing the death penalty aspects of this case.

46. State v. Smith, 909 P.2d 236 (Ut.Sp.Ct. 1995).

47. See J. Robertson and C.B.M Kidd: "The Transfer of Textile Fibres during Simulated Contact," *J. of the Forensic Sci. Soc.*, Vol. 22 (1982), at 301–308; J. Robertson, C.B.M. Kidd , and M.P. Parkinson: "The Persistence of Textile Transferred during Simulated Fibre Contact," *J. of the Forensic Sci. Soc.*, Vol. 22, (1982), at 353–360; H.G. Scott, "The Persistence of Fibers Transferred during Contact of Automobile Carpets and Clothing Fabrics," *J. of the Canadian of Forensic Sci.,* Vol. 18 (1985), at 185–199; M.C. Grieve, J. Dunlop, and P.S. Haddock: "Transfer Experiments with Acrylic Fibers," *Forensic Sci. Int.*, Vol. 40 (1989), at 267–277.

48. In addition, blood of the victim's type, found in 18% percent of the population, and semen of defendant's type, found in 2% of the population, were found on the back seat of his car. A criminologist assigned to the serology DNA section of the State Criminal Forensics Laboratory testified to a DNA match. He stated that the blood in the vehicle matched the victim's and was inconsistent with defendant's. He concluded that the random probability of the match was, by conservative estimates, about 1 in 14 thousand.

49. Broeckel v. State, 1998 WL 10267 (Alaska App.).

50. *Id.* at *1.

51. *Id.* at *2.

52. *Id.* at *3.

53. Ross v. State, 231 Ga.App. 793, 499 S.E.2d 642 (Ga.Ct.App. 1998).

54. *Id.* at 794.

55. *Id.* at 647.

56. State v. Blanton, 1998 WL 310485 (Tenn.).

57. State v. Higgenbotham, 264 Kan. 593, 957 P.2d 416 (Kan. 1998).

58. A police examiner made a fracture comparison of the duct tape from the shed and the tape on Jodi's body. The examiner testified that the torn end of the duct tape around Jodi's head matched the torn end of the roll of duct tape from the shed. Another end of the duct tape from the body matched an end of the duct tape that was found with hairs in it in the Chevette. There were two ends that did not match. Tire prints near where the body was found were not made by any of Higgenbotham's cars.

59. *Id.* at 420.

60. *Id.* at 600.

61. State v. Profit, 591 N.W.2d 451 (Minn.Sp. Ct. 1999).

62. According to police, Bell was a reputed prostitute who frequented the Broadway Avenue area of Minneapolis. The autopsy revealed that Bell had ingested cocaine within a few hours before her death. Police investigators also observed that Bell's upper torso and vaginal areas were covered with mud. Police Sergeant Robert Krebs testified that the mud "appear[ed] to be packed, not just a matter of something [sic] had flowed over the body." Dr. Morey discovered mud inside Bell's vaginal vault as well, but found no other evidence of vaginal injury nor any indication of sperm or seminal fluid inside Bell's vaginal vault. Dr. Morey declined to rule out the possibility of sexual assault, however, stating that the decomposition of Bell's body and her submersion in water could have masked evidence of such an assault. *Id.* at 455

63. *Id.* On June 3, 1996, the body of Deborah Lavoie was found approximately 1 1/2 blocks from where Bell's body had been discovered. On June 19, 1996, the body of Avis Warfield was found approximately 1/2 mile from Theodore Wirth Park. Both bodies had been burned with gasoline. On July 20, 1996, the body of Keooudorn Phothisane, a male transvestite, was discovered in Theodore Wirth Park within 1 1/2 blocks of where Bell's body had been found. Although Phothisane's body was also burned, police determined that he had been bludgeoned to death. Several juveniles claimed to have seen an African-American man running from the scene where Phothisane's body was found. The juvenile witnesses provided a composite sketch of the man to police. Profit is an African-American.

64. *Id.* at 456. This case also contains an extensive discussion of the admissibility of other crimes evidence and the value of a confession by a friend who had access to the car where the ligature-related fibers were discovered.

65. Floudiotis v. State, 726 A.2d 1196 (Del.Sup.Ct. 1999).

66. *Id.* at 1200.

67. *Id.* at 1209.

68. Eaton argued that Detective Johnson seized his boots without sufficient probable cause to arrest him. The court concluded that while a very close issue factually, they need not decide the issue since Eaton's boots were admissible under the exigent circumstances exception to the search warrant requirement.

69. State v. Young, 1999 WL 771070 (Ohio App. 7 Dist.)

70. *Id.* at *9.

71. *Id.* at *14. The forensic scientist testified that while some of the blood stains on the concrete chunk could have come from a 13 foot fall, the blood spatters on a tree stump located near Heidi's body could not have been created by Heidi's impact with the concrete after the fall and that two impacts by a blunt force were made to an already exposed blood source on Heidi. Those impacts occurred more than 30 inches above the ground level where the tree stump was located.

72. Woodward v. United States; 1999 WL 645111 (D.C.).
73. *Id.* at *1.
74. State v. Timmendequas, 161 N.J. 515, 737 A.2d 55 (1999).
75. *Id.* at 544, 70. The autopsy found, among other things, petechial hemorrhages in both eyes, a common indicator of death by strangulation, and a ligature mark on the neck that was consistent with the leather belt found in defendant's room. Over 30 hairs found near defendant's bed, on a dishcloth, on the carpet, and in the black felt cloth had the same physical and microscopic qualities as Megan's. There were 4 head hairs on Megan's blouse that were consistent with defendant's hair and inconsistent with Cifelli's and Jenin's. A pubic hair on Megan's blouse compared favorably to defendant's. The forensic chemist examining fluid evidence found blood on defendant's bedsheets, the black belt, swabs taken from defendant's bedroom door, oral and anal swabs taken from the victim, and on her blouse and earring.
76. See discussion of the Locard principle in Chapter 2.
77. State v. Goney, 1999 WL 960585 (Ohio App. 2 Dist.).
78. At trial, defendant's defense was that he and the victim had consensual sex, defendant having testified that two had intercourse. Here, however, in his post-conviction petition his position was that he did not have intercourse with Canton, and did not penetrate or ejaculate. However, court observed, DNA results had eliminated and belied such a claim.
79. *Id.* at *8.
80. *Id.*

5 Ballistics and Tool Marks

[T]his left-handed twist bullet, No. III, was fired by a Colt .32. Was it fired by this Colt .32? Some one of the learned counsel for the defendant has said that it is coming to a pretty pass when the microscope is used to convict a man of murder. I say heaven speed the day when proof in any important case is dependant upon the magnifying glass and the scientist and is less dependant upon the untrained witness without the microscope. Those things can't be wrong in the hands of a skilled user of a microscope or a magnifying glass.

Closing Argument by the Commonwealth
Massachusetts v. Sacco and Vanzetti (1921)

I. INTRODUCTION

It has been observed in the earlier chapters of this book that the bulk of the forensic sciences are, at their core, observational disciplines supported by modern microscopy. It has also been noted that, other than DNA settings, there is an absence of databases supporting population match probabilities of a laboratory "match" testified to by experts. This absence gives rise to considerable doubt as to the ultimate value of any such conclusions, whether couched in terms of *"similarity," "consistency," "lack of dissimilarities,"* or the like. Nonetheless, there is ongoing judicial support for forensic sciences such as hair, fiber, soil, paint, footwear, and tire impressions. This is especially the case in the area of ballistics regarding gun type and brand, and bullet and shell casing identifications. As opposed to the majority of the forensic sciences, ballistics experts may couch their matching findings in terms of certainty, and often do so.

Although the bulk of the forensic sciences do not rest upon any core scientific or mathematical principles, there has been considerable and growing interest by those outside of the criminal justice system in gathering very detailed information about many of the data compared by forensic scientist, because of the commercial value of patents. There is a tremendous amount of commercially generated information, contained in readily accessible databases, which are continually updated in the area of textile manufacture and sales, international footwear, weapons and ammunition, DNA research, glass and paint manufacture, geology and mineral identification, and many other commercially generated and maintained information sources.[1] The keen commercial interest in minor differences of their commercial products, both for marketing and intellectual property protection purposes, has supported, and will continue to support, the uses of forensic science attempts to match crime scene data to a suspect.

At the outset, a few remarks are warranted in respect to what aspects of the wider science of ballistics will be discussed here. The science or subject of ballistics

129

encompasses the study of 3 distinct areas: internal ballistics, external ballistics, and what is called terminal ballistics.[2]

Internal Ballistics — The study of striations and other marks made to a projectile as it passes through the barrel of a firearm, called *rifling* (lands, grooves, striations, manufacturing "defects," wear characteristics, caliber, gauge), which are what is actually referred to when studying the forensic discipline of "ballistics."

External Ballistics — The study of flight and angle of shot patterns (homicide, suicide, sniper, or ricochet).

Terminal Ballistics — The study of the effect of the projectile on or in the target. Wound analysis or "wound ballistics" is what is studied here.[3]

What are the recurring issues that must be considered when addressing the subject of the investigative and evidentiary value of the science of ballistics? These issues may, for convenience, be broken down into several categories:

1. *Crime Scene Recognition, Collection, and Preservation*
   - Angles of the shots.
   - Location of slugs.
   - Location of wounds.
   - Location of shell casings.
   - Damaged glass, metal, or wooden structures or surfaces.
   - Fingerprints on shell casings.
   - Physical locations of the participants.
   - Visual fix on contact vs. noncontact wounds.
   - Preliminary identification of firearm type.
   - Witness statements, ammunition, wounds.
2. *Firearm and Ammunition Identification*
   - Twists.
   - Lands and grooves.
   - Caliber of weapon.
   - Gauge.
3. *Matching Crime Scene Bullets to Defendant's Gun*
   Peculiarities of firearm types: calibers and gauges:
   - Rifles.
   - Handguns.
   - Shotguns.
   - Miscellaneous: machine guns, zip guns, tear gas guns, commercial nailers.
4. *Laboratory Examination by Ballistics Experts*
   Bullet matching: certainty is routinely achieved here:
   - Class characteristics: manufacturer's general and proprietary features.
   - Accidental characteristics: match to defendant's gun via test firing and the examination of the manufacturer's tool and die flaws, wear patterns in rifling, bone striations in some rare cases.

- Probability analyses: note that ballistics identifiers or minutiae are not as certain as fingerprints because fingerprint minutiae never change, whereas the rifling in any particular gun does change with use or even long-term storage due to rust or corrosion.[4]

Cartridge case matching: certainty is routinely achieved here also:
- Breech face.
- Firing pin impressions.
- Extractor marks.
- Chamber marks.

Same basic matching idea: class characteristics, manufacturing characteristics, wear patterns.
- Note: studies of error rate in ballistics laboratories.
5. *Wound Analyses* (especially where slugs are smashed[5])
6. *Angle of Shot or Distance of Shot*
   - Distance between shooter and victim (important in deciding suicide or homicide cases).
   - Who, of several participants, actually fired.
   - Positions of victims and shooters.
   - Shotgun dispersion pattern studies.
7. *Ricochet Patterns*
8. *Gunshot Residue Detection* (controversial[6])
9. *Excluding Function* (of all types of forensic evidence methods, including ballistics)

Microscopic comparisons of firearms evidence have changed little since the development of the ballistic comparison microscope over 70 years ago. The Sacco and Vanzetti case, tried in 1921, where the defendants, known and very vocal anarchists, were accused of murder during a robbery, is perhaps the most famous of the early uses of ballistics in U.S. law. It was then, and is now, considered a definitive proof of a suspect's involvement in a crime if a particular weapon used can be traced to the defendant:

> I say to you on this vital matter of the No. III bullet . . . Take the three Winchester bullets that were fired by Captain Van Amburgh at Lowell and take the seven United States Bullets that were fired by Mr. Burns at Lowell, and, lastly, take the barrel itself which we will unhitch for you, and determine the fact for yourself, for yourselves . . . . Take the glass, gentlemen, and examine them for yourselves. If you choose, take the word of nobody in that regard. Take the exhibits yourselves. Can there be a fairer test that I ask you to submit yourselves to?[7]

The above selection from the closing argument in the famous Sacco and Vanzetti case illustrates the long-standing belief in the certainty of ballistic matches by comparing projectile striations on bullets fired from a weapon linked to the defendant with one connected with the crime scene.[8] Since the pioneering efforts of ballistics expert Calvin Goddard in the 1920s up to the present, properly examined and supported ballistics analyses, along with fingerprint evidence, have been considered virtually unassailable.

A modern, and now staple, feature of the science of ballistics is the development of computer systems for the digitalization of striation and other markings on spent bullets and shell casings. Deployed in 1992, DRUGFIRE has been refined, improved, and expanded through developments in the imaging technology currently utilized in cutting-edge digitalization processes in criminal justice systems worldwide.[9] Lena Klasen, of the Swedish National Laboratory of Forensic Science, has recently stated in a paper presented at the 12th INTERPOL Forensic Science Symposium (October 20–23, 1998) that the main difference between evidential images and images captured at a crime scene is that between a direct information source and an indirect representation of an item of evidence. She cautions that the border between these two image types is somewhat difficult to define, a fact of great importance to lawyers whose case involves the validity of an imaging process factual conclusion linking a suspect to a crime scene:

> The introduction of digital images rapidly changed our possibilities to deal with images, and thereby also the need of methods, software and hardware. The human visual system, although superior on dealing with visual information, such as motion and dynamic changes, cannot properly distinguish small quantitative visual differences in the same way as computer aided methods. For example, we cannot resolve small geometrical differences of an object in an image, or small quantitative changes of the image resolution. For this purpose we use computers as an aid and to complement the human visual system.[10]

The presentation of this important paper at the recent INTERPOL Forensic Science Symposium underscores the future in store for the uses of digitalized imagery in the worldwide investigation, prosecution, and defense of crime.

It is to be noted that the electronic image associations made through DRUGFIRE-type computer systems, as with fingerprint identifications made through the Automated Fingerprint Identification System (AFIS), are still verified by traditional comparison microscopic examination of the firearms evidence by experienced technicians. DRUGFIRE serves as a screening tool to extend the capabilities of the examiner by facilitating the cross-referencing of thousands of stored images from across the country and informing the inquiring party of close associations. All probable associations made through the DRUGFIRE system are then, as before, verified by forensic firearms identification examiners using traditional, court-accepted comparison microscope techniques. The deployment of the FBI DRUG-FIRE system facilitated the opportunity of regional forensic laboratories to centrally store, search, and share forensic firearms data and imagery. With DRUGFIRE, digital images of these items are interchanged over high-speed cable or telephone lines, permitting different laboratories to remotely compare the data and thereby virtually eliminate jurisdictional, logistical, and chain-of-custody impediments.[11] There is considerable international interest in digitalized search systems for bullet and shell casing identification.[12]

Ballistics expertise encompasses, necessarily, the updating of material on the weapon manufacturing process and tooling, as they are the source of the striations used to match a found slug or casing to a weapon. In this important regard, it is of interest to note that the authors of the Firearms Evidence section of the report of the *Proceedings of the 12th INTERPOL Forensic Science Symposium* found no articles in world forensic literature updating manufacturing techniques:

> No literature articles were found on research into new manufacturing techniques and tools for manufacturing firearms. This is nevertheless an important subject because it may provide information about the specific characteristics of a firearm. Given the number of publications in the expert field of firearms and ammunition, more research is carried out into the improvement of recording techniques and the statistical processing thereof than into the question of whether the striae indeed have characteristic qualities.[13]

It is to be noted that the image-processing advances discussed herein are still closely allied with manufacturing profiles.

II. WEAPON IDENTIFICATION

There are no recent decisions questioning the scientific validity of the basis for firearms identification or projectile matching. Ballistics and fingerprints, at the present time, appear to be solidly accepted as being capable of providing assured "match" evidence.[14] There are still many questions as to the validity of systems for determining the presence of gunshot residue on the hands. Since ballistics is so widely accepted, this chapter will provide a basic breakdown of the many cases that are still being decided annually with ballistics as an important part of the case analysis. The lawyer must be as aware, if not more aware, of cases validating the increasingly diverse uses of ballistics disciplines, more than just the occasional attack on the disciplines themselves. Ballistics cases, like fingerprint and DNA cases, must be monitored on a regular basis to gain an understanding of the use of the disciplines by law enforcement. For example, this chapter discusses in detail a very recent decision allowing testimony that unspent bullets found in defendant's home matched the bullets fired due to a chemical analysis of the lead content in the batch of bullets in the box found in the defendant's home.[15]

In *Manning v. State,*[16] the defendant was charged with capital murder while engaged in the commission of a robbery. Manning argued that the state's ballistics expert's testimony that the projectiles taken from Tiffany Miller's body and found at the scene matched the projectiles taken from the tree at Manning's mother's house was beyond the scope of his expertise. A neighbor told police that Manning used to target-practice with a gun into trees and cans around his mother's house. She noticed him shooting into a particular tree in the first part of December of 1992. Based on this statement to the sheriff, a search warrant was obtained for the mother's house. Investigators recovered .380 projectiles and slugs out of the tree described by the witness. The ballistics expert testified that the projectile found at the scene and the two projectiles taken from Tiffany Miller's body were fired from the same weapon as the projectiles taken from the tree into which Manning fired. The testimony objected to by the defendant is set forth below:

Q: That which has been marked State's for—in Evidence Number 37 which is a projectile found at the scene of these killings, and that which has been marked State's in Evidence 63 which are the two projectiles which have already been identified as being taken from the body of Tiffany Miller, they all three were fired from the exact same firearm, is that correct?

A: That's correct.

Q: To the exclusion of every other firearm in the world, is that correct?

A: That's correct.[17]

The court noted that, later in his testimony, the expert linked the projectiles taken from the victim to the projectiles taken from the tree in Manning's yard. Since there was no speculation in the course of the expert's testimony, in that he was sure that the projectiles taken from the victims and the projectiles taken from the tree came from the same gun, any issue regarding the *degree* of certainty of the match was deemed meritless.

Some of the discrete areas where ballistics evidence is of central concern are, of course, clearcut homicide cases, and issues respecting weapon type, brand, or caliber. Ballistics is typically of great import in suicide vs. homicide inquiries, as is the related area of gunshot residue. There is also a close relationship in certain cases between ballistics and wound analysis to determine the relative positions between a shooter and victim or with surveying principles to determine the angle of shot in cases of snipers or drive-by shootings.

The introduction of a weapon not actually identified as used in a killing was approved in the case of *Smoote v. State,*[18] where the defendant was convicted of murder, conspiracy to commit robbery, robbery, and being a habitual offender. The defendant alleged error, among other reasons, in permitting a ballistics expert to demonstrate to the jury how a shotgun would be loaded and prepared for firing.

According to the state, the defendant and another man hatched a plan to rob a branch of the First America Bank. The next day, the defendant borrowed a gold Buick Electra 224 from Robert Hartley, the murder victim in this case, and met his accomplice who was driving a blue station wagon. The two men drove to a residential area, parked the Buick, and drove to the bank together in the station wagon. The shotgun used in the murder was never recovered by the police and no connection was made between the shotgun used in the demonstration and either the defendant or the victim. As such, the defendant argued that there was no relevance to the shotgun demonstration. And even if marginally relevant, the defendant contended the probative value of the demonstration was substantially outweighed by the danger of unfair prejudice or misleading the jury.[19]

The court rejected this argument, holding that at trial, the state made clear that it was not asserting that the shotgun was the one used in the murder or that it belonged to or was in any way connected with defendant. While the court thought that the demonstration was, at best, of marginal relevance and marginal probative value, it was undisputed that the victim was killed by a shotgun blast. A demonstration of how such a weapon works, the court reasoned, might have been of some benefit to the jury in understanding the details of the killing. In any event, they did not see how the demonstration prejudiced the defendant or misled the jury. While the trial court would have been well within its discretion to exclude the demonstration, it was within its discretion to admit it.[20]

In *People v. Askew,*[21] the defendant was convicted of murder and armed robbery. The victim was shot in the course of an armed robbery attempt. One Bell, a neighbor of the defendant, called police after he saw the defendant, who lived across the street in the defendant's girlfriend's house, on the porch of that house with a shotgun and a pistol. The police discovered 3 guns, including a .22 pistol, all hidden under the cushions of a couch located in the alley between Bell's home and the defendant's girlfriend's home. Ballistics tests on both the .22 pistol and the bullet recovered from the robbery victim's body revealed that the bullet had the same "class characteristics" as the pistol, but it was uncertain whether or not the bullet had been fired from the pistol. After a hearing on the defendant's motion in limine, the trial court ruled that there was an insufficient connection between the .22 pistol found in the alley and the murder weapon, or that it was ever in the possession of the defendant. However, the trial judge ruled that the .22 pistol could be used for *identification* purposes, i.e., testimony that a similar gun was used to shoot the victim or was at one time in the possession of the defendant.[22]

During closing argument the state emphasized the ballistics expert's testimony noting the consistencies present between the bullet recovered in the body and the .22 pistol, and reminded the jury of the testimony that the defendant was seen with a gun very similar to the .22 only 4 days after the murder. Thereafter, the state drew the inference that the .22 pistol was the murder weapon defendant used to shoot the victim. The defendant argued that this inference was impermissible in light of the trial judge's earlier in limine ruling. The court concluded that the inference drawn by the state was reasonable and based on facts in evidence.

The appellate court noted that weapons were generally admissible when there was proof that they were sufficiently connected to the crime and that when there was evidence that the perpetrator possessed a weapon at the time of the offense, a similar weapon could be admitted into evidence even though not identified as the weapon used.[23] Moreover, a weapon need not be positively shown to have been used in committing the crime, and any doubt whether or not it was connected to the crime or to the defendant did not bar its admission, so long as a jury could find a connection.[24]

> Here, Juan was killed by a .22 caliber bullet; the lands, grooves, and twist of which were consistent with the .22 pistol introduced at trial. Just four days after Juan's death, Bell saw defendant with a pistol resembling a .22, and soon thereafter such a pistol, along with a sawed-off rifle and a shotgun, were found in the alley between defendant's girlfriend's home and Bell's home. Irma testified that Juan was searched by a man with a shotgun. Furthermore, Irma identified the .22 as being similar to a gun that defendant fired over her head. Based on this evidence, we conclude that a reasonable jury could have found that there was a connection between the .22 and defendant or Juan's murder—or both.[25]

Regarding the inference of such connection drawn by the prosecutor, the court concluded that the inference drawn by the state was reasonable and based on facts in evidence.

In a similar setting, a New York court condemned the misuse of this concept, especially in light of ballistics testimony favoring the accused. In *People v. Walters*,[26] the defendant was convicted of attempted murder in the second degree, robbery in the first degree (three counts), robbery in the second degree, assault in the first degree, assault in the second degree, criminal possession of a weapon in the second degree, and criminal possession of a weapon in the third degree. The court ordered a reversal due to prosecutorial misconduct. Most egregious, the court stated, was the prosecutor's insinuation that the gun that had been recovered from the defendant 2 weeks after the crime in an unrelated arrest may have been the gun that was used to shoot the victim. The prosecution had persisted with this implication despite its knowledge that the ballistics test performed by police conclusively established that the gun had not been used in the crime. The prosecutor's conduct in advocating a position which he knew to be false was an abrogation of his responsibility as a prosecutor.[27]

In *People v. Jackson*,[28] the defendant was charged with aggravated battery with a firearm. The victim Rhodes testified that at about 10:30 or 11 P.M. that night, he was walking back to the Carter residence when a Nissan Maxima pulled up beside him. He claimed he recognized the driver as Jackson. He testified that the driver asked him what he was up to, to which he responded "nothing much," and then the driver shot him. Jackson was arrested. A state policeman testified that he saw a .357 Magnum pistol on a nightstand in the bedroom where he arrested Jackson, who claimed that it belonged to a friend. The bullet had not been surgically removed from the shooting victim at the time of trial so the caliber of the bullet was not established and no ballistics tests had connected the bullet to the pistol on Jackson's night stand. Additionally, no witnesses ever identified the pistol as the weapon used to shoot the victim. Nonetheless, the pistol was admitted into evidence without objection. The court here noted that the state did not offer any testimony to establish that the .357 Magnum found when Jackson was arrested was capable of producing an injury such as the one suffered by Rhodes or that it was similar to the weapon used to commit the crime. While questioning Rhodes, the state asked him about the lighting conditions, to establish that he clearly saw his shooter, but they never asked him to describe or identify the weapon used. As a matter of fact, the court observed, nowhere in the record is it established that Rhodes was shot with a handgun or pistol, as opposed to some other firearm.[29]

During the time this case had been pending on appeal, Rhodes was murdered in an unrelated incident. An autopsy was performed on Rhodes body. The bullet from the shooting at issue in this appeal was removed, and it was conclusively established that the .357 Magnum pistol found on Jackson's nightstand and introduced into evidence was not the weapon used to shoot Rhodes. The state admitted these facts, but asserted that, as a reviewing court, this court was not allowed to consider this new evidence. The court disagreed, stating this situation was one of those rare instances where the exercise of its original jurisdiction was proper. It concluded that the admission of the weapon, coupled with the emphasis placed upon it by the prosecution in its closing argument, resulted in clear prejudice to the defendant in light of the admitted fact that the weapon in question had absolutely no connection to the crime.[30]

In *Commonwealth v. Busch*,[31] a homicide case, the victims, Melvin Bonnett and Christopher Green, were shot and killed in the hallway of an apartment building in Brockton on December 13, 1991. The defendant lived in the building with his girlfriend, India Noiles, and her two daughters. Bonnett also lived in the building. A tenant found 2 handguns under some bushes 6 months after the murders and turned them over to the police. One was a .32-caliber revolver, and the other was a .22-caliber revolver. There was a sufficient evidentiary basis to permit an inference by the jury that the 2 handguns admitted in evidence were the same handguns used by the defendant to commit the murders. The 2 handguns were of the same caliber as the handguns used to kill the victims. The 4 bullets recovered from the victims, and at the scene, were consistent with 4 bullets that could have been fired from the handguns. There was testimony that the rifling systems of the 2 handguns were similar to the handguns used in the murders. Due to the "poor markings of the evidence," the police ballistics expert could not positively identify that the bullets recovered from the victims had been fired from these guns. However, both the bullet configurations and the "rifling" patterns were similar for the bullets recovered from the guns and those recovered from the victims. When shown the guns during her testimony, India Noiles stated that they looked exactly like the ones she saw in the possession of the defendant.

In *State v. Treadwell*,[32] a homicide case arose from a gang-related shooting outside a tavern. The bullets found in shooting victim Powell's car were analyzed and a ballistics report was issued that stated that, although the bullets found in a shooting victim's car could not be positively identified as having come from Treadwell's gun, the bullets were consistent with bullets fired from Treadwell's gun. The court ruled that although the physical evidence did not conclusively show that the bullets found in the car came from Treadwell's gun, it was far from correct to say that there was no physical proof of that fact. The ballistics report did state, "Items AB, AE, AF, AG, and AH [bullets removed from Powell's car] were not positively identified to any firearm submitted." The report, however, also stated, "Examination of Items AB, AE, AF, AG, and AH revealed them to be consistent with damaged bullets fired through the barrel of a caliber 9MM Luger firearm having 6 lands and grooves with a right hand twist." Viewed in its totality, the ballistics report, rather than providing "no proof" that Treadwell's shots struck Powell's car, actually corroborated the other evidence supporting the state's case against Treadwell.

The court ruled in *Commonwealth v. Spotz*,[33] that the state need not establish that a particular weapon was actually used in the commission of a crime in order for it to be introduced at trial. Rather, the commonwealth need only show sufficient circumstances to justify an inference by the finder of fact that the particular weapon was likely to have been used in the commission of the crime charged. The admission of such evidence is a matter within the sound discretion of the trial court, and, absent an abuse of such discretion, the trial court's decision to admit the evidence must stand. A weapon found in the possession of the accused at the time of his arrest, although not identified as the weapon actually used in the crime on trial, is admissible where the circumstances justify an inference of the likelihood that the weapon was used in the crime.

III. ANGLE OF SHOT

In *Jones v. State*,[34] a homicide case, police officer Szafranski's car was the third in a series of police cars turning at the intersection of 6th and Davis Streets, when shots were fired. Officer Dyal, who was driving one of the two police cars immediately preceding Officer Szafranski's vehicle, testified that after he heard the first shot, he looked back and saw "flashes" from two more gunshots emanating from Jones's apartment building. Expert testimony revealed that Officer Szafranski was shot with a .30–.30-caliber Winchester Marlin rifle and two such rifles were found in the defendant's apartment, each with one spent shell casing. His fingerprint was found on the breach area of one of the rifles. While searching the downstairs vacant apartment in the defendant's building after the shooting, police found a fresh recoil mark on the sill of one of the windows and a ballistics expert testified that the bullet's trajectory was consistent with the bullet having been fired from the downstairs apartment. The expert also testified that the bullet entered the windshield of Officer Szafranski's car around the area of the rearview mirror, traveling in an approximately horizontal plane. The court ruled that the physical evidence was consistent with the state's theory that Officer Szafranski was shot from the downstairs apartment.[35]

In *State v. Lyons*,[36] defendants Robert Lyons and Vincent Rossa were charged with robbery and several other crimes and their cases were consolidated. Lyons and Rossa committed two armed robberies of restaurants. After the report of the second robbery, police were dispatched to pursue the suspect vehicle. In the course of a lengthy pursuit, Lyons leaned out the passenger window and fired several shots from a shotgun toward the deputies. Lyons maintained that he fired his gun in the air just to frighten the deputies and to keep a distance between the two cars. One of Lyons's shots ricocheted off the suspect vehicle and hit one of the patrol cars. Lyons maintained that he accidentally discharged his gun in this instance.[37]

The state sought to introduce demonstrative evidence in the form of a videotape prepared by a ballistics expert demonstrating the effect of the shots fired toward the patrol car windshield. In attempting to duplicate the conditions of the shots fired, he obtained windshields from the same make and model as the patrol car, placed the windshields at the same angles, used the same type of shotgun and very same pistol, as well as the same type of ammunition. He also factored in the temperature and barometric pressure, and stated that they would have no appreciable difference in the demonstration. While none of the shots hit any of the windshields during the actual incident, the state offered the evidence for purposes of arguing the defendant's intent to inflict and the potential for grievous bodily harm.

Here, the trial court determination that the demonstrative experiments were conducted in "a reasonably similar manner and under substantially similar circumstances" as the alleged crime was upheld on appeal. The court observed that the demonstration would assist the jury in its deliberations.[38]

Surveyor testimony and ballistics expertise were used to convict a gang member in the case of *People v. Torres*.[39] The defendant was convicted of second-degree murder and aggravated discharge of a firearm, as a result of the death of a bystander shot during a gang-related shootout. The victim was a janitor at a school across the street from the house where the defendant and others were exchanging fire with rival gang members. He was looking out the second-floor window and was fatally struck by a stray bullet. A central issue in the case was the location of the possible shooter, given the angle of shot required to have hit the victim.

The police received a call that someone had been shot at Elgin Academy. Several officers responded to the Academy's Sears Hall, where they were directed upstairs to the second-floor cafeteria. There they found Earl Harris, a custodian, lying dead from a bullet wound to his head. Officer Michael Whitty traced the approximate trajectory of the bullet, and found small holes in the glass and screen of a window facing in the direction of 362 Franklin. He then notified the officers at the defendant's home of a probable connection between Harris's death and the shots fired at 362 Franklin. Surveyors were called, and they pinpointed the source trajectory as being within a small area immediately adjacent to the front porch at 362 Franklin, where witnesses had reported defendant Torres stood as he fired after the fleeing attackers.

At trial, forensic examiner Welty, employed by the Illinois State Police, testified that 3 of the bullets found at the school came from the same weapon that fired the fatal bullet, although he was unable to determine the same for a fourth slug because police had recovered only the inner core of the bullet, not the outer portion which would bear the unique markings of the gun that fired it. He further testified that casings found in a bucket on the defendant's porch also came from one weapon, but he was not sure whether that was the same weapon that fired the bullets found at the school. He also testified that the bullets in a clip found at the defendant's house were of the "same sort" as the spent bullets taken from the school and the victim, and that the clip would fit either a 9mm Baretta or a .380 automatic Browning.[40]

Michael Kreiser, also a forensic scientist employed by the Illinois State Police, testified that his study of the surveyors' documents and other physical evidence led him to the conclusion that the fatal bullet could only have been fired by someone standing within a narrow "window" of space immediately adjacent to the defendant's front porch. Eyewitnesses had established that only Torres and Soto had been positioned anywhere within that "window" during the shooting. However, eyewitness testimony established that defendant Soto was firing a shotgun and only defendant Torres was seen firing a handgun. Pursuant to Welty's and Kreiser's testimonies, the trial court determined that it was reasonable to conclude that Torres was the shooter:[41]

> Four projectiles were recovered in and around Elgin Academy, three of them had been
> identified as coming from a .380 semiautomatic [gun]. Four shell casings had been

recovered at the scene from a .380 semiautomatic weapon. One issue I have to deal with is . . . the missing gun theory. That is, all the ballistics reports show that the guns that had been recovered from the defendant's home, including the two pistols and the .22 rifle, were not involved [in] shooting the projectiles or the four casings. The state's theory was that basically the defendant hid the remaining gun . . . Now, I have to take into consideration several factors . . . and most importantly [sic] is that a clip was recovered from the residence. The importance of that clip is that it did not belong to any of the three weapons that had been recovered. And that clip, in fact, the testimony showed it did fit and function in a .380 Baretta [sic], not in the defendant's pistol that was recovered from the room or the other guns. Now that's significant and that's important. I also look at the fact that the defendant would have had the time to hide that particular weapon along with the fact that the four casings were hidden in a bucket by the porch. No other casings were found in the front yard where the shots were fired from. Therefore, my conclusion is that the four shots fired by the defendant were shot at the fleeing antagonists and they were fired toward the Elgin Academy.[42]

The appellate court, while recognizing the highly circumstantial nature of the evidence, found that it could not conclude that no reasonable trier of fact could have found that the defendant fired the shot that killed Harris. Missing gun notwithstanding, it appeared that Torres met all of the requisite criteria to have fired the fatal shot:

He was within the "window" of trajectory, he fired a .380 caliber handgun, and he fired in the direction of the academy. No other person met all three of these critical factors according to witness testimony and other evidence adduced at trial.[43]

The appeals thus court concluded that the state had proved the defendant guilty beyond a reasonable doubt of second-degree murder.[44]

In *Cammon v. State*,[45] the defendants were convicted of felony-murder predicated on an aggravated assault at a nightclub. On the night of the homicide, Cammon became involved in a fistfight with the deceased, Adrian Woods. Later in the evening the defendant obtained a pistol and shot Woods who was in a van carrying Woods and several others that had pulled into Wood's apartment complex. Cammon began shooting and the occupants of the van returned fire. During the shoot-out, a Ms. Ellison was struck and killed by a bullet as she stood in her living room. There was evidence that the bullet that killed Ms. Ellison "could have been" fired from a Beretta pistol.[46]

Defendants argued trial error in allowing an officer who was not qualified as an expert in ballistics to give an opinion as to the trajectory of the bullet which killed the victim. The state argued that the opinion was based upon the officer's own extensive investigation of the homicide, and was clearly admissible over any objection to lack of expertise in the field of ballistics. The ultimate issue, the court underlined, was not the bullet trajectory, but whether the defendants were guilty of an aggravated assault or not guilty by reason of self-defense:

If the three co-defendants were parties to an aggravated assault initiated against the occupants of the van, then they all were guilty of felony murder regardless of who actually fired the shot which killed the victim. If, on the other hand, they were victims of an aggravated assault initiated by the occupants of the van, then they all were not guilty by reason of self-defense even if one of them had shot the victim. The officer was not asked whether he believed that the three started the shoot-out or were justified in defending themselves against an aggravated assault begun by the occupants of the van. The officer only was asked if he had an opinion as to the path of the bullet, and his response to that inquiry was not inadmissible on the ground that it expressed his opinion the ultimate issue in the case.

In *Whites v. State*,[47] the defendant was convicted of committing first-degree premeditated murder. At trial, the defendant moved for a continuance or mistrial, arguing that the state had violated the discovery rules by failing to disclose the results of ballistics tests performed on bullet holes in the victim's sweater in a timely manner. The trial court concluded that the state had violated the rules of discovery, but determined that neither a continuance nor mistrial was required.

On the evening of the murder, Mr. Whites was involved in a brawl with two other men on a street corner in Lake Helen, Florida. During the fight, the victim grabbed Mr. Whites's neck. After the fight ended, Mr. Whites told the victim that he was going home to get his gun and that he would return, which he did. The defendant admitted that he shot and killed the victim, but contended that he acted in self-defense because he became concerned that the victim would grab him and kill him. He testified that he was between 5 and 10 feet from the victim when he fired the first shot, and his brother testified that he saw the victim grab the defendant before the first shot was fired.

Shortly before jury selection, the prosecutor gave defense counsel a copy of a ballistics report describing tests conducted on bullet holes found in the victim's sweater, the tests having been completed a full 2 years earlier. The ballistics report described the sweater worn by the victim at the time of the shooting, and belied the defendant's version of events regarding how close he was as he shot the victim:

> The left collar of the sweater displays two holes. Numerous gunpowder particles were found on the collar around these holes indicating that at least one of the holes could be an entrance hole. These residues are consistent with a distance less than the maximum for which gunpowder would be deposited.
>
> . . .
>
> The left middle back displays five holes, gunpowder was found around these holes. These residues are consistent with at least one of these holes being fired at a distance less than the maximum for which gunpowder would be deposited.

The prosecutor stated that he initially discovered the report in a police file on the Wednesday before the trial began and that he had attempted to reach defense counsel but failed. He assured the court that he did not intend to offer the report into evidence.

The appellate court agreed with the trial court that the state's failure to deliver the ballistics report in a timely fashion to defense counsel constituted a discovery violation. The only substantial issue remaining was whether the trial court abused its discretion in determining that the discovery violation was not substantial and thus did not result in prejudice or harm to the defendant. The defendant argued that the violation prejudiced his ability to present an effective defense because the ballistics report would have helped him prove his theory of self-defense, contending that the existence of gunpowder on the victim's sweater supported his contention that the victim was close enough to threaten his life when he shot him. He argued further that the report contradicted the medical examiner's report that gunpowder burns were not observed on the victim's body, and corroborated his brother's testimony that the victim had reached for Mr. Whites before the first shot was fired. The court was not convinced:

> We disagree. The ballistics report is cursory and does not estimate the distance between Mr. Whites and the victim at the time of the shooting. Importantly, the ballistics examiner did not have possession of the weapon from which the shots were fired; therefore, the weapon could not be tested to determine the maximum distance from which it would deposit powder residue. Moreover, the report is consistent with the testimony of the witnesses, including Mr. Whites, that the victim was between five and fifteen feet away from Mr. Whites at the time of the shooting . . . . It is uncontroverted that Mr. Whites retrieved his pistol after the initial altercation with the victim and that he expressed his intention "to bust" the victim; that Mr. Whites had adequate time and means to escape if he believed that he was in danger; and that Mr. Whites shot the victim at least four times.[48]

Considering those facts, the court held that it could not say that the trial court abused its discretion in determining that no prejudice was incurred by the defendant by the delay in the disclosure of the ballistics report.

IV. BULLET MATCHING

In cases of the clear application of striation matching after test firing of a gun connected to a defendant, there is generally little or no discussion of foundational ballistics issues. The cases of interest tend to focus on weapon identifications and linkage where no gun is available for comparison purposes. Several very recent cases deal with the ammunition-matching issue in the context of trying to chemically match the lead content of bullets taken from a crime victim with unspent shells or ammunition otherwise connected to the defendant. These cases and the technology discussed therein are at the cutting edge of the end-of-century relationship between law and science.

In *State v. Fulminante*,[49] the defendant was found guilty of murder and sentenced to death. In September 1982, the defendant lived in Phoenix with his wife, Mary, and his 11-old stepdaughter, Jeneane. On September 6, 1982, Mary checked into the hospital for surgery. Before leaving for the hospital, she told the defendant she would leave him if he did not have a job by the time she fully recovered from her surgery. At 2 A.M. the next morning, the defendant telephoned the Mesa Police Department to report his stepdaughter, Jeneane, missing. Later that morning, when the defendant brought Mary home from the hospital, he told her Jeneane had not come home the previous night. He said that when he realized Jeneane was missing, he first looked around the house, then went around the neighborhood door-to-door, and then went used his motorcycle to continue searching for her. When Mary questioned him on the details of his search, he admitted he had not gone door-to-door. At this point, Mary and the defendant both went through the neighborhood looking for Jeneane. Sometime after Mary returned to the house, she searched around the house and discovered that the defendant's pistol was missing. When the police visited their home on September 15, the Fulminantes reported the missing pistol.

On September 16, the child victim's body was found in a desert wash 11 miles from the Fulminantes' home. The body had two gunshot wounds to the head; a long, narrow cloth was wrapped loosely around her neck; her pants had been undone, the waistband resting below her waist, and the elastic of her underpants rolled under. Police later recovered a spent bullet from the ground near the place where her body was found. The autopsy determined that the child died of the gunshot wounds, and gunpowder in the entry wounds suggested the shots had been fired at close range. In addition, lead fragments were recovered from Jeneane's brain. Police were unable to perform ballistics testing since the defendant claimed he sold his guns while Mary was in the hospital. Police later discovered that the defendant traded his rifle for $80 cash and a second barrel for his .357 Dan Wesson revolver. The extra barrel was also missing from the family home. Ballistics tests were able to determine that the wounds on Jeneane's body were made by either .357 or .38 caliber bullets. The wounds were most consistent with a .357, and a .357 was compatible with a .38. The police were able to recover a box of .357 and .38 caliber ammunition during a consensual search of the Fulminantes' house.[50]

According to the state, the ballistics evidence was consistent with guilt:

Defendant possessed ammunition of the same caliber that probably killed Jeneane; lead retrieved from Jeneane's head was from the same batch of ammunition as the lead found in Defendant's home; the projectile jacket recovered from the crime scene could have been fired from a .357 Dan Wesson; the projectile was fired from a dirty gun, and spent .357 cartridges retrieved from Defendant's home indicated they were also fired from a dirty gun; and finally, the projectile jacket found at the scene and those retrieved from Defendant's home indicated a similar manufacturer. Defendant had a gun and ammunition of the same type used to kill Jeneane and purchased an extra barrel for the gun the day Jeneane disappeared. Both items were missing when police investigated, and Defendant could not rationally explain their disappearance—strengthening an inference they might have been used to kill Jeneane.[51]

From the above-noted facts, the court found competent evidence from which the jury could have "pieced together a web of suspicious circumstances tight enough that a reasonable person could conclude, beyond a reasonable doubt, that Defendant was the perpetrator."[52]

The defendant argued that evidence comparing the lead fragments retrieved from Jeneane's head to the lead from the ammunition recovered from the defendant's home should have been excluded because the probative value was substantially outweighed by the prejudicial impact and potential to mislead and confuse the jury. The defendant argued that the fact that fragments from Jeneane's head were of the same elemental composition as his ammunition was statistically irrelevant because there could have been as many as 40,000 boxes of such ammunition. The test for relevance, the court noted, was whether the offered evidence tends to make the existence of any fact in issue more or less probable. The court found that the lead comparison evidence here was probative in that it tended to demonstrate that the defendant possessed ammunition consistent with that used to kill Jeneane. They did not see any prejudice that would substantially outweigh the probative value of the evidence to bar its admission.

In *United States v. Davis*,[53] the defendant was convicted in the U.S. District Court for the District of Nebraska of armed bank robbery and using a firearm during a crime of violence. The case centered around the armed robbery of 3 separate, federally insured financial institutions in Omaha, Nebraska, 2 of which occurred only minutes apart on January 29, 1994. The third took place on March 12, 1994. Shots were fired during 2 of the robberies. The gun was identified as a dark-colored, short-barreled gun. The defendant Cleophus Davis was arrested and charged with all three robberies. An eyewitness and a bank teller provided the FBI with information sufficient for a rough sketch, and the defendant was eventually identified in a lineup.

When Davis was arrested, a partial box of .38-caliber wadcutter cartridges was found in the car belonging to a friend that the defendant was driving. The .38-caliber wadcutter cartridges found in a box in the Nissan were later tested against the bullets found at the crime scenes, and the bullets bore markings similar to each other, indicating that they were "possibly" fired by the same gun. The bullets from the box found in the Nissan were determined to be analytically indistinguishable from the bullets recovered at 2 of the bank robberies. A ballistics expert testified that such a finding was "rare and that the bullets must have come from the same box or from another box that would have been made by the same company on the same day."[54]

The FBI tested the gun and found it to have a very worn, heavily leaded barrel, consistent with the markings on the bullets recovered from the crime scenes. A ballistics expert witness testified that it was "possible" that the bullets recovered from the 2 crime scenes where shots were fired were fired from that weapon. The court accepted the expert's testimony as sufficiently probative and reliable because it demonstrated a high probability that the bullets spent at the first robbery and the last robbery originated from the same box of cartridges.

The district court conducted a hearing to determine the adequacy of the scientific foundation supporting expert testimony proffered by the government on inductively coupled plasma-atomic emission spectrometry (IAP), a process used in this case to analyze and compare trace elements found in the bullet fragments. John Riley, special agent of the FBI, who specializes in the analysis of various materials for their elemental and trace elemental composition was the government's witness. Mr. Riley had been doing this work for approximately 27 years, had a bachelor of science degree in chemistry and a master of science degree in forensic science, and had authored articles and lectured on this subject.

Mr. Riley testified that IAP, an analysis that the FBI has been using for approximately 10 years, is a generally accepted scientific technique that has been subjected to testing, publication, and peer review, and the technique is the same no matter who performs it. Another procedure used to accomplish the same basic analysis is neuron activation analysis. The FBI has been using the neuron activation analysis since the mid-1960s but now favors IAP for trace elemental analysis because IAP is more sensitive. IAP can determine trace elements down to parts per million (.0000001 percent). The procedure determines which of five trace elements are present in the bullets to be compared. If the same elements are present in each, then the procedure determines the percentage of each element present. If the same elements are present in the same amounts then they are analytically indistinguishable.[55]

Agent Riley described at length the bullet-manufacturing processes that supported his chemical analysis and his testimony linking defendant Davis.

Mr. Riley testified that research had been conducted on the composition and comparison of bullets manufactured at the same plant on either the same or different days and at different plants. The research revealed that while 400,000 bullets could be produced at a factory in one day, the composition of those bullets will vary vastly unless they were manufactured side by side, because lead is a heavy molten metal that cannot be mixed into a completely homogenous mixture throughout; pockets of different elemental compositions will exist and additional lead of differing elemental compositions is periodically added to the cauldron throughout a day, changing the elemental composition of the bullets produced. Based on this research and the results of the trace elemental composition IAP analysis, the expert concluded that the bullets at issue were analytically indistinguishable from some of the bullets in the box of cartridges found in the Nissan, that they were generally similar to the remaining bullets in that box, and that there was a high correlation between the two bullets found at the crime scenes. He also concluded that these bullets must have been manufactured at the same Remington factory, must have come from the same batch of lead, must have been packaged on or about the same day, and could have come from the same box.[56]

Davis's counsel, during cross-examination of Riley, cited one paragraph from a book that criticized neuron activation analysis (IAP was the analysis used here), because there was no way of knowing exactly how many bullets manufactured by the same company have this same elemental composition. Agent Riley admitted having no way of knowing how many other bullets Remington produced on the same day as these that also would have a composition that was analytically indistinguishable from the bullets tested here. The court ruled that there was a sufficient scientific basis to admit the expert's testimony. Davis, the court noted, did not attempt to show that IAP was not a scientifically valid technique for determining the trace elemental composition of bullets, nor did he try to establish that Riley improperly utilized the technique.[57]

Another important case addressing the novel lead-matching issue, where a gun is not available or the more traditional firing-match testimony is inconclusive, is *State v. Noel*.[58] Here, the defendant was found guilty of murder, possession of a handgun without a permit, and possession of a handgun with intent to use it unlawfully against another. The victim was a young man who was shot repeatedly on his front porch as he was returning to his home in the early evening. There was no known motive for the murder, nor was robbery was involved. The shooting appeared random and senseless. Informant testimony led to the arrest of the defendant. A bag containing 18 bullets was found in his locker, 9 of which were 9mm bullets stamped with the manufacturer's name, Speer. The police had also recovered spent bullets and bullet casings at the crime scene, which were stamped with the same manufacturer's name.

Charles Peters, a physical scientist with the materials analysis unit of the FBI, examined 15 bullets, 4 collected at the crime scene, 2 recovered from the decedent's body, and the 9 Speer bullets found among the defendant's belongings. The court characterized this complex testimony as follows:

> He analyzed the bullets using a process known as inductively coupled plasma atomic emission spectroscopy (IAP). IAP determines the proportions of six elements other than lead: copper, antimony, bismuth, arsenic, tin, and silver. The bullet manufacturer adds these elements to each batch of lead. From one batch to another, the proportions in bullets of the six elements vary. Thus, the chemical composition of a bullet from one batch may match that of another bullet from the same batch, but not the composition of a bullet from another batch.
>
> Peters divided the bullets into five compositional groups. Within each group, the bullets were of the same composition. Four of the five groups contained both a bullet from defendant's pouch and one recovered either from the crime scene or from the victim's body. For example, Group One included six bullets that were analytically indistinguishable: one bullet from the crime scene, one from the victim's body, and four from defendant's pouch. Group Four, which consisted of a solitary bullet found at the crime scene, did not match any other bullets. At trial, Peters testified that, in his experience and that of his unit, "bullets that come from the same box have the same composition of lead and bullets that come from different boxes . . . will have different compositions." He explained that the manufacturer fills a given box with bullets from a single batch of lead. Consequently, those bullets will possess the same chemical composition. Because mixing may occur during storage, however, bullets of different compositions may be found in the same box. Peters concluded that he would not expect random batches of lead to produce the match that existed among the subject bullets.[59]

Before conducting his analysis, Peters testified that he had visited the Speer manufacturing plant in Lewiston, Idaho to study the manufacturing processes. He limited his testimony on the manufacturing process to an explanation that each bullet was extruded from a billet, or 70-pound cylinder of lead, each of which produces a number of billets. A billet yields approximately 4,300 bullets. Peters further noted that about 5 billion bullets were manufactured in the U.S. each year, and at least 50 thousand bullets may have the same composition.[60]

The defendant argued in the appellate court that Peters failed to provide foundational evidence in the form of statistical probability evidence about the identical composition between the bullets recovered from the crime scene and the victim's body and those found in defendant's pouch. The appellate court agreed, concluding that Peters's testimony depended on the statistical probability that the 2 sets of bullets would have the same composition.

The New Jersey Supreme Court noted that the prosecutor's purpose in offering the testimony of Mr. Peters was to persuade the jury that the identical composition of the 2 sets of bullets significantly enhanced the strength of the link between defendant and the crime, that is, the link that had already been established by the identity of caliber and manufacture. That was obvious from remarks made in his summation, by which the prosecutor sought to impart scientific certainty to an implied conclusiveness of that link, also attempting, the court noted, to bolster the argument with a "patently improper" character reference for witness Peters's credibility:

Finally Mr. Charles Peters of the FBI. I realized that was some sophisticated testimony and I know I personally had trouble following it. But I hope the conclusions are what came clear. It is a very precise, scientific process that has been used for, I believe, he said about, about 30 years to test these bullet leads and his testimony is critical to this case because it completely blows away the murder theory advanced by the defense that Malika and Lamar somehow engineered the murder.

Now do you think Mr. Peters was a liar? He's not a cop. He's not even an FBI agent. Charles Peters is a scientist and he looked like a scientist; didn't he? You could almost see him in a white lab coat. You could see him in math class in a high school in the back. He had all the answers.

He's a straight shooter. Did not testify beyond what the results of his examination were. Didn't try to make it out to be more than what it was but it is something very critical in this case. Basically what he told us was that an examination of bullets, whenever a manufacturer is going to run a line of bullets, they order a source of lead from a lead smelter.

I asked him if that was like a "batch." He said it was. The scientists like using the word "source." I think it is easier to conceive of as a batch of lead and he said that there are millions, literally millions of these batches of lead out in circulation. And from those millions of batches of lead out in circulation, there are billions of bullets produced each year.

The key, I submit to you, is not what Mr. Peters said it is, not about the number of billets produced—the number of bullets produced, the key is the number of sources of lead; the number of batches. Millions of batches; each one unique like a snow flake; like a fingerprint.[61]

In initiating its analysis, the New Jersey Supreme Court noted that statistical evidence had not generally been a prerequisite to the admission of matching samples, noting, for example, that in cases involving matching blood samples, statistical evidence of the probability of a match had not been required to establish a bloodstain as a link in the chain of evidence. Similarly, the court noted that expert testimony about matching soil and hair samples has been deemed admissible, with the weight of the evidence left to the jury. Finally, the court continued, expert testimony about matching carpet fibers had been admitted in the absence of statistical evidence about the probability of the match.[62] In the present case, the New Jersey Supreme Court observed, the expert's testimony established a match among the bullets found in the defendant's belongings, at the crime scene, and in the victim's body. The defendant's contention that the large quantity of bullets produced by the manufacturer rendered the match among the bullets inconclusive went to the weight, not admissibility, as with the other observational forensic disciplines noted.

The jury in the present case, the court stated, received the guidance it needed to discharge its function. The expert explained the chemistry of lead analysis, why bullets of the same chemical composition generally come from the same box, and why a single box may contain several bullets of different compositions. The jury was left with the task of determining whether the bullets at issue came from the same box. The jury in the present case could evaluate the expert's testimony without recourse to mathematical calculations; like juries assessing samples of blood, soil, and fibers, it did not require statistical data to discharge its duties.

> IAP is an accepted method of bullet lead analysis. The compositional match among the bullets increased the probability that the bullets in the victim came from the defendant. That evidence constituted a link in the prosecution's chain of evidence. The defense attempted to undermine that conclusion by cross-examining the expert, by showing that many bullets of the same composition had been manufactured, and by arguing an alternative conclusion to the jury. Consequently, we find that the trial court did not err in permitting Peters to testify about the similarity of the composition of the lead bullets.
>
> We also conclude that Peters did not exceed the limits of his expertise in testifying about the manufacturing process. Peters testified that bullets of the same composition generally come from the same box, although a single box may contain bullets of several different compositions. He based his testimony on years of analyzing boxes of bullets and on a tour of the Speer plant. That tour may not qualify him as an expert on bullet manufacturing for all purposes. When combined with his substantial experience in analyzing bullets, however, the tour provided him with the "minimal technical training and knowledge essential to the expression of a reliable opinion." Although experts generally may not express opinions outside their areas of expertise, those areas may overlap, and in certain circumstances an expert in one area may be qualified to express an opinion in another. Here, Peters's testimony regarding the arrangement of bullets in a box provided an appropriate basis for the jury to evaluate the significance of the bullet matches.[63]

The dissenting judges saw the issue as whether Peters's testimony provided an adequate basis to support the conclusion that the bullets not only came from the same source of lead at the manufacturer's but were sold from the same box. According to them, the issue was not whether Peters's testimony regarding the matches between the bullets was admissible, but whether too many bullets were in circulation to justify any real inference of guilt.

A second concern of the dissent, with reference to a "snow flake" remark in the state's closing, was that the prosecutor's summation elevated the testimony from "a bit of circumstantial evidence that adds to the State's case" to "scientific fact," which led the jury to ignore the large number of bullets in circulation, and so prejudiced the jury that its verdict must be set aside. The Supreme Court of New Jersey observed that:

> [E]xcessive statements from both sides are a regrettable fact of life in criminal trials. In such trials, an objection by counsel remains as the first line of defense. Although the prosecutor's statement may have been more temperate, it, particularly in the absence of an objection, does not justify upsetting the jury verdict. Given the realities of adversary proceedings, the prosecutor's remarks pass as fair comment.[64]

V. INCOMPETENCY OF COUNSEL

In *Boyd v. State*,[65] the defendant was convicted for intentionally murdering Evelyn Blackmon and Fred Blackmon during the course of a robbery and kidnaping. Accomplice Milstead testified at trial that Boyd took Milstead's gun and shot the victims. Among the claims made in a postconviction petition were that his trial and appellate counsel were ineffective, in part for failing to attack the state's ballistic experts aggressively. The defendant maintained that it was essential that his attorneys impeach the credibility of the state's forensic experts who gave evidence regarding which wounds were caused by which firearms, what kind of wounds the victims suffered, and how long after the infliction of the wounds they died. Boyd maintained that such testimony was most likely used to support the trial court's finding of "heinous, atrocious, or cruel aggravating factor," justifying the death penalty, as well as to bolster the prosecutor's theory of how the murders occurred. The court ruled that the testimony of a ballistics expert would not have resolved who pulled the trigger, and thus failed to see how a court-financed ballistics expert could have impeached accomplice Milstead's testimony regarding who shot the victims.

In *Commonwealth v. Wallace*,[66] the defendant was convicted of first-degree murder and was sentenced to death. The defendant appealed, arguing, among others, on the grounds of incompetency of counsel regarding the ballistics testimony admitted against him.

On August 17, 1979, Henry Brown and William Wallace, Jr. robbed Carl's Cleaners in Cannonsburg, Pennsylvania, in the course of which defendant Wallace allegedly shot and killed the store owner and a 15-year-old employee, Tina Spalla. Wallace argued that his trial counsel was ineffective in failing to obtain an independent ballistics analysis of the bullet recovered from the body of Tina Spalla. At trial, the prosecution's theory was that Wallace had shot both victims with a .32-caliber handgun, and that while accomplice Henry Brown had carried a .38-caliber handgun, he had not fired at either victim. Brown's .38-caliber handgun was recovered and admitted as evidence at trial, but the .32-caliber murder weapon was never located.

State Trooper Daryl W. Mayfield, a ballistics expert for the State Police Crime Laboratory, examined the bullet slugs recovered from the victims' bodies and testified that they were all .32-caliber. However, Dr. Ernest Abernathy, the pathologist who performed the autopsies on the victims, testified that the bullet he removed from the body of Tina Spalla appeared to him, upon visual inspection, to be .38-caliber. Wallace argued that in light of Dr. Abernathy's testimony, and given the fact that Brown was carrying a .38-caliber weapon, his lawyer should have sought an independent ballistics analysis to assess definitively the caliber of the bullet that killed Tina Spalla.[67]

The court found this argument to be without merit, noting initially that no credible issue existed regarding the caliber of the slug. Dr. Abernathy was a pathologist who simply inspected the bullet visually and concluded that it was .38-caliber. Trooper Mayfield, on the other hand, was a state police ballistics expert who performed a laboratory analysis of the bullet and determined that it was .32-caliber. In any event, the court concluded, it was clear that counsel's decision not to pursue an independent analysis was motivated by trial strategy, counsel being concerned that if they had a ballistics analysis establishing that the bullet was indeed a .32-caliber, they would lose any reasonable doubt that they thought they could create. In light of this, the court concluded, the defendant's claim of incompetency of counsel failed.

VI. WOUND ANALYSIS AND BALLISTICS

Ballistics-related testimony is often linked with wound analysis testimony by forensic pathologists to determine the relative location of shooter and victim by way of powder residue or stippling effects. Several recent examples are briefly examined below. It should be noted here, in a related matter, that the tests utilized to determine gunshot residue on the hands or clothing of the shooter or victim remain controversial. The article, "Firearms Evidence," contained in the recent INTERPOL Forensic Science Symposium,[68] notes that the introduction of lead-free ammunition has had a noticeable impact on the testing for gunshot residue:

> Recent contacts with ammunition showed that increasingly more manufacturers include lead-free ammunition in their assortment. The use of lead-free ammunition is steadily rising, but it has not yet resulted in an increasing number of publications in the field of investigation of lead-free gunshot residues.[69]

In *Quince v. State*,[70] the body of Verbena High School English teacher and coach Michael Bernos was discovered in his home, sitting in a chair in front of his television. He had been shot 15 times, predominantly in the head and chest. At trial, the state asked a Dr. Lauridson to give his "medical opinion as to the position Coach Bernos was in as he was being shot and the existence of 1 or 2 gunmen in delivering the wounds." Defense counsel objected to Dr. Lauridson's testimony, on the basis that it was clearly outside of his field of expertise. The trial court overruled Quince's objection on those same grounds, stating that whether there were 2 gunmen was out of Dr. Lauridson's expertise, but that Dr. Lauridson could give an opinion regarding the position of the victim's body.[71]

In the case of *State v. Harris*,[72] a coroner and expert in forensic pathology testified that the victim suffered a gunshot wound to the nose, causing damage and hemorrhage to the brain which resulted in death. He testified that there were areas around the wound that were burned by the powder from the weapon, which is known as stippling, and that there was soot on the bridge of the nose and the forehead, indicating that the weapon was relatively close to the victim. He also stated that a ballistics expert would be the best person to testify regarding how close the weapon was when it was fired.

Jim Churchman, a forensic scientist at the State Police Crime Laboratory, was accepted by the court as a forensics expert with special expertise in the field of ballistics dealing with gunpowder residue and the calculation of the distance from a shooter to the target. He testified that he had considerable experience dealing with the Colt .357 revolver, the weapon used in this shooting. He described his history of performing firing tests of the Colt .357 revolver to determine the distance from the shooter to the victim. He testified that, from the amount of soot and stippling omitted when a weapon is discharged, he could determine how far away the weapon was from the target. Here, he testified that, based on the photographs of the victim and the concentrated soot residue around the entrance wound, the gun was approximately 4 to 8 inches away from the victim when fired. He also testified that the powder particles would diminish at distances of greater than 1 foot. Expert Churchman admitted that he did not actually test-fire the weapon involved in this shooting.

State v. Myszka[73] involved the murder of a woman whom police found dead in her bedroom as a result of a gunshot wound to her chest. A .32 Derringer pistol was removed from her left hand. The deceased was right-handed.

The state's ballistic firearm expert testified that he found no gunpowder residue on the shirt which the deceased wore at the time of her death. He further testified that he test-fired the gun and found that at 20 inches, gunpowder residue would be present on the garment, meaning that the gun had to have been fired at a distance greater than 20 inches from the wound. Based on this, he concluded that this gunshot would have been inconsistent with the deceased shooting herself. The medical examiner testified that it would be impossible for the gunshot wound on the deceased to have been self-inflicted, given the autopsy report on the deceased and the ballistics report. Dr. Bonita Peterson, who performed the autopsy, testified that, "with the left hand," a suicide "would be "difficult and awkward" or "may not even be possible."[74] Dr. Peterson testified that the path of the bullet was at a very slight upward angle and at about a 20 degree angle to the left. She opined that it may not have been physically possible for the deceased to shoot herself with her left hand. She also testified that there was no sooting or tattooing in the deceased's gunshot wound, indicating that the gun was not close to and not in contact with the skin. Finally, the medical examiner testified that it would be impossible for the gunshot wound on the deceased to have been self-inflicted, because the ballistics report concluded that the gun had to have been fired more than 20 inches away and because of the wound track, angle, and characteristics reported by Dr. Peterson.[75] The court concluded that the killing was neither an accident nor a suicide, but a homicide:

This is substantial evidence from which a jury could find that the death of the victim was not the result of an accident. Under the evidence at trial, a reasonable juror could find beyond a reasonable doubt that the Appellant was guilty of second degree murder. The State provided ample evidence to prove the *corpus delicti*. The evidence showed the gunshot was not self-inflicted, and certainly not a natural event. Nor was any evidence offered to show that the gunshot was the result of an accident. This leaves one possibility: Appellant shot the victim.[76]

VII. TOOL MARK CASES

Tool mark evidence continues to be part of the forensic science corpus of disciplines used in criminal case investigations and trials. The idea encompasses striation marking made in wood, putty, and other media that must be forced to gain entry to property, or, in rare cases, used to cause blunt trauma to an assault or homicide victim. Pry bars, screwdrivers, knives, pliers, crowbars, wire cutters, bolt cutters, and a host of other tools may leave striation marking in building media that can provide valuable trace evidence and possible identifications. Building materials such as paint, brick, or glass may also attach themselves to the tool itself and thereby provide a possibility of linkage.[77] Tool mark "matching" is still far from confident, given the nature of the malleable medium that typically contains the mark. Nonetheless, recent decisions have had little difficulty accepting expert opinion based upon it.

In *People v. Genrich*,[78] the defendant was convicted of use of explosives to commit a felony, third-degree assault, and two counts of extreme-indifference homicide. The disputed evidence consisted of testimony from a Bureau of Alcohol, Tobacco, and Firearms (BATF) expert that 3 different sets of pliers recovered from the defendant were used in making one or more of the bombs used. According to this witness, one set of the defendant's pliers was used to cut certain wire, the wire strippers were used to cut a different wire, and a third wire was used to fasten a cap to the pipe. The witness also testified that wires used in two of the bombs came from the same batch of wire.

The defendant, reciting the standard objections to "nonscientific" evidence, contended that the evidence was not based on a theory generally accepted in the scientific community, that no techniques in the examination were capable of producing reliable results, and that the prosecution's expert did not use tests that followed accepted scientific techniques. The prosecution offered to prove that tool mark identification evidence had been accepted in a number of courts throughout the U.S. over an extended period of time and hence an evidentiary hearing was unnecessary.

The defendant noted that the BATF agent who served as the prosecution's expert did not have any post-high-school formal education, that no standard curriculum had been developed to train tool mark examiners, and that no national certification program was available to confirm the knowledge and training of this type of expert. The defendant also pointed out that, unlike fingerprint or ballistics testing, no data bank has been established relative to the various types of hand tools. In the present case, defense counsel argued that the examination of only two consecutively manufactured tools was insufficient to support the expert's claim that every tool leaves a mark or marks different from every other tool.[79]

The court of appeal found no error in the trial court ruling, noting:

> [T]hat the record reflected that the basic premise for toolmark analysis was that hand tools used either to cut or to clamp softer materials may leave a specific and essentially permanent type of mark on that material. The softer material is examined under a microscope that magnifies the marks to 80 times their original size. The handbook can then be examined to determine whether the marks were left by that specific tool.

> According to this expert, no two tools make exactly the same mark on softer material either because of the manufacturing process or because of the subsequent use or misuse of the tool. In this regard, the witness stated that he had never encountered any research or other data indicating that any two hand tools of the same type can make the same mark.[80]

Legal research demonstrated that experts in the use and analysis of tools have traditionally and consistently been allowed to testify concerning the marks left by such instruments.[81] Hence, there was ample legal support for the trial court's conclusion that this type of evidence is accepted.

The court noted that neither college degrees nor formal training in an established curriculum were necessarily required before one may be considered an expert in a particular field. The absence of clear points of comparison or data banks relative to tool examination did not render the analysis inherently unreliable:

> The critical factors are the marks, as magnified by the microscope, on the materials used in the bombs and similar test materials and the examination of the cutting or clamping face of the tool itself . . . . The expert's premise, that no two tools make exactly the same mark, is not challenged by any evidence in this record. Hence, the lack of a database and points of comparison does not render the opinion inadmissible.[82]

The court concluded that the defendant's objections and arguments addressed the weight to be accorded the expert's opinion and that no pretrial evidentiary hearing was required.

The impact of modern forensics on the solution of old or "cold files" is demonstrated by a fascinating example in the case of *State v. Parsons*.[83] There, the defendant was found guilty and sentenced for the 1981 murder of his wife, Barbara Parsons. On the afternoon of February 11, 1981, Sherry Parsons discovered her mother's body lying at the foot of her parents' bed in their Norwalk, Ohio home. Barbara Parsons had been beaten to death. The murder investigation soon centered on appellant James Parsons, the decedent's husband, when it was discovered that the Parsons were considering a divorce.

Norwalk police interviewed several persons associated with the appellant including a mechanic who was employed at the appellant's garage. The mechanic told police of an unusual statement the appellant had made, where he announced that a "half-inch breaker bar," which had been missing from the appellant's tool set, had been left in a car he had sold to a friend 2 weeks earlier. Prosecutors labeled this statement as an attempt to establish an "alibi" for the murder weapon.

The detectives traced the car to Arizona, recovered the bar, and returned to Ohio, where the bar was examined. Criminalists, however, found no traces of blood or other material that might link the bar to the murder, and it was returned to Norwalk where it was stored in the police property room along with the bloodstained sheets, clothing, and other physical evidence taken from the crime scene. That evidence remained in storage for nearly a decade. During that time the case, although nominally still open, was not actively investigated by police.

In 1990, a new detective was assigned to review the case; he looked at the evidence collected in 1981, and believed that he saw a match of marks on the bloody sheets and the bar. The sheets and breaker bar were tested by the forensic experts at the Cuyahoga County Coroner's Office and the Ohio Bureau of Criminal Investigation (BCI). These experts testified that they found numerous impressions in blood on the sheets consistent with the breaker bar retrieved from Arizona in 1981. Importantly, the experts testified that none of the impressions were inconsistent with the breaker bar. The BCI expert testified that by chemically enhancing the bloodstains on the sheets, letters from the word "Craftsman" on the breaker bar could be seen and that the marks found in bloodstains on the nightgown Barbara Parsons was wearing "matched" "individuating" abnormalities unique to the breaker bar. This evidence gave clear support to the verdict against the husband:

> [F]rom the ferocity of the attack on Barbara Parsons it can be reasonably inferred that whoever killed her intended to do so. The only real issue at trial was the identity of that actor. It was unquestioned that appellant owned a Craftsman half-inch breaker bar. There was expert forensic testimony that a specific Craftsman half-inch breaker bar left identifiable impressions in blood at the murder scene and that the shape and design of the bar was consistent with the wounds Barbara Parsons received. This specific Craftsman breaker bar was found under the seat of a car appellant sold to Neil Burras.[84]

At a bare minimum, the court concluded, this was evidence by which reasonable minds could differ regarding appellant's culpability.

Finally, in *State v. Hill*,[85] the defendant was convicted of aggravated murder. The coroner testified that the victim, the defendant's mother, died as a result of 10 stab wounds to her chest and back. Some were inflicted with "considerable force." One knife wound perforated the heart and nicked a lung, two others punctured a lung and broke ribs, and another perforated the scapula or wing bone. No defensive-type wounds were evident. The victim, aged 61 years, had been partly paralyzed from a stroke. The defendant told detectives that around March 23 he had been driving in his mother's car and using cocaine, but denied any knowledge of his mother's death. Detectives talked with Hill's brother. Police further learned that the mother never let either son drive her car without her being present. The police searched the victim's Oldsmobile and found a tire tool, two $20 bills, and two $1 bills in the trunk. One $1 bill was stained with type A blood, which was the victim's blood type. Microscopic examination of the tire tool revealed microscopic brass flakes matching the composition of a brass door protector on the victim's apartment door and the brass protector appeared to have "fresh jimmy marks." The black paint on that protector matched the painted tire tool.[86]

RESEARCH NOTE

The Journal of Forensic Sciences is the official publication of the American Academy of Forensic Sciences. By visiting the Academy's Web site at *http://www.aafs.org* and clicking on the "Journal of Forensic Sciences" link, one can get to a searchable index of the journal from 1981 to the present that uses common search terms. The site also provides tables of contents for more recent issues of the journal, and, for a modest fee, one can download individual articles from issues published after January 1, 1999. The index, content, and article availability site is maintained by the publisher of the journal, The American Society for Testing and Materials (ASTM). There are current plans to move toward Web-based publication of the journal, although the paper copy will still be available for some time. Individual subscriptions to this essential journal are also available from ASTM for those interested.

Visiting this important Web site on a regular basis and viewing the available abstracts are essential to the early stages of forensic science/forensic evidence research. Also see the recent bibliography prepared by Dr. W.J.J. Sprangers, E. van Leuvan, R. Walunga, R. Beijer, and G.A.L. Dofferhoff, "Firearms Evidence," in *Proceedings of the 12th INTERPOL Forensic Science Symposium* (1998), at 303–331.

ENDNOTES

1. The Dialog Information Service's massive collection of bibliographic and full-text databases, accessible through Westlaw, provides a window for incredibly detailed information queries into the biotech, manufacturing, and chemical industries and research centers.
2. Generally, see Saferstein: *Criminalistics: An Introduction to Forensic Science* (6th ed. Prentice-Hall, Upper Saddle River, NJ, 1998) at 466–492; Giannelli and Imwinkelried: *Scientific Evidence* (2d ed. Michie Co., Charlottesville, VA, 1993) at 374, 375–408; Fisher: *Techniques of Crime Scene Investigation* (5th ed. CRC Press, Boca Raton, FL, 1993) at 272–303; Geberth: *Practical Homicide Investigation: Tactics, Procedures, Techniques* (3d ed. CRC Press, Boca Raton, FL, 1996) at 283–291, 513–517. Also see Sprangers et al., "Firearms Evidence," *Proceedings of the 12th INTERPOL Forensic Science Symposium*, October 2–23 1998 (The Forensic Sciences Foundation Press, New York, 1998) at 136–151 for a very extensive international bibliography of literature published between July 1995 and May 1998.
3. *Id.*
4. See Saferstein, *supra*, note 2, at 466–474; Giannelli and Imwinkelried, *supra*, note 2, at 378–382. For more recent general Internet-based discussions, see "F.B.I. Handbook of Forensic Services: Firearms Examinations," at *http://www.fbi.gov/lab/handbook/*

examfire.htm. Also see the excellent page maintained by Jeffrey Scott Doyle, a Kentucky State Police firearm and tool mark examiner located at *http://www.firearmsID.com.* This is an first-rate example of the potential for forensic science on the Internet, containing large amounts of information and excellent graphics. Also see the Firearm Image Library, a large collection of images of weapons with basic descriptions of weapon configurations and ammunition, located at *http://www.recguns.com.*

5. See Giannelli and Imwinkelried, *supra,* note 2, at 380. The authors of the recent INTERPOL study of ballistics research note the recent publication of a large number of world studies on wound ballistics. See Sprangers et al., *supra,* note 2, at 138.

6. The historical types of gunshot residue tests include paraffin testing, Harrison-Gilroy Neutron Activator Analysis (NAA), ASV, SEM, and trace metal detection technique (TNDT) for metal traces. These tests attempt to determine if the defendant shot a gun or was present and if the shooting was a suicide or a homicide. See Saferstein, *supra,* note 2, at 478; Giannelli and Imwinkelried, *supra,* note 2, at 394 et seq.; *Proceedings of the 12th INTERPOL Forensic Science Symposium, supra,* note 2, at 136; Fisher, *supra,* note 2, at 167–168, 277–280; Geberth, *supra,* note 2, at 199–201.

7. *Massachusetts v. Sacco and Vanzetti: Closing Argument by the Commonwealth.* Also see Thorvald: *The Century of the Detective* (Harcourt, Brace and World, New York, 1965) at 417 et seq.; Starrs: Once More into the Breech: The Firearms Evidence in the Sacco and Vanzetti Case Revisited, 31 *J. Forensic Sci.* 630 (1986) [Part I]; 31 *J. Forensic Sci.* 1050 (1986) [Part II]. See also Frankfurter: "The Case of Sacco and Vanzetti," *Atlantic Monthly* (March 1927).

8. See James E. Hamby: "The History of Firearm and Toolmark Identification," *Assoc. of Firearm and Toolmark Examiners J.,* 30th Anniversary edition, Vol. 31, No. 3 (Summer 1999), set out in full at *http://www.firearmsID.com/A_historyoffirearmsID.htm.* Also see Thorvald, *supra,* note 7, at 417 et seq.

9. Robert W. Sibert: *DRUGFIRE: Revolutionizing Forensic Firearms Identification and Providing the Foundation for a National Firearms Identification Network* (Federal Bureau of Investigation, April, 1996). Also see "Definitions and Guidelines for the Use of Imaging Technologies in the Criminal Justice System," Scientific Working Group on Imaging Technologies (SWGIT), located on the FBI Web site at *http://www.fbi.gov/ programs/lab/fsc/current/swgit1.htm.* A recent initiative will utilize manufacturer-supplied data to increase the "fingerprinting" capability of DRUGFIRE, leading to a known shell casing or projectile fingerprint for all weapons. See "U.S. to Develop a System for 'Fingerprinting' Guns," Fox Butterfield, *New York Times,* Monday, December 20, 1999.

10. See Lena Klasen: "Image Analysis," *Proceedings of the 12th INTERPOL Forensic Science Symposium, supra,* note 2, at 261. This is an excellent paper setting forth the history and current status of the equipment, software, and related topics in this technology of the 21st century criminal investigator.

11. Sibert, *supra,* note 9, at 2. DRUGFIRE's emphasis has been on the comparison of cartridge case imagery, rather than bullet imagery. Nevertheless, images of highly characteristic bullet striations can be stored in the DRUGFIRE system as supplemental images and compared. DRUGFIRE represents a major technological advancement in the discipline of forensic firearms identification. The same computer hardware that runs DRUGFIRE can be used to store an image database of firearm and ammunition exemplars from the FBI Laboratory's Reference Firearms Collection and Standard Ammunition File. This collection is the largest and most comprehensive in the world.

12. See, e.g., Sprangers et al., *supra,* note 2, at 138.

13. *Id.*
14. However, see In re Petition of Louis Vazquez, v. Howard Safir, 673 N.Y.S.2d 12 (N.Y.A.D. 1 Dept. 1998), where a proceeding was brought by police officer challenging his dismissal from the police department, in that the officer, while off-duty, discharged multiple rounds from a gun he owned, other than his service weapon, thereafter failed to report the incident promptly, and then made false and misleading statements concerning the incident. Although ballistics evidence established that many of the shell casings found at the scene were fired from the gun in question, other ballistics evidence stated that there was no indication of discharge present in the bore of the gun in question. The testimony and reports of investigators concerning their interviews of witnesses, either supporting or not inconsistent with petitioner's claim that he did not fire his gun, raised issues of weight of the evidence and credibility that were beyond judicial review in such proceedings.
15. See State v. Fulminante, 193 Ariz. 485, 975 P.2d 75 (1999).
16. Manning v. State, 726 So.2d 1152 (Miss.Sp.Ct. 1998).
17. *Id.* at 1181. The same level of acceptance of fingerprint identifications has resulted in modern cases increasingly discussing the failure to look for fingerprints by the police in areas where they would have been expected to be found, as inuring to the benefit of the defendant when challenging the state's crime scene investigation.
18. Smoote v. State, 708 N.E.2d 1 (Ind.Sp.Ct. 1999).
19. *Id.* at 3.
20. *Id.*
21. People v. Askew, 273 Ill.App.3d 798, 652 N.E.2d 1045 (1st Dist.App. 1995).
22. *Id.* at 809.
23. See People v. Lee, 242 Ill.App.3d 40, 42–43, 610 N.E.2d 727 (1993).
24. Askew, *supra*, note 21, at 810. Also see *People v. Lee, supra,* note 23, at 43, 729.
25. *Id.*, note 21, at 810.
26. People v. Walters, 251 A.D.2d 433, 674 N.Y.S.2d 114 (1998).
27. *Id.* at 435.
28. People v. Jackson, 299 Ill.App.3d 323, 702 N.E.2d 590 (1998).
29. *Id.* at 593, 253.
30. *Id.* Also see Commonwealth v. Dennis, 715 A.2d 404 (1998), where the commonwealth presented the testimony of 3 eyewitnesses, as well as evidence that defendant had a gun of the type used in the murder and clothing resembling that worn by the perpetrator. Although the murder weapon was never recovered, a ballistics expert testified that there was a 99% chance that the bullet that killed the victim was fired from a Harrington and Richardson handgun.
31. Commonwealth v. Busch, 427 Mass. 26, 691 N.E.2d 218 (Sp.Ct 1998).
32. State v. Treadwell, 577 N.W.2d 387 (1998).
33. Commonwealth v. Spotz, 552 Pa. 499, 716 A.2d 580 (1998).
34. Jones v. State, 709 So.2d 512 (1998).
35. *Id.* at 516.
36. State v. Lyons, 91 Wash.App. 1019, 1998 WL 293758 (Wash.App.Div. 2).
37. 1998 WL 293758, at *1.
38. *Id.* at *3.
39. People v. Torres, 269 Ill.App.3d 339, 645 N.E.2d 1018 (1995).
40. *Id.* at 345.
41. The defendant claimed that the weapon he fired was the one found by Officer Kaminski in his room. Prosecutors countered that the gun was found fully loaded

and there was no opportunity for the defendant to have reloaded the weapon between the time of the shooting and when the officer found it. Consequently, prosecutors said, that gun could not have been the one the defendant fired. Rather, the prosecution opined, the "fatal" gun may have still been on the defendant's person when he brushed past the officer who searched his room, and he may have disposed of it outside during the commotion and milling about that went on after his room was searched, but prior to his arrest. *Id.*

42. *Id.* at 347, 1024.
43. *Id.* at 348.
44. Also see State v. Ward, 712 A. 2d 534 (Md.Ct.App. 1998), for an exhaustive discussion of the issue in search warrant suppression cases, whether there was probable cause to believe that instrumentalities and evidence of a street murder could be found in the residence and/or motor vehicle of the person identified as the murderer. The court held that there was probable cause.
45. Cammon v. State, 269 Ga. 470, 500 S.E.2d 329 (1998).
46. *Id.*
47. Whites v. State, 730 So.2d 762 (Fla.App. 5 Dist. 1999).
48. *Id.* at 764.
49. Fulminante, *supra*, note 15.
50. *Id.* at 80, 490. In Fulminante II, the U.S. Supreme Court held that defendant's confession was coerced. The court found the admission prejudicial, in part because both the trial court and the state recognized that a successful prosecution depended on the jury believing the 2 confessions. Absent the confessions, the court determined, it was unlikely that Fulminante would have been prosecuted at all, because the physical evidence from the scene and the other circumstantial evidence would have been insufficient to convict.
51. *Id.* at 83, 493.
52. *Id.*
53. United States v. Davis, 103 F.3d 660 (8th Cir. 1996).
54. *Id.* at 666.
55. *Id.* at 673.
56. *Id.* at 674.
57. *Id.*
58. State v. Noel, 157 N.J. 141, 723 A.2d 602 (1999).
59. *Id.* at 145, 604.
60. IAP analysis of lead bullets is a process generally accepted by the scientific community and producing sufficiently reliable results to warrant the admission of expert testimony regarding the test and the test results. See, e.g., Bryan v. Oklahoma, 935 P.2d 338 (Okla.Crim.App. 1997); United States v. Davis, 103 F.3d 660 (8th Cir. 1996), cert. denied, 117 S.Ct. 2424, 138 L.Ed.2d 187 (1997); State v. Freeman, 531 N.W.2d 190 (Minn. 1995); State v. Strain, 885 P.2d 810 (Utah.Ct.App. 1994); State v. Grube, 126 Idaho 377, 883 P.2d 1069 (1994), cert. denied, 514 U.S. 1098, 115 S.Ct. 1828, 131 L. Ed.2d 749 (1995); People v. Johnson, 114 Ill.2d 170, 102 Ill.Dec. 342, 499 N.E.2d 1355 (1986), cert. denied, 480 U.S. 951, 107 S.Ct. 1618, 94 L. Ed.2d 802, reh'g denied, 481 U.S. 1060, 107 S.Ct. 2205, 95 L. Ed.2d 860 (1987); State v. Ware, 338 N.W.2d 707 (Iowa 1983); Jones v. State, 425 N.E.2d 128 (Ind. 1981) (Hunter, J. dissenting). See also Erwin S. Barbre: "Annotation, Admissibility of Evidence of Neutron Activation Analysis," 50 *A.L.R.*3d 117 (1973) and supplemental service.

61. *Supra*, note 58, at 162.
62. *Id*. at 604. See State v. Koedatich, 112 N.J. 225, 548 A.2d 939 (1988); State v. Hollander, 201 N.J.Super. 453, 467–68, 493 A.2d 563 (App.Div. 1985).
63. *Id*. at 150. See Hake v. Township of Manchester, 98 N.J. 302, 316, 486 A.2d 836 (1985); Landrigan v. Celotex Corp., 127 N.J. 404, 421–22, 605 A.2d 1079 (1992) (permitting epidemiologist to testify that asbestos can cause colon cancer); Rubanick v. Witco Chemical Corp., 125 N.J. 421, 426, 452, 593 A.2d 733 (1991) (allowing biochemist to testify that PCBs can cause colon cancer).
64. *Id*. at 607, 152.
65. Boyd v. State, 1999 WL 172985 (Ala.Crim.App. 1998).
66. Commonwealth v. Wallace, 724 A.2d 916 (Sp. Ct. Penn. 1999).
67. *Id*. at 925.
68. See Sprangers et al., *supra*, note 2, at 136–137.
69. *Id*.
70. Quince v. State, 721 So.2d 245 (Ala.Crim.App. 1998).
71. *Id*. at 249.
72. State v. Harris, 708 So.2d 1169 (La.App. 1998).
73. State v. Myszka, 963 S.W.2d 19 (Mo.App 1998).
74. *Id*. at 22.
75. *Id*.
76. *Id*. at 24.
77. See Fisher, *supra*, note 2, at 173–178; Saferstein, *supra*, note 2. Also see Christophe Champod and Pierre A. Margot: Fingermarks, Shoesole Impressions, Ear Impressions and Toolmarks," *Proceedings of the 12th INTERPOL Forensic Science Symposium* (The Forensic Sciences Foundation Press, New York, 1998) at 303, 313.
78. People v. Genrich, 928 P.2d 799 (Colo.Ct.App. 1996).
79. *Id*. at 801.
80. *Id*. at 802.
81. See, e.g., State v. Baldwin, 36 An. 1, 12 P. 318 (1886) (experienced carpenters permitted to testify that wood panel could have been cut by defendant's knife); A. Moenssens and F. Inbau, *Scientific Evidence in Criminal Cases* 4.24 (2d ed., Foundation Press, New York, 1978). Also, this testimony has addressed a number of different types of tools. See State v. Olsen, 212 Or. 191, 317 P.2d 938 (1957) (hammers); State v. Raines, 29 N.C.App. 303, 224 S.E.2d 232 (1976) (crowbar); State v. Wessling, 260 Iowa 1244, 150 N.W.2d 301 (1967) (screwdriver); State v. Churchill, 231 An. 408, 646 P.2d 1049 (1982) (knives).
82. *Supra*, note 78, at 802.
83. State v. Parsons, 1995 WL 29526 (Ohio App. 6 Dist.).
84. *Id*. at *8.
85. State v. Hill, 73 Ohio St.3d 433, 653 N.E.2d 271 (1995).
86. *Id*. at 275.

6 Soil, Glass, and Paint

The finest line that can be drawn upon the smoothest paper still has jagged edges if seen through a microscope. This does not matter until important deductions are made on the supposition that there are no jagged edges.

—Samuel Butler[1]

I. INTRODUCTION

This chapter addresses the efforts of forensic science to provide both general and individual linking evidence to be used in cases involving laboratory analysis of glass shards, paint, or soil taken from a crime scene. The microscopic examination of these items, found at many crime scenes, are, like the others discussed so far, basically an observational discipline, but much more involved with chemical analyses than hair, fiber, ballistics, or tool mark examinations. Nonetheless, the recurring questions posed in the preceding chapters regarding the ultimate legal value to be given the offerings of forensic science apply equally here.[2]

II. GLASS ANALYSIS

A. GENERAL

The subject of glass as forensic evidence typically involves crushed glass, glass shards, or portions of a glass pane, present at the crime scene, as a result of an illegal entry or some type of violence causing the glass to disintegrate in some form. As with all of the forensic sciences, glass analysis can offer a wealth of class characteristic as well as individual linkage evidence. Also, as with the greatest number of the forensic sciences, such information is used to place the defendant at the crime scene or somehow connect him to it. Placing the suspect at the crime scene goes a long way toward charging and convicting him.

The class characteristic data that may result from a close chemical and microscopic analysis includes, initially, a determination of the type of glass involved. What kind of glass is it? What is its source? What is there to compare with glass associated with the defendant? Does the condition of the glass located at the scene indicate how or if glass shards or spray could have been transferred to a suspect, such as on shoes, clothing, or automobile carpeting?[3]

There are many types of "glass" that may be generally identified with great precision:

- Window glass.
- Plate glass.
- Safety glass.
- Automobile window safety glass.
- Automobile headlamp glass.
- Tinted glass of all types.
- Eyeglasses glass (prescription if large enough shards).
- Bottle glass.
- Antique glass.
- Architectural glass (shower stalls).
- Glass beads.
- Pyrex and other cooking glass.
- Clay, fired surfaces plates, dishes, etc.
- Crystal.

Class characteristic information that can often be made with confidence include the kind of glass it is, to a degree, the nature of the impacting projectile, the direction of impact (in or out), type of glass cutters used, and comparisons for potential jigsaw "matching" of shards. It should be noted that the microscopic presence of glass is ubiquitous in modern urban life. Tiny glass particles are commonly found on shoe soles and clothing. Giannelli and Imwinkelried cite studies indicating that 67 of 100 men's suits examined at a dry cleaners contained glass fragments.[4] Given the extensive presence of glass particles picked up in our daily transit, it is especially important to be able to discriminate among the various types of glass products before any attempt is made to link a suspect to a crime scene. The greatest amount of manufactured glass in the U.S. has a soda-lime base, and the nature of the glass components visually and chemically differs with the proposed commercial or artistic use.[5]

As with all forensic sciences, a comparison is typically made of whatever there is to compare of crime scene material and similar material associated with a suspect, to obtain a "match." As noted throughout this book, a clear distinction must be continuously made between what the forensic scientist sees as a laboratory match and what the courts will allow to be said about any such finding. Here, as in the other forensic sciences, with the possible exception of fingerprints and DNA, the opinion in court must be couched in the language of "consistent with," "not dissimilar," etc.

Comparison of a crime scene datum with that found to be associated with the suspect is the central idea of forensic evidence. Given the extraordinary length of the DNA testimony in the O. J. Simpson murder trial, is is good to remember that the sole purpose of it was to place him at the crime scene. Like hair, fiber, ballistics, and tool marks, we need to inquire initially, what comparisons *can* be made here? Glass, paint, and soil can equally be broken down into component parts that may yield worthwhile comparisons leading to legally significant linkage testimony. As in most other of the forensic disciplines, there are no definitive databases with which to determine the frequency of any stated "match" occurring in the general population. However, because of the considerable commercial attention given to proprietary differences in the world glass industry and the consistent collection of glass data by the FBI, progress is being made in that respect.[6]

Most commonly used comparison analyses utilize a combination of physical and chemical properties, such as refraction indexes, dispersion staining, density, chemical components, mineral content, and color. As recently noted in the *Proceedings of the 12th INTERPOL Forensic Science Symposium:*

> Recent advances in analytical capabilities for the trace element characterisation of glass fragments have provided a high degree of discrimination between glass fragments that was previously not available with the physical property comparisons. There has been considerable interest in the probability of transfer of glass fragments and their retention on the clothing of a suspect of glass breaking.[7]

The increased cooperation with the glass industry and their significant proprietary databases, as with fiber, tire tracks, and shoe impressions, will allow for rapid strides in the establishment of meaningful databases with which to engage in population percentage projection regarding proffered "match" opinions.[8]

B. Glass Analysis Cases

There are a number of case reports addressing several applications of the forensic examination of glass, in one or more of the aspects noted above. The transfer of glass fragments from the crime scene with something, typically items of clothing, is most prevalent.

In *People v. Dailey*,[9] the defendant was convicted of burglary. The appellate court held that evidence of tests on bits of glass found on the defendant's sweatshirt, which were performed to establish the defendant's presence at the scene of the crime, was properly admitted.

When the victims of the burglary were returning from a family outing they noted a car parked in front of their house, which was stipulated to be the defendant's car. When they opened the overhead garage doors, the wife walked into the garage, which was attached to the house, and noticed that the rear door of the garage was open. She closed and locked the door, a wooden door with 8 panes of glass in the middle. The 9-year-old son entered the house first and made some noise. There was a 75-watt bulb lighted inside the house in the area of the door. The chain lock on the door had been broken.[10]

As the wife entered the house, she saw a man with a hooded blue sweatshirt coming down the hall toward her. The man ran toward the rear door of the garage, found it locked, and proceeded to break the 4 center sections of glass, pulled the wooden frame out, and escaped. As the man returned to get his car, the husband caught and held him until he was arrested.

Three different samples of glass were tested. The first was made of samples of glass that had fallen on the floor in the garage, and these tests showed that the glass from the garage door was different from the glass found on the defendant's sweatshirt. On the day before the trial, the victim brought some more glass from the garage door to the state's attorney, and the second test resulted in testimony that there was a high probability that the sample from the glass on the sweatshirt and the sample brought in at that time were part and parcel of the same piece of glass. Four different panes were brought in for the second test—two were from panes broken by the burglar and two were not. They were unmarked. The defendant presented the results of the third test, which allegedly determined that the glass fragments from the sweatshirt could not have originated from the immediate area of the glass taken from the defendant's storm door. The defendant argued that such tests were inconsistent and therefore threw grave doubt on the validity of the tests performed by the state's expert witness. The court rejected that argument, holding:

> However, these conclusions are truly not inconsistent, because as the trial judge noted there might have been glass on the defendant's sweat shirt from both the defendant's broken storm door and from the victims' garage door. The expert's testimony was that two samples of the glass had the same refractive indices and densities as did the matching samples and came from the same source.[11]

The defendant sought to keep this testimony out on the basis that it was irrelevant and that the tests came too late in the trial and thus were unfair to the defendant. The defendant had relied on the first test indicating no connection between the broken glass and the glass on the defendant's sweatshirt. The defense contended that this all came as a surprise and that the results of the new tests were inadmissible.

The court ruled that in the absence of a showing in the record that the defendant either requested or was refused additional time in which to prepare his case, a reviewing court would not remand for a new trial on the grounds that the defendant did not have an adequate opportunity to prepare his defense. In the case at bar, the defendant did not accept the continuance offered by the court.

In *People v. Pruitt*,[12] the defendant was convicted in Circuit Court, Winnebago County, Illinois, of armed robbery. The defendant allegedly robbed a Minit-Mart Grocery store in New Milford, Illinois. Two men armed with revolvers, and wearing gloves and disguised with false black beards, entered the grocery store and demanded money from the owner, who placed approximately $500 in a bag. The two men left with the money in a light-colored, 1960, four-door Oldsmobile, Deputy Sheriff Billy Gene Burgess received a radio alert and spotted a car that fit the description of the car used in the robbery. Burgess pursued the Oldsmobile and when the driver ignored his police light, he continued the pursuit in his own car until the Oldsmobile collided with another vehicle. Three men emerged from the Oldsmobile and attempted to escape on foot. Officer Burgess apprehended one of the men, Raymond Fuller, and other officers arrested the other two men, one of whom was the defendant in this case.

Detectives looked inside the 1960 Oldsmobile and observed a .38-caliber revolver with brown handles, and the bottom part of a beard or wig. Two guns were found nearby. A search of the car revealed a bag containing $354.90 in cash and $44.05 in checks identified by the proprietor as checks received by him in the store, a goatee-type beard and moustache, a false moustache, a pair of glasses with a rubber nose, three wigs, and a .38-caliber revolver.[13] The police combed out glass and paint particles from the defendant's hair using the defendant's comb.

Laboratory analysis of these things disclosed that the glass particles taken from the defendant's hair and clothing "matched" both the safety glass of the Oldsmobile and the glass particles taken from co-defendant Fuller's hair. The paint particles taken from the defendant's person and clothing matched the paint from the car struck by the Oldsmobile. Finally, fibers taken from the defendant's clothing matched the fibers of the false beard and moustache found in the Oldsmobile.[14] The court held that the various beards and disguises were properly admitted into evidence as they were connected to the defendant and the crime:

> The grocery store owner testified that the robbers wore beards. These beards were later found in the Oldsmobile which was identified by him as the get away car. The defendant was linked to the get away car by the automobile safety glass particles found in his hair.[15]

Additionally, the court observed, fibers found in the defendant's jacket pockets matched those in the beard found in the Oldsmobile.

In *People v. Colombo*,[16] a notorious Illinois murder case, defendants Patricia Colombo and her boyfriend Frank DeLucca were convicted in the Circuit Court, Cook County, of three counts of murder, conspiracy, and solicitation to murder. After several unsuccessful efforts to engage hired killers to murder Patricia's family, the two committed the murders themselves. Investigators discovered the bodies of Frank, Mary, and Michael Columbo. Frank Columbo, defendant Columbo's father, was found lying on his back in the living room, surrounded by broken glass with a torn and bloody lamp shade nearby, and also had a 2-inch slash across his throat. Mary Columbo, defendant Columbo's mother, was found lying on her back on the landing in front of the bathroom with a bullet wound on the ridge of her nose, right between her eyes, and a 1-inch slash across her throat. Portions of a bloodied magazine and fake fern were lying next to her body, and broken glass and beads lying near her head. Michael Columbo, defendant Columbo's 13-year-old brother, was found lying on his back on his bedroom floor, and had what appeared to be a bullet wound on the left side and a second bullet wound on the back. In addition, there were 98 puncture wounds on Michael's neck and chest.

A pair of bloodied scissors with crossed blades were found on Michael's desk and a marble-based bowling trophy, covered with blood, was lying next to Michael's body. In addition to the testimony regarding glass fragments, the jury heard evidence of blood typing and ballistics.[17] Blair Schultz, a criminalist employed by the Illinois Bureau of Identification in the trace section and trained in glass analysis, testified to her findings regarding 28 exhibits she received from the crime scene, from a 1968 Buick that the defendants had rented around the time of the murders, and from Frank Columbo's 1972 Thunderbird and 1972 Oldsmobile. Of the 28 items, 15 had glass in them. Schultz stated that there were three ways to analyze glass fragments: fit the pieces together, analyze the chemical properties and densities, or analyze the refractive index of the fragments.

By using the refraction method, Schultz concluded that two of the fragments, one from the broken lamp base found on Columbo's living room floor and one found in the 1968 Buick had "the same degree of tolerance and, thus, could have originated from the same source." Schultz buttressed her opinion by noting that only five times in 1000 previous glass tolerance tests had glass with the identical degrees of tolerance "not been" from the same source. On cross-examination, however, Schultz agreed that the matched glass fragment recovered from the Buick could have come from any of thousands of pieces of glass with the same optical properties as the lamp base.[18]

In *People v. White*,[19] the state filed a petition to revoke the defendant's probation because he committed an aggravated battery by inflicting a cut with a broken bottle. After closing arguments, the trial court examined the cut on the victim's arm and discussed the discrepancies between the witnesses' testimonies, concluding that the wound had been caused by either a knife or a piece of broken bottle:

> Now the Court can take into account its own observations and experiences of life. Most broken bottles [are] round—if there is a flat part it's on the bottom and normally when a bottle breaks it doesn't break in a perfectly straight line. Glass tends to break in a jagged fashion. The Court notes the position of the wound. The wound is not on the palms. It's not on the heel of the palms. It's down two and a half to three inches down the wrist. One would think that if a man fell the likely thing to do would be to put your palms out and break the fall. That's not where the cut is. The cut is at a place further down the wrist. The nature of the cut—it's a straight cut. I described it earlier as about an inch and a half to about an inch to three quarters in length, not the type that one would think would be made with a round bottle. It doesn't add up. If it was made by a piece on the bottom I might expect a straighter cut but I would expect it to be more jagged. This is a fairly straight cut.[20]

The defendant argued that he was denied due process of law when the trial judge based his decision in part on the differences between glass and knife cuts, since this information was not in evidence. The appellate court agreed with the defendant, ruling that the ability to examine a cut and determine the instrument that made it was beyond the province of common knowledge. Accordingly, the trial judge erred in considering facts not in evidence in entering his judgment. Additionally, the court concluded, the trial judge "spent a significant part of his analysis of the evidence on the distinction between glass and knife cuts." Given that fact and the overall weight of the evidence, they found the error to be grounds for a reversal.

Two different types of glass found on the defendant's gloves were the key to a murder conviction, in the 1996 case of *Land v. State*.[21] Michael Jeffrey Land was convicted of the capital murder of Candace Brown, and sentenced to death.

Ms. Brown's landlord observed that a window located near the rear entry to the house had been broken into, that the telephone wires to the house had been cut, and that the window on the driver's side of Ms. Brown's car had been shattered. When officers from the Birmingham Police Department arrived at Ms. Brown's residence, they established that all doors to the house were locked, that a storm window located near a rear entry to the house had been removed, and that several panes of the interior window behind that storm window had been cut and removed. One of the removed panes of glass, which was lying on the ground, contained a shoe imprint with a distinctive tread design bearing the lettering "USA." Ms. Brown's body was discovered by hikers in a rock quarry on Ruffner Mountain in Jefferson County, Alabama. She had been shot once in the back of her head. The officers also found on a bulletin board a note with the name and telephone numbers of Michael Jeffrey Land and his mother, Gail M. Land. Police informed Land that they were investigating the disappearance of Ms. Brown, and he agreed to accompany them to the police station to answer some questions.

During the interrogation, a Detective Fowler noticed that the tread design on the bottom of Land's tennis shoes appeared to match the print the officers had seen on the window glass at Ms. Brown's house. At the completion of Land's interview, Detective Fowler asked to see Land's shoes and, upon closer observation, noticed what appeared to be bloodstains. Land, in a second statement made after his first alibi-based story was disproved, stated that he had told two men that the deceased was a good robbery target, and agreed to cut and remove a window for them from her house. Land said that after Ms. Brown was injured he became frightened and left the house and that he did not know what happened to her after that.

At trial, the state's expert testimony established that a pair of wire cutters found during the search of Land's car had made the cuts on the telephone wire leading into Ms. Brown's residence. The experts also testified that the two types of glass fragments found on a pair of gloves seized from Land's car were consistent with the glass in the shattered window of Ms. Brown's car and with the glass in the broken window near the rear entry of Ms. Brown's house. Their testimony also established that Land's tennis shoe sole had the same distinctive design as the shoe print found on a removed pane of glass at Ms. Brown's house.[22]

In *People v. Noascono*,[23] the defendant was convicted of burglary, theft of property valued at less than $150, and possession of a controlled substance. Campbell's Drug Store in Marion, Illinois was burglarized on March 26, 1977, at approximately 3:30 A.M. Upon arrival, a police officer responding to an alarm found the front and rear glass doors broken, the cash drawer open, the change bin on the floor, and three pill containers on the counter near the rear door. Police collected samples of broken glass from the floor near the doors and packaged them separately. Leaving Detective Kobler and another officer at the scene, Officer Sprague returned to duty.

Police stopped the defendant's car for an alleged brake light malfunction and noticed that he fit the description received earlier of the person running from the area of the drugstore.

The state's forensic expert witness Smith, who worked in the mineralogy unit of the FBI Laboratory in Washington, D.C., testified that he was trained in the examination of glass, soil, safe insulation, and other materials. He had received the defendant's clothing and picked out what appeared to be bits of glass, whereupon he examined them under a microscope and determined from their appearance that they were glass. Smith then performed light refraction and dispersion tests on the particles from the defendant's shoes, socks, and clothing, and on samples from Campbell's Drug Store. He testified that the dispersion and refraction measurements of particles on the defendant's clothing "matched exactly the dispersion and refraction measurements of the samples" from Campbell's. Smith opined that the particles on the defendant's clothing "very probably" came from the same source as the samples from Campbell's, but he could not say positively that they came from the same source. Smith testified that no chemical tests were performed to determine if the particles on the defendant's clothing were glass or to determine the composition of these particles.[24]

In many cases, the simple breaking of glass, its location, or the presence of blood or fingerprints on a fragment, is the circumstantial key to identifying the dynamics of the crime scene, if not the actual perpetrator. In *Jensen v. State*,[25] a case where the glass evidence was central to the prosecution's theory, there was no chemical or microscopic testimony required. Here, the defendant was convicted of first-degree murder and the use of a handgun in commission of crime of violence. Theodore Daniels was murdered in his office in Woodlawn, Maryland. Dagmar E. Jensen, with whom Daniels had a business and romantic relationship, was arrested for the killing. The state hypothesized that the victim and defendant were at odds over his fidelity and his refusal to tell her where he lived. The state argued that she broke into his office building, went to his office, and shot him.

Police officers came to the scene and attempted to gain entrance to the building via the second-floor backdoor and noticed that the pane of glass in the bottom window opening of the interior door had been broken. There were shards of glass lying on the floor both inside and outside the door and more glass on the exterior side of the door. There was also blood smeared on the interior and exterior of the door and on the broken glass. The blood smears suggested that someone had been cut by the broken glass. The blood smears were heavier on the exterior portion of the door and it seemed to the police, based on where the glass landed, that the glass was broken from the inside of the building while the storm door was closed.[26]

The broken window contained 3 to 4 inches of glass on the bottom left-hand side of the window frame. One of the responding officers described it as follows: "I observed that there was in the bottom left-hand corner a triangle shape of glass that still existed. The remainder had been cleanly knocked out and there were no glass splinters." The victim's body was found lying near his desk, with bloodstained clothing, a pair of bent eyeglasses containing a shattered lens lying immediately to Daniels's right, and a tennis ball, with signs of considerable damage, was further to the right of the eyeglasses. The tennis ball, the police surmised, had been used as a "silencer" to muffle the sound of a gun as it was fired.

The court noted that this was a case with multiple strands of circumstantial evidence, including broken glass, all of which tied that appellant to the murder:

> The State's evidence, if believed, showed that it is likely that the following transpired:
> (1) Sometime between 7:30 p.m. and 9:00 p.m. on the night of his death, Daniels let

a visitor into his building, then locked the front door; (2) Daniels next unlocked his office door and escorted the visitor into his office, where the visitor turned up the volume of the television to block out the noise; (3) the visitor shot Daniels and next proceeded to the rear door but could not unlock it because Daniels had the key to the deadbolt lock; (4) the murderer kicked (or otherwise broke out) the window pane in the rear door; (5) as the glass was broken, most of the glass shards fell next to the closed storm door; (6) the murderer then crawled through the opening provided by the open window and, in doing so, was cut by glass shards still in the pane . . . the glass in the bottom window pane of the back door of Daniels's office building was intact at 7:30 p.m. at which time Daniels was still alive. Approximately an hour and a half later, the window was broken—it is reasonable to conclude that the person who broke the rear window pane was the person who killed Daniels. It is also reasonable to conclude that the person who broke the window did not possess a key to the building. Appellant's fingerprints were found on the interior side of the window panes to the rear entrance to the building. Her blood was found smeared on both sides of the rear wooden door. The glass in the rear door was mostly found on the exterior side of the dead bolted door. From this it can be inferred that a person without a key broke out the pane to get out of the building. Going through a 11½ inch high, 22½ inch wide window, thirty-eight inches off the ground at its lowest point, would take agility. Appellant was agile as demonstrated by the fact that she bragged that she could move her handcuffed hands from behind her back to her front. Even an agile person would likely be cut going through such a small opening. Appellant, by her own admission, was cut by the broken glass in the pane.[27]

In addition to this circumstantial evidence, the court noted that the jury had to weigh defendant's belated explanation for her fingerprints and blood being at the backdoor to Daniels's office, i.e., that she went to look for Daniels at his office even though she did not have a definite appointment with him and cut her hand on the already broken glass after receiving no response from Daniels. The court determined that a rational jury might conclude that it was unlikely that she was cut reaching in to try to unlock the door because she admitted that the hall lights on the second floor were on; if there were glass shards there, it seems likely that she should have seen the glass and avoided injury if she had merely reached through the open window. Moreover, a rational jury could conclude that if she cut herself as she said she did, it would be unlikely that blood would be found afterwards smeared on both sides of the wooden door and on the glass pane.[28]

In *State v. Monroe*,[29] the defendant was convicted of aggravated first-degree murder. On December 28, 1994, Michelle Smith arrived at work late, her face noticeably bruised and swollen. When asked what had happened, she became emotional and stated that the defendant Lloyd Monroe had hit and sexually assaulted her. The defendant was arrested after a supervisor at Smith's place of employment called police. The defendant was mistakenly released, and proceeded to stalk and murder Smith at her apartment. When Smith did not come to work on Monday, her supervisor called the police. The police found Smith's body in her apartment face down on a couch, clothed, and partially covered by a blanket. The cause of death was ligature strangulation. She had also suffered blunt trauma to her head prior to death.[30]

At trial, Helen Rae Griffin, a forensic scientist with the state patrol's crime laboratory, testified that four glass fragments taken from the defendant's jacket matched the glass in Smith's bedroom window. She also testified that her examination determined that the window had been broken from the outside.

In response to the defendant's challenge to her qualifications, Griffin testified that she had worked for 6 years as a forensic scientist at the state patrol crime laboratory; had worked previously for 5½ years in a similar capacity with the Royal Canadian Mounted Police; had received the standard training in glass examination from the state patrol, including training on the determination of the direction of force; and had been certified to perform casework in the field for approximately 5½ years. Although she had not received specific proficiency testing in directionality, she testified that the directionality analysis was straightforward.

[I]t's the kind of examination where I couldn't explain why you're doing it to a lay person but I could show them how to do it within an hour and have them fairly reliably be able to tell me which projectile was fired first and from which side of the glass.

The court concluded that Griffin's on-the-job training and practical experience in this type of analysis were sufficient to qualify her as an expert. Thus, the trial court did not err in admitting her testimony.[31]

III. PAINT ANALYSIS

A. GENERAL

A common instance of the utilization of forensic paint analysis is determining central facts in hit-and-run and vehicular homicide cases with respect to accident dynamics or simple identity of participating vehicles. It is also seen in burglary cases where paint residues are found on burglary tools or other devices used to gain entry to a residence or business establishment. The matching of automobile paints has risen to a highly sophisticated level across the world, again, due to the keen proprietary interest automobile and paint manufacturers have in the smallest differences between their commercial output and the competition.

However, forensic paint analyses involve different ultimate considerations. As noted in the FBI Forensic Paint Analysis and Comparison Guidelines:

Forensic paint analyses and comparisons are typically distinguished by sample size that precludes the application of many standard industrial paint analysis procedures or protocols.[32]

The forensic paint examiner must be concerned with a number of noncommercial factors, such as case investigation requirements, crime scene collection and chain of evidence considerations, environmental factors, and many others that contribute to the goal of supportable forensic evidence at trial.

These factors require that the forensic paint examiner must choose test methods, sample preparation schemes, test sequence, and degree of sample alteration and consumption suitable to each specific case.[33]

Forensic paint analysis encompasses considerable knowledge about automobile paint coating systems, as well as standard, repair, and custom paint colors. Complex chemical analyses such as pyrolysis gas chromatography, and many other chemistry-related subjects need to be understood. Color comparison is still central to forensic paint analyses. As noted by Saferstein:

> [T]he criminalist need not be confined to comparisons alone. Crime laboratories can often provide valuable assistance in identifying the color, make, and model of an automobile by examining small quantities of paint recovered at an accident scene.[34]

The microscope remains a basic tool of the forensic paint analyst as with all other forensic scientists in all disciplines:

> When one considers the thousands upon thousands of paint colors and shades that are known to exist, it is quite understandable why color, more than any other property, imparts paint with its most distinctive forensic characteristics. Questioned and known specimens are best compared side by side under a stereoscopic microscope for color, surface texture, and color layer sequence.[35]

The FBI-sponsored Forensic Paint Analysis and Comparison Guidelines, available online, are essential reading for any lawyer faced with a forensic paint issue. The guidelines include discussion of terminology used in the field, practice summaries, collection, transport, and storage procedures, and detailed description of physical match examinations. The paper, "Paint and Glass Evidence," in the *Proceedings of the 12th INTERPOL Forensic Science Symposium,* prepared by Ran Singh, Ph.D., should also be consulted for its discussion of techniques, such as infrared spectroscopy, chromatography, and UV/vis spectroscopy, X-ray fluorescence, X-ray diffraction, and other techniques currently employed in forensic laboratories around the world. This valuable paper also contains discussion of selected paint databases, books, and articles.[36]

B. Paint Analysis Cases

There are not many criminal cases centered in paint comparisons, when compared with the other forensic sciences. Nonetheless, the same components of "class characteristic" statements and "individual linkage" statements are the central features of this important forensic science discipline. The inferences put into the case by paint analysis-based testimony may, as with all of the offerings of the forensic sciences, be the weight tipping of the jury's decision to one side or the other.

For example, in *People v. Mitchell*,[37] the defendant was convicted of two counts of burglary. The court found it was proper to have admitted into evidence the defendant's plastic Social Services card, which was bent and had streaks of paint on it, since the card was not introduced to show the defendant's propensity to commit crimes, but rather was logically linked to one issue in the case—the defendant's entry, without a key, into the complainants' hotel room. There was no paint-matching testimony of the paint on the card and that on the hotel room door.[38]

In *State v. Kandies*,[39] the defendant was charged with murder. Sergeant Wilson's discovery of paint rather than blood in defendant's truck cab contradicted defendant's statement that he accidentally hit the victim Natalie with his truck and that she was bleeding when he put her in the truck. Sergeant Wilson testified that he examined the inside of defendant's truck and found some red dots in the cab to be red oxide primer (as opposed to blood). Sergeant Wilson testified that the spots in defendant's truck looked peculiar, so he sanded a spot with a knife and discovered it to be red oxide primer. He also testified that he held a part-time job doing car repair and body shop work. The court ruled that, based on his experience, it was likely that Sergeant Wilson could perceive the difference between blood and red oxide primer.[40]

The classic hit-and-run scenario was recently addressed in the important Illinois Supreme Court case of *People v. Digirolamo*,[41] where the defendant was convicted of failing to report an accident resulting in a person's death and of obstructing justice.[42] The detailed investigative, accident reconstruction, and forensic analyses merit extended examination for lawyers involved in such cases.

The victim, 72-year-old retiree William Pranaitis, arose in the early-morning hours while it was still dark outside to take his routine morning walk. A local police officer discovered Pranaitis's dead body lying next to a telephone pole near the intersection of Blackjack Road and Lebanon Road at 6:36 A.M. that day. Detective Michael Ries of the Collinsville Police Department investigated the scene of the accident and found a flashlight lying in the center of Lebanon Road, near its intersection with Blackjack Road, and a baseball hat and eyeglasses 3 to 4 feet onto the grass. He also observed a bag containing cans, which the victim routinely collected on his walks, and a single set of tire tracks which entered the grassy area alongside Lebanon Road and then traveled approximately 50 to 60 feet before reentering Lebanon Road. Ries conjectured that these tracks, which were narrow in width, were made by two right-side tires of a small car or possibly a small truck.[43]

Officer David Schneider, an accident reconstruction specialist from the Collinsville Police Department, testified that he observed a "scrub" mark on the curb, made by the smear of rubber from a tire, and a 48-foot-long tire mark in the grass alongside Lebanon Road. Later, Schneider examined the defendant's car and found scuff marks and a small dent on the edge of the rim of the right front tire, which he testified were "consistent with" the scrub mark found on the curb at the accident scene. He also observed the following damage to the defendant's car: dirt in the right front wheel rim; a "broken-out" windshield; dents on the right front quarter panel and in the right-side pillar (the support from the hood to the roof); and a small, depression-type dent on the right side of the roof above the pillar.[44] Schneider concluded that a vehicle traveling east on Lebanon Road left the road at the point of the scrub mark and that the right front corner of the vehicle struck the victim from behind. The impact flipped the victim onto the hood, with his head striking the pillar on the right side, and then propelling him into the air to a resting point at the base of the telephone pole. Officer Schneider opined that the defendant's car "could have been" the one that struck Pranaitis because it displayed damage on the right side of the vehicle, which was "consistent with" the accident that killed the victim.[45]

The state experts testified regarding the physical evidence. A forensic pathologist testified that the victim had extensive injuries, including large lacerations on the scalp and the back of his right leg in the knee area and a fracture to the left leg, which were consistent with his being struck by a motor vehicle while he was upright and moving. It was also determined that the victim's head injuries were consistent with his striking the dented right window post area of the defendant's car, although it was conceded on cross-examination that the window post damage could have been caused by removal of the windshield from the car. While admitting that she could not say that the defendant's car caused the victim's injuries, the expert nonetheless concluded that the car's damage was "consistent with the victim's injuries."[46]

Blair Schultz, an Illinois State Police forensic chemist, compared a piece of standard laminated glass from the defendant's windshield with a piece of glass from the victim's clothing and testified that they had the same refractive index, which means that the two pieces of glass could have originated from the same source. Schultz testified that the likelihood of this match was one in five, meaning that one out of every five pieces of laminated glass would have the same refractive index.[47] However, trace chemist Cheryl Cherry testified that although she found several different colors of paint on the victim's clothing, the paint chips were not large enough to determine if the paint was automotive. There was also no match between the paint from the defendant's car and the samples taken from the victim's clothing. She explained that when a person is thrown to the ground he will pick up paint and debris in his clothing. This also occurs when a person is walking around.[48]

The court determined that the evidence was more than adequate to uphold the defendant's conviction:

> Here, the circumstantial evidence against defendant showed that there was damage to the front passenger side of defendant's car that was consistent with William Pranaitis' injuries. There was also glass from defendant's car that was linked to the glass found on the victim's clothing. In addition, defendant admitted to being in an accident in an area near the scene of the accident killing the victim in this case. Following the accident, defendant appeared nervous and ultimately sought to replace the damaged windshield of his car. There was also evidence that defendant removed whitish-gray hair strands from his car's windshield. This circumstantial evidence, when viewed in the light most favorable to the prosecution, was sufficient for a rational trier of fact to conclude beyond a reasonable doubt that defendant's car struck and killed Pranaitis.[49]

Paint analyses are not restricted to automobile or injury settings, as may be exemplified by the case of *Commonwealth v. McEnany*,[50] where the defendant was convicted of second-degree murder, burglary, and robbery. Kathryn Bishop, aged 82, was found dead on the floor of her residence. Testimony of a forensic pathologist established that Mrs. Bishop had been stomped to death. Paint chips were discovered on the victim's hands, and black T-shirt fibers were found on her face, neck, and clothing. The victim's kitchen door window had been smashed, her basement window had been opened, and scuff marks were found on her clothes dryer which was located just below the basement window.

As the investigation continued, a Trooper Stansfield obtained search warrants for the appellant's van and residence and officers got possession of the clothes worn by the appellant on the day of the murder. Expert examination of the clothing revealed paint chips in the pocket of his jacket, which a forensic paint analyst testified at trial "were consistent" with chips found on Mrs. Bishop's hands. The chips found in the defendant's jacket and on the victim's hands were also found to be "consistent with" the peeling paint around the broken basement window. Chemist Lee Ann Grayson testified that fibers found on Mrs. Bishop's body matched those of the T-shirt the appellant wore on the day of the murder.[51]

The court found that the evidence was sufficient to place the defendant and fellow chimney sweep at the customer's residence at the time of the homicide and, therefore, supported convictions for second-degree murder of their elderly customer.

IV. SOIL ANALYSIS

A. GENERAL

Forensic examination of soil samples is quite common in a variety of criminal cases, especially in instances of kidnaping by vehicle and the disposing of bodies in rural or semi-rural areas or a wide variety of burial sites. Geologic surveys, archaeology, environmental concerns, oil and gas exploration, and the worldwide commercial interest in building materials originating in whole or in part from mineral substances have generated a wealth of information available to those engaged in forensic soil analyses. The definition of soil for forensic science purposes is necessarily broad. As observed by Saferstein:

> [F]or forensic purposes, soil ma be thought of as including any disintegrated surface material, both natural and artificial that lies on or near the earth's surface.[52]

Such a necessarily broad net would encompass naturally occurring rocks, all manner of minerals, vegetation,[53] and animal matter.[54] The subject also encompasses the recognition and analysis of a large number of commercial products, such as glass, paint chips, asphalt, brick fragments, cinders, ceramics, and a host of other building materials that may serve as indicators of where all or part of a crime occurred.

Soil examinations can be relatively straightforward and conclusive:

Most soils can be differentiated and distinguished by their gross appearance. A side-by-side visual comparison of the color and texture of soil specimens is easy to perform and provides a sensitive property for distinguishing soils that originate from different locations.[55]

As with glass, fiber, hair, blood products, and finger, foot, or tire impressions, soil analysis can often impart important information linking a suspect to a crime scene. Also, as in all forensic science crime scene investigations, recognition and collection issues are paramount.[56]

The broad nature of soil analysis and its increasingly detailed nature was recently noted at the *Proceedings of the 12th INTERPOL Forensic Science Symposium*:[57]

> As soil particles are one of the major components of air borne dust, it can be frequently transferred by a suspect touching the dusty surface of items such as a door, a windowsill, etc. This report, therefore, includes not only soil materials, but also dust and other earth related materials, such as plant chips, diatoms, pollen and spores, and concrete or brick fragments.[58]

In cases where unique items such as glass are embedded in both comparison samples, a comparison may be readily made. However, as noted in the same paper:

> The more difficult situations occur where there is a variation in components and composition among the samples from the same site. It requires tedious long work and patience with a lot of examiners' experience and statistical consideration.[59]

Examining soil and decayed matter from a landfill area would be a prime example of the above observations. The above-noted symposium is well worth consulting for its comprehensive overview of this subject as well as its current world bibliography on soil analysis and related subjects.

It is incumbent on lawyers involved in the criminal justice system to become familiar with the key information points and players in the scientific field of soil analysis. Very few of the forensic sciences are or were ever created and developed for strictly forensic purposes. As noted above, the keen commercial interest involved is typically the primary generator of detailed data sourcing. Soil analysis stems from and depends upon the sciences of geology as well as anthropology. There are several recent excellent books[60] and Web sites[61] now available to get the investigator on his way in a soils-related criminal case. Several excellent case studies of soil-based kidnaping and homicide incidents are available for study. Extensive articles on the murder investigation in the death of DEA Agent Enrique Camarena and the kidnap and murder of Adolphe Coors provide both extremely instructive and interesting reading.[62]

B. Soil Analysis Cases

There are not many cases where soil analysis is at the center of the investigation, but soil analysis often is an important part of the circumstantial physical evidence leading to acquittal or conviction. Several of this type of cases are set out below.

In *People v. Begley*,[63] the defendant was convicted in the Superior Court, Shasta County, California of conspiracy to injure an archaeological object. In an attempt to apprehend looters of Native American artifacts, the U.S. Forest Service set up a sting operation in Shasta County where a Forest Service special agent opened a booth at a flea market and advertised as a broker of Native American artifacts.

The defendant contacted Agent Price and informed Price that he had excavated a number of arrowhead projectile points, beads, obsidian chips, and other artifacts from a burial site. The agent eventually bought several arrowheads later examined by Dr. Eric Ritter, an archaeologist for the Bureau of Land Management, who testified that these items contained a teshoa flake, used by prehistoric Native Americans for cutting and scraping, a late prehistoric arrow point known as a Gunther barb, and obsidian chips, a form of volcanic glass. The items were consistent with those one would expect to find in archaeological sites in Shasta County, including the Ono site.[64]

The defendant's residence was searched and officers seized trade beads, various midden-covered rocks, and documents and other materials. Some of the items had characteristics consistent with recent removal from an archaeological site. Midden was described by an archeologist as "a trash mound, that is composed of materials that have built up over time from cooking ovens and fires, house structures that have been built and either decomposed or have burnt, resulting in soil that is very dark colored and distinctive from surrounding soil." Possession of such material suggested that the defendant was also in the business of fabricating Native American archaeological treasures.[65]

In *People v. Davenport*,[66] the defendant was convicted before the Superior Court, Orange County, California of the vicious murder of a young woman with the special circumstance that the murder was intentional and involved infliction of torture. The defendant was sentenced to death.

Gayle Lingle, the victim, spent the evening of March 26, 1980, at the Sit 'N Bull Bar in Tustin. Between approximately midnight and 1 A.M., she and the defendant left the bar. The victim's body was found the next morning lying in a large, uncultivated field south of the I-5 Freeway near Tustin. There were motorcycle tracks in the area.[67] The body bore signs of extreme cruelty and mutilation.

Bonnie Driver, a criminalist employed by the Orange County Sheriff's Department, testified that she had examined vegetable matter taken from the defendant's motorcycle and compared it with vegetation taken from the area where the victim's body was found. Driver found the gross morphology of the plants in both samples to be "consistent with each other."[68]

Forensic microscopist Skip Pallinick examined and compared the heavy mineral content of soil samples taken from the defendant's bike with samples taken at the murder scene and testified that the samples were "generally consistent" with each other. In fact, he testified, one of the samples from the motorcycle contained sufficient similarity to the murder scene samples that he concluded they were "virtually indistinguishable." Both of these witnesses admitted they had not compared the samples taken from the defendant's bike with samples taken from other parts of Orange County. Dr. Stephen Dana, a geologist retained by the defendant, examined the same soil samples and found similarities and differences in all of them, and based on his knowledge of the geology of the area, he opined that the samples could have come from anywhere in Orange County.[69]

In *State v. Lee*,[70] the defendant was charged, along with a co-defendant, with the second-degree murder of one Peter Weber. On April 21, 1997, a partially decomposed body was found in a wooded area in St. Bernard Parish, Louisiana. Dental records were used to identify positively the body as that of Peter Weber. Bruising and broken bones in the neck area indicated that the victim died of strangulation.

A North Lopez Street residence, the defendant's former abode, was searched pursuant to a warrant and under the house the officers saw what appeared to be a shallow grave. Several articles were taken from both inside and underneath the house that were linked to the body of the victim. Analysis of soil samples indicated that the soil found in the soles of the victim's shoes was the same as that found underneath the house.[71]

RESEARCH NOTE

The Journal of Forensic Sciences is the official publication of the American Academy of Forensic Sciences. By visiting the Academy's Web site at *http://www.aafs.org* and clicking on the "Journal of Forensic Sciences" link, one can get to a searchable index of the journal from 1981 to the present that uses common search terms. The site also provides tables of contents for more recent issues of the journal, and for a modest fee, one can download individual articles from issues published after January 1, 1999. The index, content, and article availability site is maintained by the publisher of the journal, the American Society for Testing and Materials (ASTM). There are current plans to move toward Web-based publication of the journal, although the paper copy will still be available for some time. Individual subscriptions to this essential journal are also available from ASTM for those interested.

Visiting this important Web site on a regular basis and viewing the available abstracts are essential to the early stages of forensic science/forensic evidence research.

Also see the bibliography on paint and glass prepared by Ran B. Singh, "Paint and Glass Evidence," and that on soil evidence, "Soil Evidence," in *Proceedings of the 12th INTERPOL Forensic Science Symposium* (1998) at 199 and 242.

ENDNOTES

1. Desmond MacHale, *Comic Sections: The Book of Mathematical Jokes, Humour, Wit, and Wisdom* (Dublin, Ireland, 1993).
2. See, generally, Saferstein: *Criminalistics: An Introduction to Forensic Science* (6th ed. Prentice-Hall, Upper Saddle River, NJ, 1998) at 97–126; Giannelli and Imwinkelried: *Scientific Evidence* (Michie Company, Charlottesville, VA, 1993), Vol. 2, at 24–6;

Ran B. Singh: "Paint and Glass Evidence," *Proceedings of the 12th INTERPOL Forensic Science Symposium* (The Forensic Sciences Foundation Press, New York, 1998) at 199; Yoshiteru Marumo and Ritsuko Sugita: "Soil Evidence," *Proceedings of the 12th INTERPOL Forensic Science Symposium* (The Forensic Sciences Foundation Press, New York, 1998) at 242; Geberth: *Practical Homicide Investigation* (3rd ed. CRC Press, Boca Raton, FL, 1996) at 522; Fisher: *Techniques of Crime Scene Investigation* (5th ed. CRC Press, Boca Raton, FL, 1993) at 195; "F.B.I. Forensic Paint Analysis and Comparison Guidelines," Scientific Working Group on Materials Analysis (SWGMAT), available at *http://www.fbi.gov/programs/lab/fsc/current/painta.htm.*

3. See, T. Hicks, R. Vanina, and P. Margot: "Transfer and Persistence of Glass Fragments on Garments," *Science and Justice* 1996; 36(2): 101–107.

4. Giannelli and Imwinkelried, *supra*, note 2, at 380.

5. *Id*. Also see Saferstein, *supra*, note 2, at 101.

6. There is a small but growing "third database" for glass and paint chips in the FBI Laboratory regarding density and refraction indexes. See *Id*. at 115. Also see Max M. Houck: "Statistics and Trace Evidence: The Tyranny of Numbers," *Forensic Science Communications*, Vol. I, No. 3, October 1999, available at *http://www.fbi.gov/programs/lab/fsc/current/houck.htm.*

7. See Ran B. Singh, *supra*, note 2, at 209. Similar studies have been successfully conducted involving fiber transfers. See J. Robertson and C.B.M. Kidd: "The Transfer of Textile Fibres During Simulated Contact," *J. of the Forensic Sci. Soc.,* Vol. 22 (1982), at 301–308; J. Robertson, C.B.M. Kidd, and M.P. Parkinson: "The Persistence of Textile Transferred during Simulated Fibre Contact," *J. of the Forensic Sci. Soc.,* Vol. 22 (1982), at 353–360; H.G. Scott: "The Persistence of Fibers Transferred during Contact of Automobile Carpets and Clothing Fabrics," *J. of the Canadian of Forensic Sci.,* Vol. 18 (1985), at 185–199; M.C. Grieve, J. Dunlop, and P.S. Haddock: "Transfer Experiments with Acrylic Fibers," *Forensic Sci. Int.,* Vol. 40 (1989), at 267–277.

8. A significant amount of information on the technical and compositional aspects of fiber, weapons manufacture and glass and paint is available in the hundreds of full-text or bibliographic databases accessible on the Dialog Information Service through Lexis-Nexus or Westlaw.

9. People v. Dailey, 15 Ill.App.3d 214, 304 N.E.2d 156 (1973).

10. *Id*. at 216.

11. *Id*. at 217.

12. People v. Pruitt, 16 Ill.App.3d 930, 307 N.E.2d 142 (1974).

13. *Id*. at 147.

14. *Id*. at 935.

15. *Id*.

16. People v. Colombo, 118 Ill.App.3d 882, 455 N.E.2d 733 (1983).

17. Susan M. Twardosz, criminalist at the Illinois Bureau of Identification and specialist in the firearms and tool mark section, testified that Officer Gonsowski gave her four complete bullets and a fragment of a fifth to identify. By using a comparison microscope, Twardosz identified the bullets and fragments as .32-caliber. Further, she identified the nonmutilated bullets as coming from the same weapon which, in her opinion, was a .32-caliber gun. She could not discern with certainty whether the projectiles were fired from a rifle, automatic, or revolver. In addition, Twardosz testified that her examination of four locks taken from the doors of the Columbo house revealed that nothing but a key had been used to open them. On cross-examination, however, Twardosz admitted that a lock could be opened with a shim device such as a credit card or a thin-bladed knife and escape detection. Some of the locks

taken from the Columbo house were equipped with an anti-shim device. Michael Podlecki, criminalist employed by the Illinois Bureau of Identification, testified to his examination of the hair standards found on Michael Columbo's T-shirt. *Id.* at 752, 905.

18. *Id.* at 905

19. People v. White, 183 Ill.App.3d 838, 539 N.E.2d 456 (1989).

20. *Id.* at 840.

21. Land v. State, 678 So.2d 201 (Ala. Sp. Ct.1996).

22. *Id.* at 230. Expert testimony also established that the bullet recovered from Ms. Brown's head had been fired from a .45-caliber handgun, that it matched a bullet test-fired from the .45-caliber handgun found in Land's car, that a DNA profile of a semen stain found on Ms. Brown's blouse matched Land's known blood sample, and that only 1 in 20,620,000 white males would have those same DNA characteristics (Land is white).

23. People v. Noascone, 80 Ill.App.3d 921, 400 N.E.2d 720 (1980).

24. *Id.* at 722. Also see McNish v. State, 1999 WL 604436 (Tenn.Crim.App. 1999), where defendant was convicted of the murder of a 70-year-old victim, Gladys Smith, who was brutally beaten about the head and face with a glass vase, the fragments of which were found in her apartment. Scientific tests of the blood found on appellant's trousers showed that it matched that of the victim, Mrs. Smith, and that it was not the blood of the appellant. Some blood particles taken from his fingernails were found to be human blood, but it was in quantities too small to test. An analysis performed at the Tennessee Bureau of Investigation laboratories showed that a fragment of glass found inside the packaging material in which appellant's trousers had been transmitted matched the glass particles found on the rug and floor of Mrs. Smith's apartment.

25. Jensen v. State, 127 Md.App. 103, 732 A.2d 319 (1999).

26. *Id.* at 323.

27. *Id.* at 328.

28. *Id.* at 330.

29. State v. Monroe, 1999 WL 211823 (Wash.App. Div. 1, 1999).

30. *Id.* at *1.

31. *Id.* at *7.

32. "Forensic Paint Analysis and Comparison Guidelines," Scientific Working Group on Materials Analysis (SWGMAT), F.B.I. Forensic Science Communications (January 1999), available at *http://www.fbi.gov/programs/lab/fsc/current/painta.htm*, at *1.0.

33. *Id.* at *1.1.

34. Saferstein, *supra*, note 2, at 239.

35. *Id.* at 241.

36. Ran B. Singh, *supra*, note 2, at 199–223.

37. People v. Mitchell, 224 A.D.2d 316, 637 N.Y.S.2d 733 (N.Y.A.D. 1 Dept. 1996).

38. *Id.* at 734.

39. State v. Kandies, 342 N.C. 419, 467 S.E.2d 67 (N.C. Sp. Ct. 1996).

40. *Id.* at 444.

41. People v. Digirolamo, 179 Ill.2d 24, 688 N.E.2d 116 (1997).

42. In an important doctrinal ruling, the court held that the offense of failing to report an accident resulting in a person's death requires proof that accused driver had knowledge that he was involved in accident that involved another person. Accordingly, the trial court's instruction that the state had to prove defendant's knowledge that he was involved in an accident, and omitting the requirement of a finding that another person was involved, constituted reversible error. *Id.*

43. *Id.* at 119.

44. *Id.* at 30. There was no blood on defendant's car.
45. *Id.* at 30.
46. Kenneth Knight, an expert in hair and fiber evidence, analyzed Pranaitis's clothing, samples of his hair, and debris removed from the windshield glass of defendant's car. In the debris from the windshield, Knight identified animal hair from a dog and human Caucasian hair, which was not suitable for comparison. After comparing a cotton fiber found in the debris with Pranaitis's clothing, he concluded that they did not match. *Id.*
47. *Id.* at 32.
48. *Id.*
49. *Id.* at 44. Also see State v. Buterbaugh, 1999 WL 717268 (Ohio App. 10 Dist., 1999), where defendant was convicted of two counts of involuntary manslaughter, growing out of a drag-racing automobile accident. An analysis of paint scrapings from the two Firebirds involved at the scene showed that the vehicles, one of which was defendant's, made contact leading to the death of passengers in a third vehicle.
50. Commonwealth v. McEnany, 446 Pa.Super. 609, 667 A.2d 1143 (Pa. Sup. Ct. 1995).
51. *Id.* at 616–617.
52. Saferstein, *supra*, note 2, at 121.
53. The separate forensic discipline of forensic limnology focuses on plant life as related to questions of place of a murder, the movements of bodies, and other location-based concerns in a wide variety of crimes. See, e.g., D.M. Bate, G.J. Anderson, and R.D. Lee: "Forensic Botany: Trichome Evidence," *J. Forensic Sci.* 1997; 42:380–386.
54. This is especially important in cases of poaching and other illegal hunting cases. See U.S. Fish and Wildlife Service Web site at *http://www.fws.gov/*.
55. Saferstein, supra, note 2, at 122.
56. See Bruce Wayne Hall, "The Forensic Utility of Soil," F.B.I. Law Enforcement Bulletin (September 1993) at 16.
57. Marumo and Sugita, *supra*, note 2, at 242–252.
58. *Id.* at 242. Also see Saferstein, *supra*, note 2, at 122.
59. *Supra*, note 57.
60. See McPhee: *Annals of the Former World* (Farrar Strouse & Giroux, New York, 1998). This volume collects John McPhee's majestic study of the geology of America, composed of *Basin and Range* (1981), In *Suspect Terrain* (1983), *Rising from the Plains* (1986), *Assembling California* (1993), and *Crossing the Craton* (1998). A number of books on the geology of very specific areas of the U.S. may be located at travel stores as well as libraries. The Roadside Geology series can be of great educational value in criminal investigations involving soil analyses.
61. See, e.g., the following Web sites for good information and valuable links: National Soil Information System (NASIS) at *http://www.itc.nrcs.usda.gov/nasis*. National Soil Survey Center, at *http://www.statlab.iastate.edu/soils/nsdaf*. Soils Explorer, at *http://www.itc.nrcs.usda.gov/soils_explorer/soils_ex.htm*.
62. See Michael Malone: "The Enrique Camarena Case: A Forensic Nightmare," F.B.I. Law Enforcement Bulletin (September 1989); John McPhee, "The Gravel Page," The New Yorker, January 29, 1996, at 45. The McPhee article is especially informative and interesting.
63. People v. Bealey, 46 Cal.Rptr.2d 279 (Cal. Ct. App. 1995).
64. *Id.* at 282.
65. *Id.* at 283.
66. People v. Davenport, 11 Cal.4th 1171, 906 P.2d 1068, 47 Cal.Rptr.2d 800 (1996).

67. *Id.*, Jack Leonard, the production manager for the International Sport and Rally Division of Dunlop Tire Company, testified that the tracks of the rear tire at the crime scene had the same highly unique and distinctive characteristics as the rear tire of the motorcycle. See Chapter 7, Footprints and Tire Impressions.
68. *Supra*, note 66, at 1189.
69. *Id.* at 1190.
70. State v. Lee, 1999 WL 1078733 (La.App. 4 Cir. 1999).
71. Also, a piece of green carpet taken from the house matched the carpet in which the body was wrapped and police found pieces of cord and two knives under the house. Inside the house, the officers observed a red substance on the wall and a stain on the floor. Id., pages unavailable.

7 Footprints and Tire Impressions

There is no branch of detective science which is so important and so much neglected as the art of tracing footsteps. Happily, I have always laid great stress upon it, and much practice has made it second nature to me. I saw the heavy footmarks of the constables, but I saw also the track of the two men who had first passed through the garden. It was easy to tell that they had been before the others, because in places their marks had been entirely obliterated by the others coming upon the top of them. In this way my second link was formed, which told me that the nocturnal visitors were two in number, one remarkable for his height (as I calculated from the length of his stride), and the other fashionably dressed, to judge from the small and elegant impression left by his boots. [Sherlock Holmes to Doctor Watson.]

— Arthur Conan Doyle:
A Study in Scarlet (1887)

I. INTRODUCTION

The case reports each year contain many instances of the use of foot impression evidence, in a wide variety of settings including *both* two-dimensional and three-dimensional impressions, whether it is footprints in dust, plaster, blood, glass panes, paper, carpeting, oils or other petroleum products, or impressions in soil, mud, or snow.[1] With each, preservation issues are paramount. Crime scene photography and casting techniques are central to footwear impression cases. Like the other forensic disciplines, footwear impression science offers valuable class characteristic and individual or linking information. Here, as with ballistics and tool mark cases, manufacturing technology and machine tooling are of cardinal importance. There is a significant and growing body of knowledge contained in books,[2] articles,[3] and Web sites,[4] with respect to the manufacture and styles of footwear of all kinds, ranging from sandals and moccasins to athletic shoes and expensive dress shoes.

The World Wide Web provides an enormous amount of information on both footwear and tire retailers, manufacturers, conferences, etc. For example, a simple search on the Yahoo search engine for "footwear" will bring up links to numerous sites in the areas of accessories, athletic shoes, boots, brand names, children's shoes, clogs, custom-made shoes, manufacturer's directories, retailers, and trade associations. Each of those in turn will lead to numerous other useful sites for lawyers beginning research on a footwear-related issue. Likewise, a Yahoo search on "tires" will bring up numerous links in the areas of brand names, distributors and wholesalers, importers, exporters, and manufacturers of automobiles, trucks, and motorcycles.

II. FOOTPRINTS

A. GENERAL

An initial issue of importance to investigators is, as with fingerprints, an understanding of what surfaces or media *could* hold an impression? Footwear impressions can be two or three dimensional; in the latter case, some medium capable of a sinking down, allowing for a depth measurement along with length and width, is necessary. Two-dimensional impressions refer to footwear impressions made in or on dust, glass, paper products, human skin, paint, blood, and oil or other petroleum products. Impressions made in a three-dimensional medium include carpeting, dirt, mud, snow, drywall, and other media capable of depth when trod upon.[5]

Given the original quality and integrity of the impression, examiners can often determine such important class characteristics as shoe type, shape, brand, and size. As noted by footwear expert William J. Bodziak, all crime scenes should be approached with the expectation that they contain footwear impressions in some form, whether visible or latent. Investigators must be, according to Bodziak, "aggressive" in their search for such impressions.[6] Bodziak lists five areas deserving special attention: actual point of commission, the party's point of entry, the route to and through the crime scene, the exit point, and the area in and around other visible impressions.[7]

Many supportable assumptions can be made from class characteristic categories, such as a person's general height, weight, ambulatory difficulties, loads being carried, whether the footwear is new, capable of retaining crime scene media such as soil, mud, plant life, construction materials, etc.

The preservation of the impression is of keen interest, given the typically transitory nature of footwear impression evidence. This is especially true in crime scenes, where human traffic is so ubiquitous, even when efforts are made to limit personnel, equipment, or vehicles. Photography and casting methodologies are the typical methods used to preserve impression evidence for laboratory testing and subsequent use at trial. There is a growing international interest in footwear impression evidence.[8] There have also been great strides in the effort to perfect computerized databases of footwear images.[9] In the important crime scene investigative area of collection and preservation, lawyers need to know how the experts photograph, cast, or otherwise preserve an impression.

Consulting Bodziak's treatise or one of the growing number of articles[10] that address the important subject of forensic photography can go a long way toward familiarizing the neophyte with these key preservation methodologies.[11] Forensic photography is, of course, central to most of the forensic sciences, not the least of which are forensic pathology, fingerprints, forensic anthropology, and blood spatter pattern analyses.[12] There are a number of very useful Web sites addressed to forensic photography issues.[13] The FBI has just electronically published a paper entitled "Definitions and Guidelines for the Use of Imaging Technologies in the Criminal Justice System,"[14] prepared by the Scientific Working Group on Imaging Technologies (SWGIT). These guidelines as all other FBI pronouncements in the area of forensic science will receive considerable respect in future court discussions of forensic photography issues.

Basic information regarding modern impression casting techniques is also required of lawyers if they are to interact effectively with forensic scientists and criminalists in footwear and tire track settings.[15] There are a number of important references in Bodziak and forensic science articles on various procedures used to preserve an impression other than straight photography. Some of these include the use of electrostatic or adhesive-lifting techniques and new casting mediums such as Traxtone and Ceramass RC (ceramic gypsum), magnetic powders, chemical agents, and cyanoacrylate fuming, and Luminol for prints in blood.[16]

An excellent source for information on footwear impression cases, in particular the individual, linking characteristics essential to tying a suspect to a particular crime scene, can be obtained by examining some of the testimony given by Agent William Bodziak himself in the recent notorious O. J. Simpson homicide trial. The famous size-12 Bruno Magli shoe print was the centerpiece of that expert testimony, and bears brief examination here, prior to a discussion of recent footwear and tire impression cases.

The efforts related by Agent Bodziak in the *Simpson* case were extraordinary, and do not represent the standard in such cases, especially with regard to foreign travel to inspect the machinery used to manufacture the shoe type and size involved. Forensic shoe print examiners do not normally go as far as locating the machine on which the shoes were run. Also, if they do so in major profile cases like O. J. Simpson, their extraordinary efforts are as good as the photography used to memorialize the burr marks, striations, etc., since they obviously cannot haul the foreign machine to court. The testimony of Agent Bodziak, available for download from Westlaw, especially the foundation laid for the testimony, is very extensive and most instructive.[17] A very brief selection will be excerpted here as an example of translating forensic theory to practical courtroom work.[18]

Agent Bodziak began his testimony by explaining the class and individual characteristics in forensic footwear impression analyses:

A: One of the primary purposes of footwear comparison is ultimately to examine the footwear impressions from the crime scene, which is depicted here on the right side, (indicating), with shoes of suspects that might be obtained during the investigation.... This comparison involves the class characteristics first of the shoe, that is, the physical shape and size, the design or pattern on the bottom of the shoe, which leaves its print in the impression, and then subsequently we will draw its attention to wear characteristics. Maybe the heel may begin to wear on the edge and other wear that might be evident and would change the pattern of the shoe.

The fourth area of comparison, after the size, design and wear, would be things such as accidental characteristics, such as a cut mark that would also show up in the impression and would be found on both the test impression and the known shoe. These cut marks or changes to the pattern of the shoe are what makes a shoe unique and would possibly enable, if there was an adequate number of these, the positive identification of this shoe having made the impression at the crime scene.[19]

Proceeding to an analysis of the crime scene datum in the *Simpson* case, Bodziak noted that that typical type of analysis was not done due to the fact that no shoe associated with the defendant was available to him. Continuing, he testified:

Q: All right. Now, in cases that are submitted to you for analysis at the FBI, since 1973 when you've been working there, can you give us an estimate as to what percent, where they are submitted to you, they do not have shoes of a suspect?

A: Approximately forty percent of the case work that is submitted to us initially does not have the shoes of the suspect. A few of those may be submitted later after we provide them additional information.

Q: And are there some where the shoes are never recovered?

A: Absolutely, yes.

Q: Now, in cases where the shoes are not recovered, is it, nevertheless, possible to do other kind of analysis on the shoes?...[20]

A: Yes. The second and third portions of the chart draw the attention to those kind of requests we get in situations where we do not have the shoes of a suspect, and we are asked to provide the brand name and manufacturer of the shoe and we do this by accumulating, in a reference collection, thousands of designs of shoes and searching a particular pattern from the crime scene print through that reference collection, and hopefully we will be able to determine the manufacturer and brand name of that shoe. After that, depending on the quality of the impression and the completeness of the impression at the crime scene, as well as the kind of manufacturer of the shoe in question, we may be asked to give either a general estimate of the size and that would be just through a linear measurement, or an actual specific sizing of the shoe by directly working with the manufacturer.

. . .

Q: Now, during your involvement in this case, when you first became involved in the case, what type of analysis were you asked to perform?

A: Initially I was asked to determine what type of shoe, what brand or manufacturer, type of shoe made the impressions that were located in blood on the Bundy sidewalk.

Q: And did you consult any reference collections of the sort that you mentioned previously in order to do that?

A: Yes, I did. I initially consulted the FBI's reference collection which involves thousands of impressions on computer and in photographs and catalogues, but I was unable to find that particular design.

Q: And how long has this reference collection been in existence?

A: Well, we have changed it over the years, but it was initially started in 1937 basically as a rubber heel file.

Q: Is it a computerized system?

A: Part of it is computerized, yes, sir.

Q: All right. You also were unable to locate the design in your reference catalogue?

A: That's correct.

Q. After you were unable to locate the design based upon your own resources, did you take some additional steps?

A: Yes, I did.

Q: What did you do?

A: In looking at the detail in the shoe impressions in the thirty photographs which I was submitted which were the impressions from the Bundy location, I observed that there were certain features about that shoe that strongly suggested that it was a high end — that is a very expensive Italian brand shoe. So I looked through our written reference material and I identified approximately 75 to 80 manufacturers and importers of high end Italian shoes and some South American shoes or Brazilian shoes, and I prepared a sketch and a — one of the photographs, a composite photograph — excuse me —- a composite sketch and three photographs of heel impressions from the Bundy scene, along with a letter, and contacted those manufacturers and importers to see if they recognized or knew the origin of that particular design.

Q: Did you get any information back as a result of that?

A: Yes. On August 17th I received a reply from a Mr. Peter Grueterich of the Bruno Magli Uma shoe store in New Jersey.

Q: And did he send you anything?

A: Yes. He sent me two shoes that were left over from a Bruno Magli distribution of his in 1991 and 1992. These were both right shoes. One was a size 9 and a half and one was a size 12. And I believe from looking at them they were probably samples that were just left over.[21]

Q: Now, in addition to the information that you sent out that you just told us about to these shoe manufacturers, did you send out any other inquirers to law enforcement agencies?

A: Yes. Also sending — I sent an inquiry to eight international laboratories which I knew had computerized reference collections such as the FBI and I sent them pictures of the sole of the shoe as well as the pictures from the crime scene, a couple pictures from the crime scene at Bundy, and asked them the same question, could they identify the brand name or manufacturer of this shoe.

Q: Were any of those countries with computerized systems similar to the FBI's able to provide you with any information?

A: Yes. Seven of them responded and said they did not have this shoe in their collection. The eighth one, the national police agency in Tokyo, Japan, responded and advised that they had a shoe that they had obtained from a merchant of this design that was distributed in Europe and was made in Italy.[22]

Q: Now, as a result of the information that you have just talked to us about, did you determine who the manufacturer was of the Bruno Magli shoe?

A: Yes. Well, if I could comment on the bottom of the shoe, which has the manufacturer's name on it?

Q: Sure.

A: The bottom of the shoe has design elements.... The bottom of the shoe has design elements which are repeated across the entire sole area, as well as the heel, and these design elements, which repeat after one another across the width and length of the shoe, are identical in size in both the heel and the sole, and they are surrounded by a perimeter, a little raised line, and then there is an outer perimeter which does not actually touch the surface of the ground, but which is a little bit raised but can touch it if there is enough weight or other factors. The same is true of the heel and the leading edge of the heel is curved and has the notch cut off of the medial side, the inner side. This is a reverse photograph so this is actually the left — an enlargement of the left shoe, and this would be the outside of the body and this would be the inside to the right as you look at it (indicating) and in the center arch area. Also is the name "Bruno Magli," that is B-r-u-n-o M-a-g-l-i, as well as the capital "M" for Bruno Magli, their logo in the middle of that, and at the very bottom in the shadow here, which is probably hard to see, is the words "made in Italy" and up in the top corner here is the word "Silga," s-i-l-g-a, which to answer your question, this is the manufacturer in Italy of this outsole.

Q: Okay. Now, is that common in the footwear industry, that the company whose name goes on the shoe doesn't necessarily have their own factories that they own?

A: That is very common in the footwear industry, to have one company make the outsoles and sell those to another company that will then create the upper, which are attached and glued and stitched to the bottoms.[23]

Q: So what is the Bruno Magli company? If it is not a shoe factory, it is a what?

A: Well, it may also be a shoe factory, but they may — I don't know their full habits of purchasing, but with regard to this shoe, they had this mold made by Silga. For their shoes and these molds — these molded bottoms which were sent to another factory which is called 4c also in Italy, in the same area of Italy, and then the uppers were stitched and placed into the bottom and made and sold as a shoe.

Q: ... As to the manufacturer of the sole of the Bruno Magli shoe and also the upper, did you decide to visit the factories, these two factories?

A Yes, I did.

Q: And before getting into that, did you have some training and experience specifically in shoe manufacturing?

A: Yes. Over the years, since the late seventies, I have been to approximately ... footwear manufacturers approximately 25 occasions.

Q: And what is the purpose of trying to gather information about how shoes are manufactured from the standpoint of a forensic shoe examiner?

A: In some cases the purpose is because of the need to, in a particular case that I might be working, but as a general training tool it is important to learn the various ways that shoes can be manufactured, because there is quite a lot of differences between a direct attach injection molded shoe or a cut shoe that is made of unvulcanized rubber or a composition molded shoe.

Q: Okay. And are you able to use this information in your analysis in determining shoe size that left impressions at a crime scene?

A: Yes, sir.

Q: Now, is this something that you are routinely able to do based on that kind of information and other information?

A. Yes, sir.

Q: Now, in cases where you do have the information as to who manufactured the shoe, what can you do?

A: In that case we can specifically size the shoe if it has been made in certain manners. If it has been cut from a sheet of goods and then just glued to the bottom, that is usually not possible with an absolutely 100 percent certainty, but if the shoe has been molded and the molds have been made with a hand-milled method, where the person is actually guiding the milling device and creating the molds through their personal direction, as opposed to a computer method, then each of those molds, both in different sizes, as well as molds that may be duplicated in the same sizing, each of those will come out slightly different. And those differences will manifest themselves in impressions at the crime scene and enable a direct comparison to eliminate the molds that did not make the shoe and identify the mold which did make the shoe.[24] Different runs with same mold can yield minute differences;

Q: So does that mean, sir, that if you have two molds that were created with the same template, that as a forensic shoeprint examiner you would be able to distinguish those two molds?

A: Yes, sir.

Q: And is that based upon the placement, the exact placement of the mold with respect to the perimeter of the shoe?

A: It is based on the fact that in the hand milling process, as opposed to a process where you make duplicate molds from the beginning, or a computer process where the computer of course is going to do exactly the same thing every time with a CAD/CAM device, in the hand milling process each of these patterns will result in a slightly different position each time.

Q: Okay. And are there some other factors that are — in addition to the ones that are on this chart — that also go into the issue of shoe size?

A: Yes. There is other factors. One that is very important is the personal preference for fit. Some people, for instance, if they are buying a soccer shoe, may prefer it to be very tight. If they are buying a dress shoe, they may prefer it to be loose so they don't have to go into that breaking-in. If the shoe is in very expensive leather shoe, they may know in a couple wears it will be very soft and pliable and very much to their foot and they may like that fit, so they may intentionally buy it a little snug, so there is a lot of factors involving personal preference that play into account.

Q: Okay. Would it be just fair to say, to summarize this issue of shoe sizing, that there are more factors that go into it than a lay person might imagine?

A: Absolutely.[25]

After an extensive discussion of the foundation for his "matching" of the Bundy shoeprint to a Bruno Magli size 12, Agent Bodziak concluded:

Q: And with respect to the print on the right that says "Shoeprints FBI Q68" even though only a heel of that is visible, you were able to determine that was a 46 European sole?

A: Yes.

Q: How?

A: Because the heels, like the rest of the shoe, are distinctly different and so no other heel in the other sizes could have made that impression.

Q: Were you able to determine whether these shoe prints were made with a shoe that was manufactured on that precise mold that you saw at the Silga factory, the 46 mold?

A: Yes, it was — it had to have been made in that mold. There would be no other mold like it. So it was made — the shoe that made the impressions that I have addressed here, q107 and q68, were positively shoes that came from the Silga mold size 46.[26] [Extensive testimony followed: See total transcript].

B. FOOTWEAR CASES

There are a significant number of reported cases each year that involve footwear impression expert testimony. As noted above, there is bound to be some such data in virtually every crime scene involving the physical presence or movement of one or more persons. The value of any such impressions depends on the integrity of it and the preservation methods used by police and forensic technicians. In addition to class characteristic information, wear marks, embedded glass or stone, cuts, and gouges can provide individual characteristics unique to an individual. Differences and similarities vie for the attention of prosecuting and defense lawyers. What follows is a brief analysis of some of the more informative and important decisions in the area of footwear impression evidence.

The visual comparison of shoe impressions for purposes of size estimations or comparisons by police officers in the course of active crime scene investigations has been readily approved by the nation's courts. The analogy to permissible areas of lay person opinion is often seen.

In *People v. Ricketts,*[27] defendant was convicted of home invasion, robbery, burglary, and felony-theft. The defendant, accompanied by his friends, Ted Lucas and Elmer Cusick, went to the rural home of the victim for the stated purpose of getting a part for an air conditioner. The state contended that the defendant Ricketts, Lucas, and Cusick returned to the farm home; that Lucas and Cusick forced Griff Miller into the bathroom so violently that he suffered a broken hip and other injuries; and that defendant Ricketts then entered and took firearms, silverware, and jewelry.

Sheriff's Officer Busby testified concerning a boot print found in the dust on the dark wooden floor of a second-story bedroom. He measured its length at 11½ inches and sketched the details observed, including ridges across the sole and areas which appeared to be worn. Subsequently, the print was photographed to scale and the picture was introduced into evidence. When the defendant was arrested his boot was seized and at trial introduced into evidence. The defendant admitted that he was wearing the boot in January 1981.

Busby testified that he had measured the respective lengths of the boot and of the boot print, and that each was 11½ inches long, and he testified to the apparent worn spots on the sole and heel. The examination continued with the question:

Q: Do those worn spots correspond to the spots on the photograph being a representation of the footprints as you saw it?[28]

The objection made and overruled was "No foundation." The defendant argued that a nonexpert police officer could not give an opinion on shoe size or comparisons. The court ruled that the testimony objected to was merely illustrative of the observations to which Busby testified, and did not undertake to state as a matter of expert opinion that the boot in evidence made the print shown by the photograph in evidence. Assuming *arguendo* that a factor of lay opinion is found in the record, such testimony came within the rule holding that a lay witness may express an opinion where such opinion is one that people in general were capable of making and accustomed to make.[29]

In *People v. Lomas*,[30] the defendant was convicted of the early-morning burglary of a Goodyear service store in Rock Island, Illinois. A witness led police to the defendant. After booking the defendant at the station and asking him to remove his shoes, Officer Woodburn testified that he and Officer Pauly took the defendant's shoes to the scene of the burglary, where about 3 inches of snow covered the ground. There Officer Pauly put on the defendant's shoes and made a set of tracks in the snow parallel to those made by the perpetrator. At the hearing defense counsel objected to additional testimony from Officer Woodburn concerning the footprints, since he had not been shown to be an expert. The trial judge overruled this objection, stating that one need not be an expert to give an opinion concerning footprints.[31]

Woodburn then indicated that the original prints and the test prints were generally the same size and shape, with rounded toes and plain soles and heels. He also noted that the right shoe in both sets of prints revealed a round gouge in the sole near the ball of the right foot. An elongated gouge near the ball of the right foot showed up in some of the test prints but not in any of the suspect's prints. No additional witnesses were called by the state. No measurements or photographs of the footprints were made. The appeals court validated the trial court's overruling of defendant's objection to the evidence of the two officers:

> In the case at bar, we cannot say that the trial judge's determination was contrary to the manifest weight of the evidence, nor was his ruling to permit testimony by Officer Woodburn concerning the footprints erroneous, as the defendant alleges. Where the matter to be determined is one upon which the fact finder is competent to make a decision, expert opinion is unnecessary and inadmissible.... In the present case, evidence concerning the two sets of footprints did not warrant the services of an expert. For this reason, the trial judge correctly overruled the defendant's objections to the testimony of Officer Woodburn concerning the prints.[32]

At the close of all the evidence the trial judge examined the defendant's shoes and that the elongated gouge which showed up in some of the test prints but in none of the original prints was of recent origin and may have been made after the defendant's arrest.

The appeals court ruled that the judge's viewing of the defendant's shoes was properly within the scope of his responsibilities as the trier of fact.[33]

In *People v. Lawson,*[34] the defendant was convicted of first-degree murder and was sentenced to death. On July 28, 1989, between 7 and 8 A.M., the body of 8-year-old Terrance Jones (known as T.J.) was found lying face down approximately 15 or 16 feet inside a small, abandoned church in East St. Louis, Illinois. He had been stabbed several times in the back, chest, and arm, and his throat had been cut. He was clothed in a T-shirt with his underpants were pulled down around the knee area and on only one leg.[35]

The interior of the small church was dusty, dirty, and in a state of complete deterioration. During the morning hours following the discovery of the body and before the arrival of the police at around noon, many people in the surrounding neighborhood entered the church and observed the body, the defendant being among them. During the investigation, a police crime scene analyst observed several shoe prints in a substance which appeared to be dried blood. Subsequent forensic tests revealed the substance to be human blood consistent in type with the victim's. The bloody shoe prints were on two pieces of wooden paneling located immediately to one side of the body and bore the legend "Pro-Wing," a brand of gym shoe indisputably worn by many individuals in the immediately surrounding neighborhood. At the direction of the crime scene analyst, police looked for persons in the crowd wearing Pro-Wing gym shoes. Police saw no one in the crowd other than the defendant wearing the Pro-Wing shoe and requested that he give them his shoes for purposes of elimination, which he did.[36]

David Peck, a forensic scientist, testified as the state's fingerprint and footwear analysis expert. Peck testified that he found 5 of 12 bloody shoe print impressions on the two pieces of wooden paneling as identifiable to either the defendant's right or left Pro-Wing gym shoe. Peck testified that the seven remaining shoe print impressions could have been made by the defendant's shoes. Peck also opined that the shoe print impression found on the page from the allegedly pornographic magazine could also have been made by the defendant's shoe. Peck testified that the additional shoe print impression, in the white, chalky substance on the wooden paneling, could not have been made by the defendant's shoes.[37]

Peck showed the jury photographic enlargements of the shoe print impressions, which he relied on as exhibits. Peck then directed the jury's attention to a prepared chart pointing out eight different individual characteristics of the bloody shoe print impressions on the boards. He then matched each shoe print impression on the boards with photographic enlargements of defendant's Pro-Wing gym shoes. Peck stated that he could not determine when the bloody shoe print impressions were made.

The defendant contended that the trial court erred in denying his motion for funds to obtain the services of a fingerprint and shoe print expert. The defendant asserted that the denial of funds for such expertise denied him due process of law, effective assistance of counsel, and the right to obtain witnesses for his defense.[38] The state acknowledged the possible constitutional and statutory dimensions of the claimed error,[39] but claimed that the defendant, as required, failed to provide the trial court with the name of a specific expert and an estimate of the fees involved.

The court ruled that in analyzing the particular circumstances of each case, whether deciding statutory or constitutional issues, a standard had evolved that there must be some showing that the requested expert assistance was necessary in proving a crucial issue in the case and that the lack of funds for the expert would therefore prejudice defendant. The Illinois Supreme Court noted that the U.S. Supreme Court in *Ake v. Oklahoma*,[40] held that when an indigent defendant shows that his sanity at the time of an offense is to be "a significant factor at trial," the state must, at a minimum, assure access to a competent psychiatrist who can examine the defendant and assist in his defense.

Here, defense counsel had filed a Motion to Provide Funds for Experts and Investigative Assistance, which stated that the defendant was indigent, was represented by appointed counsel, could not afford to pay for experts pending reimbursement by the county, and that the defendant would need a fingerprint expert to examine and compare shoe prints and fingerprints found at the crime scene. The court here noted that the state's expert Peck directed the jury's attention to enlarged photographic exhibits of the bloody shoe print impressions found on the wooden paneling and of the bottom of the defendant's Pro-Wing gym shoes and described in considerable detail the manner in which he was able to identify the impressions:

> What I've done again is put eight numbers on here and drawn them to areas which contain either one or numerous individual characteristics on the unknown bloody footwear impression on the paneling and the test impression of the bottom of this shoe. Number one is a little nick in a circular area in the ball of the shoe area.
>
> ...
>
> Again, I can point out eight different areas in—for instance, number five on the heel area I circled an area, and they are basically two or three individual cuts or gouges within that small circular area there. What I also do when I'm comparing is ... look microscopically or very close at each of these individual characteristics to make sure that the cut or gouge, the outlying contours are the same between the unknown and the known.
>
> ...
>
> Of course, you look closely you can see that the ... the class characteristics are also the same. You have the small linear bars in the heel area with a type of rectangular squares in both the unknown and the known.
>
> ...
>
> So I was able to, by looking at the class, in other words, the type of pattern, is the same and the number of individual characteristics being the same, was able to positively

say that the footwear impression—laid footwear impression on the paneling was positively made by the left shoe of People's Exhibit No. 5.[41]

Peck then demonstrated to the jury how he matched each individual shoe print impression found on the paneling to each of the defendant's shoes and that based on wear characteristics of the two pieces of wooden paneling, he was able to align the wood as it was aligned at the murder scene.

At the close of the state's case, the court noted, the defendant renewed his motion, requesting funds to hire a shoe print and fingerprint expert and the trial court again denied it. During closing arguments, the prosecutor stated that "[t]he most important evidence in this case is the scientific evidence which was presented to you" and that "[t]he single, strongest piece of evidence in this case, and it's a piece of evidence that you can't get around, is that piece of wood with defendant's fresh footprints in it."

Considering that record before it, the Illinois Supreme Court ruled that there was no question that the defendant's indigency was established or that the opinion of a defense shoe print expert was necessary to proving a crucial issue in the case and that the defendant was prejudiced without such assistance. The expert's opinion of the shoe print evidence, as acknowledged by the prosecutor, was also the strongest evidence presented by the state because it was the only evidence capable of establishing the defendant's actual presence at the scene at the time of the murder. The state's remaining evidence consisted of highly inconsistent eyewitness testimony and circumstantial witness testimony going only to motive and opportunity.[42]

Another important and comprehensive case in the footwear area is another decision by the Illinois Supreme Court in *People v. Campbell*,[43] where the defendant was charged with residential burglary. The case warrants extended discussion here.

Jeffrey Miller testified that on the evening of March 9, 1989, when he returned home from work, he found the front door wide open, most of the lights inside the home on, the house in disarray, and wet, muddy footprints throughout the living room and kitchen. Bills, which he had placed on the kitchen table that morning, were scattered over the kitchen and living-room floors. When Miller and Buchanan left home, however, only a small lamp in the living room had been left burning. Miller noticed also that a television and VCR were missing. He then summoned the police. At about 10:30 P.M., after police completed their investigation, Miller left the house and picked up Buchanan from work.[44] Miller testified that when he arrived, there were wet, muddy prints on the linoleum kitchen floor and on the living room carpet.

During his investigation, police officer Provensale found an empty, Illinois Bell Telephone bill envelope lying on the floor in the living room/dining room area and that there was a shoe print on the envelope. Provensale examined Miller's shoes, as well as those of the other investigating officers at the scene, and concluded that their shoes did not match the print on the envelope.

Officer Richard Fonck testified that on March 12, 1989, he was on duty as an evidence technician at the Joliet police station when he encountered defendant, who was at the station on an unrelated matter. Officer Fonck noticed that the defendant was wearing tennis shoes, which when compared with a photograph taken by Provensale of the print on the telephone bill envelope, appeared similar in design. Fonck secured the defendant's shoes, and forwarded them to the state crime laboratory for examination.[45]

A forensic scientist employed by the Illinois State Police crime laboratory, Walter Sherk, testified that he had been with the forensic bureau of the crime laboratory for about $14^{1}/_{2}$ years, working in the specific area of firearms, tool marks, and shoe prints. He further testified that he received a bachelor's degree in forensic science, had 2 years' on-the-job training in his field of expertise; had attended an FBI course in shoe print identification, and that he attends annual lectures and meetings regarding shoe print identification. In his career, he had performed approximately 300 shoe print comparisons and testified in approximately 15 cases on his shoe print analyses.[46]

The expert testified that, for purposes of shoe print analysis, class characteristics refer to the size and pattern of the shoe, and individual characteristics refer to such things as nicks, cuts, and scratches, which are picked up after the shoe has been worn over a period of time. In comparing shoe prints, a forensic shoe impression analyst looks for both types of characteristics. Here, he testified that the Illinois Bell envelope bore two separate shoe impressions made by what appeared to be dust or dirt. He performed a comparison of the Nike brand tennis shoes taken from the defendant with the prints on the envelope, and on the basis of dissimilar patterns, he concluded that the smaller of the two prints on the envelope could not have been made by the defendant's shoes.

The expert then made a "test print" from the defendant's right shoe for comparison with the larger print on the envelope, by inking the sole of the shoe and stepping on white paper. The larger print showed two thirds of the middle portion of a shoe. Based upon his comparison, Sherk found the shoe size and patterns "consistent with" the defendant's shoe. In addition, he identified six "matching individual class characteristics." From this analysis, he testified that he could "positively identify" the defendant's right shoe as having made the larger shoe print on the envelope.[47]

On cross-examination, he testified that there was no requisite number of characteristics necessary for an identification, since each identification depended upon the uniqueness of the individual characteristics. Depending on what the marks look like, he continued, an identification could be made based on as little as two or three marks. He further testified that he could say neither where the envelope was when the print was made nor when the print was made.

The expert observed that if a shoe is worn for some period of time after the shoe print was placed on an exhibit, some change in the shoe's characteristics could occur. On cross-examination, the following exchange occurred:

Q [Defense attorney]: Are there any dissimilar points in the shoe and in the print on the envelope?

A: There are points, yes. There are dissimilarities, obviously, that may not show up on the test print or the evidence.

...

Q: I'm saying did you find some dissimilar points, some things that were on the envelope that weren't on the shoe?

A: Well, there may be, but I didn't look for dissimilarities. I mean. It's granted that there are dissimilarities in the shoe. There are points that are not going to possibly match up. You're talking about the wear, after the shoe print was on the shoe. And there may be—

The Court: ... How can you know if a dissimilarity is wear or how can you know if a dissimilarity was there before or after the offense?

A: There are a number of factors that come into play. There could be dirt on the portion of the shoe that is not there when I have the shoe, that was there at the time the shoe print was made.

The Court: But how would you know that?

A: I don't know that, if there was or there wasn't.

The Court: Would you presume that if there was a dissimilarity?

A: I would presume it could be that, or it could be the fact that the shoe was worn after the shoe impression was made, and therefore it changed.

...

If you have the correspondence of individual characteristics that are present on both, then you have to assume that the areas, the one little nick or something that may not show up on the test print, then that area was possible [sic] distorted after the original impression was made, or there may be dirt or something that was present at the time the shoe print or the test print with the impression on the evidence with the sufficient correspondence of individual characteristics that are present on both that are present and you can see them, then those are identifying marks that enable you to positively identify that shoe.

Q: So, you can't tell us here now whether there is any dissimilar things on the print on the envelope and the shoe print?

A: Well, again, I didn't mark and specifically identify any dissimilarities. There may well be some though.[48]

During cross-examination, the trial judge asked the expert whether he meant that the second print on the envelope was smaller because it was a smaller size shoe or just a smaller print because of the way it was on the envelope. He responded that it was just a smaller print, to distinguish it from the larger print on the envelope.

Initially, the court noted that research had not revealed any recent Illinois case that addressed whether shoe print evidence, standing alone, was sufficient to convict. It is the case in both state and federal courts that forensic evidence alone, with the possible exceptions of ballistics and fingerprints, to be soon joined by DNA evidence, is insufficient to sustain a conviction.[49]

The court noted defendant's argument that the strength of the expert's opinion on the similarity between the shoe and the test print was subject to doubt because, unlike fingerprint, bite mark, or ballistics evidence, shoe prints lacked original uniqueness and that their characteristics change over a period of time, which should result in a general distrust of shoe print evidence. The court refused to find shoe print evidence unreliable, as a matter of law:

> We believe that where there are significant general and individual characteristics, such as would provide a basis for a positive identification, shoeprint evidence may be as reliable and as trustworthy as any other evidence. Indeed, our review of the relevant case law lends no support to defendant's argument that shoeprint evidence is "generally distrusted." We note that in Illinois, correspondence of footprints found at the scene of a crime with the sole of one accused of the crime has long been admissible as competent evidence in an attempt to identify the accused as the guilty person.... It simply does not follow that since, as defendant concludes, shoeprint evidence lacks the "original uniqueness" of certain other types of demonstrative evidence it is untrustworthy.[50]

The court, while acknowledging that "general problems" with the probative value of shoe print evidence may arise in a particular case where an attempt is made at positive identification of an accused in the absence of sufficient unique, distinctive characteristics, found no "general problems" with shoe print evidence such as would support a conclusion of unreliability as a matter of law.[51]

The court took note of the fact that most shoes today have been mass-produced, and identical shoes may be sold to many people, and that new shoes generally differ very little from one to another. Therefore, pattern and other general characteristics, alone, would seldom be sufficient for identification purposes. However, the court recognized, "when shoes are worn, even for a limited period of time, the soles begin to show peculiar signs of wear, nail marks, cuts, and other accidental markings. Consequently, shoeprints may offer sufficient individual, unique markings and characteristics upon which to base a positive identification."[52]

In this case, the court recalled, the expert testified not only to the general pattern and size of the shoe, but also to "peculiar signs of wear," and, thus, the evidence here did not suffer for lack of evidence of peculiarities.

Finally, the defendant argued that the time between the occurrence of the crime and the police seizure of his shoes, wherein the shoes had been worn, may have resulted in a coincidental accumulation of any so-called distinguishing features. The court rejected any such argument:

> We find it unlikely, as apparently did the trial court, that the six similar individual characteristics could all be the result of coincidence. Were there only one similar characteristic, we would be more inclined to accept this argument. However, we believe that even one individual characteristic, depending on the nature and uniqueness, could be enough for a valid comparison. Defendant urges another point on the issue of coincidence as it relates to the lack of evidence of dissimilarities. He states that the expert "ignored" dissimilarities, explaining that any dissimilarity would be attributable to wear upon or injury to the shoe occurring after the test print had been impressed. Defendant argues that if subsequent wear caused dissimilarities, it is reasonable that the same wear attributed to "coincidental" similarities. He further maintains that since the expert "ignored" the dissimilarities, the appellate court properly discounted his comparison.[53]

The court noted that in shoe print comparison, the first step in the analysis is to note any fundamental differences between the shoe and the shoe print. A fundamental difference is one such as size, shape, or make, that precludes any further comparison. Absent fundamental differences, points of similarity are located and recorded and explainable dissimilarities are differences between the shoe and the shoe print which may have resulted from dust or dirt.[54]

The defendant also attempted to analogize fingerprint evidence to shoe print evidence by pointing out that fingerprint analysis depended upon similarities, and that a dissimilarity between a test print and a defendant's fingerprint defeated an identification. It would seem, the defendant opined, that the same should be true for interpretation of the far less precise science of shoe print impression analysis. The court quickly rejected this argument, observing that fingerprints do not essentially change and no two fingerprints are the same. Shoeprints, on the other hand, as conceded by the defendant, do change. Therefore, while a dissimilarity in a fingerprint may not be subject to explanation, such was not the case with shoe print evidence.[55]

The defendant also argued that a comparison consisting of only six individual characteristics was way too few upon which to base any credible "match" testimony. The court noted that there are no cases that expressly state a requisite number of points of similarity for either shoe print or fingerprint evidence. The court also noted that cases with varying number of points in fingerprint ranging from 4, 5, 10, and 20 had been approved.[36] In this case, the court concluded, the expert testified that the six individual characteristics were a sufficient number upon which to base a positive identification.[57]

Finally, the defendant contended that to connect the defendant with the offense, as with fingerprint evidence, there must be proof that the shoe print was made at the time the offense was committed. The court agreed, stating:

[D]efendant is correct in his assertion that in order to sustain a conviction solely on fingerprint evidence, fingerprints corresponding to those of the defendant must have been found in the immediate vicinity of the crime under such circumstances as to establish beyond a reasonable doubt that they were impressed at the time the crime was committed.... Further, we agree with defendant that the same time/placement requirement should exist for shoeprint evidence. However, in either case, the State is not required to seek out and negate every conceivable possibility that the print was impressed at some time other than during the commission of the offense.... In some cases, evidence of the particular location of the fingerprint satisfies the time/placement requirement, as does the prosecution's proof of the chain of contact of the touched item, which would show that the item could have been touched only at the time of the crime.... Additionally, attendant circumstances may well support an inference that the print was made at the time of the commission of the offense.[58]

Here, the court determined that there were sufficient attendant circumstances here to support the inference that the shoe print was made at the time the offense was committed, inasmuch as Miller testified that when he left the house for work, the Illinois Bell envelope was on the kitchen table. He gave no permission to anyone to enter the house during his absence and, upon his returning home, the envelope was on the floor. The expert testified that the shoe print on the Illinois Bell envelope shared sufficiently similar individual characteristics with shoes in the possession of the defendant for him to make a positive identification. This evidence, the court stated, while not conclusive on the issue of when the print was impressed, has some tendency to establish that the defendant was at the scene of the crime, and further that the impression was made at the time the offense was committed.[59]

In *People v. Robinson*,[60] another case dealing with foot impressions on paper products, the defendant was convicted of a first-degree murder and an armed robbery committed while he was a prisoner at the Stateville Correctional Center. He was accused of murdering a fellow inmate and stealing his cigarettes. When officer Jessie White came out of the commissary, she found the victim's body. It was subsequently determined that victim Troeng died from a severe head injury due to blunt-force trauma. A partial shoe impression was found on a paper sack on the floor of the commissary.

Walter Sherk, an expert in footprint comparisons, testified that he compared the footwear impression on the paper sack with the boots recovered from the defendant and stated that, while the boots recovered from the defendant were standard issue at the Department of Corrections, the impression was consistent with defendant's right boot. The defendant alleged that the prosecutor misstated the boot-impression testimony of the state's expert witnesses. Specifically, the defendant objected to a statement in the prosecution's closing that defendant's boot impression was found in the commissary:

The important thing about what Walter Sherk said [the state's expert in footprint comparisons] is the boot [imprint] is consistent with the boots that Wesley is wearing. But the most important thing Walter Sherk said is they're the same size boots as Wesley. So what we're saying is that Wesley is not eliminated by the boot impression.[61]

The court determined that the remarks in the present case did not substantially prejudice the defendant. This correct statement regarding the relevance of the boot impression effectively alleviated any harm which was done by the immediately following isolated boot-imprint statement about which the defendant complained.

In *State v. Kortbein*[62] the defendant was convicted of first-degree intentional homicide of a 77-year-old veteran whose habit was to stop in at a gas station near where he lived every morning to read the paper. He was found bludgeoned to death in his apartment on August 2, 1990 after notification to police by the gas station owner that he hadn't stopped at the station. A pathologist concluded that the murder weapon was a blunt instrument such as a crowbar, tire iron, hammer, or numbchucks. The amount of force required to depress the skull caused the pathologist to opine that the murderer had been highly agitated. No fingerprints or murder weapon were found at the scene; however, there were several partial footprints recovered from newspapers that had been scattered on the floor near the body. The prints appeared to have been made in blood by British Knight tennis shoes.

After receiving a tip about the defendant, after police interviewed him and observed a pair of British Knight tennis shoes in defendant Kortbein's apartment. He agreed to turn his shoes over to the police for analysis. A forensic serologist at the state crime laboratory found no evidence of blood on the shoes, and then turned the shoes over to shoe print analyst Steve Harrington, for comparison with the imprints made at the crime scene.[63] Upon analysis, he concluded that Kortbein's left tennis shoe "positively matched" one of the footwear impressions from the crime scene. He also testified that the shoes were consistent with four other impressions recovered from the scene but did not cause two other patterns observed in photographs from the scene. Based upon this shoe identification information, Kortbein was charged with the murder.[64]

An example of Bodziak's advice to trace the dynamics of the crime scene as a means of locating foot impressions may be seen in *State v. Washington*,[65] where defendant was convicted of simple burglary. Police received an anonymous call reporting that someone was coming in and out of the True Hope Church of God and Christ. The caller said that the man was dressed in a red jacket, blue jeans, and a plaid shirt. When Deputy John Baptiste arrived on the scene, he saw a man in the field next to the church. After returning to the church with the defendant, a police officer entered the church and observed a piano with a footprint on it and testified that the burglar would have had to stand on the piano to remove the speaker that was tied to the ceiling. The officer compared the shoes that the defendant was wearing with the footprints and observed that they were a visual match.

Another deputy observed a footprint in the mud outside of the church kitchen window. She, too, saw the footprint on the top of the church's piano. When the officers brought the defendant back to the church after he was stopped, she compared the defendant's shoes with the prints and concluded that the impression in the ground and the one on the piano and another near the amplifier were all made by the defendant's shoes.[69]

Many cases have been reported where mention is made of police having followed footprints or boot prints made in the snow to track a perpetrator.[67] Less common are cases where an attempt has been made to present linking evidence regarding an impression in snow that was either preserved or, more commonly, where police testify to a visual match between a snow print and the defendant's footwear.[68] A number of articles have been published on the subject of the preservation of shoe-wear impressions made in snow.[69]

In the footwear area, as with all others, too often the admissibility of such evidence is effected without any serious challenge. Nonetheless it, like the other areas of forensics, carries very significant circumstantial weight in the midst of a variety of nonforensic evidence.

In *State v. Delucca*,[70] the defendant was convicted of armed robbery, conspiracy to commit armed robbery, and weapons offenses. On December 20, 1995, at approximately 8:15 P.M., a car stopped near a gas station, an armed man exited the vehicle, walked into the food store, and demanded money from the owner. The perpetrator beat the victim and fled. Police Officer Steven Gonzalez responded to a police dispatch and went to the crime scene. As Gonzalez headed in the direction where a witness reported the suspect in the street, he noticed footprints with a distinctive pattern in the snow. Gonzalez testified that there was about 12 inches of snow, and that the temperature was "possibly below zero" the night of the incident. He further testified that the footprints appeared "consistent" and described them as a "vibrum type sole, a particular, like a triangular like pattern of the wearer."[71]

The appellate court held that the trial judge did not err in allowing officer Gonzalez to testify about footprints found in the snow, since a nonexpert may give an opinion on matters of common knowledge and observation. The testimony of a police officer regarding his observations of footprints in the snow and his conclusion that the footprints were similar to the prints left by the defendant's boots is not a matter of expert opinion.[72] In *State v. Patterson*,[73] the defendant was convicted of first-degree murder for the homicides of his ex-girlfriend's mother, Ida Strouth, Ida's 9-year-old son, Jacob Strouth, and the Strouths' 13-year-old neighbor, Jeremiah Sponsel. At the crime scene, police found several impressions consistent with a bloody, gloved hand. Police also found two sets of footprints in the basement. One set was from an unknown source, but the other matched a pair of shoes later seized from Patterson's truck and those footprints were also consistent with an imprint on victim Ida's face.

In *Lewis v. State*,[74] the defendant was convicted of two counts of capital murder for the double murder and robbery of Gertrude and Willie Woods, the elderly great aunt and uncle of the appellant. The two victims were brutally attacked in their home. Both victims had been repeatedly stabbed. The attacker fled the scene with one or more of Mrs. Woods's purses. Based on physique and voice, one neighbor positively identified Lewis as the assailant. The neighbor also identified Lewis's car as the getaway car. The police seized clothing from Lewis's house, which was similar to that worn by the assailant.

A criminalist testified that a bloody shoe print from the scene of the crime matched one of Lewis's shoes "to the exclusion of any other shoe in the world." The defendant argued that the trial judge erred by admitting the testimony of one Joe

Andrews, an employee of the Mississippi Crime Laboratory, who had compared the bloody footprints found at the scene of the crime with Lewis's shoes and concluded that one of the bloody prints was made by Lewis's shoe, to the exclusion of every other shoe in the world.

As in the O. J. Simpson case, Lewis also argued that he should have been allowed to don Exhibit 66 (a pair of black Fila tennis shoes) in order for the jury to consider the fit of the shoes. There were two pairs of black Fila tennis shoes in this case: (1) Exhibit 66, size 12 shoes, which the police contended were worn by Lewis at the time of his arrest, and (2) Exhibit 75, shoes with white paint on them, which the police contended were seized from Lewis's room with a search warrant. However, the court ruled, it was undisputed that both pairs of shoes belonged to Lewis (whether they were taken from his bedroom or his feet). The right shoe from Exhibit 66 was identified as having made the bloody footprint at the scene of the crime. Later, during Lewis's case-in-chief, the defense attorney attempted to have Lewis don the shoes. The state objected to Lewis exhibiting the fit of the shoes, unless Lewis took the stand, under oath. The trial judge held that exhibiting the fit of the shoes would waive Lewis's Fifth Amendment right against self-incrimination. That is, the trial judge would allow Lewis to make the demonstration, but only if Lewis took the stand and subjected himself to cross-examination.[75]

On appeal, Lewis argued that he should have been allowed to put the shoes on his feet, and that such a demonstration would not waive his Fifth Amendment right against self-incrimination. The court rejected this argument, stating:

> Clearly, the defendant can be required to make such demonstrations, without violating the Fifth Amendment.... [L]ong ago, the United States Supreme Court held that an accused's Fifth Amendment rights are not offended when the accused is compelled to put on clothing identified with a crime, to see if it fits, because "the prohibition of compelling a man in a criminal court to be witness against himself is a prohibition of the use of physical or moral compulsion to extort communications from him, not an exclusion of his body as evidence when it may be material."... The Fifth Amendment privilege "is a bar against compelling 'communications' or 'testimony,' but that compulsion which makes a suspect or accused the source of 'real or physical evidence' does not violate it." [76]

Lewis argued that, because the state could have compelled him to demonstrate the fit of the shoes, he was entitled to a level playing field, and could not be denied the right to make the same demonstration before the jury. In the case at hand, the court observed, the ownership of the shoes is not at issue. Also, it was undisputed that the defendant was wearing the shoes when he was arrested. And all of the officers present at the arrest identified the shoes (in Exhibit 66) as those worn by the Lewis at the time of his arrest. The right shoe from this pair was identified by the expert as having made the bloody footprint at the scene of the crime—to the exclusion of every other shoe in the world.

Clearly, the court ruled, the defendant does not waive his Fifth Amendment protections by offering demonstrative evidence, if appropriate and relevant. That is, if the state could require the demonstration without violating the Fifth Amendment, then the defendant may make the demonstration without waiving his Fifth Amendment protection against self-incrimination. Here, however, since the demonstration requested by defendant was irrelevant, his argument on this point was without merit.

In *State v. Matney*,[77] defendant was convicted of first-degree murder, armed criminal action, and first-degree robbery. The bodies of Cecil Phillips and Ethel Phillips were discovered inside their house at Malden, Missouri, late in the afternoon of December 18, 1996. Mrs. Phillips had multiple stab and slash wounds to the head, neck, and upper part of her body. Mr. Phillips had multiple skull fractures and incisions to the neck. Evidence officers discovered blood smears and spatter on the wall and footwear impressions in bloodstains on the carpet near the feet of the victims. The footprints in the carpeting were photographed and sections of the carpeting with the bloodstained footprints removed. There was a bloodstained vacuum cleaner in the hallway.[78]

A police officer who participated in the search of defendant's residence testified that he seized an empty boot box from underneath a bed, but did not locate the boots that belonged with the box. The box was for "Brahma brand, Canyon Split, size 8 boots."

Andy Wagoner, a firearms and tool marks examiner at Southeast Missouri Regional Crime Laboratory, testified that he received the part of the carpet from the Phillips house that had bloody footprints and compared the imprints on the carpeting with the tread on the soles of a pair of Brahma brand, Canyon Split, size 8 boots secured from a Wal-Mart store for that purpose. Mr. Wagoner testified as follows:

Q: Okay. And what were your findings with respect to the comparisons that you made?

A: The findings were that the lug design of the outer sole on the boots that were submitted produced a similar lug design as that on this carpet.

Q: Now, would you be able—do you have any opinion as to a reasonable scientific certainty as to whether there are class comparisons that are a match?

A: Yes.

Q: And what is that opinion?

A: The class comparisons of the lug design as well as the measurement of the width are the same.[79]

Pamela Johnson, a criminalist employed by Southeast Missouri Regional Crime Laboratory, testified that she compared fingerprints of defendant to an unidentified fingerprint from the tags that were inside the boot box recovered from the defendant's residence. She gave the opinion that "the latent print that was on the tag that was contained inside Item 18 [the boot box]" was made by the left index finger of defendant.

In *Miller v. State,*[80] the defendant was convicted in the District Court, Oklahoma County, Oklahoma of first-degree murder and sentenced to death. Kent Dodd worked as the night auditor for the Central Plaza Hotel located in Oklahoma City. Dodd registered a guest at approximately 3:15 A.M., September 17, 1994. Soon after Dodd was attacked by an assailant who stabbed him repeatedly, beat him with hedge shears and a paint can, and poured muriatic acid on him and down his throat. Bloody footprints were found near the body of the victim. Defendant Miller had worked as a maintenance man at the Central Plaza Hotel for 2 weeks about a month before the murder and had been known to the victim under an alias, Jay Elkins.

All of the evidence against George Miller was circumstantial. Experts testified that Miller's sandals "could have" left the bloody footprints found at the scene, but could not be exclusively identified. A microscopic drop of blood found on Miller's sandal was consistent with Dodd's blood, but also could not be exclusively identified. Miller told police he was home with his wife at the time of the murder. Photographs of the crime scene revealed what appears to be finger writing in the blood on the floor and wall which could be the letter "J" and the word, "Jay." The court stated that while Miller correctly pointed out that no eyewitness, fingerprint, or hair evidence connected him to the crime and no blood evidence conclusively placed him there, that there was a substantial amount of circumstantial evidence against him.[81]

The state's shoe print expert, FBI criminalist Sarah Wiersema, created an acetate overlay of a life-size imprint of the sole of Miller's sandal, State's Exhibit No. 96. During her testimony, she placed it over a life-size photograph of a bloody shoe print found at the scene of the crime. The size and shape of the prints matched. The defense objected on the grounds the overlay had not been provided to the defendant prior to trial. The trial court overruled the objection and admitted State's Exhibit No. 96 on the grounds the state had provided the defense with the sandal, the state's photograph of the sandal's sole, and photographs of the bloody footprints left at the scene.

The court found the evidence sufficient to sustain the conviction:

> Bloody footprints left at the scene could have been made by sandals owned by Miller. The State's expert carefully explained that while the size and "interlocking dog bone" pattern of the sole was "consistent" with the footprints found at the scene, Miller's sandal could not be identified conclusively as the source of the print, for no unique flaws in the sole of the sandal were present in the footprint. The expert explained blood is an imperfect medium for the forensic identification of footprints, for it fills in the very flaws used for exclusive identification.[82]

"Consistency" between the sole of Miller's sandal and the crime scene footprint was sufficient to meet the evidentiary standard of relevance.

III. TIRE IMPRESSIONS

A. GENERAL

Tire impression analysis works on principles quite similar to shoe impression analyses, i.e., style, brand and class, individual wear pattern, and other use factors.[83] There are a respectable number of reported decisions addressing this mode of forensic identification.

B. TIRE IMPRESSION CASES

In *People v. Sutherland*,[84] the defendant was convicted of aggravated kidnaping, aggravated criminal sexual assault, and murder, and was sentenced to death. The case arose out of the brutal sexual assault and murder of a 10-year-old child. Among many other types of forensic evidence, the court admitted tire cast testimony.

Illinois State Police forensic scientist David Brundage examined the plaster casts of the tire print impressions made at the scene of the crime. He concluded, and testified at trial, that the tire impressions left at the scene were consistent in all class characteristics with only two models of tires manufactured in North America, the Cooper "Falls Persuader" and the Cooper "Dean Polaris."

Several months after the discovery of Amy's body, the police at Glacier National Park in Montana called Jefferson County Deputy Sheriff Michael Anthis regarding Cecil Sutherland's abandoned car, a 1977 Plymouth Fury. At the time of Amy's murder, Sutherland had been living in Dix, Illinois, in Jefferson County, on the county line between Dix and Kell. Deputy Anthis determined that the car in question had a Cooper "Falls Persuader" tire on the right front wheel. Deputy Anthis and David Brundage then traveled to Montana where they made an ink impression of the right front wheel of Sutherland's car.

After comparing the plaster casts of the tire impression at the scene with the inked impression of the tire from Sutherland's car, Brundage concluded that the tire impression at the scene corresponded with Sutherland's tire and could have been made by that tire. Brundage, however, could not positively exclude all other tires due to the lack of comparative individual characteristics, such as nicks, cuts, or gouges.[85]

Similarly, Mark Thomas, the manager of mold operations at the Cooper Tire Company, concluded that due to the "mal" wear similarity, Sutherland's tire could have made the impression found at the crime scene. Thomas compared the blueprints of Cooper tires with the plaster casts of the tire impressions and concluded that the "probability" was "pretty great" that a size P2175/B15 tire—the same size as Sutherland's Falls Persuader tire—had made the impression. He conceded, however, that there was a significant number of such tires on the road.[86]

In *People v. Davenport*,[87] the defendant was convicted before the Superior Court, Orange County, California of murder in the first degree with the special circumstance that the murder was intentional and involved infliction of torture. The jury fixed the defendant's sentence at death.

Gayle Lingle, the victim, spent the evening of March 26, 1980, at the Sit 'N Bull Bar in Tustin. Between approximately midnight and 1 A.M., she and defendant left the bar. The victim's body was found the next morning lying in a large, uncultivated field south of the I-5 Freeway near Tustin. The victim suffered extremely violent injuries prior to death at the hands of her attacker. There were motorcycle tracks in the area.

Defendant owned a "350 cc" Honda motorcycle, and his nickname was "Honda Dave." The prosecution produced three eyewitnesses who placed a motorcycle similar to one owned by the defendant at the murder scene between 12:30 and 1:30 A.M. on March 27. Three expert witnesses testified to facts that connected the defendant's motorcycle to the crime.

Jack Leonard, the production manager for the International Sport and Rally Division of Dunlop Tire Company, testified that the tracks of the rear tire at the crime scene had the same highly unique and distinctive characteristics as the rear tire of the motorcycle. Both were Dunlop brand motorcycle tires, size 4.00-18 with a K-70 tread pattern, and both were characterized by a rare defect in a portion of the tread pattern known as the cross-slot. The degree of wear of the defendant's tire was consistent with the tracks at the scene. The track of the front motorcycle tire at the scene showed a tread pattern which he recognized as a Bridgestone tire, similar to the front tire on the defendant's motorcycle.[88]

IV. BITE MARK CASE LISTING

A relatively recent phenomenon in the general area of impression expertise is the forensic odontology specialty of bite marks. While still controversial, an increasing number of courts are accepting bite mark testimony as a scientifically sound basis for attempts to link a suspect to a crime scene, typically homicide and sexual assault settings. A brief description of cases is provided here.

Brewer v. State of Mississmippi, 725 S0.2d 106 (1998)
The defendant was convicted of capital murder while in the commission of the crime of sexual battery of a 3-year-old child. On appeal, the court found that the dentist qualified as an expert in forensic odontology even though he had been suspended from the American Board of Forensic Odontology for testifying beyond his expertise. In addition, this court found that a videotape showing the defendant's dentitions was not reversible error, because it showed the same thing as photographs.

State v. Cazes, 875 S.W.2d 253 (1994)
In a first-degree felony murder case, the forensic odontologist's testimony matching the bite marks on the victim to the defendant was admissible despite the lack of absolute certainty.

Harrison v. State, 635 So.2d 894 (1994)
The court held that the defendant in a capital murder case was denied due process and fundamental fairness when he was denied funds to obtain a forensic odontologist's expert opinion when the state's expert was the only one to testify.

Keko v. Hingle, 1999 WL 155945 (1999)

The court held that the plaintiff's Fourth Amendment rights were violated when a warrant was sought for his dental impressions. Dr. West's (forensic odontologist) technique for examining bite mark evidence was used in this case. Evidence was brought to Dr. West to persuade him to find that the plaintiff was responsible for his wife's murder. As a result, Dr. West's expert opinion that the bite marks on the victim matched the plaintiff's bite marks was used to obtain a warrant for Keko's arrest.

State v. Landers, 969 S.W.2d 808 (1998)

The court ruled that defense counsel was not ineffective in failing to ask the defendant if he had chipped his tooth before or after the date of the incident. The dentitions taken of the defendant's mouth showed a gap where a tooth was chipped, and the defendant alleged that the chip occurred after the event in question.

Malone v. Camp, 22 F.3d 693 (1994)

In a murder case, "potential prejudice did not so greatly outweigh probative value of evidence comparing bite mark on the murder victim's thigh with dental impressions taken from the defendant as to deny the defendant fundamentally fair trial, even though at the time of murder prosecution, science of forensic odontology was still in its infancy; evidence had some probative value, and the defendant cross-examined state's witnesses and presented witnesses of his own to testify that he could not have made the bite mark." U.S.C.A. Const.Amend. 6.

People v. Payne, 667 N.E.2d 643 (1996)

In this first-degree murder case, the defendant contends that the grand jury erred by compelling the defendant to produce dental impressions because there was no showing of probable cause. The court held that "relevance and individualized suspicion" are required for the request for dental impressions, because it qualifies as a nonintrusive procedure and does not threaten one's bodily integrity.

People v. Shaw, 664 N.E.2d 97 (1996)

"Trial court did not abuse its discretion in admitting doctor's testimony that mark on defendant's shoulder was caused by victim's braces despite doctor's characterization of bite as toolmark where doctor was expert in bitemark identification, doctor had previously been qualified as toolmark examiner, doctor was familiar with comparing dental appliances with injuries, and doctor's methodology was reliable."

State v. Tankersley, 956 P.2d 486 (1998)

The defendant was sentenced to death for the first-degree murder and sexual assault of a 65-year-old woman. The victim was found with bite marks on her face and breasts. Her right earlobe had been bitten off, and a tooth was discovered under her body. A forensic odontologist testified that it was "highly probable" that the defendant bit the victim's breast. Another expert said that the defendant's teeth matched the bite marks. Saliva with H antigens were found in the bite wounds, consistent with the defendant's saliva. In addition, alternative suspect Tyman was excluded when evidence showed that Tyman had no teeth and no dentures due to a fire that destroyed them 5 years before the murder. The experts determined that someone with teeth made the bite marks.

State v. Ortiz, 502 A.2d 400 (1985)

During a prosecution for manslaughter, the court held that the expert testimony of forensic odontologist Lutz that bite marks preserved in pieces of an apple scattered about the crime scene were the defendant's was admissible. Lutz said that the pieces of the apple "fit together like a jigsaw puzzle," and he was able to identify a human bite mark belonging to the defendant.

State v. Patterson, 509 S.W.2d 857 (1974)

The court held that requiring the defendant to produce a mold of his teeth did not violate any of his constitutional protections; the expert testimony comparing the teeth marks on the victim's body to the mold of the defendant's teeth was admissible; and the state did not suppress evidence by not preserving the original tissue from the victim's left breast where the bite mark was found because the defendant testified that he bit the victim's left breast, and there was no way to preserve the original tissue for the defendant's expert.

People v. Jordan, 469 N.E.2d 569 (1984)

Forensic odontologist's testimony of the "pink tooth theory" as the cause of the victim's death in a murder case was not an abuse of discretion when both the state's experts and the defendant's experts acknowledged its existence in their area of expertise, stated that strangulation could have caused the pink tint to the victim's teeth, and when it is beyond the knowledge of a layperson.

People v. Prante, 498 N.E.2d 889 (1986)

The defendant's knowledge of the location of bite marks on the murder victim's body was enough to establish criminal agency on the defendant's part, and the expert odontologist's comparison of the bite marks on the victim's body showing gaps in between each one of the defendant's front six teeth to the defendant's matching dentitions was admissible.

People v. Slone, 143 Cal.Rptr. 61 (1978)

Dentition evidence matching the defendant to the bite mark on the victim's thigh was admissible after passing the three-prong test established in *Kelly*: (1) general acceptance in the scientific community; (2) determination that witness was qualified to testify as an expert; and (3) correct scientific procedures were used.

People v. Smith, 479 N.Y.S.2d 706 (1984)

A comparison of a photograph of a bite mark from a previous murder victim to a photograph of a bite mark from the victim in this murder case was admissible to show that the bite mark on the victim in this case is from the defendant.

People v. Stinson, 397 N.E.2d 136 (1986)

Bite marks were found on the breast, abdomen, and pubic region of the 73-year-old murder victim. Both forensic odontologists concluded that the bite marks were made at or near the time of death, and defendant was the only one who could have inflicted these wounds. Experts found eight complete or partial bite marks. To preserve the bite marks, a rubber impression of the victim's breast was made because it contained the most three-dimensional indentations. Deeper bite marks were preserved by affixing an acrylic ring to the tissue surrounding the indentations and then removing that block of tissue. As part of a forensic workup, a special camera photographed the biting and facial surfaces of the defendant's teeth. Rubber impressions of the defendant's teeth were made, and an expert examined the defendant's teeth to observe any defective or decayed teeth or any teeth that may have been artificially restored. An overlay technique consisting of a black-and-white negative of the defendant's teeth over a color transparency of the bite mark was used to compare teeth patterns.

People v. Vigil, 718 P.2d 496 (1986)

The court held that the prosecution did not suppress evidence when pictures of marks on the murder victim's body were not taken until a few days after the body was discovered. The defendant claimed that this did not allow him to show that the bite marks on the victim did not come from him. The court reasoned that the importance of the marks of the victim's body was not obvious to the police, and the defendant did not have any evidence showing that the marks were in fact bite marks.

Wade v. State, 490 N.E.2d 1097 (1986)

The court held that the defendant's right against self-incrimination was not violated by requiring him to submit to an oral examination and an impression of his teeth for comparison to the bite marks on the murder victim.

Wilhoit v. State, 816 P.2d 545 (1991)

In a first-degree murder trial, the court held that the defense counsel's failure to pursue bite mark evidence or to use the bite mark expert hired by the defendant's family was ineffective assistance of counsel because the outcome of the defendant's case may have been different with the bite mark evidence. Counsel was suffering from alcohol abuse and brain damage while representing the defendant.

People v. Williams, 470 N.E.2d 1140 (1984)

In a murder and rape case, a witness who had 19 years' experience in dentistry, had taken two courses specifically in bite mark comparison, and had taught courses on the subject qualified as an expert in bite mark comparison, even though the witness was not board-certified in the field of forensic odontology and had never made a comparison of a bite in human tissue.

People v. Malone, 356 N.E.2d 1350 (1976)

In a homicide case, bite mark evidence taken from the victim's thigh shortly after death was admissible, and there was no invasion of the defendant's right to privacy when photographs and impressions of his teeth were taken. This did not violate the defendant's Fifth Amendment right against self-incrimination because dental impressions, like fingerprints, are fixed characteristics of the body and do not receive Fifth Amendment protection.

Walters v. State, 720 So.2d 856 (1998)

Bite marks found on murder victim McCoy's shoulder, wrist, and forearm matched a cast made of Walter's teeth, but defense counsel did not provide ineffective counsel by failing to file any pretrial motions to obtain funds for an odontologist because bite mark evidence was only one bit of evidence used to identify the defendant.

Kinney v. State, 868 S.W.2d 463 (1994)

The defendant was convicted of the murder and rape of a 7-month-old child. The victim had bite marks on his penis, and the court held that the trial court did not abuse its discretion in allowing the photograph of another infant with bite marks on his penis for comparison.

State v. Lyons, 924 P.2d 802 (1995)

In this murder case, a DNA expert took saliva samples from the bite marks on the victim's body and determined that the marks were made by an individual with type A blood who secretes A antigens into bodily fluid other than blood, consistent with the defendant. A forensic odontologist also compared a mold of the defendant's teeth to the bite marks on the victim and determined that they matched.

RESEARCH NOTE

The Journal of Forensic Sciences is the official publication of the American Academy of Forensic Sciences. By visiting the Academy's Web site at *http://www.aafs.org* and clicking on the "Journal of Forensic Sciences" link, you can get to a searchable index of the journal from 1981 to the present that uses common search terms. The site also provides tables of contents for more recent issues of the journal, and, for a modest fee, one can download individual articles from issues published after January 1, 1999. The index, content, and article availability site is maintained by the publisher of the journal, The American Society for Testing and Materials (ASTM). There are current plans to move toward Web-based publication of the journal, although the paper copy will still be available for some time. Individual subscriptions to this essential journal are also available from ASTM for those interested.

Visiting this important Web site on a regular basis and viewing the available abstracts are essential to the early stages of forensic science/forensic evidence research. Also see the recent bibliography prepared by Christopher Champod and Pierre Margot, "Fingermarks, Shoesole Impressions and Toolmarks," in *Proceedings of the 12th INTERPOL Forensic Science Symposium* (1998), at 303–331.

ENDNOTES

1. A small selection of citations of very recent case reports illustrate the continuation of this pattern. See, e.g., Regan v. State, 1999 WL 1980973 (Tex. Crim. App.) (footprints in dust in a warehouse); People v. Mandez, 1999 WL 1023939 (Co. App.) (bloody footprints all over house, indicating a search for valuables); Hinjosa v. State, 1999 WL 974918 (Tex. Crim. App.) (muddy footprint "match."); Brooks v. State, 1999 WL 798599 (Miss. Sp. Ct.) (bootprint on body parts); State v. Frank, 1999 WL 793677 (Neb. App.) (bloody footprints); U.S. v. Garcia, 179 F.3d 265 (5th Cir. Ct. App.) (depth of dirt/mud print indicated a small man carrying a heavy load, i.e., drug backpacks). See detailed discussion of case reports *infra.*

2. See Bodziak: *Footwear Impression Evidence* (CRC Press, Boca Raton, FL, 1995); Saferstein: *Criminalistics: An Introduction to Forensic Science* (6th ed. Prentice Hall, Upper Saddle River, NJ, 1998) at 492–499; Fisher: *Techniques of Crime Scene Investigation* (5th ed., CRC Press, Boca Raton, FL, 1993) at 90; Geberth: *Practical Homicide Investigation* (3rd ed., CRC Press, Boca Raton, FL, 1996) at 524–532; Giannelli and Imwinkelried: *Scientific Evidence* (2d ed. The Michie Company, Charlottesville, VA, 1993) at Vol. 2, Chap. 16.

3. See Christopher Champod and Pierre Margot: "Fingermarks, Shoesole Impressions and Toolmarks," *Proceedings of the 12th INTERPOL Forensic Science Symposium* (New York, 1998) at 303–331.

4. See, e.g., Ernest Hamm's comprehensive bibliography of footwear impression literature available for download at Zeno's Forensic Site, *http://www.forensic.to/hamm.html.* Zeno's site is by far the most comprehensive Web site available, loaded with important links and routinely updated. Also see "Recording, Enhancement and Recovery of Footwear Marks," a comprehensive overview of the subject, a class based upon the report to the National Conference for Scientific Support (1997), available at *http://www.nfstc.org/footwear.htm.*

5. See, generally, Giannelli and Imwinkelried, *supra,* note 2 at 479 et seq. Also see "Recording, Enhancement and Recovery of Footwear Marks," *supra,* note 4, at 4.

6. Bodziak: *supra,* note 2 at 16. William J. Bodziak's treatise is an essential volume in the library of all police and private investigators, prosecutors, defense lawyers, and forensic evidence teachers. It is deservedly the bible of footwear impression investigators and contains information in a wide variety of areas not easily accessible.

7. *Id.* at 18–19.

8. See, e.g., A. Yitti and H. Majimaa: "Survey of the Conclusions Drawn of Similar Footwear Cases in Various Crime Laboratories," *Forensic Science International* 1996; 82(1):109–120; A. Yitti, H. Majimaa, and J. Virtanen: "Survey of the Conclusions Drawn of Similar Shoeprint Cases, Part II," Information bulletin for shoeprint/toolmark examiners–*Proceedings of the 2d European SP/TM Conference* 1998; 4(1):157–169. Also see citations to recent European footwear studies at Champod and Margot, *supra,* note 3 at 326–329.

9. See Z. Geradts and J. Keijzer: "The Image-Database REBOZO for Shoeprints with Developments on Automatic Classification of Shoe Outsole Designs, *Forensic Science International* 1996; 82(1):21–31; A. Girod: "Computerized Classification of the Shoeprints of Burglars Soles," *Forensic Science International* 1996; 82(1):59–65; S. Mikkonen, V. Suominen, and P. Heinonen: "Use of Footwear Iimpressions in Crime Scene Investigations Assisted by Computerized Footwear Collection System," *Forensic Science International* 1996; 82(1):67–79; M. Tart: "United Kingdom SICAR:

Shoeprint Image Coding and Retrieval," *Forensic Science in Europe ENFSI Bulletin* 1996; 30(5):24.

10. See Bodziak, *supra*, note 2, Chap. 2, "Photography of Footwear Impressions," at 25.
11. *Id.*
12. See the following texts for references of the importance of forensic photography in their various disciplines: DiMaio and DiMaio: *Forensic Pathology* (CRC Press, Boca Raton, FL, 1993); Pickering and Bachman: *The Use of Forensic Anthropology* (CRC Press, Boca Raton, FL, 1997), Fisher: *supra,* note 2; Geberth, *supra,* note 2; Stuart James, Ed.: *Scientific and Legal Applications of Bloodstain Pattern Interpretation* (CRC Press, Boca Raton, FL, 1999); Bevel and Gardner: *Bloodstain Pattern Analysis* (CRC Press, Boca Raton, FL, 1997).
13. See, e.g., the excellent Web site primer on crime scene photography entitled "Forensic Photography for the Crime Scene Technician." This excellent site also contains a wealth of important links to governmental and commercial sites of interest to the crime scene photographer. This site is sponsored by the University of California at Riverside Police Department, and is located at *http://www.police.ucr.edu.* The photography course page is located at *http://www.police.ucr.edu/fet-ol.html.*
14. Located at *http://www.fbi.gov/programs/lab/fsccurrent/swgit1.htm.*
15. A related casting issue occurs with increasing frequency in recent cases involving bite mark testimony. See G.S. Golden, "Use of Alternative Light Source Illumination in Bite Mark Photography," *J. For. Sci.,* 1994; 39(3): 815–823.
16. See Bodziak, *supra*, note 2 at Chap. 3, Casting Three Dimensional Footwear Impressions, and Chapter 4, Lifting Two-Dimensional Footwear Impressions. Also see Champod and Margot, *supra*, note 3, at 311–312.
17. The O. J. Simpson criminal and civil cases trial transcripts are available for download on Westlaw at the OJ-TRANS and OJCIV-TRANS databases.
18. The complete testimony along with the full testimony of Dr. Henry Lee on crime scene analysis, Dr. Robin Cotton and Gary Sims on DNA, pathologists and crime scene technicians, not to mention the cross-examinations throughout the case should be in the library of all lawyers interested in the realities of a forensic science–centered prosecution.
19. See The People of the State of California v. Orenthal James Simpson, Official transcript. Examination of William Bodziak, Docket-Number: BA097211, Superior Court, Los Angeles County, Monday, June 19, 1995 9:05 a.m., Judge: Hon. Lance A. Ito, at 8.
20. *Id.*
21. *Id.* at 10.
22. *Id.* at 11.
23. *Id.* at 12.
24. *Id.* at 13.
25. *Id.* at 17.
26. *Id.* at 23–24.
27. People v. Ricketts, 109 Ill.App.3d 992, 441 N.E.2d 384(1982).
28. *Id.* at 997.
29. *Id.* at 998.
30. People v. Lomas, 92 Ill.App.3d 957, 416 N.E.2d 408(1981).
31. *Id.* at 960.
32. *Id.*
33. *Id.* at 961.
34. People v. Lawson, 163 Ill.2d 187, 644 N.E.2d 1172(1994).

35. *Id.* at 190. Forensic tests revealed no physical evidence of sexual assault, and no presence of seminal fluids. Although an autopsy was performed on the body, it was impossible for medical examiners to determine the time of the child's death.
36. *Id.* at 191.
37. *Id.* at 204.
38. *Id.* at 219.
39. Defendant cited in support, U.S. Supreme Court in Ake v. Oklahoma, 470 U.S. 68, 105 S.Ct. 1087, 84 L.Ed.2d 53 (1985), which held that an indigent defendant's right to fair opportunity to present a defense, partially grounded in Fourteenth Amendment due process, required psychiatric evaluation and assistance at state expense where defendant's mental condition was a significant factor at trial. Also see People v. Watson, 36 Ill.2d 228, 221 N.E.2d 645 (1966), holding that defendant's right to summon witnesses in his behalf under section 8 of article II of the Illinois Constitution and Sixth Amendment of U.S. Constitution required reasonable funds for expert assistance where expert opinion may have been crucial in the case.
40. Ake v. Oklahoma, *supra*, note 39.
41. *Supra*, note 34, at 227.
42. *Id.* at 229–230.
43. People v. Campbell, 146 Ill.2d 363, 586 N.E.2d 1261 (1992).
44. *Id.* at 370.
45. *Id.* at 371.
46. *Id.*
47. *Id.* at 372.
48. *Id.* at 373.
49. See, e.g., Carlton v. People (1894), 150 Ill. 181, 187, 37 N.E. 244, where, quoting *Wharton's Criminal Evidence* s 796 (8th ed.), the court stated: "The evidence of the footprints and their correspondence with the defendant's feet was competent, and, though 'not by itself of any independent strength, is admissible with other proof as tending to make out a case.' " Also see Gilbreath v. State, 158 Tex.Crim. 616, 617, 259 S.W.2d 223, 224 (1953) ("ordinarily, identity of an accused may not be established alone by tracks"); see also Ennox v. State (1936), 130 Tex.Crim. 328, 94 S.W.2d 473.
50. *Supra*, note 43, 376-377. Also see, e.g., Schoolcraft v. People (1886), 117 Ill. 271, 7 N.E. 649; Carlton v. People, 150 Ill. 181, 37 N.E. 244 (1894); People v. Zammuto, 280 Ill. 225, 117 N.E. 454 (1917); People v. Hanson, 31 Ill.2d 31, 198 N.E.2d 815 (1964); People v. Diaz, 169 Ill.App.3d 66, 119 Ill.Dec. 527, 522 N.E.2d 1386 (1964); People v. Henne, 165 Ill.App.3d 315, 116 Ill.Dec. 296, 518 N.E.2d 1276 (1988); People v. Howard, 130 Ill.App.3d 967, 86 Ill.Dec. 148, 474 N.E.2d 1345 (1985); People v. Ricketts, 109 Ill.App.3d 992, 65 Ill.Dec. 471, 441 N.E.2d 384 (1982); People v. Lomas, 92 Ill.App.3d 957, 48 Ill.Dec. 377, 416 N.E.2d 408 (1981); People v. Robbins, 21 Ill.App.3d 317, 315 N.E.2d 198 (1974); People v. Kozlowski, 95 Ill.App.2d 464, 238 N.E.2d 156 (1968).
51. *Supra,* note 43, at 378. But see the concerns expressed by Dean Wigmore, where, in concluding his discussion about the weakness of such evidence, states: "This is because the features usually taken as the basis of inference—size, depth, contour, etc.—may not be distinctive and fixed in type for every individual, but may apply, even in combination, to many individuals. Hence their probative significance is apt to be small. ... No doubt a witness to identity of footmarks should be required to specify the features on which he bases his judgment of identity, and then the strength of the inference should depend on the degree of accurate detail to be ascribed to each

feature and of the unique distinctiveness to be predicated of the total combination. Testimony not based on such data of appreciable significance should be given no weight." J. Wigmore, *Evidence* Vol. 2 § 415, at 488-489 (rev. ed. Chadbourn, 1979).

52. *Supra*, note 43, at 379.

53. *Id*. at 382.

54. See, 43 Proof of Facts 2d s 7, at 237–38 (Minneapolis, 1985).

55. See People v. Lomas, *supra*, note 30, where the trial court, in rendering its decision, made certain findings regarding dissimilarity of markings made by a right shoe. Specifically, the judge suggested that an elongated gouge which showed up in some of test prints but in none of the original prints was of recent origin and may have been made after defendant's arrest.

56. *Supra*, note 54, at 298. Also see, People v. Cheek, 93 Ill.2d 82, 93, 66 Ill.Dec. 316, 442 N.E.2d 877 (1982) (10 fingerprint comparison points); People v. Reno, 32 Ill.App.3d 754, 757, 336 N.E.2d 36 (1975) (fingerprint technician testified that he found 20 different points of identical comparison.); State v. Pinyatello, 272 N.C. 312, 158 S.E.2d 596 (1968) (expert testified that he identified between 20 and 25 points that were built into the shoe, no points of dissimilarity, and 11 different identifying points or marks that were not built into the shoe heel); Giacone v. State, 124 Tex.Crim. 141, 62 S.W.2d 986 (1933) (21 points of similarity observed). Also see Chapter 8, Fingerprints, for a discussion of this issue.

57. *Supra*, note 43, at 385.

58. *Id*. at 386.

59. *Id*. at 388.

60. People v. Robinson, 157 Ill.2d 68, 623 N.E.2d 352 (1993).

61. *Id*. at 74.

62. State v. Kortbein, 1999 WL 144754 (Wis.App.).

63. *Id*. Harrison waited $3^{1}/_{2}$ years before examining the shoes, for which he was later disciplined. At trial, the trial court prohibited the defense from questioning Harrington about the disciplinary action taken against him for his delay in examining the shoes. The appellate court saw no misuse of discretion or constitutional error in the trial court's decision to exclude the evidence.

64. *Id*. at *1, 2.

65. State v. Washington, 1999 WL 31241 (La.App. 5 Cir.).

66. *Id*. At trial, Captain Merrill Boling of the Jefferson Parish Sheriff's Office Latent Print Division testified that he was unable to match the fingerprints taken at the scene to the defendant's, because the fingerprints from the scene did not contain enough points of identification for comparison.

67. Also see State v. Keith, 79 Ohio St.3d 514, 684 N.E.2d 47 (1997), at a snowbank where a witness witnessed a getaway car slide, investigators made a cast of the tire tread and of the indentation in the snowbank made by the car's front license plate number—"043." The indentation from the license plate matched the last three numbers of a 1982 Oldsmobile Omega seized from Melanie Davison shortly after she visited appellant in jail, under the pseudonym of Sherry Brown, a few weeks after the murders.

68. See, e.g., Martin v. Commonwealth, 1999 WL 10088 (Va.App.) (footprints, which appeared to be made from a "lug-soled" or "mountain climbing-type" boot or shoe, that led from the broken glass to the back of the cleaners and then to the back of Kmart, another store located in the shopping center similar to shoes of defendant); Corliss v. Vermont, 1998 WL 44853 (defendant's *found in snow* near body of homicide victim.).

69. See "A New Improved Technique for Casting Impressions in Snow," S.M. Ojena: *J. For. Sci.,* 1984; 29(1): 322–325; Frank Daulby: "An Evaluation of Snow Casting Materials," *Identification Canada,* 10:1 (1987); Lawren Nause: "Casting Footwear Impressions in Snow: Snowprint-Wax vs. Prill Sulphur," *R.C.M.P. Gazette* (Cand.), 54:12 (1992); James R. Wolfe and Chris W. Beheim: "Dental Stone Casting of Snow Impressions," *FBI International Symposium on FWTT Evidence* (1994); Raymond L. Kenny: "Identification of a Footwear Impression in the Snow," *FBI International Symposium on FWTT Evidence* (1994); J.W. Allen: "Making Plaster Casts in Snow," *International Criminal Police Review,* No. 89 (1955); Edward E. Hueske: "Photographing and Casting Footwear/Tiretrack Impressions in Snow," *Journal of Forensic Identification,* 41:2, (1991); Gaylan Warren: "Snowprint — Wax Casting Material Information," *AFTE Journal,* 15:2 (1983). Also see Bodziak, *supra,* note 2, at 87 ("Casting Footwear Impressions in Snow").

70. State v. Delucca, 1999 WL 1018647 (N.J.Super.A.D.). [To be reported at 325 N.J. Super 376, 739 A.2d 455 (1999).]

71. *Id.* at 9. The morning after the crime, the state police conducted a search of the area near the store and recovered from a mailbox on Hamilton Road: a blue ski mask, two latex gloves, and a revolver. The revolver had two spent .38-caliber rounds and four live rounds in the chamber. Subsequent ballistics tests confirmed that the bullet recovered from the gas station window frame had been fired from this gun. Also, two hairs discovered on the ski mask were found to be consistent with hair removed from defendant. In addition, DNA markers extracted from saliva stains on the blue ski mask were consistent with markers found in defendant's blood.

72. Also see United States v. Wilderness, 160 F.3d 1173 (7th Cir. Ct. App. 19998), where defendant was convicted of carjacking and of using a firearm during a crime of violence. Edward Dame of the Gary, Indiana police found the car and followed footprints in the snow to a house about a block and a half away. Another officer came in response to a call for assistance. The two found Wilderness asleep in the house. His shoes matched the footprints they had followed. No challenge was made to this testimony on appeal. See also State v. LaBrutto, 114 N.J. 187, 197, 553 A.2d 335 (1989); State v. Johnson, 120 N.J. 263, 294–95, 576 A.2d 834 (1990); State v. Harvey, 121 N.J. 407, 427, 581 A.2d 483 (1990), cert. denied, 499 U.S. 931, 111 S.Ct. 1336, 113 L. Ed.2d 268 (1991); Johnson v. State, 59 N.J.L. 535, 543, 37 A. 949 (E. & A. 1896) (finding that a witness's testimony about a footprint's appearance "involved in no sense the knowledge of an expert...").

73. State v. Patterson, 587 N.W.2d 45 (Minn. Sp. Ct. 1999).

74. Lewis v. State, 725 So.2d 183 (1998).

75. *Id.* at 188.

76. *Id.* at 188. See United States v. Craft, 691 F.2d 205, 206–7 (5th Cir.1982). Also see, e.g., Porter v. State, 519 So.2d 1230, 1232 (Miss.1988) (defendant can be required to demonstrate scar on his hand); McCrory v. State, 342 So.2d 897, 899 (Miss.1977) (defendant can be required to give fingerprints and handwriting exemplar, because "the Fifth Amendment only bars the compelled production of testimonial evidence, as opposed to identifying physical characteristics"); Thames v. State, 221 Miss. 573, 73 So.2d 134, 137 (Miss.1954) (defendant can be required to stand).

77. State v. Matney, 979 S.W.2d 225 (Mo. Ct. App 1998).

78. *Id.* at 230.

79. *Id.*

80. Miller v. State, 977 P.2d 1099 (Okla.Crim.App.).

81. *Id.* at 1104.

82. *Id.* at 1108. See the important polymerase chain reaction (PCR) DNA discussion in this case in Chapter 10, DNA Analysis. PCR DNA testing conducted on Miller's right sandal revealed human DNA consistent with that of the victim, Kent Dodd. The state's expert testified the DNA could not be used to identify Dodd as the donor conclusively. It could have come from 1 in 19 Caucasians, 1 in 16 African-Americans, or 1 in 55 Hispanics. Miller argued that this evidence was not admissible.

83. See the ENFSI Working Group Marks car database, maintained by the Judicial Police in Ghent, Belgium, a system for searching the makes and models of cars based on the measurements of tire track widths. The site includes data on tires, track widths, wheelbases and other specifications of 4,500 vehicles sold in Europe from 1969 to date. See also the publication called *Tread Design*, referenced by tire tread analysts.

84. People v. Sutherland, 155 Ill.2d 1, 610 N.E.2d 1 (1992).

85. *Id.* at 9.

86. *Id.* See the extensive discussion of the Sutherland case in Chapter 2, Science and the Criminal Law.

87. People v. Davenport, 11 Cal.4th 1171, 47 Cal.Rptr.2d 800 (1995).

88. *Id.* at 1191.

8 Fingerprints

> Although this may seem a paradox, all exact science is dominated by the idea of approximation.
>
> —Bertrand Russell[1]

I. INTRODUCTION

U.S. courts accepted fingerprint identification evidence long before there was an FBI laboratory or any hint of computerized fingerprint image retrieval systems. Fingerprint identification methods were briefly preceded by the famous Bertillon system introduced by the Paris police in 1882. The Bertillon method involved the recording and subsequent matching of scrupulous measurements of bodily structures, such as height, length, and width of head, fingers, feet, etc., from the recorded data and current suspects. This system was briefly utilized in the United States for purposes of identifying military deserters in the early 1890s.[2] The first attempt to formalize a system for using the ridge characteristics of fingers is generally recognized as that of Sir William Herschel in the Indian state of Bengal in 1877 to check forgeries. In 1892 Frances Galton published the famous book *Finger Prints,* setting forth a statistical basis for supporting a friction ridge identification system. Since its publication, it has remained in the literature as one of the formulistic bases for the modern science of fingerprint identification. Its system of classification of finger skin patterns, labeled arches, loops, and whorls, still serves today as a basis for modern fingerprint systems.

The FBI Identification Division was initiated in 1924, with the receipt of over 8,000,000 fingerprint files, mostly from the Leavenworth Penitentiary. Currently, the FBI collection contains well over 250 million sets of fingerprint records, composed of both criminal and civil prints. The civil file includes the prints of current government employees and applicants for federal jobs. More will be said of this collection below.

There are a number of standard forensic science texts available with excellent introductions to the forensic discipline of fingerprint impression recognition, retrieval, and identification processes.[3] International interest in fingerprint impression evidence is growing and new publications are appearing that need to be in the library of any law firm or governmental unit addressing fingerprint theory, collection procedures, or the utilization of digital impression technology.[4] An increasing number of Web sites also contain valuable introductory and specialized fingerprint impression information[5] that should be regularly consulted for new information.[6] Also, the rapid addition of new sites in the forensic science and law and science areas makes it imperative for lawyers to be current with the available Internet sites.[7]

Dean Wigmore noted the growing importance of fingerprint evidence in the 1913 second edition of his famous treatise, *The Principles of Judicial Proof*.[8] Interestingly, the third edition, published in 1937, changed its title to *The Science of Judicial Proof*,[9] with a substantial increase in coverage of what would be considered today forensic evidence. This is a still valuable and extensive treatise on proof of fact. Throughout all editions, the book is subtitled, *As Given by Logic, Psychology, and General Experience and Illustrated in Judicial Trials*. It contains not only numerous and generous quotations from a host of classic texts on philosophy, psychology, logic, and law, but selections from transcripts of famous trials from the 17th century to the Knapp trial of 1830. It is centered in the idea that at the ground level of a trial, the scholastic delineation of the rules of civil and criminal liability theory and the rules of evidence[10] await the presentation of fact and inferences, which drive the daily operation of the U.S. justice system.

In the 1913 edition, in the section entitled "Circumstantial Evidence, Proof of Identity," Wigmore provides two selections—an excerpt entitled "Finger-Print Iden- tification," from a 1911 book entitled *Science and the Criminal* by Ainsworth Mitchell, and the full text of the famous fingerprint case of *People v. Jennings*,[11] decided by the Illinois Supreme Court in 1911. Mitchell notes that the work of Galton, at the end of the 19th century, set the standard for estimating the match capability of fingerprints:

> [E]ven after making all allowance for ambiguities and for possible alterations caused by accident or disease, a complete, or nearly complete, agreement between two prints of one finger and infinitely more so between two or more fingers, afforded evidence, which did not stand in need of corroboration, that the prints were derived from the fingers of one and the same person.[12]

The first major criminal case recognizing the scientific and, hence, legal viability of fingerprint evidence was the case of *People v. Jennings*,[13] decided by the Illinois Supreme Court in 1911. Given its importance, extensive discussion of its thoughts on this new and apparently definitive method of identification is warranted.

The defendant Thomas Jennings was convicted of the murder of a Mr. Hiller, the owner of a home that Jennings had illegally entered. At the head of the stairs, near the door leading to a daughter's room, a gaslight was kept burning at night. Shortly after 2 A.M. on Monday, September 19, 1910, Mrs. Hiller was awakened and noticed that this light was out. She called her husband's attention to the fact and he went in his nightclothes to the head of the stairway, where he encountered an intruder, with whom he grappled, and in the struggle both fell to the foot of the stairway, where Hiller was shot twice, dying in a few moments.

The house had recently been painted, and the back porch, which was the last part done, had been completed on the Saturday preceding the shooting. Entrance to the house had been gained by the murderer through a rear window of the kitchen, from which he had first removed the window screen. Near the window was the back porch, whose railing would support a person entering the window. On the railing in the fresh paint was the imprint of four fingers of someone's left hand. This railing was removed in the early morning after the murder by officers from the identification bureau of the Chicago Police Force, and enlarged photographs were made of the prints. Jennings was arrested after several eyewitnesses[14] identified him. Earlier, when he was returned to the penitentiary for violation of parole in March 1910, he had had a print of his fingers taken, and another print was taken after this arrest. These impressions were enlarged for the purpose of comparison with the enlarged photographs of the prints on the railing.

The defendant argued that the evidence of the comparison of photographs of the finger marks on the railing with the enlarged fingerprints of him was improperly admitted. No question were raised about the accuracy of the photographic exhibits, the method of identifying the photographs, the taking of the fingerprints, or the correctness of the enlargements. The defendant argued that fingerprint comparison evidence was not admissible under the common-law rules of evidence, and since there was no statute authorizing it the court should have refused to permit its introduction.

The court noted that as of 1913 there had been no reported cases or state statutes addressing the admissibility of this class of evidence, although such evidence had recently been accepted in England.[15] The Illinois Supreme Court noted that while the courts of this country did not appear to have passed on the question, "standard authorities on scientific subjects" did discuss the use of fingerprints as a system of identification, and had concluded that experience had shown it to be reliable.[16] These authorities, the court observed, found this system of identification to be of very ancient origin, having been used in Egypt when the impression of the monarch's thumb was used as his sign manual and that it has been used in the courts of India for many years. More recently, its use had become very general by the police departments of the large cities of this country and Europe. The court was particularly impressed with the apparent great success of the system in England, where it had been used since 1891 in thousands of cases without error. They also noted that this success has resulted in the sending of an investigating commission from the U.S., upon whose favorable report a bureau was established by the U.S. government in several departments.[17]

The court began its analysis of the *Jennings* case by reviewing the proffered qualifications of the four fingerprint witness employed here by the prosecution. William M. Evans testified that he began the study of the subject in 1904; had been connected with the bureau of identification of the Chicago Police Department in work of this character for about a year; had personally studied between 4,000 and 5,000 fingerprints and had himself made about 2,000; that the bureau of identification had some 25,000 different impressions classified; that he had examined the exhibits in question, and on the forefinger he found 14 points of identity, and on the second finger 11 points; that in his judgment the fingerprints on the railing were made by the same person as those taken from the plaintiff.

Edward Foster testified that he was inspector of the dominion police at Ottawa, Canada, connected with the bureau of identification; that he had a good deal to do with fingerprints for 6 years or more; that he had done fingerprint identification work in Vancouver and elsewhere in Canada; had studied the subject at Scotland Yard; that he began the study in St. Louis in 1904 under a Scotland Yard representative and had taken about 2,500 fingerprints; that he had studied the exhibits in question and found 14 points of resemblance on the forefinger; that the two sets of prints were made by the fingers of the same person.

Mary E. Holland testified that she resided in Chicago and began investigation of fingerprint impressions in 1904, studied at Scotland Yard in 1908 and passed an examination on the subject, and started the first bureau of identification in this country for the U.S. government in Washington, D.C. She stated that her work at Scotland Yard involved a collection of over 100,000 prints. She also testified that she had examined the two sets of prints here and believed them to have been made by the fingers of the same person.

Finally, Michael P. Evans testified that he had been in the bureau of identification of the Chicago Police Department for 27 years; that that bureau had been using the system of fingerprint impressions since January 1, 1905, while they also used the Bertillon system. He had studied the subject since 1905 or 1906 and had made between 6,000 and 7,000 fingerprints. He had been in charge of the taking of the photographs of the prints on the railing, and in his judgment the various impressions were made by the fingers of the same person.[18]

The court noted that all of these witnesses testified at varying lengths regarding the basis of the system and the various markings found on the human hand, stating that they were classified from the various forms of markings, including those known as "arches," "loops," "whorls," and "deltas," the same as noted by Wigmore and Mitchell.

The court observed that when photographs were first sought to be admitted, it was seriously questioned whether photographs thus created could properly be introduced in evidence, but that method of proof, as well as proof by means of X-rays and the microscope, were now admitted without question.[19] The court found equal acceptability here:

> We are disposed to hold from the evidence of the four witnesses who testified, and from the writings we have referred to on this subject, that there is a scientific basis for the system of finger print identification, and that the courts are justified in admitting this class of evidence; that this method of identification is in such general and common use that the courts cannot refuse to take judicial cognizance of it. Such evidence may or may not be of independent strength, but it is admissible, the same as other proof, as tending to make out a case. If inferences as to the identity of persons based on the voice, the appearance, or age are admissible, why does not this record justify the admission of this finger print testimony under common-law rules of evidence?[20]

After an examination of the rules guiding when expert testimony is to be allowed, the court ruled that this category of expertise clearly qualified as an admissible area of expertise:

> From the evidence in this record we are disposed to hold that the classification of finger print impressions and their method of identification is a science requiring study. While some of the reasons which guide an expert to his conclusions are such as may be weighed by any intelligent person with good eyesight from such exhibits as we have here in the record, after being pointed out to him by one versed in the study of finger

prints, the evidence in question does not come within in the common experience of all men of common education in the ordinary walks of life, and therefore the court and jury were properly aided by witnesses of peculiar and special experience on this subject.[21]

The court also concluded that the four witnesses here were qualified to testify on the subject of fingerprint impression evidence.

It was further argued that some of the witnesses testified positively that the fingerprints represented by the photographs were made by a certain person whose fingerprint impressions had been photographed, enlarged, and introduced in evidence, when they should have only been permitted to testify that such was their opinion. The court noted that on questions of identity of persons and of handwriting it was everyday practice for witnesses to swear that they believed the person to be the same or the handwriting to be that of a particular individual, although they will not swear positively, and the degree of credit to be attached to the evidence was a question for the jury. The modern case law does indeed support a more positive statement of identity in fingerprint and ballistics settings than in those disciplines such as hair, fiber, glass, and soil, considered more inconclusive in nature.

Issues that are standard fare for lawyers involved in crime scene investigations usually include the following categories of inquiry:

• What surfaces can hold a print?

Smooth, nonporous surfaces such as glass, painted or varnished surfaces, plastic molded surfaces, paper, cardboard, polyethelene-based products, vinyl, rubber, leathers, some metal surfaces, untreated wood products, waxed surfaces, and human skin.

• What is a fingerprint?

The capture on an accepting surface of several clusters of ridge characteristics or "minutiae" present on the fingers of the human hand, as a result of natural oils and secretions of the human finger that leave an image of such minutiae on the surface at issue.

• What methods and chemicals are routinely used to recognize and preserve a print image for analysis?

Flake powders such as silver latent print powder, varied fluorescence techniques such as ultraviolet illumination, iodine, ninhydrin, silver nitrate, small particle reagents, cyanoacrylate (superglue) fuming, and vacuum metal deposition (gold and zinc).[22]

• What are the comparison points for attempting a fingerprint "match"?

Comparison of ridge characteristics (minutiae: short ridges; dots; bifurcations; deltas; trifurcations; ridge endings). There are 150 "comparison points" potentially available for comparison. Realistically, all prints are partial in the sense of there always being fewer than 150 points. The courts in the U.S. generally only require six to eight points, while other nations require 14 or more.[23]

World fingerprint experts agreed in 1995 that there was no requisite number of comparison points to allow for positive identification of a suspect:

The Ne'urim Declaration approved June 19, 1995 have been positively approved in the main fingerprint journals. No objection were raised for accepting that no scientific basis exists for requiring that a pre-determined minimum number of friction ridge features must be present in two impressions in order to establish a positive identification.[24]

Some jurisdictions, such as Australia, are moving to a nonnumerical method of expressing sufficient criterion for a match statement.[25]

The SWGFAST (formerly TWGFAST) guidelines issuing from that FBI-sponsored group are receiving increased attention. The focus for the immediate future appears to be on uniformly accepted minimum-qualifications guidelines, training-to-competence guidelines, and quality assurance guidelines, as bases for ongoing confidence in international fingerprint identification. It is felt that accomplishing these goals will go a long way toward instilling continued confidence while the debate over numerical or non-numerical "ridgeology" comparison methods continues.[26]

- What about AFIS, the Automated Fingerprint Identification System? Does it provide the eventual match using computer technology?[27]

It is important to understand that the AFIS system does not itself provide match identification that serves as the basis for a fingerprint expert's identification testimony. That is still the result of close visual examination of ridge characteristics and experience. It is quite definitely an inference as with all of the other forensic opinions delivered daily in courts around the globe. AFIS has the amazing capability of searching through millions of digitalized images of prints originally provided by ink cards or, more recently, by initial digitalized recordings, and kicking out the 10 closest "matches" in the collection. These then must undergo close examination by experienced fingerprint examiners. AFIS makes possible the heretofore impossible task of comparing millions of images from all over the country and narrowing the candidates. If nine of the selections seem totally unrelated, but the tenth is the victim's estranged husband, the value of the AFIS system is evident. AFIS systems are being utilized worldwide. The FBI IAFIS, the Integrated Automated Fingerprint Identification System, is intended to assist local authorities greatly by speeding up the digitalization of inked cards as well as by integrating criminal record data with the imprint data and providing for increased speed and accuracy in performing AFIS searches.[28]

- What about current statistics and/or "population" databases for ruling out other suspects on something other than the match by an experienced fingerprint examiner?

Here, as with most other forensic science offerings, there are no databases to utilize for a statistical projection to determine the existence in the general population of an identical "match." The assumption has always been that the theoretical basis for fingerprint identification established by Galton and his successors internally provides the assurance of uniqueness to the identification. Dr. Saferstein, in his text *Criminalistics: An Introduction to Forensic Science,* cites three basic principles or assumptions that have historically supported this position.

1. To date, after almost a century of fingerprint experience, no two fingers have ever been found to possess identical ridge characteristics.
2. A fingerprint will remain unchanged during a person's lifetime.
3. Fingerprints have general ridge characteristics that permit them to be systematically classified and examined with great efficiency and efficacy.[29]

The long-standing acceptance of fingerprint evidence as being conclusive for identification has resulted in a dearth of cases even approaching an attack on its claim to be scientifically sound. What has occurred, because of the tremendous esteem of fingerprint identification as an identifying process, are a series of cases addressing whether the absence of fingerprints of the suspect, when they would be expected to be there, is entitled to any evidentiary value or should serve as the basis for a defense-oriented jury instruction.

The state's failure to collect and preserve potentially exculpatory evidence violates a defendant's due process rights only if defendant demonstrates that the officers acted in bad faith.[30]

II. FINGERPRINT CASES

In *People v. Towns,*[31] a jury found defendant Sherrell Towns guilty of five counts of first-degree murder and sentenced him to death. The case arose out of the execution-style murder of five men in Madison, Illinois in a drug-related incident. Among other points, the defendant claimed that his attorney should have presented the testimony of a forensic expert to dispute the state's fingerprint evidence. The trial testimony indicated that the state's expert, Garold Warner, and two of his associates concluded that there were 25 "points of agreement" between the defendant's fingerprints and those found at the scene of the crimes. According to Warner, fingerprint examiners in the U.S. tend to use between 8 and 10 points of agreement before arriving at a conclusion. Based on that evidence, the court concluded that it could not be said that defense counsel's decision not to call an independent expert constituted ineffectiveness. The court observed that the failure may very well have been a matter of trial strategy not to call an expert—"a withering cross-examination as to the points of agreement could only serve to reinforce the strength of the fingerprint identification in the eyes of the jury."[32]

The taking of fingerprints is a "search" for purposes of the Fourth Amendment to the U.S. Constitution.[33] In an interesting case involving two sets of prints taken from a defendant, where the first set was found to be improperly taken because the defendant had not been told that he need not supply prints, a court ruled that the use of both sets by an examiner did not prevent testimony on a match from the second set. In this decision, *Hooker v. State,*[34] the defendant was convicted of murder in a trial based entirely on circumstantial evidence.

Around 5:30 A.M. on the morning of March 14, 1991, the Sheriff's Office responded to a call reporting a comatose man in a car, and upon arriving at the rural crime scene, a deputy discovered Walter Johnson's dead body behind the steering wheel of his vehicle. Investigators discovered that Johnson had been shot twice.

Investigators searched Johnson's car and found three .25-caliber shell casings, a bag containing several unopened cans of Coors Light beer, and one opened, partially full can of Coors Light beer sitting on Johnson's dashboard.[35]

After questioning various people, investigators from the Sheriff's Office were led to Hooker, who, it was learned, was a teacher at the middle school where Johnson had been principal. During the investigatory process, Hooker supplied the sheriff with several fingerprint cards. These prints were sent to the crime laboratory in Jackson, and ultimately the crime laboratory matched a latent print found on the half-full Coors Light beer can to Hooker.

Hooker argued that all fingerprint evidence should be suppressed as the "fruit of the poisonous tree,"[36] because the state did not prove that it informed Hooker prior to taking the first set of prints that he had the right to refuse the request that he give the police his prints. Hooker provided two sets of fingerprints to the sheriff, the first on March 19, 1991, and the second on March 28, 1991. The trial court did suppress the first set of prints, but refused to suppress the second set, ruling that Hooker had been properly informed at that time that he had the right to refuse to give his prints. On appeal, Hooker argued that because the second set of prints were not "independently obtained," they too should be suppressed.

The court held that the second set of fingerprints was not gained by exploiting alleged illegally seized first set of fingerprints, and, thus, the second set of fingerprints was admissible to identify the defendant and not the fruit of the poisonous tree. The first set of prints was, as claimed by the defendant, taken without informing him that he had right to refuse. The first set being found to be smudged, the state crime laboratory informed the sheriff it would need a second set, and the defendant, upon his return to provide second set, was informed of right to refuse the request for prints. This was so, even though the fingerprint examiner testified that when she initially identified the defendant's thumbprint she had both set of prints before her and did not know whether she had used the first set of prints or the second, legally obtained, set, because during trial she compared the second set of prints with the thumbprint obtained from the crime scene container and testified before the jury that it matched the defendant's.[37]

A number of jurisdictions require the state, if it wishes to rely solely or substantially on fingerprint evidence, to establish to some degree that the prints were made at a point contemporaneous with the commission of the crime. In *People v. Campbell*,[38] a 1992 Illinois Supreme Court decision, the court agreed with the defendant that, to sustain a conviction solely on fingerprint evidence, fingerprints corresponding to those of the defendant must have been found in the immediate vicinity of the crime under such circumstances that establish beyond a reasonable doubt that they were impressed at the time the crime was committed.[39] The court also agreed with the defendant that the same time/placement requirements exist in many states for shoe print evidence. However, in either case, the court explained, the state was not required to seek out and negate every conceivable possibility that the print was impressed at some time other than during the commission of the offense.

In some cases, the court noted, evidence of the particular location of the fingerprint might satisfy the time/placement requirement, as would the prosecution's proof of the chain of contact of the touched item, which could establish that the item could have been touched only at the time of the crime.[40] Additionally, the court observed, a wide variety of attending circumstances might support an inference that the print was made at the time of the commission of the offense.[41]

In *State v. Montgomery*,[42] the defendant was convicted of first-degree murder, first-degree burglary, robbery with a dangerous weapon, and attempted first-degree rape. At approximately 11:05 P.M., the victim's friends returned to the victim and discovered the body of Kimberly Piccolo lying on the floor next to her bed. When Piccolo's body was found, she was dressed in a sweatshirt, sweatpants that were inside out, and socks, but she was not wearing panties. The sofa on which Piccolo had been sitting when her roommates left had been moved out of place. The officers found a pair of panties lying on the sofa. A butcher knife was missing from the kitchen. Piccolo's eyeglasses were found on the coffee table. A fingerprint, which matched a print of the defendant's left ring finger, was lifted from one of the lenses.

An autopsy showed that Piccolo had received nine stab wounds that were clustered in her chest, arm, back, and abdomen and several defensive wounds on her hands. One stab wound went completely through her right hand. A fingerprint lifted from a lens of the victim's eyeglasses found in the apartment matched one of the defendant's fingerprints.[43]

The defendant argued that the state failed to prove that the fingerprint found on the victim's eyeglasses was impressed at the time the crimes were committed. The court stated that regardless of the confidence attending fingerprint-matching testimony, it is usually insufficient, alone, to sustain a conviction:

> This Court has considered the sufficiency of fingerprint evidence to identify defendant as the perpetrator in a number of cases. Where the State has relied solely on fingerprint evidence to establish that the defendant was the perpetrator of the crimes charged, this Court has held that the defendant's motion to dismiss should have been granted.[44] On the other hand, where the State presented other evidence tending to show that the fingerprints could only have been impressed at the time the crimes were committed, this Court has found that the case was properly taken to the jury.[45]

The cases referenced stand for the proposition that testimony by a qualified expert that fingerprints found at the scene of the crime match the fingerprints of the accused, when accompanied by substantial evidence of circumstances from which the jury could find that the fingerprints could only have been impressed at the time the crime was committed, is sufficient to withstand a motion for dismissal and carry the case to the jury:

> The soundness of the rule lies in the fact that such evidence logically tends to show that the accused was indeed present and participated in the commission of the crime.

In the present case, the court ruled that the state submitted substantial evidence of circumstances from which the jury could find that the defendant's fingerprints could only have been impressed at the time the crimes charged were committed:

> The evidence showed that the victim was wearing her eyeglasses all day on the day the crimes charged were committed; was studying or reading most of that day; that

she was reading when the group left at around 10:00 p.m. for a party, leaving her alone in the apartment. When the group left, the furniture was in order and the victim was sitting on the sofa with her eyeglasses on, reading the newspaper. When the group returned approximately an hour later, the apartment was in disarray, the victim's lifeless body was lying on the floor away from the sofa, which had been moved, and her eyeglasses were on the coffee table. No one else was in the apartment. Defendant's fingerprint was found on the inside lens of the victim's eyeglasses. This evidence, disclosing the circumstances under which the eyeglasses were found, when combined with other testimony placing defendant in the vicinity of the victim's apartment, constitutes substantial evidence from which the jury could find that defendant's fingerprints could only have been impressed on the lens between the hours of 10:00 p.m. and 11:05 p.m. Since the evidence also showed that the crimes charged were committed during the same time period, the fingerprint evidence logically tends to show that defendant was present and participated in the commission of the crimes. Thus, we hold that the evidence was properly admitted and the trial court did not err in denying defendant's motion to dismiss for insufficiency of the evidence.[46]

The defendant also argued that the portion of the state expert's testimony indicating that he had prepared his report with the aid of a previously prepared print card at the local jail was not prejudicial since he used the same card in cross-examination to challenge the accuracy of the expert's testimony.[47] This is common problem faced by defendants with prior records.

Similar issues of contemporaneity were raised in *People v. Zizzo*,[48] where defendant was convicted of felony theft, arising from the defendant's collusion with a bank employee to obtain and use false automatic teller machine (ATM) cards.

The state's first witness, Carol Carl, testified that, in May 1996, while updating her family's financial records, she discovered a series of unauthorized ATM withdrawals from her account totaling over $62,000. The withdrawals were traced to the defendant.

In addition to bank employees and the defendant's accomplice, the state called Dr. Jane Homeyer, executive director of the Northern Illinois Police Crime Laboratory. She testified that she performed a fingerprint analysis on the Daryl Simson ATM account file. She found two prints suitable for comparison, both of which matched the defendant's. Homeyer noted, however, that her analysis could not establish either when or in what context the fingerprints had been left.

The defendant contended that because an innocent explanation was available for the discovery of her fingerprints on the Daryl Simson ATM file, those fingerprints could not be used to support her conviction. The defendant relied upon a 1991 case, *People v. Gomez*,[49] in which the court had held that, to support a conviction, fingerprint evidence must satisfy both physical and temporal proximity criteria. The fingerprints must have been found in the immediate vicinity of the crime and under such circumstances that they could have been made only at the time the crime occurred.[50] Although the court did not dispute defendant's reading of *Gomez*, it stressed that the physical and temporal proximity criteria came into play only when a conviction was based solely upon circumstantial fingerprint evidence. Here, the court observed, discovery of the defendant's fingerprints on the Daryl Simson ATM file was not the sole basis for the defendant's conviction, as it was introduced to corroborate co-defendant Carr's prior inconsistent statement. Accordingly, the jury properly could have considered the discovery of the defendant's fingerprints on the Daryl Simson ATM file as evidence of the defendant's guilt.

Contemporaneousness and proximity were also issues in *State v. Monzo,*[51] a 1998 Ohio decision. There, the defendant was convicted of two counts of rape, one count of aggravated burglary, and one count of kidnaping. The victim had been assaulted in 1987, but the defendant was not identified until a fingerprint run under a newly installed AFIS system kicked out his card. Police found a knife beside the victim's bed, and her open wallet and purse in her bedroom, although she had left those items on the kitchen counter before going to bed, with the wallet inside the purse.

A fingerprint examiner testified that in 1987 he performed a preliminary examination of the fingerprint lifts from the victim's house, but had no known suspect to whom the lifts could be compared, so the prints were simply retained in the police file for future reference. Subsequently, the police put in place an AFIS system which kicked out the defendant's prints several years later. The expert conducted a visual comparison of the defendant's file fingerprints with the lifts from the basement door trim, and determined that these matched the defendant's right middle and ring finger. He later determined that the lift from the victim's wallet matched the right thumbprint of the defendant. He testified that the lift from the wallet would be a relatively fresh print because dusting for prints on a porous surface would be effective in developing prints for perhaps only 15 days after the prints were made.[52]

A housepainter, Donald Fraime, testified that shortly before the date of the 1987 attack, he painted the middle room in the victim's house, including new wood trim around the new basement door. A Columbus police officer testified that he worked for the crime scene search unit in October 1987, and collected fingerprints from the victim's house, dusting for and eventually lifting a total of 11 prints from the house. According to him, the most definitive print impressions were one lifted from the outside of the victim's wallet found in her bedroom and ones lifted from the door frame of the door leading from the basement to the middle room. An FBI forensic and fingerprint expert found that these two prints were the most valuable for comparison purposes. Comparing the lifts to the known fingerprints of the defendant, he concluded that the single fingerprint lifted from the wallet was the right thumbprint of the defendant, and the prints taken from the door trim were the right middle and right ring fingers of defendant. The agent testified that painting the door trim would have destroyed any fingerprints previously left there, so that the prints lifted from the door trim could not predate the last time the trim was painted, and that repeated handling would degrade or leave overlapping prints on an item. He saw no overlapping prints on the lift taken from the wallet, which was the victim's everyday wallet. It was pointed out that any print more than a few days old would have probably been obliterated or overlapped by her frequent handling of the wallet.[53]

As noted above, the uniform acceptance of the certainty and solidity of fingerprint evidence has resulted in claims by defendants that police failure to search for and to preserve such evidence, where it could be reasonably expected to be present, denies them of due process by removing from consideration potentially exculpatory evidence. If the state fails to produce evidence that is reasonably available to it or fails to explain why it has not produced the evidence, a defendant is permitted to comment about the missing evidence in closing argument to the jury.

In *Eley v. State*,[54] a 1980 Maryland decision, the defendant was convicted on charges arising out of a shooting and robbery. The state failed to produce fingerprint evidence against Eley and relied solely on eyewitness testimony for establishing his identification. In closing argument, defense counsel sought to argue that the state's failure to utilize the more reliable fingerprint identification, and its failure to explain why it did not produce such evidence, gave rise to an inference that Eley's fingerprints were not at the scene of the crime and, thus, he was not there. This court reversed stating, "one can reasonably draw some adverse inference from the use of an inferior method when a superior [one] was readily available."[55] The court held that possibly relevant evidence not introduced, or its absence explained, could be used against the state.

This issue was again addressed in the case of *United States v. Hoffman*,[56] where defendants were convicted of narcotics offenses. The primary issue on appeal was whether a defense lawyer must lay some evidentiary foundation before arguing in closing that the jury should infer, based upon the absence of fingerprint evidence, that such evidence could have been obtained and would have been exculpatory. The court answered that question in the affirmative, and therefore affirmed the convictions.

On the afternoon of February 14, 1990, defendants Hoffman and Smithen went to Penn Station in New York City to catch an Amtrak train bound for Charlotte, North Carolina. While in the station, they attracted the attention of two Amtrak police officers, which eventually led to search on the train of a red duffel bag that Hoffman had identified as his. Inside, police observed a pair of tennis shoes with socks stuffed into them; closer examination revealed plastic bags containing cocaine base hidden inside the socks. They also found a spray deodorant can that proved to have a false bottom containing narcotics. At trial, the government's case consisted primarily of the testimony of the arresting officers, who recounted the events that occurred aboard the train. None of the government's witnesses made any mention of fingerprint evidence, and the attorneys representing Hoffman and Smithen did not cross-examine on that point.

During closing argument, Hoffman's counsel argued that the unknown passenger who had been seated next to Hoffman was actually a drug courier who left the narcotics under a pillow on his seat when he saw the officers enter the train in Washington, D.C. According to Hoffman's counsel, Detective Hanson had lied about finding the drugs in Hoffman's bag to be able to secure a conviction. Hoffman's attorney then raised the the question of fingerprint evidence:

> If Officer Hanson had told you the truth in this case, wouldn't he after sending the drugs to the laboratory to be analyzed have sent them to be examined for fingerprints? I mean I wouldn't be here making any argument at all if this bag containing cocaine had been examined by the police lab like they should have done.[57]

The government objected to this line of argument on the ground that the record contained no evidence regarding whether the plastic bags containing the narcotics had been tested for fingerprints and, if so, what result was obtained. The district court sustained the objection and instructed the jury to disregard the comments about the lack of fingerprint evidence.

The court ruled that defense attorneys must be permitted to argue all reasonable inferences from the facts in the record, including the negative inferences that may arise when a party fails to call an important witness at trial, or to produce relevant documents or other evidence, where it is shown that the party, such as police, had some special ability to produce such witness or other evidence. However, the court continued, it was equally well established that counsel may not premise arguments on evidence that has not been admitted. In this case, the only "evidence" on the fingerprint issue was purely negative—i.e., the fact that the government did not introduce any fingerprint evidence at all. As the government conceded here, the absence of such evidence was a relevant "fact" that properly could have been argued to the jury. Hence, it would not have been improper for defense counsel to point out to the jury that the government had not presented any evidence concerning fingerprints.

Here, the court noted:

> Hoffman's attorney attempted to go far beyond merely pointing out the lack of fingerprint evidence and arguing that its absence weakened the Government's case. Rather, his argument was that because the Government had not produced fingerprint evidence, the jury should infer that: (1) the police did not attempt to obtain fingerprints from the plastic bags containing the narcotics; (2) this failure violated standard police procedures; and (3) the fingerprint evidence, if obtained, would have been favorable to Hoffman. Defense counsel further asserted that these three inferences supported the additional inference that Officer Hanson's trial testimony was false.... By making these assertions, Hoffman's attorney moved from arguing fair inferences from the record to arguing the existence of facts not in the record—viz., that the police did not look for fingerprints, that fingerprints could have been obtained from the plastic bags containing the narcotics and that standard police procedure required fingerprint analysis.[58]

Because neither defense counsel had laid any evidentiary foundation for such claims, by, for example, asking one of the officers on cross-examination whether the plastic bags were or could have been tested for fingerprints, and whether standard procedure required such testing—Hoffman's closing argument in that regard was improper. The court ruled that the Eley case was distinguishable because the defense lawyer's argument in that case was limited to the contention that the absence of fingerprint evidence weakened the prosecution's case against his client—an argument that the government conceded in Hoffman.[59]

In *People v. Mafias*,[60] defendant was convicted in a bench trial of possession of a controlled substance with intent to deliver and unlawful use of a weapon by a felon. At trial, Chicago Police Officer Thomas Horton testified that on February 5, 1996, he saw the defendant enter the apartment building, a multiple-unit building containing a security door that led to a common entry to front and rear apartments.

After obtaining a search warrant the officers, with a key recovered from the defendant, opened the security door to the common entrance, entered the building, and secured the apartment. The officers noticed that a bedroom door next to the kitchen was locked with a padlock and, using a fourth key from the defendant's set of keys, the officers unlocked the bedroom door. The officers then searched the bedroom and found weapons and, underneath a pile of clothes next to two dressers, $3^1/_2$ kilograms of cocaine.

During their search of the apartment, the officers found no evidence that the defendant resided there, nor did they find any fingerprints of the defendant within the apartment. Defendant was then arrested. The trial court found the defendant guilty of possession with intent to deliver and unlawful use of a weapon by a felon. In its ruling, the trial court emphasized that the defendant had keys not only to the apartment but to the padlock on the bedroom door, where the drugs and guns were found, and no evidence indicated that anyone else had a key to the bedroom padlock, supporting the possession charge.[61]

The appeals court noted that to sustain a charge of unlawful possession of a controlled substance, the state is obligated to prove knowledge of the possession of the substance and that the narcotics were in the immediate and exclusive control of the defendant. For both charges, possession may be actual or constructive. Here, the court found that the evidence was insufficient to prove defendant guilty beyond a reasonable doubt. The state relied heavily on the testimony of Officer Horton and the keys recovered from defendant. The state argued that the fact that the keys were on a single ring demonstrated the defendant's guilt on a constructive possession basis. Here, the court ruled, there was no corroborating evidence, such as the defendant's fingerprints in the apartment, offered to link the defendant with the narcotics and weapons other than the testimony of Officer Horton. No utility bills in the defendant's name were discovered in the apartment, no fingerprint evidence was offered, and the record indicates that others had access to the apartment. The prosecution has the burden to prove that the defendant was responsible for the presence of the narcotics. The court concluded that these facts, combined with the defendant's testimony which was corroborated, cast doubt on the defendant's knowledge of the possession of the contraband and cast doubt on the defendant's immediate and exclusive control of the contraband.[62]

III. LIP AND EAR PRINT IMPRESSIONS

This chapter will conclude with the analysis of two very recent decisions addressing the general acceptability of lip print and ear print impression testimony. Given the novelty of both approaches, they will be examined in detail.

Judicial recognition of the general acceptability of lip print identification testimony may be seen in a 1999 Illinois appellate decision involving lip prints allegedly left on duct tape in a homicide case. In *People v. Davis*,[63] the defendant was convicted of first-degree murder while attempting to commit armed robbery, attempted armed robbery, and armed violence.

On December 18, 1993, Patrick "Pall Mall" Furgeson was shot and killed at the Burnham Mill apartment complex in Elgin. According to the forensic pathologist who performed the autopsy, Dr. Joseph Cogan, Pall Mall died as a result of a gunshot wound to the abdomen from a 12-gauge shotgun fired at close range.

Elgin Police Officer Michael Gough testified that he arrived at the Mill at 6:45 P.M. on December 18, 1993, to gather evidence. He found a shotgun leaning on a bush with the stock sawed off and one spent 12-gauge shotgun shell in the magazine. Around the side of the building, he also found a pair of black nylon hose, a pair of work gloves, and a roll of duct tape. Because the ground was wet but the items were dry, Gough concluded that the items were recently placed there.

Leanne Gray, an Illinois State Police laboratory forensic scientist specializing in latent print examination, testified as an expert in impression evidence. Gray testified that she had found an upper and lower lip print on the first 6 to 8 inches of the sticky side of the duct tape and photographed the impression to preserve it. She testified that lip prints, like fingerprints and other impression evidence, are unique and can be used to identify someone positively. Gray further testified that she took standards of defendant's lips, using the sticky side of duct tape and lipstick on paper. She performed a side-by-side comparison of the standards and the photograph for about a month and a half, focusing on the lower part of the lower lip, and could not determine whether the defendant made the impression found on the tape. She then mailed the photograph and standards to Steven McKasson of the Southern Illinois forensic science laboratory in Carbondale, Illinois. On January 3, 1995, she traveled to Carbondale, where she conducted additional comparisons with McKasson and concluded that the lip print was made by the defendant.

McKasson, a document examiner for the Illinois State Police, was qualified as an expert after testifying in *voir dire* outside the presence of the jury. He testified that lip prints are unique and that lip print comparison is an accepted form of identification. After comparing the lip prints, McKasson found at least 13 points of similarity between a standard and the photograph. He admitted that part of the latent print on the duct tape was not suitable for comparison. McKasson concluded that the person who gave the standards left the duct tape print.

The defendant argued that the trial court erred in admitting the lip print evidence and the testimony of the state's experts Gray and McKasson, contending that the trial court was required to conduct a *Frye* hearing before admitting the lip print identification because it was novel scientific evidence. While agreeing that a *Frye* hearing is typically required to determine the general acceptability of novel scientific evidence, the court observed that the attorneys had an opportunity to question the state's witnesses outside the presence of the jury during *voir dire*. The first witness, Gray, was an experienced latent print examiner with 10 years experience, which adequately established her qualifications to discuss the matter of lip print impressions. The court them noted her support for this relatively rare form of impression evidence:

> Although this was the first time she was asked to conduct a lip print comparison, she completed over 100,000 latent print examinations, has been qualified as an expert in the area of fingerprint or impression evidence over 35 times, and she has given talks and in-house training on latent print evidence. Gray testified that lip print comparison is not a new form of identification but it is seldom used because lip prints are not

readily available. Although this print is the only case of which she is aware in Illinois in the past 10 years, the methodology of lip print comparison is very similar to fingerprint comparison. She testified that lip print comparison is a known and accepted form of scientific comparison. The methods used in her comparisons are accepted within the forensic science community, regardless of whether the comparison is a lip print or fingerprint. She opined, in accord with the Federal Bureau of Investigation (FBI) and Illinois State Police, that lip prints, like fingerprints, are unique and a positive means of identification.[64]

The state's other witness was Stephen McKasson, a document examiner and training coordinator for the Illinois State Police, where he had been employed in the area of forensic science for 25 years, 18 of those years with the Illinois State Police. While employed by the U.S. Postal Inspection Service, he performed thousands of fingerprint examinations each year. He stated that he had previously compared lip prints in other cases. Regarding lip print impression technology, the court noted that:

> According to McKasson, the basis for identification of impression evidence is that everything is unique if looked at in sufficient detail, and if two things are sufficiently similar, they must have come from the same source. He testified that lip print comparison is an accepted method of scientific identification in the forensic science community because it appears in the field literature. He is unaware of any dissent in the field regarding the methodology used to make a positive identification of a lip print.[65]

After each witness testified, the trial court had held that the state met its burden to qualify the witnesses as experts, while admitting that this was a "unique comparison," in that lip prints have not gone into evidence "too often" in the history of the court system. Nonetheless, the court found that the witnesses were qualified as experts based on the scientific procedures followed and the witnesses' experience.

The appellate court agreed, while recognizing the rarity of such testimony:

> The question of the admissibility of lip print identification is a matter of first impression in Illinois. Thus, because lip print identification is novel scientific evidence and has yet to be accepted in a court proceeding, the trial court was required to hold a Frye hearing. A Frye hearing determines the admissibility of novel scientific evidence based on whether the scientific principle on which it rests has gained general acceptance in the relevant scientific community. As the experts testified, the scientific principle upon which lip print identification rests is the same as fingerprints and other impression evidence, i.e., that lip prints are unique and that by employing a side-by-side comparison of a known standard to a latent print, an expert will be able to positively identify whether the lips in the standard made the latent print.... The experts also testified that lip print identification was generally accepted within the forensic science community. They testified that the FBI and the Illinois State Police consider lip prints as means of positive identification, that the technique has been around since 1950, that articles have been written about the subject, and that they did not know of any dissent inside the forensic science community on their methodology or whether lip prints were positive identification.[66]

In reviewing the witnesses' uncontroverted testimony, it was apparent that the trial judge considered the necessary facts to make a *Frye* determination during the *voir dire* questioning and that defendant failed to demonstrate any abuse of discretion.[67]

As a fitting end to this subject, and this chapter, an extensive analysis will now be had of a 1999 decision rejecting the admissibility of forensic ear impression identification testimony. The decision merits detailed study, in that it provides one of the relatively rare instances of an in-depth analysis of the methodology of a proffered forensic discipline, let alone an outright rejection, based on a lengthy *Frye/Daubert* discussion. As noted throughout this book, there has been, until the advent of DNA, a judicial readiness to accept the methodological bases of virtually all of the forensic sciences. The contemporary examination of RFLP, PCR, PCR-STR, and MtDNA has demonstrated a very rapid acceptance of these complex DNA technologies. The case, *State v. Kunze*,[68] was preceded by one unreported 1985 Florida trial court decision which rejected an earlier claim for the legitimacy of ear print impression identification testimony.

In the Florida trial court decision in *State v. Polite*,[69] an extensive analysis was made by the judge in the process of refusing to accept ear print identification as a recognized subspecialty in the field of forensic anthropology and impression evidence. In excluding the ear print evidence as scientifically inadequate, the Florida trial judge stated:

> The State's witness claims to have made a positive identification of the Defendant by comparing a latent earprint found at the crime scene with a known earprint of the Defendant. This appears to be a case of first impression not only in Florida but also in the United States. There is almost no literature on earprint identification and certainly no case law on this issue of earprint identification to guide the Court. The State has offered two witnesses as "experts" to support the admissibility of the earprint identification. The Court finds that one of the State's witnesses, Alfred V. Iannarelli, is not to be recognized as an expert by the Court in determining the admissibility of this evidence.
>
> The Court notes that there were no true scientific tests performed in making the earprint identification. This identification was performed strictly as a comparison test between a known earprint and a latent earprint. The State bases its data on the alleged uniqueness of ears between individuals to establish the reliability of the results of this type of identification. Forensic anthropologists recognize the possible uniqueness of an individual's ears but not as a means of identification.
>
> The testimony presented to the Court suggests that there is a significant difference between comparing actual ears and photographs of ears and the comparing of earprints to each other. Earprints are impressions of an ear. The evidence shows that the ear is a three dimensional object and is malleable. There are no friction ridges as in fingerprints. Different pressures may cause different results with the same ear or different ears to have similar earprints. Furthermore, there are no studies concerning the comparisons of earprints to establish their reliability and validity as a means of identification. The reliability and validity of the results of comparisons of earprints are not recognized or accepted among scientists. There appears to be no science, as in odontology, existing at this time which makes the comparison of earprints possible due to

the alleged uniqueness of an individual's ear characteristics. Furthermore, the comparison techniques used in this case are not sufficiently established to be deemed reliable. The comparison of earprints has not passed from the stage of experimentation and uncertainty to that of reasonable demonstrability.[70]

In *State v. Kunze,*[71] decided 15 years later, in November of 1999, the situation has not improved regarding the acceptability of ear impressions as a legitimate tool in the identification of the perpetrators of a crime. In *Kunze,* the defendant was convicted of aggravated murder. The court of appeals held that the state did not establish that latent ear print identification was generally accepted in the forensic science community, as required for admissibility under the *Frye* test.

In the early morning hours of December 16, 1994, an intruder entered the home of James McCann, who was asleep in the master bedroom. His son Tyler, age 13, was asleep in another bedroom. The intruder bludgeoned McCann in the head with a blunt object, killing him, and also bludgeoned Tyler in the head, resulting in a fractured skull.

The police were immediately interested in Kunze, who had been married to one Diana James from 1976 to April 1994. James told Kunze, 4 days before the intruder entered McCann's home, that she and McCann were planning to be married. She testified that Kunze was upset by the news.

George Millar, a fingerprint technician with the Washington State Crime Laboratory, processed the home for evidence. He discovered a partial latent ear print on the hallway-side surface of McCann's bedroom door. He "dusted" the print by applying black fingerprint powder with a fiberglass brush. He "lifted" the print by applying palm-print tape first to the door and then to a palm-print card. The resulting print showed the antitragus and portions of the tragus, helix, helix rim, and antihelix. Michael Grubb, a criminologist with the Washington State Crime Laboratory, compared the latent print from McCann's bedroom door with photographs of the left side of Kunze's face. He concluded that the latent print "could have been made by Dave Kunze." He also thought that "[i]t may be possible to obtain additional information by comparing the [latent print] to exemplar impressions."[72]

Millar and Grubb met with Kunze to obtain ear print exemplars. The court recited the steps taken by them, noting that neither had taken an ear print exemplar before, although each had practiced on laboratory staff in preparation for meeting with Kunze:

> For each of the seven exemplars they took, they had Kunze put hand lotion on his ear and press the ear against a glass surface with a different degree of pressure ("light," "medium," or "hard"). They then dusted the glass with fingerprint powder and used palm-print tape to transfer the resulting impression onto a transparent plastic overlay. The reason Millar and Grubb took multiple exemplars is that they were consciously trying to produce one that would match (i.e., "duplicate") the latent print from McCann's door. They knew that earprints of the same ear vary according to the angle and rotation of the head, and also according to the degree of pressure with which the head is pressed against the receiving surface. They did not know the angle and rotation of the head that made the latent print, or the degree of pressure with which that head

had been pressed against McCann's door. Hoping to compensate for these difficulties, they told Kunze to use a different degree of pressure each time ("light," "medium," or "hard"), and they looked at the latent print as they worked.[73]

Grubb, the one who testified, concluded that "David Kunze is a likely source for the earprint and cheekprint which were lifted from the outside of the bedroom door at the homicide scene." Grubb testified to his extensive qualifications as a criminalist. He had been working as a criminalist for more than 20 years, was currently the manager of the state crime laboratory's Seattle office, although he had never before dealt with ear prints, he specialized in firearm and tool mark identification, and had analyzed "impression evidence" of other kinds. The court recited his basis for providing an ear print opinion. He admitted that he had not seen any data or studies on ear prints, or on how often an ear having the general shape of the questioned print in this case appeared in the general human population. He had used transparent overlays to compare the latent and the exemplars in this case, and stressed that the use of overlays was a generally accepted method of making comparisons. When he compared the latent print with the exemplars taken from Kunze, he admitted accentuating the exemplars taken with "a lighter amount of pressure," because those "more closely approximated … the impression from the crime scene." He opined that latent ear print identification was generally accepted in the scientific community, reasoning that "the earprint is just another form of impression evidence," and that other impression evidence was readily accepted in the scientific community.[74]

Cor Van der Lugt testified to extensive qualifications as a police evidence technician in the Netherlands. He had been a Dutch police officer since 1971 and a crime scene officer since 1979, had trained other crime scene officers for many years, and had written "a lot of letters all around the world to people who did something with earprints." He admitted that he had not gotten much response to his inquiries. He testified he had adopted methods used by one Professor Lunga of Germany, who had investigated what parts of the ear look alike between parents and their children. He also testified to have relied on methods used by a Mr. Hirschi of Switzerland, who had investigated the relation of the height of an ear print and the body length of the offender. He testified that he had received over 600 cases for comparative analysis and had made an identification to his own satisfaction in "somewhere between 200 and 250 cases." On the basis of "somewhere between 100 and 200 prints," he had concluded that pressure distortion is not a problem that prevents one from making an identification or a comparison between ears, even though you must "get the same pressure on the ear as the ear that was found on the scene of a crime." He opined that the solution was merely to take several exemplars under different degrees of pressure, then "pick the one that comes closest" to the latent print.

He had been to court in six ear print cases, all in Holland, and the judges in those cases had not been concerned about his methodology; indeed, they had accepted that an identification of an individual can be made by an ear print. The witness did not present or refer to *any* published literature stating that ear print identification was generally accepted in the scientific community, but testified, none-theless, as follows:

> Q: [D]o you have an opinion as to whether ... the uniqueness of the human ear as a basis for personal identification is a notion that is generally accepted in the Netherlands and elsewhere amongst those engaged in forensic identification?

> A: It is accepted, yes.[75]

Alfred V. Iannarelli testified to his extensive qualifications as a law enforcement officer. He had worked as a deputy sheriff in Alameda County, California for 30 years, as the chief of campus police at California State University at Hayward, and in several other law enforcement positions, and had worked as a consultant on ear identification. He stated he became interested in ears in 1948, and over the next 14 years classified perhaps 7,000 ears from photographs (but not from latent prints). In 1964, he published a book describing his system, which he called "earology" or the "science of ear identification."[76] In 1989, he stated, he published a second edition through a different publisher.[77] He admitted that he had been prohibited from testi-fying in a 1985 Florida case on the ground that his system of ear identification was not generally accepted in the scientific community,[78] but had testified without objec-tion in a 1984 California murder case.

He stated that he did not know of any published scientific studies that confirmed his theory that individuals can be identified using ear prints, nor did he assert that his system was generally accepted in the scientific community:

> Q: Are you aware of any scientific research at all that would confirm your theory that ears are so unique that individuals can be positively identified by comparing known earprints with latent ear impressions?

> A: Ear photographs, not earprints. Counsel, this is relatively a new science.[79]

Dr. Ellis Kerley testified to extensive qualifications as a physical anthropologist. He had a doctorate in anthropology from the University of Michigan and was a professor of long standing in that subject. He had taught the anatomy of the human ear and had been President of the American Academy of Forensic Sciences, and President and First Diplomate of the American Board of Forensic Anthropology. He had worked on prominent cases such as the assassination of President John F. Kennedy. He testified that while the human ear was probably different for each person, he had no information "indicating whether one ear could be differentiated from another by observing the ear's gross external anatomy." He did not consider Mr. Iannarelli's work scientific, but rather, simply narrative, not reported in a scien-tific manner, and not subjected to any statistical analysis. He also rejected Van der Lugt's approach of applying pressure until you could make the exemplar prints look about the same as the latent print in issue, concluding, "we don't do that in science ... [b]ecause we're not trying to make them look alike." He also stated that ear print identification had not been presented in general scientific sessions or publications, and that he was not aware of any scientific research or authoritative literature concerning ear print identification. It was his opinion that ear print identification had not achieved "general acceptance" in the forensic science community.

Professor Andre Moenssens testified to extensive qualifications as a fingerprint examiner and law professor.[80] Professor Moenssens testified in part:

Q: [D]o you have an opinion whether or not earprint identification is generally accepted as reliable in the forensic science community?

A: [T]he forensic sciences … do not recognize as a separate discipline the identification of ear impressions. There are some people in the forensic science community, the broader forensic science community, who feel that it can be done. But if we are talking about a general acceptance by scientists, there is no such general acceptance.

Q: Is there any evidence that earprint identification has ever been tested by scientific methodology?

A: To my knowledge, it has not been.

Q: Or adequately subjected to scientific peer review?

A: If by peer review, you mean inquiry and verification and studies to confirm or deny the existence of the underlying premise, that is, ear uniqueness, to my knowledge that has not been done.

…

Q: With respect to earprint identification, has it ever been shown that results can be reliably obtained in terms of an acceptable rate of error?

A: To my knowledge, there has been no investigation in the possible rate of error that comparisons between known and unknown ear samples might produce.[81]

While he agreed that one ear print could always be compared with another, he noted that "[t]he question is whether that comparison means anything." He testified that he did not know of any generally accepted methods for recording ear characteristics or determining the significance of a "match."

George Bonebrake, a latent fingerprint examiner, testified that he worked for the FBI from 1941 to 1978, that during his last 3 years with the FBI, he was in charge of its latent print section, supervising 100 examiners and 65 support people, and was currently in private practice. He testified that he never identified anyone based on ear prints, and to his knowledge no one else at the FBI had either:

Q: Is there anything in the materials that you have read that indicates earprint identification has been generally accepted in the forensic science community?

A: No, sir.

Q: What is your impression of the state of earprint identification at this point in forensic science history?

A: That there have been a few cases of individuals making earprint comparisons and identifications, but I'm not aware of any study or research that would indicate to me the uniqueness of earprints when it comes to the comparison of [known] earprint impressions ... with the latent earprint impressions; that's based on class characteristics.

...

Q: Does the literature indicate that there are problems in attempting to obtain earprint exemplars?

A: Especially when it comes to pressure, yes, sir.

...

Q: Have you ever seen any authoritative text published in any discipline of forensic science that's gone on record claiming that earprint identification is generally accepted in the forensic science community?

A: No, sir.[82]

Tommy Moorefield testified that he was a fingerprint specialist with the FBI in Washington, D.C., had worked for the FBI for 36 years as of December 1996, had conducted advanced latent fingerprint courses throughout the U.S., had instructed new agents on collecting and preserving evidence, and had worked on both the Waco disaster and the TWA Flight 800 disaster. He testified that he was not "real sure" that ear print identification was generally accepted in the community of forensic scientists, and was not aware of the FBI collecting any data on ear prints.

William Stokes testified that he was a special agent and chief of all photographic operations for the FBI in Washington, D.C. and had identified individuals from photographs of their ears, but not from latent ear prints. He stated that he had no knowledge of whether latent ear print identification was generally accepted by the scientific community.

Ralph Turbyfill testified that he is the long-time chief latent fingerprint examiner for the Arkansas State Crime Laboratory and was able to identify a person from an ear print in one case, because of hair follicles that were peculiarly located. He had, however, tried unsuccessfully to identify people from ear prints in two other cases. He did not believe that ear print identification was generally accepted in the forensic science community, and he did not know of any publication or treatise that asserted that is was so accepted.[83]

Gary Siebenthal testified that he had been an officer with the Peoria, Illinois, police department for 23 years and a crime scene technician and, although he had identified a defendant from an ear print on one occasion, he did not know of anyone who had proclaimed that ear print identification was generally accepted as reliable in the forensic science community. He also did not know of any scientific research on reliable techniques for making ear prints or dealing with pressure distortions in any such attempts.

Ernest Hamm testified that he had been a crime laboratory analyst-supervisor in Jacksonville, Florida, for approximately 16 years and had made an ear print identification in one case. He testified that he had been able to do that because the defendant had a very peculiar mark in the lobe area of the ear. Although he personally believed that ear prints could be identified, he knew of nothing to indicate that ear print identification was generally accepted in the forensic science community.

At the end of this extensive *Frye* hearing, the trial court nevertheless concluded that the principle known as "individualization" through the use of transparent overlays applied to the comparison of the latent impression in the present case with the known standards of the defendant, and was based upon principles and methods which were sufficiently established to have gained general acceptance in the relevant scientific community, and as such was admissible.

At the ensuing trial, the state called Grubb and Van der Lugt, but not Iannarelli, to compare the latent print to the exemplars and to render an opinion regarding the results of the comparison of the defendant's ear print and that lifted from the home of the victim. The court set out this crucial testimony:

> Grubb testified that the latent print showed "the antihelix, the interior portion of the ear; the helix rim, that is the top of the rim of the ear; tragus and antitragus, two portions of the ear down below"; that he had compared those anatomical features using transparencies; and that he had found "very good correspondence of those features." … He opined, to a reasonable degree of scientific certainty, that "Mr. Kunze's left ear and cheek [were] the likely source of this [ear print] impression at the [crime] scene."
>
> Van der Lugt testified that he also compared the latent ear print and the exemplars by using transparencies and found "a few parts that correspond completely," but also some "differences." He believed that the differences were insignificant, because investigators would never find a 100% fit and that any dissimilarities were caused "by pressure distortion." Although he conceded that no study had ever been published in the world that could tell the jury how much correspondence was actually required to declare a match, he nevertheless testified:
>
> Q: Mr. Van der Lugt, as a result of your comparison of the Grubb standards and your independent comparison of your own standards with the crime scene tracing earprint that was taken in this case, do you have an opinion as to the probability that the defendant's left ear is the source of the latent impression which was left at the scene of the crime in this case?
>
> A: I do have an opinion, yes.
>
> Q: What is your opinion, then?
>
> A: I think it's probable that it's the defendant's ear is the one that was found on the scene.
>
> …
>
> Q: [H]ow confident are you of the opinion that you just expressed?

A: I'm 100 percent confident with that opinion.[84]

Kunze was convicted of aggravated murder, burglary, and robbery. He was sentenced to life without possibility of parole on the murder conviction, and to standard-range sentences on the other convictions.

The court of appeals ruled that the main issue was the scientific acceptability of ear imprint testimony:

> The main question on appeal is whether Grubb and Van der Lugt could properly opine, based on the similarities and differences that they observed in the overlays, that Kunze was the likely or probable maker of the latent print. Kunze says they could not, because they were relying on scientific, technical or specialized knowledge not generally accepted in the relevant scientific, technical or specialized community. The State says they could, either because they were not relying on scientific, technical or specialized knowledge, or because they were relying on scientific, technical or specialized knowledge that was generally accepted in the relevant scientific, technical or specialized community. We inquire (A) whether Grubb and Van der Lugt were relying on scientific, technical or specialized knowledge, and (B), if so, whether that knowledge was generally accepted in the relevant scientific, technical or specialized community.[85]

The court noted that a forensic scientist must make clear the difference between individualizing and class characteristics when opining about the maker of a latent print. On the basis of class characteristics alone, a forensic scientist could say that a suspect "cannot be excluded" as the maker of a latent print, that the suspect "could have made" a latent print, or that a latent print was "consistent with" exemplars. However, the court continued, on the basis of individualizing characteristics—and *only* on the basis of individualizing characteristics—was a forensic scientist allowed to opine that a suspect made or probably made a latent print.

Here, the court observed, Grubb and Van der Lugt claimed that Kunze probably made the latent print taken from McCann's door, and therefore were necessarily claiming that they had found, and were relying on, at least one individualizing characteristic. However, the court emphasized, both Grubb and Van der Lugt lacked personal knowledge of any individualizing characteristic:

> They could not have observed an individualizing characteristic like a scar, tear, mole, or abnormal hair follicle, because the overlays did not show any such feature. They were able to observe the antitragus, tragus, helix, helix rim, and antihelix, insofar as shown in the latent print, but each of those features was a class characteristic, not an individualizing one. They were able to observe the relationship between the antitragus, tragus, helix, helix rim, and antihelix, insofar as it was shown in the latent print, but a lay person using common knowledge would have had no idea whether such relationship was an individualizing characteristic; to conclude that it was, Grubb and Van der Lugt necessarily had to be employing scientific, technical or specialized knowledge. We turn, then, to whether that knowledge was generally accepted in the relevant community.[86]

In this case, the court observed, 12 long-time members of the forensic science community stated or implied that latent ear print identification was not generally accepted in the forensic science community. Criminalist Grubb's assertion of general acceptance was not based on solid ground:

> He reasoned, essentially, that latent earprints are a form of impression evidence; that other forms of impression evidence are generally accepted in the forensic science community; and thus that latent earprints must be generally accepted in the forensic science community. . . . We reject his premise that latent earprints automatically have the same degree of acceptance and reliability as fingerprints, toolmarks, ballistics, handwriting, and other diverse forms of impression evidence.[87]

The court concluded that the trial court erred by allowing Grubb and Van der Lugt to testify.

RESEARCH NOTE

The Journal of Forensic Sciences is the official publication of the American Academy of Forensic Sciences. By visiting the Academy's Web site at *http://www.aafs.org* and clicking on the "Journal of Forensic Sciences" link, one can get to a searchable index of the journal from 1981 to the present that uses common search terms. The site also provides tables of contents for more recent issues of the journal, and, for a modest fee, one can download individual articles from issues published after January 1, 1999. The index, content, and article availability site is maintained by the publisher, The American Society for Testing and Materials (ASTM). There are current plans to move toward Web-based publication of the journal, although the paper copy will still be available for some time. Individual subscriptions to this essential journal are also available from ASTM for those interested.

Visiting this important Web site on a regular basis and viewing the available abstracts are essential to the early stages of forensic science/forensic evidence research. Also see the recent bibliography prepared by Christopher Champed and Pierre Margot, "Fingermarks, Shoesole Impressions and Toolmarks," in *Proceedings of the 12th INTERPOL Forensic Science Symposium* (1998), at 303–331.

ENDNOTES

1. W. H. Auden and L. Kronenberger: *The Viking Book of Aphorisms* (Viking, New York, 1966).
2. Galton: *Finger Prints* (Macmillan, New York, 1892).
3. See, e.g., Saferstein: *Criminalistics: An Introduction to Forensic Science* (6th ed. Prentice-Hall, Upper Saddle River, NJ, 1998) at 437; Giannelli and Imwinkelried: *Scientific Evidence* (2d ed. The Michie Company, Charlottesville, VA, 1993), Vol. 2, at Chap. 16, p. 479; Geberth: *Practical Homicide Investigation* (3d ed. CRC Press,

Boca Raton, FL, 1996), at 524 et seq.; Fisher: *Techniques of Crime Scene Investigation* (5th ed. CRC Press, Boca Raton, FL, 1993) at 90 et seq. Also see Lee and Gaensslen: *Advances in Fingerprint Technology* (CRC Press, Boca Raton, FL, 1994).

4. See J. Almog and E. Springer (Eds.): *Proceedings of the International Symposium on Fingerprint Detection and Identification* (Ne'urim, June 26–30, 1995, Hemed Press, Jerusalem, Israel) (contact Israeli National Police, Investigations Department, Division of Identification and Forensic Sciences, Jerusalem, Israel). Also see Christopher Champed and Pierre Margot, "Fingermarks, Shoesole Impressions, Ear Impressions and Toolmarks," *Proceedings of the 12th INTERPOL Forensic Science Symposium* (New York, 1998) at 303–331.

5. See the Home Page for the FBI-supported forensic sciences working groups, located at *http://www.for-swg.org/home.htm*, particularly here, the page for SWGFAST, the Scientific Working Group on Friction Ridge Analysis and SWGDE, the page for the Scientific Working Group for Digital Evidence. Also see Scientific Working Group on Imaging Technologies (SWGIT), "Definitions and Guidelines for the Use of Imaging Technologies in the Criminal Justice System," located at *http://www.fbi.gov/programs/lab/fsc/current/swigit1.htm*. The SWGFAST site contains a current listing of minimum latent print examiner's qualifications guidelines, training-to-competency guidelines, and quality assurance guidelines for such examiners. These materials are located at *http://onin.com/twgfast/twgfast.html*.

6. The Center for Law and Science of DePaul University College of Law maintains a Web site that tracks recent forensic science Web sites as well as recent decisions in the entire area of forensic evidence. Also see Zeno's Forensic Page, at *http://forensic.to/forensic.html*.

7. The Southern California Association of Fingerprint Officers (SCAFO), located at *http://www.scafo.org*, has a searchable database of over 800 fingerprint book and article references. The Forensic Science Society (U.K.) also provides a searchable index of articles in the *Journal of the Forensic Science Society*, whose name was changed to *Science and Justice* in 1995. The searchable index for the *Journal of Forensic Sciences* from 1981 to date, noted and utilized throughout this book is located at *http://www.aafs.org*. The Arkansas State Crime Laboratory site has an interesting introduction in the form of FAQs on the basics of fingerprint identification and very good graphics examples of print characteristics. It is located at *nttp://www.state.ar.us/crimelab/index.htm*.

8. D. Wigmore: *The Principles of Judicial Proof* (Little, Brown, and Company, Boston, 1913).

9. D. Wigmore: *The Science of Judicial Proof* (Little, Brown, and Company, Boston, 1937).

10. Dean Wigmore's 10-volume treatise, *Wigmore on Evidence,* remains the greatest scholarship on that subject that we possess.

11. People v. Jennings, 252 Ill. 534, 96 N.E. 1077 (1911).

12. Wigmore, *supra,* note 8 [quoting C. Ainsworth Mitchell: *Science and the Criminal* (1911)] at 79–83.

13. *Supra*, note 11.

14. *Id.* The defendant challenged the admissibility of eyewitness testimony per se, a claim that has returned with gusto as we close out this century.

15. In re Castleton's Case, 3 Crim. App. 74 (1909).

16. *Supra*, note 11. The court cited *Encyclopedia Brittannica* (11th ed.) Vol. 10 at 376; Nelson's Encyclopedia, Vol. 5 at 28; *Gross' Criminal Investigation* (Adams' transl.) at 277; *Fuld's Police Administration*, at 342; and *Osborn's Questioned Documents* at 479.

17. *Supra*, note11.
18. *Id*. at 548.
19. *Id*., citing, *Wharton on Criminal Evidence* *549 (8th ed.) §544; *Wigmore on Evidence,* Vol. 1 §795; *Rogers on Expert Testimony* (2d ed.) §140; *Jones on Evidence* (2d ed.) 581.
20. *Supra*, note 11, at 549. The court noted the general rule that whatever tends to prove any material fact is relevant and competent. They also observed that testimony as to footprints has frequently been held admissible. See *Wharton on Crim. Evidence* (8th ed.) §796; *Wigmore on Evidence,* Vol.1, §413; State v. Fuller, 34 Mont. 12, 85 Pac. 369, 8 L. R. A. (N. S.) 762, 9 Am. & Eng. Ann. Cas. 648, and note.
21. *Supra*, note 11 at 549.
22. See Almog and Springer, *supra*, note 4, for a comprehensive series of articles on the detection and enhancement of latent prints by specialized lighting techniques, short-wave ultraviolet reflection photography, superglue, vacuum methodologies, DMAC (dimethylaminocinnamaldehyde), PDMAC, amino acid reagents, reflected ultraviolet imaging systems, ninhydrin, black powder, iodine and alpha-naphthoflavone. There are also recent studies of obtaining latent prints from human skin, plastic bags, and cartridge cases.
23. See Saferstein, *supra*, note 3, at 440–448; Giannelli and Imwinkelried, supra, note 3, at 503–510; Fisher, *supra*, note 3, at 99–118. Also see *F.B.I. Handbook of Forensic Sciences*: Latent Print Examinations, located on the FBI Web site, available at *http://www.fbi.gov/programs/lab/labhome.htm*.
24. Champed and Margot, *supra*, note 4, at 304.
25. *Id*. at 305. Also see, Evett, I.W., and Williams R.L., "A Review of the Sixteen Points Fingerprint Standard in England and Wales," *Proceedings of the International Symposium on Fingerprint Detection and Identification* (Jerusalem, 1995).
26. *Id*.
27. See J. Peterson: "The Status of AFIS Systems Worldwide: Issues of Organization, Performance and Impact," *Proceedings of the International Symposium on Fingerprint Detection and Identification* (1995); Also see Dr. Peterson's description of this conference in J. Peterson: "Israel Fingerprint Conference Draws 22 Countries," Crime and Justice International, located at *http://www.acsp.uic.edu/oic/pubs/cji/110505.htm*.
28. The five key IAFIS services are Ten-print Based Identification Services; latent fingerprint services; subject search and criminal history services; document and image services; and remote search services. IAFIS will consist of three integrated segments: Identification Tasking and Networking (ITN); Interstate Identification Index (III); and Automated Fingerprint Identification System (AFIS). See "NCIC 2000, Linking It All Together, Fingerprint Matching Subsystem" (FMS) (1997) and "Fingerprint Identification and Related Information Services" (1997), both of which may located through a search on the FBI homepage, located at *http://www.fbi.gov*.
29. See Saferstein, *supra*, note 3, at 440–446.
30. Arizona v. Youngblood, 488 U.S. 51,58,109 S.Ct. 333, 337–38,102 L.Ed.2d 281 (1988); Miller v. Vasquez, 868 F.2d1116,1120 (9th Cir. 1989), cert. denied, 499 U.S. 963,111 S.Ct.1591, 113 L.Ed.2d654 (1991).
31. People v. Towns, 174 Ill.2d 453, 675 N.E.2d 614 (1996).
32, *Id*. at 468.
33. Davis v. Mississippi, 394 U.S. 721, 724, 89 S.Ct.1394, 22 L.Ed.2d 676 (1969).
34. Hooker v. State, 716 So.2d 1104 (Miss. Sp. Ct. 1998).
35. *Id*. at 1108.
36. Wong Sun v. United States, 371 U.S. 471, 83 S.Ct. 407, 9 L.Ed.2d 441 (1963).

37. *Id.* at 1113. During a break in the trial, examiner Morgan was allowed to compare the second set of prints with the latent print removed from the Coors Light beer can. At trial, and before the jury, Morgan testified that the thumbprint matched the known thumbprint of Hooker.

38. People v. Campbell, 146 Ill.2d 363, 586 N.E.2d 1261 (1992).

39. *Id.* at 387. Also see People v. Rhodes, 85Ill.2d 241,422 N.E.2d 605 (1981); People v. Gomez, 215 Ill.App.3d 208, 574 N.E.2d 822 (1991).

40. See People v. Donahue, 50 Ill.App.3d 392, 394, 365 N.E.2d 710 (1977).

41. *Supra*, note 38, at 1272. Also see People v. Taylor, 32 Ill.2d 165, 204N.E.2d 734 (1965) (defendant's fingerprints on the inside of a window sash in the apartment of a rape and burglary victim was sufficient evidence to establish guilt, since the presence of defendant's prints was unexplained); People v. Reno, 32Ill.App.3d 754, 336 N.E.2d 36 (1975) (the unexplained presence of defendant's thumbprint on a package of cigarettes found in a purse which had been stolen from the residence of murder, standing alone, was sufficient evidence to support conviction of murder.

42. State v. Montgomery, 341 N.C. 553, 461 S.E.2d 732 (1995).

43. *Id.* at 561.

44. See, e.g., State v. Bass, 303 N.C. 267, 278 S.E.2d 209 (1981) (where the only evidence tending to show that the defendant was ever at the scene of the crime was four of defendant's fingerprints found on the frame of a window screen on the victim's home; the state produced no evidence tending to show when they were put there, and the defendant offered evidence that he was on the premises at an earlier date); State v. Scott, 296 N.C. 519, 251 S.E.2d 414 (1979) (where the only evidence tending to show that defendant was ever in the victim's home was a thumbprint found on a metal box in the den on the day of the murder, and the niece of the deceased testified that during the week, she had no opportunity to observe who came to the house on business or to visit with her uncle); State v. Smith, 274 N.C. 159, 161 S.E.2d 449 (1968) (where the state had no evidence tending to show that the fingerprint of the defendant found on the victim's wallet could only have been impressed at the time the money was allegedly stolen from her wallet); State v. Minton, 228 N.C. 518, 46 S.E.2d 296 (1948) (where the defendant's fingerprint was found on broken glass from the front door of a store that had been unlawfully entered, and the defendant was lawfully in the store on the day the crime was committed).

45. See, e.g., State v. Irick, 291 N.C. 480, 231 S.E.2d 833 (1977) (where the defendant's fingerprint was found on the window sill of the victim's house, the defendant was apprehended near the scene of the crime, and other evidence tied defendant to the break-in); State v. Miller, 289 N.C. 1, 220 S.E.2d 572 (1975) (where the state's evidence established that the defendant's right thumbprint was found on the lock at the scene of the crime, no other fingerprints were found at the scene, and the defendant falsely stated to the police that he had never been in the building that was broken into); State v. Jackson, 284 N.C. 321, 200 S.E.2d 626 (1973) (where the state's evidence showed that the defendant's fingerprint was lifted from the lower sash of the window inside the kitchen of the apartment occupied by the victim, the victim identified the defendant's voice, and nothing appeared in the record to show that the defendant had ever been in the apartment occupied by the victim prior to the morning of the crimes charged); State v. Foster, 282 N.C. 189, 192 S.E.2d 320 (1972) (where the victims testified that they did not know the defendant and had never given him permission to enter their home and the defendant testified he had never been in their home, and the evidence showed that the flowerpot where the defendant's fingerprints were found had been frequently washed); State v. Tew, 234 N.C. 612, 68 S.E.2d 291

(1951) (where the defendant's fingerprints were found at the scene of the crime and the testimony of the owner and operator of the service station tended to show that she had not seen the defendant before the date of the crime); State v. Reid, 230 N.C. 561, 53 S.E.2d 849 (1949) (where the defendant was never lawfully in the apartment of the victim, and the defendant's fingerprint was present on the inside of the window sill in the sleeping quarters of the victim), cert. denied, 338 U.S. 876, 70 S.Ct. 138, 94 L.Ed. 537 (1949).

46. State v. Montgomery, *supra*, note 42, at 564.
47. *Id*. at 565.
48. People v. Zizzo, 301 Ill.App.3d 481, 703 N.E.2d 546 (1998).
49. People v. Gomes, 215 Ill.App.3d 208, 158 Ill.Dec. 709, 574 N.E.2d 822 (1991).
50. *Id*. at 212.
51. State v. Monzo, 998 WL 66942 (Ohio App.).
52. *Id*. at *3.
53. *Id*. at *4.
54. Eley v. State, 288 Md. 548, 555–56, 419 A.2d 384, 388 (1980).
55. *Id*. at 388, quoting People v. Carter, 73 Ill.App.3d 406, 410, 29 Ill.Dec. 631, 392 N.E.2d 188, 192 (1979) (alteration in original).
56. United States v. Hoffman, 964 F.2d 21 (Dist. Col. Ct. App. 1992).
57. *Id*. at 24.
58. *Id*. at 25.
59. See Patterson v. State, 1999 WL 112.5162 (Md. 1999), where defendant was convicted of possession of cocaine with intent to distribute and various driving offenses. The appellate court ruled on defendant's claim that the trial court erred in refusing to give his requested "missing evidence" instruction. The court concluded that a party generally is not entitled to a missing evidence instruction, and affirmed the conviction. This is an excellent case that provides a very comprehensive analysis of the current status of the "missing evidence" issue, especially in regard to a defendant's right to a "missing evidence" jury instruction.
60. People v. Mafias, 299 Ill.App.3d 480, 701 N.E.2d 212 (1998).
61. *Id*. at 482.
62. *Id*. at 488.
63. People v. Davis, 304 Ill.App.3d 427, 710 N.E.2d 1251(1999).
64. *Id*. at 436.
65. *Id*.
66. *Id*. at 437.
67. Also see Smallwood v. State, 907 P. 2d 217 (Ct. Crim. App. Okla. 1995) (cups located in the living room and bedroom showed bloody lip prints, suggesting the victim had been conscious enough to drink from containers before finally being bludgeoned to death).
68. State v. Kunze, 97 Wash.App. 832, 988 P.2d 977 (1999).
69. State v. Polite, No. 84-525 (14th Judicial Circuit, Fla. Jun. 10, 1985). This case is noted and referenced in State v. Kunze, *supra*, note 68; discussed in detail below.
70. State v. Polite, *supra*, Clerk's Papers at 1073–74. This case did not result in a published appellate opinion.
71. *Supra*, note 68.
72. *Id*. at 981.
73. *Id*. After Millar and Grubb took the exemplars, they were asked to compare them with the latent print. Millar declined because his laboratory supervisor thought that earprint identification was "out of the expertise of the [crime laboratory's] latent unit."

74. *Id.* at 982–983.

75. *Id.* at 983.

76. *Id.* at 984.

77. The court noted the 1989 edition of Iannarelli's book was introduced along with his oral testimony. Titled *Ear Identification*, it was published by the Paramont Publishing Company of Fremont, CA and, the court observed, contained no bibliography or other indicia of scientific verification or acceptability.

78. See State v. Polite, *supra.*

79. *Supra*, note 68.

80. Professor Moenssens is coauthor of the leading text, Moenssens, Starrs, Henderson and Inbau: *Scientific Evidence in Civil and Criminal Cases* (4ᵗʰ ed. Foundation Press, Minneapolis, 1995), still the leading law school casebook and treatise on scientific evidence.

81. *Supra,* note 68 at 984–985.

82. *Id.*

83. *Id.* at 985.

84. *Id.* at 987.

85. *Id.* at 977–978.

86. *Id.* at 989.

87. *Id.*

9 Blood Spatter Analysis

I. INTRODUCTION

Arterial spurting, expired blood, flight paths, misting, wave casting, blood dripping, satellite patterns, low-, medium-, and high-velocity deposits, backspatter, wipes, swipes, angular deposits, and off patterns are just some of the body of terms[1] utilized in the very telling discipline of bloodstain pattern analysis. This strictly observation-based forensic tool is a highly specialized crime scene procedure that is combined with the equally important skills involved in forensic photography.[2] It is commonly used in homicide and suicide settings to determine the sequence of events, the distance of shooter to victim, self-defense, mental states such as intent, and a number of important crime scene dynamics that can be of inestimable use to both prosecutors and defense counsel. Considerable attention to this subject was given in the recent O. J. Simpson and the Lyle and Eric Menendez murder prosecutions.[3]

Blood transfer mechanisms, blood sequencing, whether the nose or mouth was involved in expired blood, and blood spatters are the stock in trade of analysts in this area. Photography and string arrangements tracking the type, shape, extent, and direction of blood material, whether large or microscopic, can reprise the fatal event with an impressive degree of accuracy. As evidenced in the second Menendez prosecution, a clear reconstruction of just how a crime occurred can eliminate any number of defense arguments based on accident, recklessness, or sudden panic by illustration of cold calculation or the minimal amount of premeditation required to convict.[4] For example, "arterial gushing" produces characteristic bloodstain patterns on a surface as a result of blood exiting under pressure from a breached artery;

249

medium-velocity impact spatter is produced when an object, such as a baseball bat, strikes a bloody object, such as a victim's head, at a velocity of approximately 25 feet per second; and high-velocity impact spatter occurs when the velocity of the impact is at least 100 feet per second. This phenomenon is typically associated with gunshot wounds.

A pioneering study in this century was made by MacDonnell and Bialousz, "Flight Characteristics and Stain Patterns of Human Blood," National Institute of Law Enforcement and Criminal Justice of the Department of Justice (1969), although important judicial acceptance came as long ago as 1922.[5] There are now several excellent texts, bibliographies, Web sites,[6] and training courses that address all aspects of this important forensic discipline.[7] The presence or absence of blood in and around a crime scene has been discussed in cases since the beginning of the nation, although the type of discussion concerning bloodstain pattern analysis is a phenomenon of the last quarter of this century.

In *People v. Davis*,[8] decided by the Michigan Supreme Court, the defendant was convicted of murder in the first degree, growing out of the killing of one Earl Zang, who was found on the sidewalk near the corner of Fort and Sixth Streets, in the city of Detroit, about 5 A.M., March 7, 1921. His death was caused by two knife wounds, one in the side, and the other in the neck. The defendant was one of the deceased's companions earlier in the evening and was eventually charged with his murder.

Dr. John E. Clarke, a county chemist, had examined spots of blood on the defendant's coat. He explained the difference in appearance when the blood was dropped on a garment and when it "squirted from a bleeding artery." He was then asked:

Q: Can you say that the blood was dropped on, or was squirted on, ... as by a bleeding artery? ...

A: My opinion is it was spread on.

Q: Sprayed?

A: Squirted.

This testimony was accepted without challenge or discussion by the court.[9]

The initial step is, of course, to identify the presence of blood at various points in the crime scene. Luminol has been used by police for years as an investigative tool to accomplish this. It has been subject to debate about the utility of such identifications as forensic evidence because of its tendency to indicate false-positive results. Luminol and phenolphthalein are used as presumptive tests in the field to identify potential bloodstains, but they can generate false-positive reactions. The tests can react to metal surfaces, cleansers containing iron-based substances, horse-radish, and rust. Neither test can distinguish between animal blood and human blood, and they cannot determine how long the substance has been at the scene. When a positive reaction occurs, a criminalist must do a confirmatory test to determine conclusively that the test sample is human blood. The potential for Luminol destroying important markers needed for certain blood analyses was also cited as a concern in the early part of the 1990s.[10]

Chapter 2, Science and the Criminal Law, contains an extensive discussion of very recent cases accepting Luminol as sufficiently grounded to support blood spatter testimony in cases involving the legal implications of crime scene procedures. The FBI has recently published an important paper entitled "Critical Revision of Presumptive Tests for Bloodstains," which addresses this necessary step in the use of bloodstain pattern analysis testimony.[11]

II. BLOOD SPATTER CASES

In *State v. Ordway*,[12] the court set out the basic profile of an acceptable presentation of a forensic bloodstain pattern analysis. Here, the defendant proffered an insanity defense to charges of first-degree murder and theft in the deaths of his parents and the theft of their automobile. A jury found him guilty of two counts of second-degree murder and one count of felony theft.

Betty and Clarence Ordway lived approximately a mile west of Stockton, Kansas. On Saturday evening, November 20, 1993, in response to a call from the Ordways' nieces, a sheriff's officer went to the Ordway house. Investigation disclosed drag marks leading to the garage where the officer found Clarence Ordway's body wrapped in bedding and partially concealed behind some garbage cans. The body of Mrs. Ordway was found several days later in the trunk of their stolen car. A search revealed blood spatters, sometimes combined with what appeared to be tissue or fat, in a number of different locations in the home. Betty Ordway died as a result of shotgun wounds in her right chest and one entry wound in her back, which caused damage to her lungs, heart, liver, ribs, vertebrae, and aorta. In addition to the shotgun wounds, the pathologist found bruises, lacerations, abrasions, and fractures caused by impact with a blunt object.[13]

Ordway, among other trial errors, contended that the trial court abused its discretion in admitting the blood spatter testimony of Kelley Robbins, an expert witness for the state. The core of the objection at trial was the state's failure to show that an adequate procedure for blood spatter analysis was followed by the witness, since she was neither qualified to testify as an expert in blood spatter identification nor had laid a sufficient foundation to show that she conducted the blood spatter testing in conformity with the generally accepted standards in the scientific field. The trial court was satisfied with the expert's qualifications and proffered methodology.

Out of the hearing of the jury, Robbins described blood spatter analysis and explained its uses:

> Blood stain pattern analysis is the evaluation of the size, shape and distribution of patterns that are identified in blood. The purpose is to possibly identify the activities that took place to deposit the blood, and also possibly to identify the location of the individual during the bloodshed.... The first step involved is identifying basic patterns. By identifying patterns I can then draw conclusions as far as what type of activity took place to create those patterns. Those are recognizable patterns and they are reproducible patterns.[14]

The witness proceeded to display some pattern standards, linking each with its source. She exhibited and discussed examples of patterns created by blood dripping from a wound, blood being pumped from an artery, a bloody item coming into contact with a nonbloody item, blood spattered by the force of a bullet, and blood cast off a swinging object. She elucidated the procedure for finding the point of origin for the blood by noting the direction stains point and measuring the width and length of stains. She also explained that faint and trace stains could be detected by spraying them with Luminol, a chemical that emits light in reacting with blood.

At the time of trial, Robbins had been a forensic scientist in the biology unit of the KBI Crime Laboratory for more than 9 years, had satisfactorily demonstrated proficiency in blood spatter analysis after taking a 40-hour class on the technique and later attending a 3-day refresher course. Her primary duties were in bloodstain pattern analysis, and her educational background included a graduate degree combining administration of justice, investigation, and chemistry. The court noted that Robbins was nationally certified as a medical laboratory technician, had been regional vice-president of the International Association for Blood Stain Pattern Analysts, and had been an assistant instructor in bloodstain pattern analysis. The court concluded that she was a qualified expert whose testimony established that the tests were reliable and were accepted by the scientific community.[15]

In *Eason v. United States*,[16] the defendant was convicted of second-degree murder of his fiancée while armed and in possession of a firearm while committing a violent or dangerous crime. Eason argued on appeal that the trial court erred in admitting expert testimony on blood spatter from individuals not qualified in the field of blood spatter analysis.

Detective Thomas Campbell of the Metropolitan Police Department Homicide Branch arrived at Eason's apartment and found Lenear "in a supine position on her back with her legs bent underneath her." Lenear had been shot in the left temple. Campbell observed a small tack hammer near the body, and a Browning automatic .22 with a sawed-off barrel was found in a backpack behind a door in the apartment. At trial Eason testified that he and Lenear had been fighting, that Lenear had swung a hammer at him which he knocked out of her hand, and that she had retrieved a gun out of the closet. Eason testified that he attempted to take the gun out of her hands and during the course of the struggle the gun discharged.

Detective Campbell testified that based on his observations of the position of the body, the blood spatter, and other things on the scene he concluded that Lenear was kneeling when she was shot. Dr. Silvia Comparini, the medical examiner who performed the autopsy, also testified that based on examining the wound and photographs from the crime scene she concluded that Lenear was most likely kneeling. Eason argued that the trial court erred in finding Campbell qualified as a blood spatter expert and in allowing Dr. Comparini to give a blood spatter opinion, since she was only qualified as a forensic pathologist.

The trial court had concluded that Campbell could testify in this trial as an expert in the area of the appearance and recognition of blood splatter, the transfer of blood, and his conclusions in regard to the positioning of the decedent at the time the blood spatter and transfer occurred. Campbell was a member of the Metropolitan Police Department for 16 years, including 4 years as a homicide detective, and had attended both investigator's school and homicide school, where he learned to analyze the position of victims and any blood at homicide scenes, including specific instruction and experiments regarding blood spatter. Campbell had worked with more-experienced detectives analyzing blood spatter, and he had analyzed it himself at innumerable crime scenes.[17] The court noted that "blood spatter" referred to blood that is ejected from the body after force has been applied. "Blood transfer" or "smudge" occurred when something came into contact with blood and smeared it on a surface. For example, a hand that touches spatter and then smears it across a surface or makes a mark on a wholly new surface creates a blood transfer or smudge.

The court found his opinion amply supported by his expertise when combined with the case facts here:

> When Campbell testified that in his opinion the victim was kneeling when she was shot, he stated that his opinion was based on the position of the body and that in relationship with the blood spatter. Campbell previously testified that he found the victim "lying in a supine position on her back with her legs bent underneath her." He also testified as to the location of the blood spatter on her body including the underside of her foot which led him to believe that at the time of the shooting her feet were not flat on the floor. Finally Campbell testified that he saw no blood spatter on the upper part of the door.[18]

The court noted that Detective Campbell did not attempt to engage in sophisticated blood spatter analysis involving more-complicated calculations or experiments; rather, his testimony concerned only the location of spatter and transfers, the direction of the drip, and his opinion as to the position of the body based both on the spatter and his visual observations of the victim at the scene.[19]

The court allowed Dr. Comparini's testimony that in her opinion the victim was most likely kneeling because her head had to be at a lower level when the gun was fired. Comparini based her opinion on photographs of the victim on the scene, where she noted that there were blood spatters on the lower portion of the door. She pointed out how the blood dripped onto the body consistent with the victim kneeling. She further testified that in performing her autopsy she observed a muzzle imprint and soot at the site of the wound indicating the muzzle of the gun was right against the skin. Comparini also discussed the trajectory of the bullet once inside the victim's head.

The trial court allowed this testimony after Comparini's qualifications had been reviewed. She had been a deputy medical examiner for 10 years, had studied and practiced anatomic and clinical pathology and serology, and had conducted at least 2,000 autopsies involving gunshot wounds and witnessed another 12,000 autopsies. Based on her experience the court could not find the trial judge erroneously exercised discretion in allowing her to testify regarding the position of the victim at the time of the gunshot.

In *State v. Perkins*,[20] the defendant was charged with murder. In the late evening hours of January 19, 1997, Lillian Perkins left the apartment of a friend and drove, in her cab, to her apartment, where her husband, Robert Perkins, attacked her with a hammer. After striking Lillian's head at least 15 times with the hammer, the defendant put on a long-sleeved sweatshirt, shirt, and coat to cover the blood spattered on his T-shirt. After returning to the apartment with his son, the defendant allegedly faked an exhibition of shock and grief.

The state presented evidence of Perkins's guilt, including expert testimony regarding the blood spattered on Perkins's T-shirt and jeans. The expert testified that the blood spatters on Perkins's T-shirt and jeans appeared to be the result of a "casting-off motion" of the object used to strike the victim, such as a motion used by hittting someone with a hammer, and that such evidence was consistent with the trauma injuries suffered by the victim.[21]

In *State v. Fleming*,[22] defendant was convicted of first-degree murder and sentenced to death. The defendant entered the home of the victim and assaulted him with a blunt object. Based upon the blood spatter marks found at the crime scene, Anthony Jernigan, a special agent with the State Bureau of Investigation (SBI) and a crime scene specialist, testified to the dynamics of the assault. He concluded that the assault began in the victim's den and that the victim moved from the middle of the love seat to the north end of the love seat. While the assault continued, the victim moved from the den, to the kitchen, and finally to the main hallway. Based upon an examination of the level of the blood spatter marks, the victim rose and fell approximately six different times as his assailant hit him on the head.[23]

The court determined that this blood spatter analysis testimony established that the victim's assailant entered the victim's house and repeatedly hit the victim on the head as the victim tried to escape, leaving a trail of blood spatter marks leading from the den, into the kitchen, and down the main hallway. Then the assailant manually strangled the victim while the victim unsuccessfully attempted to defend himself. The defendant's watch and a shoe impression that identically matched defendant's shoe were also found at the crime scene. While the watch and shoe impression were not discovered until 3 days after the scene was initially examined, they were present in photographs taken at the initial examination. This evidence supported a reasonable inference that defendant was the perpetrator of the murder.[24]

Another case that centered on the location or position of a body when shot is the important 1997 Texas decision in *Ex parte Freda S. Mowbray a/k/a Susie Mowbray*,[25] where defendant was convicted of murder. She subsequently petitioned for habeas corpus, alleging denial of due process and the state's knowing failure to disclose a blood splatter expert's report supporting the defendant's position that the victim committed suicide.

The deceased was shot in bed at night. The only occupants of the room in which the shooting occurred were the deceased and the defendant. The defense theory was that she and the deceased were lying in bed with a pillow barrier between them when she saw the deceased's elbow point upward. When she reached to touch it, the gun went off. She made a taped statement about the shooting, and the tape was admitted into evidence. Witnesses to the defendant's statements recalled that she indicated that she had used her left hand to reach toward the deceased. The state, however, introduced a crime laboratory supervisor's analysis of defendant's night-gown showing traces of lead or gunshot residue on the lower right sleeve. That witness, Steve Robertson, conducted tests with the gun found at the scene and opined that the residue was consistent with someone firing that gun.

Estella Mauricio, who was dispatched to the Mowbray residence just after the shooting, testified that she found the deceased, still alive and shot through the head, lying on his left side and covered all the way up to his shoulder. The bullet had entered the right side of his head, exited to the left, and wounded his left hand, which was under his head with a pillow between his head and left hand. The right hand was lying across his chest under the covers. There was no blood or brain matter on the right hand and she did not ever see his hand being washed at home or at the hospital. Dr. Dahm, the pathologist, testified that if the deceased had shot himself, his right hand would have been covered with blood and brain matter. He found no such blood or brain matter on the deceased's right fingers, hand, or forearm. Dahm testified it would have been impossible for the deceased to have shot himself and the hand to be clean, and concluded that the death was a murder.[26]

Additionally, two blood spatter experts testified. Sergeant Dusty Hesskew, of the Austin Police Department, testified on behalf of the state and Captain Tom Bevel, of the Oklahoma City Police Department, testified on behalf of defendant. Generally, blood spatter experts inspect the physical evidence to determine the injuries suffered and their location with respect to the other physical evidence. In the instant case, both experts examined the nightgown for "high velocity impact [blood] staining" which commonly occurs within a short distance from a contact gunshot wound. Hesskew testified that he identified and measured, through "Lumi-nol testing," high-velocity impact bloodstains on the nightgown, which were invis-ible to the naked eye. Hesskew concluded the cause of death in the instant case was probably homicide. Bevel testified that his examination of the physical evidence led him to conclude the deceased could have died in the manner in which she testified, i.e., suicide.[27]

The habeas judge heard a third blood spatter expert, Herbert Leon MacDonell, the director of an independent forensic laboratory in Corning, New York, who is viewed as the preeminent authority on the science of blood spatters.

MacDonell was retained to review the photographs and physical evidence in the instant case by the Cameron County District Attorney's office approximately 7 months prior to trial. MacDonell's examination of the nightgown revealed no blood stains either visible to the naked eye or under a microscope, and concluded that it was very unlikely that the defendant's nightgown was in close proximity to the victim's gunshot wound at the time of his shooting, or it was protected from spatter in some manner if it were. After reviewing the crime scene, the physical evidence and the photographs, MacDonell's expert opinion was that it was more probable than not that the deceased died from a suicide rather than a homicide.[28] At the prosecutor's request, MacDonell prepared and mailed to the Cameron County District Attorney a written report of his findings approximately 2 weeks before trial.

MacDonell took issue with Hesskew's use of Luminol to measure blood spattering. Noting that while Luminol is a substance that can react with blood that is invisible to the naked eye, it was not accepted as a positive test for blood. Luminol testing, he continued, was merely presumptive because Luminol reacts with substances other than blood. In MacDonell's opinion, the luminescence from a Luminol reaction could not be accurately measured. He stated:

> I think it would truly be an exercise to futility. I don't think you can put any reliability on it—I certainly wouldn't—and I've seen Luminol sprayed many times. I've never heard of anyone trying to measure it, count it, other than saying there appears to be a dozen or more.... You could do it, but the validity of your conclusion would be highly suspect in my opinion.

In MacDonell's view, Hesskew did not understand the chemistry behind Luminol testing.[29]

Hesskew had testified he was retained by the Cameron County District Attorney's office as a blood spatter expert and closely examined defendant's nightgown at the Department of Public Safety laboratory prior to the time it was shown to MacDonell. Hesskew stated that he was present when the nightgown was treated with Luminol, and counted 48 small stain areas around the stomach and chest of the nightgown which appeared consistent with high-velocity stains. He even put on a similar nightgown and fired test shots into a CPR dummy's head filled with blood in an attempt to duplicate the staining he observed through the Luminol testing. Although Hesskew could not remember how he was able to duplicate the blood staining, in his expert opinion, the defendant, wearing her nightgown, could not have been lying beside her husband at the time of his death. Thus, Hesskew's testimony contradicted the defendant's defensive theory.

Expert Hesskew admitted that his testimony included several assumptions that involved more than his own test results, most important of which was that someone tested the invisible stains and determined them to be human blood. At the hearing on the instant habeas application, Hesskew conceded his trial testimony was scientifically invalid because no such confirmation was ever made. In other words, he conceded that his ultimate opinion that the victim died as a result of a homicide, and that her statements were impossible, had no scientific basis.

Captain Tom Bevel, defense expert, testified that it was impossible to measure high-velocity impact blood spatter in the manner utilized by Hesskew. He, like Hesskew, only performed presumptive tests on defendant's nightgown because Hesskew had informed him that the Department of Public Safety laboratory confirmed human blood on defendant's nightgown. Because his trial testimony was based upon this erroneous premise, Bevel concluded, "with the inability to determine that ... is blood that is there, especially since we are talking about blood that is only invisible to the unaided eye, I don't think you can really say anything."[30] Bevel believed the failure to conduct confirmation tests undermined his examination and earlier testimony, and agreed with Hesskew that their trial testimony was scientifically invalid.

Steve Robertson, a chemist in the Texas Department of Public Safety (DPS) crime laboratory, testified that he examined the defendant's nightgown and was present on three different occasions when the nightgown was sprayed with Luminol. The nightgown was also sprayed with three chemicals to determine the presence of lead residue and treated with heat and chemicals to determine the presence of gunshot residue. His examination of the nightgown revealed very small red stains, visible to the naked eye, lead residue, and a yellowish stain. Robertson conducted two confirmatory tests on the red stains to determine if they were human blood. Both tests resulted in *negative* results. Robertson testified that, if the stains were blood, the tests for the gunshot residue could have destroyed the protein in the blood and would cause a negative reaction. Further, the chemicals sprayed on the nightgown could have diffused or dissolved the red stains to the extent they were undetectable without a microscope.

Prosecutors claim that they forwarded a copy of Dr. MacDonell's reports to the defendant's trial counsel 10 days to 2 weeks prior to trial, but did not contact MacDonell to testify. A defense trial review expert also voted against calling Mac-Donell out of concern that he might change his mind about his opinion in favor of the defense.

The habeas judge found that there was was a rationale for both murder and suicide and that the rationale for suicide was at least equally persuasive: the deceased had vowed to kill himself, had attempted suicide at least twice prior to his death, and on one occasion had shot himself. The court ruled that the linchpin of the state's case was the high-velocity impact spatter allegedly found on the front of the defendant's gown, that, if there, meant she could not have been prone in the bed at the time the shot was fired and was thus lying.

Under these facts, the habeas judge determined the state violated the defendant's due process right to a fair trial by suppressing evidence favorable to the defendant. The appeals court here held that the habeas judge's factual determinations were supported by the record and, therefore, would be accepted by it. Accordingly, the court ruled that the defendant's due process rights were violated, and she was entitled to relief and her conviction was set aside.[31]

In *State v. Gattis*,[32] defendant Robert Allen Gattis was convicted of first-degree murder and sentenced to death for the homicide of Shirley Y. Slay, shot when she opened the door of her apartment.

Gattis argued to the Delaware Supreme Court that a forensic scientist would, if given the opportunity, testify that the prosecution's theory of the case was physically impossible. Based on these assertions, the supreme court remanded the case, directing the court to hold an evidentiary hearing if Gattis's expert produced an affidavit to the effect that the state's theory of the homicide was impossible. Mr. Stuart James submitted an affidavit stating that, based upon the evidence he had reviewed, the state's version of the events leading to Shirley Slay's death was "not plausible" to a reasonable degree of scientific certainty. He also stated that opinions on forensic matters are rarely formulated in empirical terms such as "impossible."

James offered expert opinions on three fact questions: (1) the distance the door to Slay's apartment was open when the fatal shot was fired; (2) the significance of certain bloodstain evidence, known as high-velocity backspatter; and (3) Gattis's opportunity to see Slay and enter the apartment. These questions of fact, the court noted, were highly relevant to the legal issue of intention, and, ultimately, to the question at present before the court, which was whether trial counsel was ineffective for not calling a witness such as James to testify on Gattis' behalf. The court addressed several key fact questions: the distance the door was open; when the shot was fired; what was indicated by the high-velocity backspatter; and could Gattis see the victim before shooting her and whether he ever fully entered the apartment.

Conflicting evidence was gathered on the question of the distance the door was open when Slay was shot. The evidence showed that by the time the victim's position on the floor was marked, six people had come and gone from the apartment. When asked about this evidence, Dr. Galicano Inguito, the Medical Examiner, stated that Slay probably fell where she stood. However, he could not tell where the victim and the shooter stood when the shot was fired because (1) the victim may have been moving away from the shooter to protect herself and (2) a reflex may have allowed her to move or shift her position even after she was shot if she did not die instantaneously. He also stated that, based on the bloodstains around Slay's head, her head may have been moved as much as 7 inches after the murder by either paramedics or other witnesses.

High-velocity backspatter was found on Slay's telephone receiver but not on the door, the adjacent closet wall, or the floor near the door. Expert James in his affidavit concluded that the backspatter on the phone receiver indicated that the receiver was within a few feet of Slay when she was shot, and, in fact, the State and the defense agreed that Slay was on the phone when she was shot. James also concluded that the lack of backspatter on the door or wall indicated that Slay had probably not been standing near the door when she was shot. Regarding the defendant's argument that he was denied due process by not having been able to avail himself of expert James's opinion, the court ruled that it actually supported the state, not him:

> It appears to the Court that if James had testified at trial this portion of his testimony would have allowed the prosecution to argue that Gattis' testimony was contradicted by the forensics and inconsistent with the opinion of his own expert, as follows. James relied on the lack of blood spatter on the door or adjacent wall to show that Slay was probably not standing near the door when the gun discharged. However, the medical examiner testified that the stippling and soot on Slay's skin showed that the gun was fired at a distance of 4 to 18 inches. If, as Gattis testified, he was standing outside the door and, consistent with the forensics, Slay was within 18 inches of the gun (and hence even closer to the door which was between them if Gattis was outside the door), the chances are greatly increased that the door and/or wall would have shown blood spatter, which typically travels no more than 2 to 3 feet.[33]

Expert James was also not able to resolve the question of Gattis's position when the gun discharged, and acknowledged that it was possible that Gattis got all the way into Slay's apartment. Thus, the court concluded, the crux of James's testimony was that Gattis's version was more plausible than the state's, but that he could not say that the state's version was impossible. Viewing these opinions in light of the other testimonial and physical evidence, the court concluded that James's testimony would not have altered the result of the trial.

In *State v. Laws*,[34] the defendant was convicted in the Superior Court, Durham County, Farmer, J., of first-degree murder. Earl Handsome died on June 27, 1993 as a result of multiple stab wounds to his chest and back. After interviewing potential witnesses at the scene, police were directed to the defendant, who subsequently confessed to the murder,

The defendant, in his confession, stated that on the night of the murder, he was walking home when the victim drove up and started a conversation, whereupon the defendant went to the victim's apartment and drank vodka and smoked marijuana with the victim. According to the defendant, the victim made several sexual advances toward him, and after trying unsuccessfully to stop him, the defendant grabbed a nearby knife and stabbed the victim in the neck. The defendant stated that he ran for the door and tried to open it, but the victim pushed it, at which point the defendant grabbed a ceramic vase and hit the victim twice, knocking him to the ground. When the victim started to get back up, the defendant ran to the kitchen, got another knife and started stabbing the victim again. When that knife broke off inside the victim, the defendant got a pair of scissors and continued stabbing him.

Dr. Deborah Radisch, a forensic pathologist, performed an autopsy on the victim, which revealed several blunt-force injuries on the scalp and at least 18 stab wounds to the victim's chest and back. The blunt-force injuries consisted of numerous abrasions and lacerations and a fracture of the bones at the base of the skull, of a type and number to cause a loss of consciousness for a short period of time. Dr. Radisch opined that the victim died from a loss of blood due to severe damage to his lungs and heart caused by multiple stab wounds to the chest.

Della Owens-McKinnon, a certified bloodstain pattern analyst testified that her examination found that most of the bloodstains were found in the bedroom, with "overcast patterns" on the bedroom wall over the bed. She testified that this type of bloodstain pattern occurs when blood is being thrown off the tip of an object as it is being swung back and forth. She also testified to finding "back patterns" on the bedroom wall, which occurs as an object is being released or pulled out of the body. The bedroom stains reflected the infliction of a minimum of three or four blows in the area of the bed. She also observed "impact patterns" at the entrance to the bedroom, which indicated to her that two or three blows were inflicted at that location. She also found a trail of dripping blood and bloody handprints along the hallway leading to large "transfer patterns" and smudges on the front door, indicative of someone attempting to leave the apartment. Finally, she testified to impact spatters on the front door, which indicated to her the infliction of a minimum of two to three blows at that location.[35]

The court concluded that when viewed in the light most favorable to the state, the evidence shows three clear indicators of premeditation and deliberation, i.e., the defendant dealt lethal blows to the victim after he had been felled, the killing was done in a brutal manner, and the victim suffered an excessive number of wounds.

The defendant's actions after the attack were also indicative of premeditation and deliberation, inasmuch as the defendant did not seek help or medical assistance for the victim and did not call the police. After this brutal killing, the defendant stole the victim's jewelry and car and exchanged them for cash to buy drugs. This evidence belied any spontaneous action in response to an attempted sexual assault and implies a clear-headed decision to kill for a purpose.[36]

In *State v. Baston*,[37] the defendant was convicted of aggravated robbery and capital aggravated murder and, after a penalty hearing, was sentenced to death.

Chong Mah, a retail merchant in Toledo, was found dead by his wife in a rear storage room. He had been shot once through the head. Police found a single .45-caliber hollow-point slug behind the wall paneling in the room where the victim was found. An autopsy disclosed that he had been shot in the back of the head at a range of 2 to 3 inches. Further investigation led police to the defendant.

Among other issues, Baston argued that three evidentiary rulings by the trial court deprived him of his constitutional rights. First, he argued that the trial court erred in allowing Dr. Diane Scala-Barnett, a deputy coroner in Lucas County, to provide expert testimony regarding (1) the distance from gunshot to wound; (2) blood spatter, pooling, droplet, and transfer patterns; and (3) cause of death. Baston argued that she was not qualified as an expert.[38]

The court noted that since 1985, Dr. Scala-Barnett had been a forensic pathologist and a deputy coroner whose responsibilities include attending scene investigations and performing medical-legal autopsies to determine the cause and manner of death. She was board-certified in both pathology and forensic pathology. The court stressed the fact that, although the state never formally tendered Dr. Scala-Barnett as an expert regarding the distance between the gun's muzzle and the wound, during the course of questioning to qualify her as an expert defense counsel never objected or challenged her qualifications to testify, thus waiving any objection now. The court ruled that her experience as a deputy coroner and her board certifications in pathology and forensic pathology qualified her to testify regarding the cause of death and the distance between the gun's muzzle and the victim's head at the time the gun was fired.

The court noted that, although defense counsel did object to Dr. Scala-Barnett's testimony as not being expert in blood spatter and the trial court sustained the objection, when the witness returned to the subject of blood spatter, counsel did not object. Dr. Scala-Barnett then testified how the blood spatter evidence led her and the police criminologist Detective Chad Culpert to discover the spent slug behind the paneling. The court also observed that her testimony was similar to that of Detective Culpert, whose qualifications were not questioned. Furthermore, the court concluded, the testimony concerning blood spatter was helpful to an understanding of how the victim was shot and ended up in a supine position, but it was not crucial to any issue in dispute in this case. Assuming the admission of this evidence was error, it was harmless beyond a reasonable doubt.[39]

In *State v. Jacques,*[40] the defendant was convicted of attempt to commit murder and carrying a pistol without a permit. Deborah Messina, a state criminalist, testified about blood found on the gun sight found on a gun seized from the defendant, and on the defendant's jeans. She testified that a bloodstain pattern made up of 24 high-velocity blood spatters on the lower right front of the jeans was consistent with a gunshot. Additionally, she continued, blood spattering from an entrance wound, also referred to as backspatter, sprays backward toward the weapon and the individual. Blood spatter would travel approximately 3 to 4 feet from an entrance wound.[41]

In *Mills v. Commonwealth,*[42] the defendant was convicted of murder, first-degree burglary, and first-degree robbery and was sentenced to death. On August 30, 1995, Arthur L. Phipps was stabbed to death. Phipps's son-in-law, Terry Sutherland, discovered Phipps's body. On the day of the murder, Sutherland twice went to Phipps's house. On the first occasion, he left Phipps alive and in good spirits. Upon arriving the second time, he discovered a trail of blood leading up the front steps. He followed the trail of blood through the house. Sutherland found puddles of blood in the living room, and more blood in Phipps's bedroom and bathroom. He followed the blood trail to the kitchen where he found a pair of pants lying on the floor. Unable to locate Phipps inside the house, Sutherland went back outside where he found Phipps's body. While securing the crime scene, State Trooper Clyde Wells discovered a trail of blood leading away from Phipps's body. Wells and another police officer followed the blood trail to the front of a house rented from Phipps by Mills. Wells saw blood on the exterior walls of the house, on the front door, and a trail of blood crossing the front porch which led to a window.[43]

A videotape of the crime scene was introduced with the testimony of Detective Partin. During the playing of the videotape, Partin commented on the images being displayed. Additionally, the videotape showed images of the victim. There was no objection to the playing of the videotape, nor was there any objection to Partin's commentary. Prior to the playing of the videotape, the following exchange between Partin and the Commonwealth's Attorney (CA) occurred:

CA: During your state police training, have you been trained in the science of understanding blood patterns?

Partin: Yes sir.

CA: In doing so, are blood spatters part of the training?

Partin: Yes sir.

CA: Explain to the jury what that is.

Partin: Blood spatter training is when you look at the pattern of blood on an object and being able to see how that pattern may have gotten there. For instance, in a lot of stabbing cases, for instance, if someone is stabbing someone they would bring the knife back this way, blood would be in like a streak, a dotted streak. That's called "cast off." Other type of spatters would be like swabs of hair—hair type imprints against ... walls, that type of thing. Blood drops would be able to tell ... whether this was a drop coming straight down or [were] drops coming from a moving object.[44]

The defendant argued that this testimony was insufficient to establish Partin's qualifications as an expert witness in blood spatter evidence.

Initially, the court noted that defense counsel did not object to Partin's qualifications as an expert witness and that, while the trial court did not expressly recognize Partin as an expert witness, it did so implicitly by allowing Partin to testify concerning blood spatter evidence. The court ruled that while it believed that Partin was qualified to render expert testimony on blood spatter evidence, even assuming that the defendant was correct, any error was harmless.

Partin referred to blood spatter evidence only once during the narrative of the videotape. Referring to blood spots seen on a wall in a particular room, Partin concluded that Phipps was attacked in this room with a knife. This conclusion was based on his interpretation of the blood spots, which he characterized as being "cast off." There was no dispute that Phipps was stabbed repeatedly. Given all the other evidence linking Mills to the murder and to the house, testimony that Phipps was stabbed with a knife in a particular room hardly could have been prejudicial to Mills's case.[45]

The rest of Partin's testimony in connection with the narration of the videotape, the court concluded, did not rely on any blood spatter expertise, but was based on Partin's own personal observations and perceptions of the crime scene, which was proper lay testimony. The court observed that, with the exception of the brief reference to blood spatter evidence outlined above, Partin's testimony about the location of where the attacks occurred was rationally based on his perceptions of the crime scene, e.g., the pooling and the amount of blood evidenced on the videotape.[46]

An interesting point of evidence law in relation to the admissibility of forensic reports prepared by nontestifying experts is seen in *State v. Tomah*,[47] where the defendant was convicted of murder and robbery. The defendant's blood spatter expert, after submitting a report supporting the defendant's position that he simply observed his codefendant beat the deceased, refused to appear to testify. Because it was a written statement made outside of the courtroom prior to trial that Tomah sought to offer in evidence to prove the truth of its contents, and to support its conclusion that the blood spatter patterns illustrate that Tomah did not participate in the beating, Dr. Miller's report fell within the definition of hearsay. The court rejected his argument that such reports were admissible under the business record exception to the hearsay rule:

Forensic expert reports are the antitheses of the business records meant to be addressed by Rule 803(6). They are advocacy reports, expressly prepared for litigation to support one party to the litigation. Although the preparation of such a record is in the course of the expert's business of advocacy support, the preparation is not routine and the record is not of the type that is contemplated by the business records exception to the hearsay rule set out in Rule 803(6). Indeed, that it is prepared in anticipation of litigation is a common reason for a finding that a report lacks trustworthiness.... The trustworthiness and reliability of the report is not free from doubt.[48]

Here the court noted Dr. Miller was an expert hired by Tomah. She prepared the report, as an advocate, specifically for the purpose of its use at Tomah's trial. She had not viewed the blood-spattered pants on which she based her report, but relied instead on photographs and statements made by Tomah and the codefendant Chesnel. Moreover, Dr. Miller, who was the authenticating witness for the report, refused to appear at Tomah's trial at the appointed time.[49]

In *State v. McClendon*,[50] the defendant was convicted of manslaughter with a firearm. The victim, who was the defendant's roommate, was fatally shot while standing near the door of their apartment, the defendant testifying that he was asleep on the couch when he heard a loud noise. He awoke to find the victim standing in the doorway, clutching her side and saying she had been shot. There were no eyewitnesses to the shooting. Despite a search of the surrounding area, no weapon capable of shooting the fatal bullet was ever found. The testimony of the state's blood spatter expert allowed for the possibility that the shots came from outside the room where the defendant was sleeping, and the testimony of the neighbor explicitly disclaimed observation for the entire period of time in question. Under these circumstances, the court ruled, the defendant's motion for judgment of acquittal should have been granted.

In *State v. East*,[57] the defendant was convicted of two counts of first-degree murder and sentenced to death, for the dual murder of his aunt and uncle after a dispute about money.

The defendant objected to the qualifications of one Agent Tulley. The record showed that Agent Tulley had extensive training and experience in crime scene collection and processing, had earned a bachelor's degree in criminology, during which she took a crime laboratory class, and a master's degree in criminal justice. She also had numerous hours of training in crime scene collection and processing at the State Bureau of Investigation (SBI), specialized in forensic crime scene collection and processing at the SBI, and she had testified as a crime scene specialist in over 75 cases.

In *People v. Bolin*,[52] the defendant was convicted of two counts of first-degree murder and sentenced to death. When sheriff's deputies went to defendant's cabin, they found victim Huffstuttler's body lying near a truck and the body of victim Mincy was in the creek bed in a fetal position. Both had several fatal gunshot wounds, and Huffstuttler had been shot with both a revolver and a rifle. Over defense objection, the trial court admitted into evidence three photographs of Mincy's body, which criminalist Greg Laskowski utilized to illustrate his testimony about blood spatters and drips found at the crime scene. Utilizing the photographs of the crime scene, he testified regarding the various positions of Mincy's and Huffstuttler's bodies when they were shot. Based on blood spatters and drips depicted in the photographs, he indicated one shot was to Mincy's body while in a "fetal-like" position on its left side; as to the others, his body was in a vertical position. He also concluded Mincy "was moving at a relatively rapid pace" after being initially wounded. With respect to Huffstuttler, he determined that for several shots the body was prone and not moving.

Blood spatter testimony is often encountered in cases centered on the question of whether a death was the result of homicide or suicide. A good recent example may be seen in the 1998 Texas case of *Horinek v. State*.[53] Blood spatter is also commonly utilized in the death penalty aspects of cases to demonstrate the attribution of visciousness or extreme cruelty or heinousness.[54]

ENDNOTES

1. See Stuart James: *Bloodstain Atlas and Terminology, Scientific and Legal Applications of Bloodstain Pattern Interpretation* (CRC Press, Boca Raton, FL, 1999) at 177 (bloodstain atlas and terminology).
2. See Training in Crime Scene Photography and Crime Scene Investigation, a very useful site that has numerous links to photography sites. It is located at *http://www.staggspublishing.com/training.html*. Also see Bevel and Gardner: *Bloodstain Pattern Analysis* (CRC Press, Boca Raton, FL, 1997); Stuart James (Ed.): *Scientific and Legal Applications of Bloodstain Pattern Interpretation* (CRC Press, Boca Raton, FL, 1999) at 289 (stop-motion photography techniques).
3. See the extensive testimony of famed criminalist Dr. Henry C. Lee in the O. J. Simpson criminal case regarding blood spatter analysis. Dr. Lee provides extensive information about both general and specialized aspects of bloodstain pattern analysis. This is an excellent introduction to the subject as well as a model for laying a solid foundation for expert witness testimony. See People v. Simpson, Official Transcript, Examination of Henry C. Lee, Docket Number BA097211, Superior Court, Los Angeles, Tuesday, August 22, 1995. Also see a wide variety of blood pattern analysis testimony available in the O. J. Simpson Civil Case, Rufo v. Simpson, Docket Number SC031947, Superior Court, Los Angeles. Another interesting source for actual blood spatter testimony is the second trial of Lyle and Erik Menendez, in People v. Menendez, Docket Number BA068880, Superior Court of Los Angeles. These transcripts are available for searching and downloading on the Westlaw database, Legal News, Highlights and Notable Trials.
4. Menendez, *supra*.
5. See the discussion of People v. Davis, 217 Mich. 661, 187 N.W. 390 (1922), *infra*.
6. See "Collection and Preservation of Blood Evidence," by George Schiro of the Louisiana State Police Crime Laboratory, an excellent overview that addresses blood recognition and collection issues, located at *http://police2.ucr.edu/evidenc3.htm*.
7. See treatises listed above. Also see Herbert L. MacDonell: "Crime Scene Evidence—Blood Spatters and Smears and Other Physical Evidence," 1 *Quinnipiac*

Health L.J. 33 (1996) for a brief overview of the subject by one of its most eminent practitioners. Dr. MacDonell proves a very extensive bibliography on the subject, as an appendix to the article. A 40-hour course in bloodstain pattern analysis is offered by the Midwest Association of Forensic Scientists, under the auspices of the Minnesota Criminal Apprehension Bureau Crime Laboratory.

8. Davis, *supra,* note 5.
9. Also see People v. Planagan, 65 Cal.App.2d 371, 150 P.2d 927 (1944), where extensive blood spatter evidence was also neither challenged nor discussed by the California Supreme Court. Defendant's conviction was upheld in large part because of the introduction of a substantial interview, over several days, between the defendant and a state forensic chemist about blood spots on defendant's leather jacket. This case makes for a fascinating example of the total lack of investigatory rights by suspects in that early World War II era.
10. Laux, D.L.: "Effects of Luminol on the Subsequent Analysis of Bloodstains," *Journal of Forensic Sciences,* Vol. 36, No. 5, Sept. 1991, pp. 1512–1520; Grispino, R.R.J.: "The Effects of Luminol on the Serological Analysis of Dried Bloodstains," *Crime Laboratory Digest,* Vol. 17, No.1, Jan. 1990, pp.13–23.
11. Ponce and Pascual: "Critical Revision of Presumptive Tests for Bloodstains" (1999), located at *http://www.fbi.gov/programs/lab/fsc/backissu/july1999/ponce.htm.* The authors are members of the Department of Legal Medicine at the College of Medicine and Odontology of the University of Valencia, Valencia, Spain.
12. State v. Ordway, 261 Kan. 776, 934 P.2d 94 (1997).
13. *Id.* at 97.
14. *Id.* at 800.
15. *Id.* at 809.
16. Eason v. United States, 687 A.2d 922 (D.C. Ct. App. 1996).
17. *Id.* at 925. See, generally, Maj. Samuel J. Robb: "A Trial Attorney's Primer on Blood Spatter Analysis," *The Army Lawyer,* Vol. 36, 38 (August 1988) (defining blood spatter terminology). Also see Cathleen C. Herasimchuk: "A Practical Guide to the Admissibility of Novel Expert Evidence in Criminal Trials under Federal Rule 702," 22 *St. Mary's L.J.* 181, 246 (1990) (noting blood spatter analysis has recently become an accepted area for expert witness testimony and that "[w]hile the scientific theory and techniques employed in blood spatter analysis depend upon a subjective interpretation, the testimony deals with evidence that is inherently understandable"). Cf. C. Wecht: *Forensic Sciences,* Vol. 3, §37.03[c]–[f], 37.04–.09 (1996) (suggesting formal scientific training may be necessary for blood spatter analysis involving calculations of velocity, volume, and trajectory, and geometric determinations).
18. *Supra,* note 16.
19. *Id.* at 926.
20. State v. Perkins, 1999 WL 334974 (Ohio App. 1 Dist.).
21. *Id.* at *6–7.
22. State v. Fleming, 350 N.C. 109, 512 S.E.2d 720 (1999).
23. *Id.* at 118.
24. *Id.* at 120.
25. Ex parte Freda S. Mowbray, 943 S.W.2d 461 (Ct. Cr.App.Tex. 1997).
26. *Id.* at 462.
27. *Id.* at 463.
28. *Id.*
29. *Id.*

30. *Id.*
31. *Id.* at 466.
32. State v. Gattis, 697 A.2d 1174 (Del.Sup.Ct. 1997).
33. *Id.* at 1186.
34. State v. Laws, 481 S.E.2d 641(N.C.Sp.Ct. 1997).
35. *Id.* at 643.
36. *Id.* at 646.
37. State v. Boston, 85 Ohio St.3d 418, 709 N.E.2d 128 (1999).
38. *Id.* at 130.
39. *Id.* at 423–4.
40. State v. Jacques, 53 Conn.App. 507, 733 A.2d 242 (1999).
41. *Id.* at 519. Also see De La Cruz v. Johnson 134 F.3d 299 (5th Cir. Tex. 1998) (where Jose De La Cruz was convicted of stabbing Domingo Rosas to death. Blood spatters on De La Cruz's pants indicated that the wearer had forcefully stabbed a seated victim. The deceased victim was paralyzed and confined to a wheel chair); U.S. v. Veal, 153 F.3d 1233 (11th Cir. Fla. 1998) (where defendant claimed noninvolvement in a murder involving a total of four assailants. Blood spatter analysis evidence was used to demonstrate that the defendant struck the victim multiple times using medium to high force and the victim's blood spatter on walls in the corner of the room above the bed were consistent with the assailant having been in the immediate vicinity of a direct impact of the victim's head while the victim was in an upright position in the corner of the room).
42. Mills v. Commonwealth, 996 S.W.2d 473 (Sp.Ct.KY. 1999).
43. *Id.* at 479.
44. *Id.* at 487.
45. *Id.*
46. Also see State v. Fleming, *supra*, note 22 (blood spatter testimony admissible to show the progress of the victim's progress through the house to escape and that the victim rose and fell on six different times while being struck on the head. This blood spatter testimony was relevant to the applicability of the atrocious and cruel death penalty factors); Sturgeon v. State, 719 N.E. 2d 1173 (Sp.Ct.Ind. 1999) (blood found on top of table and blood spatters on a wall calendar, admissible proof of a beating and stabbing in that room); State v. Pilot, 595 N.W.2d 511 (Sp.Ct.Minn. 1999) (where defendant was convicted of attempted first-degree murder, attempted first-degree murder while committing criminal sexual assault, and first-degree criminal sexual assault. Analysis of blood spatter patterns performed on the defendant's jacket and jeans was consistent with the blood spatter patterns at the H.T. crime scene—an impact spatter from an object striking a source of blood and the blood then projecting off from that source onto the jeans. The blood spatter pattern on the jacket was a hair swipe, a pattern created when bloody hair strikes a surface).
47. State v. Tomah, 736 A2d 1047 (Sp.Ct.Maine 1999).
48. *Id.* at 1051.
49. *Id.* In addition, although Tomah sought to have Dr. Miller's report admitted as a business record, his codefendant Chesnel, whom the report inculpated and who had a constitutional right to cross-examine the preparer of the report, objected to its admission.
50. State v. McClendon, 707 So.2d 800 (Ct.App.Fla. 1998).
51. State v. East, 481 S.E.2d 652 (Sp.Ct.N.C. 1997).
52. People v. Bolin, 956 P.2d 374, 75 Cal.Rptr.2d 412 (Calif.Sp.Ct. 1998).

53. See Horinek v. State, 977 S.W.2d 696 (Tex.App.-Fort Worth 1998) for extensive discussion of blood spatter analysis as well as the psychological profiling of an alleged suicide.
54. See, e.g., Zakrzewski v. State, 717 So. 2d 488 (Fla.Sp.Ct. 1998) (Zakrzewski was charged with the first-degree murder of his wife, Sylvia, and his two children, Edward, age 7, and Anna, age 5. The blood spatter expert testified that the only conclusion that could be drawn from the positioning of Anna's blood in the bathroom was that Anna was forced to kneel over the ledge of the bathtub—in execution-style fashion—before Zakrzewski delivered the deadly blows. Zakrzewski pled guilty to all three charges, and the case proceeded to the penalty phase).

10 DNA Analysis

> If we possessed a thorough knowledge of all the parts of the seed of any animal (e.g., man), we could from that alone, bereasons entirely mathematical and certain, deduce the whole conformation and figure of each of its members, and conversely, if we knew several peculiarities of this conformation, we would from those deduce the nature of its seed.
>
> —Rene Descartes
> *Discours de la Method (1637)*

I. INTRODUCTION

The history of DNA as a method to identify participants in a crime has been a rapid and relatively noncontroversial one. The judicial acceptance of various DNA technologies, up to and including mitochondrial DNA, has been even more rapid, to the point where judicial discussions are becoming centered on lengthy case citations rather than on actual DNA analyses. This chapter will begin with brief coverage of a recent 1999 decision that illustrates this observation.

In *State v. Bowers*,[1] the defendant was found guilty of first-degree burglary and statutory rape of a 14-year-old girl. Suzanne Barker, a forensic serologist at the State Bureau of Investigation laboratory, analyzed stains found in the female minor's panties and identified the stains as spermatozoa. Also, Ms. Barker prepared slides of the defendant's blood samples and transferred the slides to Michael Budzynski, a DNA analyst. Mr. Budzynski examined the blood samples and determined that the defendant's DNA could not be ruled out as being the same DNA found in the victim's panties and sweatpants. According to Mr. Budzynski, the probability of finding the same DNA profile in another person is at least 1 in 5.5 billion.

Mr. Budzynski testified that his professional background as an expert in forensic DNA analysis included a bachelor of science degree in biochemistry and zoology; postgraduate studies in molecular biology; attendance at numerous scientific meetings and workshops of the American Academy of Forensic Scientists and the Southern Association of Forensic Science; 2 years of in-house training at the State Bureau of Investigation laboratory; advanced DNA training at the FBI laboratory in Quantico, Virginia; performance of DNA analysis in over 200 cases; and service as an expert in DNA analysis on approximately 35 prior occasions.[2]

In the case at bar, the court ruled, none of the scientific methods employed by the expert was a new method where reliability was at issue. Therefore, any analysis of the DNA methods used, which were not even identified in the appeal, was not necessary. Indeed, the issue getting the most attention was what does "nighttime" mean? "The elements of the crime of burglary in the first degree required a breaking and entering *in the nighttime* into a dwelling house or a room used as a sleeping apartment of another which was actually occupied at the time of the offense, with the intent to commit a felony therein."[3] Because the pertinent element at issue was the nighttime element, the court focused, in the absence of a statutory definition on the common-law definition of *nighttime,* which defined it "as a condition when it is so dark that a man's face cannot be identified except by artificial light or moonlight."[4]

The DNA-related progression of judicial acceptance of what was heretofore referred to as blood products or semen analyses has advanced from blood typing and enzyme matching to approval of DNA laboratory testing methodologies regarding RFLP, PCR, STR, RAPD, and mitochondrial DNA testing. We are now becoming very familiar with quick DNA profile information through the use of computerized systems for rapid DNA profile matching via the NDIS and CODIS database systems.

What do courts, prosecutors, defense counsel, and others interested in the place of DNA technology and identification claims in the criminal justice system need to know as we begin the 21st century? The DNA story in this regard is a very short one when compared with the long history of Anglo-American criminal trials. The first appellate court validations of DNA matching testimony were not even seen until 1988, in the decision by a Florida appeals court in the case of *Andrews v. Florida,*[5] where the court accepted DNA identification evidence linking the defendant to a sexual assault. During the 12 years since that decision, U.S. courts have rapidly accepted the standard DNA testing methods of RFLP, PCR, PCR-STR, the product method of conducting DNA statistical analyses, a variety of very specific laboratory procedures, and related issues such as the general acceptability of commercially produced DNA kits. The courts are also quickly moving toward a general acceptance of the previously challenged mitochondrial DNA identification technology.

There are now a respectable number of authoritative texts,[6] articles,[7] downloadable transcripts,[8] and Web sites[9] addressing basic[10] and specialized[11] DNA subjects. This chapter identifies some of the most recent cases beneficial to lawyers in the course of the discussion.

There is also a rapidly developing international consensus among DNA laboratories[12] respecting standards for laboratories as well as DNA technicians,[13] as a result of major support from the FBI for working groups and conferences[14] addressing these issues across the world, especially in Europe. These working groups are discussed below.

There remains a body of information that courts and lawyers will need to know, and keep informed of progress in, if they are to be effective participants in the 21st-century world criminal justice system. As recently noted by DNA expert Dr. Charles Strom:

> Lawyers must learn the historical context of DNA testing, the chronology of testing methods, and the implications of recent advances in DNA technology. For example, a vaginal swab that five years ago did not yield sufficient DNA for RFLP analysis — the only DNA technology available at the time — would probably yield more than enough material for a PCR analysis today.[15]

It is not the purpose of this chapter to attempt a technical analysis of the history and current status of DNA laboratory methodologies or the considerable database-centered statistical analyses associated with them. There are a number of recent articles that are excellent primers on where we have been, where we are, and where we appear to be headed in regard to DNA identifications in criminal cases.[16]

Dr. Strom's article succinctly describes five of the contemporary state-of-the-art DNA technologies and compares and contrasts their strengths and limitations and overall process differences. The five DNA technologies discussed are (1) "multi locus probe testing," traditionally referred to as DNA fingerprinting; (2) "single locus restriction fragment length polymorphism," better known as RFLP testing; (3) "polymerase chain reaction," or PCR, testing using "amplified length polymorphism" (AMPFLP); (4) PCR testing using dot-blot technology; and (5) mitochondrial DNA sequencing.[17]

II. QUESTIONS LAWYERS NEED TO ASK AND ANSWER

- What is DNA, in both a theoretical, and, most importantly, a physiological sense? What is it that gives DNA laboratory and statistical identification models their great and growing authority? Why is there no ability to make a positive statement of identity rather than a "negative" response utilizing extremely high numbers in estimating the chances of any such "match" appearing in the general population being considered?
- How and where can DNA reside at a crime scene?
  — Blood
  — Semen
  — Hair pulp
  — Saliva
  — Tissue
- What are the contemporary and prospective views on crime scene DNA collection, storage, and transportation procedures? The FBI is issuing a number of proposed standards, which will invariably be adopted by courts.[18] The "FBI Handbook of Forensic Services" is available on the Internet and is a steady source of information in regard to both data collection standards and FBI laboratory procedures.[19] The FBI site, in particular the Forensic Communications section, should be consulted on a regular basis.[20]
- What does the concept of DNA laboratory testing mean in regard to:
  — The actual physical manipulation of the subject crime scene material?
  — The preparation of the material for a laboratory "matching" procedure?
  — What are the visual results of any such procedure and what do they mean?
  — What is being compared preparatory to a proffered laboratory "match" opinion? How many markers, loci, etc. are there than can be compared? If a "match" opinion is based on less than all, then how many and why? U.S. courts generally accept six to seven points as sufficient for a fingerprint "match." Is that a useful analogy here?
  — What test methodology is being used and how do the methodologies differ in physical and procedural terms? What are the significant

differences among RFLP, PCR, PCR-STR, mitochondrial, or nonhuman DNA tests, such as RAPD for plant comparison? Why is one test used over another? Are some better than others in certain settings? Why?

- How much of a match is any DNA laboratory "match" conclusion? Is it any less tentative than hair, fiber, footprints, ballistics, or any of the other conclusions reached by forensic scientists?
- What is involved in a discussion of population statistics, *the second half* of a DNA identification effort? What does it mean to testify to a laboratory DNA profile match if its uniqueness cannot be determined? What is the current thinking in regard to the appropriate ways to get to some answer to this question? It is not possible to answer such a question in instances of the other forensic sciences, and has never been required. Is such an analysis always required in DNA cases? Why? In instances where such queries are made, what databases containing a body of previously tested DNA profiles are used? Who or what categories of individuals are in any such collections? Do racial or ethnic differences matter here?
- What is mitochondrial DNA? How do its processes differ from the more familiar and judicially approved methods of RFLP and variants of PCR technology? Why was it downplayed for so long? Why is it receiving rapid judicial approval as we enter the early days of the 21st century?
- What about nonhuman DNA matching technologies, such as for dog, cat, deer, whale, or plant DNA? How will these fare in the new century? How do DNA analyses in animals or plants differ from that of humans or each other that would exclude them from judicial approval at this time? Are those technologies any less able to provide solid circumstantial proof of presence at a crime scene that RFLP, PCR, or even mitochondrial DNA investigations?
- What are some of the likely legal issues surrounding DNA identifications in the early years of the 21st century?
  — Post-conviction DNA testing opportunities for prisoners convicted in blood-centered cases where identity was a central issue.
  — The legality of DNA registration schemes for convicts, arrestees, or the general population and the inclusion of any such DNA profiles into national or international databases.
  — The expanded utilization of nonhuman DNA profiling technologies.
  — Increasingly sophisticated DNA laboratory procedures that must pass muster under *Frye* and/or *Daubert* reliability criteria.

III. DNA CASES

A. POSTCONVICTION DNA TESTING

The results of a DNA test were recently used to free an inmate who had spent 18 years in a Louisiana prison for a rape that the DNA study showed he did not commit. The inmate was the 66th person in this country to be released from prison after testing, according to experts in the field.[21] The growing legal and popular perception of the certainty of DNA identifications or exclusions has caused an outcry, resulting in the passing of state statutes providing for limited postconviction DNA testing for inmates, albeit under limited circumstances. While these efforts are being expended on behalf of incarcerated felons whose trials occurred before DNA testing was either known or accepted by the courts, equal pressure is being placed on the nation's court systems to provide adequate funding for accused persons awaiting trial.

In Illinois the state has just established a fund to pay for attorneys and expert witnesses in death penalty cases. An examination of the recently enacted Illinois statute and the first appellate decision to address it will be beneficial, given the great likelihood of this issue being a major one as the first decade of the 21st century proceeds. The Illinois statute reads as follows:

§ 116-3. Motion for fingerprint or forensic testing not available at trial regarding actual innocence.

(a) A defendant may make a motion before the trial court that entered the judgment of conviction in his or her case for the performance of fingerprint or forensic DNA testing on evidence that was secured in relation to the trial which resulted in his or her conviction, but which was not subject to the testing which is now requested because the technology for the testing was not available at the time of trial. Reasonable notice of the motion shall be served upon the State.
(b) The defendant must present a prima facie case that:
    (1) identity was the issue in the trial which resulted in his or her conviction; and
    (2) the evidence to be tested has been subject to a chain of custody sufficient to establish that it has not been substituted, tampered with, replaced, or altered in any material aspect.
(c) The trial court shall allow the testing under reasonable conditions designed to protect the State's interests in the integrity of the evidence and the testing process upon a determination that:
    (1) the result of the testing has the scientific potential to produce new, noncumulative evidence materially relevant to the defendant's assertion of actual innocence;
    (2) the testing requested employs a scientific method generally accepted within the relevant scientific community.[22]

As noted by Public Defender Gregory O'Reilly in his article on the new Illinois statute, the new Illinois law only applies to cases where identity was the issue at trial. Thus, as he points out, a rape case defended on the basis of consent conceivably would not meet this threshold, whereas a case involving a crime scene with DNA datum where the defendant claimed a false identification would so qualify.[23]

As can be seen, the statute creates a two-part process by initially providing a mechanism for a post-trial motion wherein a convicted felon may petition the court for fingerprint or DNA testing of evidence collected before trial, but, importantly, only if any such test was not obtainable at that earlier date. There is no deadline for filing. In the event that the motion is granted and the test results tend to exculpate the inmate, then he or she may file a petition for a new trial based on this forensic evidence. In deciding whether to grant a new trial, the court will apply the existing standard for cases involving newly discovered evidence, which raises interesting issues regarding the circumstantial or direct character of DNA or fingerprint evidence.

The Illinois law authorizes DNA and fingerprint testing if the new test meets the *Frye* standard for evidence based upon methodologies generally accepted in the relevant scientific community. The general acceptance of the more accurate and accessible PCR and PCR-STR, not to mention mitochondrial DNA testing in some instances, provides good opportunity for helping to keep alive current concerns over the wrongful incarceration of many, especially, death row, inmates. As noted by O'Reilly:

> Courts in most states are likely to recognize RFLP testing and should recognize PCR testing, although there are new methods of PCR testing that may be subject to dispute. In the future, courts may routinely recognize mitochondrial DNA testing, which has the ability to profile hair samples without the roots.[24]

The very positive reception that DNA and fingerprint analyses have received in recent years raises doubts about the conclusions of the other forensic sciences discussed in this book. As noted by Dr. Charles Strom:

> The press is full of reports of innocent men being set free based on results of DNA testing, introducing the possibility of "second generation" DNA testing. The smaller amount of DNA needed for PCR testing will undoubtedly encourage attorneys to seek to reopen cases where there was not enough DNA for interpretable results under RFPL testing. PCR should theoretically make DNA testing scientifically possible in almost all cases where samples have been stored.[25]

The postconviction statutes around the country vary greatly in terms of time limits, forensic sciences included, and the standards that must be met to receive forensic testing. It is a considerable leap of faith for most states to assume that inmates are educated about the latest developments in DNA testing and population projection theories to respond adequately to the strictures of most of these statutes. A dissenting judge in a recent Florida case on this issue put it well:

> Frankly, I think it is a very harsh reading of the two-year time limit in rule 3.850 to bar testing and perhaps relief from conviction under the circumstances of this case. Rule 3.850(b) bars relief in non-capital cases unless the facts on which the claim is predicated were unknown to the movant and could not have been ascertained by the exercise of due diligence. DNA testing is a recent, highly accurate, application of scientific principles unknown at the time of Dedge's trial. It is not well known to or understood by most lawyers and judges, I would wager, even in 1998. I think it unfair and unrealistic to expect an indigent, serving two life sentences in prison, to have had notice of the existence of PCR-based testing, and possible application to his case prior to 1995 when it was first discussed by a Florida court. One of my worst nightmares as a judge is, and has been, that persons convicted and imprisoned in a "legal" proceeding are in fact innocent. If there is a way to establish their true innocence on the basis of a highly accurate objective scientific test, like the PCR, in good conscience it should be permitted. This case calls out for such relief: the evidence of Dedge's guilt

at trial was minimal; the PCR test had not been developed at the time of his trial. Even as this dissent is being written, admissibility of PCR tests in Florida courts is still being debated and the results of the tests, if successfully performed, will likely be absolutely conclusive of either his guilt or innocence. Not to do the testing consigns a possibly innocent man to spend the rest of his life in prison. I would reverse the order and direct release of the evidence for the purpose of DNA testing.[26]

Computerized fingerprint or shell casing searches now provided by the unified FBI AFIS and CODIS systems should be equally available in an appropriate case. However, as noted above, the expense and prospect of questioning the finality of convictions will certainly be a force against the expansion of this, itself nascent, national effort to achieve what has been referred to as "genetic justice."[27]

In addition to those concerns, there are the equally important issues revolving around the storage of crime scene evidence for use in postconviction proceedings. Practices vary greatly around the country regarding how long and under what circumstances crime scene materials and laboratory samples are kept. New techniques in all of the forensic sciences, but especially in respect to DNA, require a reassessment of such practices to prevent contamination and to otherwise support the intention of the host of postconviction forensic evidence testing statutes that we will undoubtedly see come onto the books in the next several years.

As noted by public defender O'Reilly:

Under the Illinois and New York forensic testing laws, the petitioner must show that the evidence had been collected for trial and had not been altered. Police, prosecutors, and clerks sometimes destroy old evidence for innocuous reasons such as space limitations. Sometimes such evidence is mistakenly destroyed, and it is possible that it could be intentionally destroyed. This could leave a wrongfully convicted petitioner who seeks testing in such a case without a remedy. Defense counsel should therefore ask the court to order forensic evidence impounded after trial and to take similar steps to make sure police, prosecutors, and court clerks also do not destroy or alter old evidence.[28]

This issue of postconviction DNA testing, and the variance in statutes or court rulings respecting it, bears close watching by those involved in the criminal justice system. A very recent decision under the new Illinois statute is now examined.

In *People v. Dunn,*[29] the defendant, who had been convicted of rape and aggravated battery, sought DNA testing on petition for postconviction relief, pursuant to the recently enacted DNA statute discussed above.

As noted above, limited postconviction forensic DNA testing has been recently authorized in Illinois by statute. Here, defendant petitioned the court for genetic testing of the Vitullo rape kit that was taken in his original proceedings. The court stated:

Nearly all of the decisions which have considered whether DNA test results are admissible, including those in Illinois, have permitted such evidence to be admitted.... Based on the accuracy and definitiveness of DNA testing, and the recent enactment of section 116-3 of the Code of Criminal Procedure, we agree with defendant that he is entitled to such testing, provided that the required prima facie case has been made.[30]

Accordingly, the court remanded the case to the trial court for consideration of defendant's motion for genetic testing.

In reaching its conclusion, the court stressed that here there was only one attacker, and that the trial court made no finding whether there was evidence that the assailant ejaculated during the attack. On remand, the trial court was to determine whether any conclusive result was, indeed, obtainable from DNA testing. This would encompass a determination whether there was ejaculation and whether the essential evidence was preserved and is available. If the available DNA evidence was capable of supporting such a determination there was no valid justification to withhold such relief if requested on postconviction review.[31]

B. SAMPLES VOLUNTARILY GIVEN USED IN OTHER CASES

Once given, a DNA sample remains in the system, available to police in other cases, although the basis for any earlier voluntary submission needs to be scrutinized. In *Pace v. State*,[32] a jury convicted Lyndon Fitzgerald Pace of four counts of malice murder, four counts of felony murder, four counts of rape, and two counts of aggravated sodomy. A DNA expert determined that Pace's DNA profile matched the DNA profile taken from the sperm in the McAfee, Martin, McLendon, and Britt murders. The expert testified that the probability of a coincidental match of this DNA profile is 1 in 500 million in the McAfee, Martin, and Britt cases, and 1 in 150 million in the McLendon case.

The defendant, while under investigation for another murder, of one Mary Hudson, had signed a consent form that states, in part: "I fully understand that these hair and bodily fluid samples are to be used against me in a court of law and I am in agreement to give these hair samples for further use in this particular investigation." The form further stated that Pace was a suspect in a murder which occurred on September 17 and the "name of the murder victim in this case is Mary Hudson." There was no mention of the other four murders. The FBI and the Georgia Bureau of Investigation (GBI) crime laboratories were subsequently unable to match Pace's DNA or hair to any evidence from the Hudson murder, but were able to obtain matches with evidence from the McAfee, McLendon, Martin, and Britt cases.[33]

Pace claims that he did not voluntarily consent to the drawing of his blood for use in the investigation of the four murders for which he was convicted and argues that the police thus exceeded the bounds of his consent by using his blood in investigations of murders other than the Hudson murder. However, the court observed, unlike an implied consent warning, the form does not limit the use of the blood or hair to only the Hudson murder investigation or to any particular purpose, and there is no evidence that Pace placed any limits on the scope of his consent:

> The police were not required to explain to Pace that his blood or hair could be used in prosecutions involving other victims, or that he had a right to refuse consent.... Further, like a fingerprint, DNA remains the same no matter how many times blood is drawn and

tested and a DNA profile can be used to inculpate or exculpate suspects in other investigations without additional invasive procedures. It would not be reasonable to require law enforcement personnel to obtain additional consent or another search warrant every time a validly obtained DNA profile is used for comparison in another investigation.[34]

In a recent editorial in the *Chicago Tribune* entitled, "When Innocence Isn't Good Enough," criticism is raised toward cases where a postconviction DNA test excludes a prisoner, but the state refuses to drop charges due to the existence of other trial evidence indicating guilt. This is in response to such a setting in the Clyde Charles and Roy Criner cases being handled by Professors Barry Scheck and Peter Neufeld's Innocence Project. As stated by the Texas court in the Criner case, such defendants need more than an excluding DNA test.[35]

The rapid judicial acceptance of DNA identification technologies does not mean that all legal issues involving it are resolved. It must be remembered that DNA evidence, as powerful and definitive as it is characterized, is just evidence nonetheless. In fact, it is typically categorized as "circumstantial evidence," like fingerprints, ballistics, hair, fiber, and the rest of the forensic evidence corpus, as opposed to "direct evidence" of the fact for which it is offered, typically presence and/or participation at a crime scene. This is an important conceptual difference, which may be belied in the eyes of juries by the reputation that DNA, like fingerprints, has gained over the past decade.

In *Thomas v. State*,[36] a capital murder appeal, the court addressed the important issue of whether DNA evidence is direct or circumstantial proof of the fact or facts for which it is offered to prove. Here, DNA extracted from vaginal fluid recovered from the victim's body and from Thomas's blood were compared to determine whether he could have been the source of the semen present in the victim's body. The DNA profiles from the vaginal fluid matched the DNA profiles from Thomas's blood. Statistically, the probability of finding an unrelated individual at random from the population who would match the particular DNA of the semen recovered from the victim's body was approximately 1 in 323,533,000 whites and 1 in 322,149,000 African-Americans. A forensic examination of the victim's husband's car and the all-white outfit he was wearing the evening before and the morning after his wife's murder, however, revealed no blood. A DNA profiling expert was provided a dried stain of the victim's husband's blood and excluded the husband as the contributor of the semen on the vaginal swabs. Defendant Thomas called no witnesses in his defense. His theory of defense was that the victim's husband caught him and the victim in the act of consensual intercourse, that he ran away to avoid an altercation with the husband, and that the husband, in a jealous rage, killed his wife.[37]

An important issue, i.e., whether DNA is now to be raised to the level of direct as opposed to circumstantial evidence, was discussed here under the aegis of the *plain error rule* since trial counsel raised no objection to the DNA evidence presented at trial. All of Thomas's issues on appeal, with the exception of the issue relating to the sufficiency of evidence, in regard to the murder-burglary charge, were not preserved for appellate review. However, because the death penalty was imposed in this case, the court felt the need to review the record for plain error, although these issues were not brought to the trial court's attention.

With regard to the defendant's allegation of plain error in the trial court's failure to issue a circumstantial evidence instruction, the court here observed that defense counsel did not request any instruction regarding circumstantial evidence, either orally or in writing. The rule in Alabama, and a number of other jurisdictions, is that the standard-of-proof instruction specifically regarding circumstantial evidence is required if the evidence is wholly circumstantial, but not if the evidence consists of both direct and circumstantial evidence.[38]

The court here noted that the threshold question was whether the evidence against Thomas was entirely circumstantial, requiring a circumstantial evidence instruction, or consisted of circumstantial as well as direct evidence, where many courts do not require such instruction. Thomas argued that the trial court erred in failing *sua sponte* to instruct the jury on the degree of proof necessary for a conviction based solely on circumstantial evidence, i.e., an instruction that Thomas could not be convicted unless the circumstances were not only consistent with his guilt, but inconsistent with every other reasonable hypothesis, and that no matter how strong the circumstances, Thomas could not be convicted if they could be reasonably reconciled with the theory that Thomas was innocent. The rule in Alabama was that the standard-of-proof instruction specifically regarding circumstantial evidence is required if the evidence is wholly circumstantial, but not if the evidence consists of both direct and circumstantial evidence.

Thomas argued that the state's evidence

was entirely circumstantial, consisting of his presence under suspicious circumstances at the scene of the murder, during the approximate time frame when the murder occurred; the semen found in [the victim's] vagina containing his DNA; his fingerprints being found on broken glass from the window of the [victim's] apartment; and on the night of the murder, he was seen in possession of property substantially similar to that stolen from the victim's.

The attorney general, without citing any authority, responded that Thomas's argument completely ignored very "direct" evidence presented by the state, such as DNA matching, DNA population statistics, and fingerprint evidence.[39]

The court observed that contrary to the attorney general's assertion, fingerprint evidence was still generally considered circumstantial evidence. This characterization applied equally well to DNA evidence. The court observed that a limited search of case law on the question of the nature of DNA evidence found more cases that refer to DNA evidence as circumstantial than as direct. Because there was some, albeit little, legal authority for the conclusion that DNA evidence was "non-circumstantial" or "direct" evidence, there was some validity to the position that any error in not instructing the jury on the "reasonable-hypothesis-of-innocence" instruction is not "plain," i.e., not "clear" or "obvious" under the law. Therefore, the plain error test was not satisfied.[40]

The court observed that this case was neither close nor doubtful. The defendant's guilt was clearly and convincingly established by compelling and overwhelming evidence. Taken as a whole, the evidence did not support any reasonable hypothesis consistent with his innocence; the evidence presented no other reasonable hypothesis that could account for the circumstances presented here. The evidence and all reasonable deductions therefrom were completely inconsistent with a reasonable hypothesis of innocence. To reverse on a finding of plain error under the facts before it, the court concluded, would be a perversion of justice.

Since DNA is evidence, it must comport with all of the rules of evidence, including specialized chain-of-custody proffers,[41] and a host of nonscientific constitutional and evidence rules.[42]

C. RFLP and the Product Rule

RFLP, which until recently was the most widely used DNA analysis technique, stands for "restriction fragment length polymorphism." As noted above, there are any number of competent texts for lawyers to acquaint themselves with the technical end of DNA testing and RFLP testing in particular. An excellent case to get an overview of DNA testing is the lengthy decision of the Maryland Court of Appeal in the case of *State v. Armstead*.[43] This section discusses several important recent cases involving RFLP DNA testing and population statistic projections under the product rule model, to be followed by similar discussions of new cases utilizing PCR, mitochondrial, and nonhuman DNA methodologies.

In *People v. Miller*,[44] the defendant was convicted of first-degree murder. In September 1993, the nude bodies of three women, Marcia Logue, Helen Dorrance, and Sandra Csesznegi, were found in rural Peoria County, Illinois. The body of Marcia Logue was found in a drainage ditch in the 500 block of South Cameron Lane on September 18, with a pillowcase stuck in her mouth. The body of Helen Dorrance was found 50 feet from Logue's body on the same date. The body of Sandra Csesznegi was found in a drainage ditch near Christ Church Road on September 26. Csesznegi's body was in a state of advanced decomposition. All three women were known prostitutes in the Peoria area.

On September 29, 1993, at approximately 11:30 P.M., Detectives Rabe and Pyatt of the Peoria Police Department and Detective Hawkins of the Peoria County Sheriff's Department went to the defendant's Peoria apartment to question him about crimes in the Peoria area. The search of the defendant's apartment revealed two robes, female underwear, a broken miniblind rod, and a brown and white cloth covered with what appeared to be dried blood. The police also recovered pillows and a mattress from the defendant's bedroom. These items had reddish-brown stains. Blood spatters were also found on a wall of the bedroom and the bed's headboard. A later search revealed a glove, a throw rug, and more women's underwear. During the second search, the police collected hair and fibers.[45]

The state's DNA expert, William Frank, testified that seminal fluid recovered from Logue matched that of defendant. Such a match would occur in 7% of the Caucasian population. Blood recovered from underneath Logue's fingernails also matched that of defendant and such a match could be expected in 1 in 465 million

Caucasians. Bloodstains from a magazine, mattress, pillow, and towel found in the defendant's apartment and from the seat of the car the defendant used matched that of Logue. Such matches would occur in 1 in 1.1 trillion Caucasians. Further, blood found on a napkin and a pillow taken from the defendant's apartment matched Dorrance's DNA profile, with such a match occurring in 1 in 466 billion Caucasians. Another bloodstain on one of defendant's pillows matched the DNA profile of Csesznegi with such a match occurring in 1 in 1 billion Caucasians. On cross-examination, Frank conceded that there were only 5 billion people in the world.

The defendant argued that the trial court erred in qualifying Frank to testify about the general acceptance and reliability of DNA evidence and in admitting the DNA evidence at his trial. The trial court held a pretrial hearing on the state's motion to admit DNA evidence. Frank was the only individual to testify at the hearing on behalf of the state. The defendant chose not to present any witnesses or evidence, notwithstanding that he had been provided the time and funds to secure an expert. After hearing testimony on Frank's background and training, the trial court qualified him as an expert. Frank then testified regarding the restriction fragment length polymorphism (RFLP) method of testing DNA and the manner in which DNA matches are calculated, including the manner in which such calculations are made at the Illinois State Police Bureau of Forensic Sciences, where Frank was employed. Frank testified that the techniques used by his laboratory in calculating DNA matches and their frequency in a population are similar to those used by the FBI. After hearing Frank's testimony, the trial court held that based on prior precedent in Illinois, the DNA procedures outlined in Frank's testimony were generally accepted in the particular scientific field and such testimony and DNA calculations would be allowed at defendant's trial.[46]

The court in addressing defendant's arguments gave a brief account of DNA profiling:

> DNA is the genetic code which is found in the cells of the human body. A DNA molecule is composed of over three billion "base pairs" of four different chemicals: adenine, thymine, cytosine and guanine. The particular pattern of these base pairs dictates an individual's genetic characteristics. Most of a DNA molecule is the same from person to person. DNA profiling focuses on those parts of the DNA molecule where there is a significant variation of a base pair pattern. The areas of significant variation are referred to as "polymorphic," and base pair patterns in polymorphic areas are called "alleles." There are approximately 3 million distinguishable polymorphic sites between individuals. Although an examination of all of these polymorphic sites is not currently feasible, an examination of a small number of polymorphic sites can establish a DNA profile which can be compared to that from another DNA sample.[47]

RFLP was the laboratory methodology used to achieve a match here and testified to by expert witness Frank. The court made the following observations in accepting this technique:

> Restriction Fragment Length Polymorphism is a six-step process which allows an analyst to physically see the results of a DNA profile in the form of bands. Since the

length of polymorphic DNA fragments differs between individuals, individuals also tend to have different positioning of their bands on a DNA print, called an autoradiograph or autorad. An analyst makes a visual comparison of DNA band patterns to determine whether known and unknown DNA samples came from the same source, whether the samples did not come from the same source or whether the comparison was inconclusive. If an unknown DNA sample has not been excluded from a comparison, a computerized measurement program is used to compare the lengths of the DNA fragments. If the DNA band patterns fall within a certain range, the samples are declared a match.

For a match to be meaningful, a statistical analysis is required. The statistical analysis determines the frequency in which a match would occur in a database population. In this case, Frank used the fixed bin method of determining the frequency of an occurrence. The process of binning is a way of counting or grouping bands and determining the frequency of the bands. The Hardy-Weinberg Equilibrium is used to determine the frequency of a particular band combination. Stated simplistically, the frequency of one band is multiplied by the frequency of a second, and so on. The product from this calculation is then multiplied by two to account for an individual inheriting one strand of DNA from his mother and one strand from his father. This result constitutes the statistical frequency of a match within a certain population. This process of binning and determining the frequency is also known as the product rule.[48]

The court, in the instant case, held that expert Frank was clearly qualified to explain and give an opinion regarding a "match" based upon RFLP/product rule methodology. The court noted that he had a bachelor's degree in chemistry and biology, was working toward his master's degree in biology with his thesis being on DNA extraction methods, that he had taken several genetics courses and attended seminars and classes on DNA methods at both the FBI and private laboratories. In addition, he had been certified by the American Board of Criminalistics and been subject to periodic testing on DNA issues.[49]

Respecting the RFLP/product rule methodology used by Frank as the basis of his opinion, the court ruled that the trial court did not abuse its discretion in relying on the cases that supported the use of the RFLP technique and the product rule. In addition to several Illinois appellate decisions accepting this method,[50] the court noted that Frank testified that the procedures he used were the same as those used by the FBI. The court also observed that the majority of courts deciding the issue of the admissibility of evidence on the six-step RFLP process had found such evidence to be admissible under several standards of admissibility, including *Frye* and *Daubert*.[51] There was little question that the RFLP technique itself was generally accepted in the relevant scientific community.

In *Ross v. State*,[52] the defendant was convicted by a jury of two counts of rape, two counts of kidnaping, two counts of aggravated sodomy, two counts of armed robbery, violation of the Georgia Controlled Substances Act, and possession of a firearm by a convicted felon. The charges arose from a crime spree in which two young women were kidnaped, repeatedly raped, sodomized, and tortured, but escaped with their lives.

Immediately after the incident, the victims were taken to a medical center for a medical examination, and a "rape kit" procedure was performed on each of them. At trial, the results of DNA testing were introduced by the state to support the victims' identification of Ross. It is important here to note that fingerprint, fiber, and hair analyses were not introduced by the state because they failed to connect Ross to the crimes.

The defendant argued that he was denied effective assistance of counsel because trial counsel failed to obtain and use an expert in the field of DNA analysis after the trial court had granted a motion for funds for that purpose. The GBI Crime Laboratory serologist testified that she was unable to use RFLP technology to match any of the DNA from victims N.X.'s or S.B.'s "rape kit" with Ross's DNA due to insufficient DNA samples. However, she testified, using PCR testing she had been able to find DNA that potentially could have been contributed by Ross on at least one item of clothing from each of the victims. She further testified that the frequency of Ross's blood pattern in the black population was 1 in 100. During cross-examination, the expert restated that she had found no match between Ross's DNA and either victim's "rape kit" using RFLP testing, and that, at the request of the state, she had not performed PCR testing on the "rape kit" samples to confirm the RFLP results even though she could have done so.[53]

The trial court first addressed the defendant's claim of incompetency of counsel for failing to call an independent expert DNA witness to testify at trial that the GBI Crime Laboratory's PCR testing and test results were unreliable. The court noted the defendant's failure to introduce any evidence at the hearing on the motion for new trial demonstrating that an independent expert witness would have testified as he claims. The court also noted that trial counsel testified at the hearing on the motion for new trial that Ross's first trial counsel had, in fact, retained a DNA expert in Alabama who had provided a report stating that he had nothing to add to the GBI Crime Laboratory's report and certainly could not disagree with it. Accordingly, he could not demonstrate prejudice from the failure to call this expert witness to testify at trial.[54]

In *Chapel v. State*,[55] the defendant police officer was convicted of malice murder, armed robbery, and possession of a firearm in the commission of a felony. The defendant was accused of the robbery and murder of a woman he lured to a meeting. The state amassed a considerable amount of circumstantial evidence against the defendant: witnesses saw two cars, one of which was a Gwinnett County police car, at the muffler shop between 9:30 and 10:00; Chapel was at the fire station that evening and he left between 9:20 and 9:30; a witness saw Chapel driving on Peachtree Industrial Boulevard near the muffler shop around 9:30 or 10:00; evidence proved that Chapel was facing an IRS verification audit with the potential of $4,000 in additional tax liability and that he owed a friend $1,400; a witness saw Chapel spending $100 bills; a witness saw a large sum of money in the purse of Chapel's wife; and a witness said that Chapel responded to a call a little after 10:00 the night of the murder, refused to assist the complaining witness, and left, saying he had problems of his own. The state also presented DNA evidence showing that a spot of blood in Chapel's police car matched the blood of the victim.

Chapel argued that the admission of DNA evidence was improper because the "partial digestion" testing method used was not generally accepted in the scientific community. According to the state's expert the DNA testing was performed using the RFLP methodology, which had been accepted in this state. During one of the steps of the testing procedure there was a failure of the restriction enzyme to completely cut the DNA sample, which is known as "partial digestion," and it results from a contaminant in the sample. The state's expert testified regarding the protocols that the state crime laboratory follows when dealing with partial digestion. After reviewing the record, the court concluded that the trial court did not abuse its discretion in holding that the evidence was admissible, since the conflicting expert opinions on the test results went to the weight rather than the admissibility of the testimony.[56]

In *State v. Brown*,[57] the defendant was convicted of aggravated rape. The victim was taken to Louisiana State University Medical Center that same morning where she was examined and a rape kit was completed. The kit included all of the victim's clothing that she was wearing at the time of the attack, as well as biological samples. The kit was sent to the North Louisiana Crime Laboratory along with a sample of defendant's blood. At trial a DNA expert, Ms. Dawn Tingle, testified that the defendant's DNA, which was found to be present in a sample tested from the victim's panties, was narrowed to a field of 1 in over 622,500 members of the black population.[58] The defendant questioned the reliability of the DNA evidence as well as the identifications of him as the assailant.

The court ruled that the results of DNA and RFLP analysis were generally admissible in Louisiana so long as the trial court's gatekeeping function has been performed in accordance with *Daubert*. Defendant alleged that Ms. Tingle altered the reagents and protocols from the recommended levels in performing the tests and that the statistical number linking him to the rape of the victim was increased by testing several probes on the samples. He also complained that the amount of the solution used in extracting the DNA from the semen stain found in the victim's panties was altered, making the tests unreliable.

The court rejected this claimed error, noting:

> While being cross-examined, Ms. Tingle testified that since the semen stain was large, more than the recommended amount of solution had to be added to the stain in order for the stain to dilute it. She stated that the company which produced the DNA kit made a recommendation concerning the amount of solution to use. She added that most of their testing procedures followed a set protocol, but that some procedures could be altered if necessary. This does not show that the procedure used in the DNA test was non-uniform or unreliable.[59]

The defendant's allegation that the number of probes used in testing for DNA matches made the statistical number higher than it would have been had fewer probes been used, and therefore made the tests unreliable, was also rejected since the expert had testified that the probes were actual locations on a chromosome. By running more probes you could either eliminate the suspect because there are fewer matches out of those tested or more accurately confirm a suspect because you would have more matches to compare.

The court concluded that:

> The DNA test concluded that the DNA in defendant's blood matched the DNA in the semen found in the victim's panties to the likelihood that only 1 in approximately 622,000 people in a black population would have those characteristics. Ms. Tingle testified that running all seven probes was standard procedure and that all seven probes were run in all cases if enough semen was present. Defendant offered no evidence showing that this varies from standard practice or is in any way unreliable. These assignments are without merit.[60]

In *People v. The Almighty Four Hundred*,[61] the defendant was convicted of first-degree murder and the concealment of a homicide. The court ruled that the "product rule" for establishing that DNA from a crime scene and the DNA of a suspect were the same was sufficiently well established within the scientific community to allow admission of expert testimony that the defendant was the perpetrator of the murder.

The state presented Therese Finn, a forensic biologist for the Chicago Police Department (CPD) Crime Laboratory, who testified that blood taken from the defendant's pants matched that of the victim. Finn was a forensic biologist for the CPD Crime Laboratory and had a bachelor of science degree in biology from the University of Illinois. She had received training in forensic DNA at the Forensic Science Research and Training Center of the FBI and had attended numerous workshops, seminars, and meetings conducted by other forensic laboratories throughout the country. At the CPD, Finn was trained in serology, the analysis of blood and other bodily fluids such as semen and saliva and was one of three analysts who established the DNA program at the CPD. Finn had conducted hundreds of DNA analyses. In addition, she had given numerous presentations and lectures to members of the legal and scientific communities on various aspects of DNA testing.

Finn testified that the likelihood of that blood coming from someone other than the victim was characterized as "less than one in a billion." Finn also testified that blood recovered from the jacket the defendant was wearing on the night of the murder also matched that of the victim and the likelihood of such a match was "less than one in a billion." She also testified that blood taken from the kitchen area of the hotel office matched the victim's blood. The probability of such a match is "less than one in a billion." The defendant's expert, Sandy Zabell, a professor of mathematics and statistics, testified that, according to his calculations, the frequency of seeing a match between the blood at the crime scene and the victim's blood was 1 in 3 to 4 million, or 1 in 1.2 million if the most conservative calculation was done.

The court first addressed the defendant's claim that it was error for the court to admit statistical probability testimony, where no single method had been generally accepted within the scientific community. The state contended that the trial court properly admitted Finn's testimony and that evidence concerning alternate methods of computing statistics went to the weight to be given that evidence, not its admissibility.[62] The court's recounting of Finn's testimony was in considerable detail and bears repeating here:

Finn testified that the chemical deoxyribonucleic acid (DNA) is the genetic material that is found in a person's cells which contains a "blueprint" of all genetic information necessary for life. Except in the case of identical twins, each person's DNA is totally unique. In the human body, DNA is present in every single cell that has a nucleus. Finn defined forensic DNA analysis as conducting DNA tests on blood samples and comparing the results with the DNA of known blood standards for the purpose of determining if an individual can be included or excluded as a possible contributor of the sample. Finn explained that in forensic DNA analysis, DNA is first isolated from blood cells. Following a series of steps, a pattern of DNA bands is generated by which different DNA fragment lengths can be compared. This process is referred to as Restriction Fragment Length Polymorphism (RFLP) analysis. A DNA molecule is composed of 3 to 4 billion "base pairs" of four different chemicals. The particular pattern of these base pairs dictates an individual's genetic characteristics. RFLP profiling focuses on the areas of the DNA molecule where there is a significant variation between individuals of a base pair pattern. Finn explained that, in this case, DNA was isolated from the blood cells. The base pairs seen in the DNA in the blood collected at the crime scene were then compared visually and mathematically with base pairs in the DNA from blood taken from the victim and the defendant. In this case, DNA in blood found on defendant's clothes and in the hotel matched the DNA in the victim's blood.[63]

After determining that such a laboratory match exists, Finn explained, investigations must be made respecting the frequency with which such a DNA profile would occur in a random match in the DNA profile population database chosen. She testified that, to make the matches meaningful, statistical analysis is required. After a match is determined visually and mathematically, she explained, analysts calculate the frequency or rarity of seeing a particular DNA pattern to the frequency of seeing this combination in the general population. To accomplish this, DNA analysts have generally used either the "product rule" or the "ceiling principle."[64]

Finn testified that she performed DNA analysis on a large stain on the pants police recovered from defendant. The DNA in this blood was compared with the victim's blood. A match was determined visually and mathematically:

The rarity of seeing this match in the population was then calculated using the "product rule." Finn testified that the likelihood of a randomly selected individual having the same DNA profile that was generated from the victim's blood was "less than one in a billion." In other words, the likelihood that the blood on defendant's pants came from someone other than the victim is less than one in a billion. A DNA profile was also generated from the blood found on the jacket that defendant was wearing on the night of the murder. The DNA profile of the blood on defendant's jacket also matched the victim's profile, and the likelihood of a randomly selected individual having the same DNA profile is "less than one in a billion." A DNA profile was also generated from the blood found in the kitchen. The DNA profiles from these three samples also matched the victim's DNA. Finn testified that the probability of this DNA profile being found in a randomly selected individual is "less than one in a billion." Finn testified that if the "ceiling principle" were used in calculating these statistics, the resulting frequency would be 1 in 3.4 million.[65]

At trial, Finn testified that after two evidence samples are deemed to have matched after a laboratory procedure, a statistical value is attached to the match to illustrate the rarity or frequency of seeing such a match. To do this, she testified, DNA samples are taken from a random population of individuals and the frequency of seeing certain patterns of DNA in the random population is determined. The random population is gathered into a database. Finn testified that in 1991, she and two other DNA analysts compiled the 600 DNA samples that are used for the CPD population database. Since the "product rule" was based upon the presumption that the samples in the database are randomly gathered and therefore independent of each other, it was necessary to validate that the samples in the database were independent and random. She testified that to validate the database, human population geneticists subject the database to tests known as "equilibriums."[66]

After the CPD compiled its database, she continued, the database was given to Dr. Michael Keneally, who was a human medical geneticist. He performed what is known as the "Hardy–Weinberg" equilibrium test on the database to validate the independence of its data. At trial, the following exchange was had:

Q: The Chicago database that was compiled, was that then statistically reviewed or analyzed by human population geneticists?

A: Yes it was.

Q: Who analyzed or reviewed that database?

A: Doctor Michael Keneally from Indiana University.

Q: And do you know who Dr. Keneally is, his background?

A: Yes.

...

Q: Who is Dr. Keneally?

A: Dr. Keneally is a human medical geneticist.

Q: And was he given the information, the statistical review and analyze [sic] the Chicago database?

A: Yes, he was given all the data from our database.

...

Q: Did the Chicago database meet the Hardy–Weinberg equilibrium?

The court agreed that this aspect of the testimony was hearsay, but allowed Finn to testify as to Keneally's findings after concluding that the testimony constituted a business records exception to the hearsay rule.[67]

After a brief recess, the examination of Finn continued and she was allowed to testify that the database had met the Hardy–Weinberg equilibrium test, thus rejecting defendant's argument that in cases involving DNA probability statistics experts such as Keneally have always been required to testify. Here Finn was allowed to note the Keneally materials as an exception to the hearsay rule.

> We hold that, in the instant case, Finn's testimony was properly admitted ... for the limited purpose of explaining the basis of her opinion. Keneally's review of the database was similar to the population databases in [other cases] and was the type of information reasonably relied upon by experts in the field of forensic DNA analysis, genetics and serology. Furthermore, we conclude, as did the courts in Lipscomb and Contreras, that it was defendant's responsibility to challenge the reliability of the basis of Finn's statistics on cross-examination, as statistics are admissible as relevant to identification and any challenges to their reliability go only to the weight to be given the evidence.[68]

In *Thomas v. State*,[69] a capital murder appeal, the court, noting continuing affirmative findings in previous cases, concluded, under the facts of this case, that the "product rule" technique used to arrive at the DNA population frequency statistical evidence in this case was reliable under *Daubert*. Expert Brewer testified:

> Q: Are the statistical methods used in your laboratory to calculate an estimate of the significance of a DNA match generally accepted in the relevant scientific community?

> A: Yes. The standard statistical procedures that we use are routinely used in medical and research laboratories as well as forensic laboratories. The 1996 report from the National Research Council specifically endorsed these measures.[70]

The court noted that while expert Brewer did not use the precise term "product rule," by his testimony that he used the "standard statistical procedures" endorsed by the 1996 report of the National Research Council (NRC), along with his cursory description of the method, they concluded that he indeed used the product rule.[71]

Thomas did not dispute the reliability of the application of the product rule in the context of DNA forensic analysis; indeed, he recognized in his brief that the product rule was the only valid method of computing the frequency of DNA patterns. The court also noted that the reliability of the product rule had been recognized by a significant number of jurisdictions.[72]

The *Thomas* case also contains a detailed analysis of the potential chain-of-custody issues rising from the increased use and importance of DNA crime scene collecting procedures and laboratory testing. Here, again, the issues are raised by way of an alleged violation of the plain error rule. Here, the court noted, the defendant did not raise any chain-of-custody objections at trial. The court observed:

The presentation of a chain of custody is such a basic tenet in the admission of evidence, it would be incredulous to assume that defense counsel was not aware of the prosecution's responsibility or of his client's right to have evidence sought to be introduced properly authenticated. We can assume only that he intentionally chose to relinquish any insistence that the prosecution present any further authentication. Otherwise, we would be promoting the practice of "sandbagging.[73]

The court recognized that the increasing volume of DNA testing has considerably increased the importance of proper handling procedures.

In regard to chain-of-custody requirements for critical DNA evidence, the court noted the following:

Even the strongest evidence will be worthless—or worse, might possibly lead to a false conviction—if the evidence sample did not originate in connection with the crime. Given the great individuating potential of DNA evidence and the relative ease with which it can be mishandled or manipulated by the careless or the unscrupulous, the integrity of the chain of custody is of paramount importance.[74]

There are an increasing number of decisions addressing DNA-related chain-of-custody issues, as defense arguments challenging DNA laboratory testing and population projections continue to fall on deaf ears.[75]

D. PCR AND STR

The PCR method involves the copying or amplification of a short section of a strand of DNA, and it allows tests to be performed on very small quantities of genetic material. In this method, the DNA is extracted from a sample of cellular material such as blood or sperm cells. Then, depending on which genetic markers are being tested for, a particular location or set of locations on the strand of DNA is isolated and copied over and over until a sufficient quantity exists for testing.[76] Unlike the RFLP procedure, which is a much more accurate test used to establish a statistical match, the PCR technique is generally used as an exculpatory tool to "exclude certain individuals as possible contributors to a particular sample."[77] It can also be used on much smaller sample obtained from a crime scene and may replicate samples to allow for multiple testing opportunities. The PCR method harnesses cellular enzymes to replicate portions of the DNA so that a sufficient number of copies of the DNA may be obtained to perform testing.[78]

The recently published *Proceedings of the 12th INTERPOL Forensic Science Symposium* noted that most laboratories are concentrating on DNA evidence as the main form of biological evidence. The author of the paper on DNA evidence, D. J. Werrett, concluded:

The trend is now firmly established towards PCR STR based technology and, in particular, to multiplexing. There appears to be widespread agreement as to the best choice of STRs and future opportunity for world-wide collaboration on STRs that are being added to current systems.[79]

The ability of PCR testing to reach results in cases where the amount of testable material is small and/or partially degraded may be illustrated by a brief summary of a recent Illinois Supreme Court decision. In *People v. Davis*,[80] the defendant was convicted of first-degree murder, aggravated criminal sexual assault, aggravated kidnaping, robbery, and concealment of homicidal death, and was given the death penalty. The state's evidence showed that, on Monday, August 21, 1995, Laurie Gwinn was reported missing after she failed to arrive at her job with the county health department. The next day, sometime after 11 A.M., Gwinn's dead body was found floating in the Hennepin Canal north of Annawan, Illinois. She was nude and was missing several pieces of expensive jewelry that she always wore.[81]

A vaginal swab taken during Gwinn's autopsy contained seminal material and sperm cells. Kristin Boster, a forensic scientist and expert in DNA analysis, testified that she isolated the DNA taken from the swab and determined it to be too degraded for an RFLP analysis. Elizabeth Benzinger, a molecular biologist and also an expert in DNA analysis, agreed that there was insufficient DNA to perform an RFLP analysis. She explained that the DNA was degraded because the murderer had placed Gwinn's body in the canal. Benzinger therefore analyzed the DNA using the PCR technique. She compared the DNA taken from the swab with samples taken from defendant, one Linsley, who was a close acquaintance of the victim, and the victim. Benzinger concluded that Linsley could not have contributed to the vaginal swab. Benzinger could not, however, exclude the defendant as the source of the semen on the swab. According to Benzinger, the percentage of the U.S. population that could have contributed the DNA recovered from the swab was 2.6% of white persons and 3.6% of black persons.[82]

In *Miller v. State*,[83] the defendant was convicted in the District Court, Oklahoma County, Oklahoma of first-degree murder and was sentenced to death. Kent Dodd, aged 25, worked as the night auditor for the Central Plaza Hotel located at the intersection of I-40 and Martin Luther King Drive in Oklahoma City. Dodd registered a guest at approximately 3:15 A.M. September 17, 1994. Shortly thereafter, Dodd was attacked by an assailant who stabbed him repeatedly, beat him with hedge shears and a paint can, and poured muriatic acid on him and down his throat. Bloody footprints were found near the body of the victim. After 2½ hours a housekeeper arrived for the morning shift. She called for Dodd when she saw he was not at the front desk. In response, she heard "animal moans" from the unused restaurant area of the hotel. She ran to a nearby restaurant and had the police summoned. Dodd was still alive when the police found him.

The court agreed with the defendant Miller that no fingerprint or hair evidence connected the defendant to the crime, no blood evidence conclusively placed him at the scene, and there were no eyewitnesses. However, the court noted that there was nonetheless a substantial amount of circumstantial evidence: microscopic amounts of DNA consistent with that of the victim were found on Miller's right sandal; footprints left at the scene could have been made by Miller's sandals; the size and interlocking dog-bone pattern of the sole and prints were consistent; two buttons found at the scene were consistent with those of Miller's shirt, which disappeared after the murder; and Miller's khaki shorts disappeared after the murder.[84]

Miller first argued the trial court failed to conduct a *Daubert* hearing to determine admissibility of the PCR evidence used against him. The court noted that at the time of Miller's trial, PCR DNA analysis was a novel scientific procedure, and an *in camera* hearing to determine admissibility should have been conducted, but was not. The failure to hold a *Daubert* hearing was deemed error, but harmless and not sufficient for reversal. The court observed that PCR DNA analysis had been accepted in Oklahoma as admissible in criminal trials, and therefore the failure to hold a hearing to determine admissibility was harmless beyond a reasonable doubt.

Next, the defendant argued that the PCR DNA evidence used in his case was unreliable, but in support of his position he relied on testimony by a defense witness who had never worked with the PCR method of DNA testing. Dr. Hanas testified the photocopy of the test result indicated the test was inconclusive because a necessary control dot was not visible. The trial court took evidence which established this control dot, although faint, was visible on the original test. The basis for Dr. Hanas' conclusion thus was discredited, and the state presented sufficient evidence to prove reliability of the PCR test.

The state's witness, Dr. Moses Schanfield, testified to the ability of PCR analysis to test extremely small samples, and explained that of four tests conducted on the sample of DNA obtained from Miller's right sandal, only the PCR test, the most sensitive test, yielded any results. The court opined that the expert, Dr. Hanas, seriously weakened his own credibility when he also admitted he had no experience with PCR DNA analysis. Nonetheless, the court ruled that the state had presented sufficient evidence to establish the reliability of PCR DNA testing sufficient to warrant admission at trial.

Finally, the defendant challenged the admissibility of the PCR DNA analysis in his case on the basis that the results were not exclusive enough to be reliable. State expert, Dr. Schanfield, testified the DNA found on Miller's right sandal could have been produced by 1 in 19 Caucasians, 1 in 16 African-Americans, and 1 in 55 Hispanics. The court agreed that the large pool of possible donors weakened this evidence considerably. However, it observed that defendant did not suggest the PCR DNA evidence did not replicate DNA sequences and determine the frequency of these sequences in the population. Rather, he argued that the pool of potential donors in this case is so large, that the evidence was simply not reliable. The court ruled that that argument appeared to address the relevance of the evidence rather than its reliability, noting that to be admissible as relevant, evidence need only have any tendency to make the existence of a fact of consequence more or less probable than it would be without the evidence. The population frequency statistics met that very liberal standard and hence left the issue to be the weight of the evidence. Here, the PCR DNA evidence was properly admitted and the defense appropriately exposed its weakness to the jury.

A combination of DNA laboratory methods was successfully used to convict the defendant in *People v. Buss*,[85] a 1999 Illinois Supreme Court decision involving a particularly gruesome murder of a child. The defendant was convicted of six counts of first-degree murder, three counts of aggravated kidnaping, and one count of aggravated unlawful restraint, and was sentenced to death. The defendant was accused of luring a young male victim from a popular Kankakee River dockside park and brutally murdering him.

Deputy Scott Swearengen testified that he and another deputy were searching the hunting areas of the Kankakee State Park during the early morning hours of August 15. In a clearing at the end of a path leading from the parking area of Hunting Area 7, they found the body of a small child in a shallow grave under a sheet of plywood. Forensic evidence presented by the State established that the body was that of Christopher and that he had died from multiple stab wounds prior to sunset on August 7.

Other forensic evidence connected defendant to Christopher's murder. Experts testified to forensically important similarities between hairs, soil, and footprint data taken from the area where the body was found and items seized from the defendant's possessions.[86]

Forensic scientists from the Illinois State Bureau of Forensic Sciences testified that there was human blood on the dent puller found in the trunk of the defendant's car, that blood was found on the carpet from the trunk, and that a stain of human blood had soaked through the carpet. There was also human blood on a box found at the grave site, as well as on the boots the defendant had placed in a motel dumpster, although the test to determine whether the blood on the boots was human was not positive.

The court here accepted without discussion the testimony of William Frank, the DNA Research Coordinator for the Illinois State Police Forensic Sciences Command and an expert in forensic DNA analysis, who testified that he analyzed DNA extracted from an inhaler prescribed for Christopher, from carpet from the trunk of the defendant's car, from a piece of Christopher's right femur, and from a bloodstained box found at the grave site:

> Frank used two methods of DNA analysis: PCR (polymerase chain reaction) and RFLP (restriction fragment length polymorphism). Each of these methods is used to identify particular characteristics of a given sample of DNA. Those characteristics are referred to as the "profile" of that DNA. Because each method of analysis, PCR and RFLP, identifies different characteristics, two different profiles are obtained by subjecting a sample of DNA to both types of analysis.... Frank used the PCR method to analyze DNA found on the inhaler, carpet, femur, and box. The PCR profile of the DNA from each of these items was the same. Frank calculated that this particular DNA profile could be found in one out of 19,000 Caucasian individuals.
>
> Using the RFLP method, which is more discriminating, Frank compared the DNA in blood samples from Christopher's parents and defendant to the DNA in blood found on the box and carpet. (Because the amount of DNA extracted from Christopher's inhaler and femur was insufficient for the RFLP method of analysis, Frank used DNA from Christopher's parents to determine whether the blood from the box and carpet belonged to Christopher.) By comparing the DNA profiles he obtained, Frank determined that the blood on the box and the carpet came from a child of Mika Moulton and James Meyer, Sr., Christopher's father. Frank calculated that the chance of two Caucasian parents producing a child with the same RFLP DNA profile as the DNA found on the carpet and box was one out of 3.8 million.[87]

After preparing both a PCR and an RFLP profile for the DNA found on the box and carpet, associated with the defendant's vehicle, Frank proceeded to estimate the frequency of DNA with both of these profiles in the population, concluding that a person with such DNA would occur in the Caucasian population only 1 out of 419 million times.

In *State v. Carter,*[88] the defendant was convicted of the murder and sexual assault of a 9-year-old female. The case centered on the admissibility and force of DNA testimony utilizing PCR DNA methods.

An autopsy on the victim's body revealed that she had been subjected to vaginal and anal penetration shortly before her death. The autopsy further indicated that the most likely cause of death was asphyxiation, due to compression of the chest which prevented the victim from breathing. Dr. Jerry Wilson Jones, the pathologist who conducted the autopsy, testified that his examination detected the presence of sperm in the victim's anus.

The state conducted DNA tests on semen and blood found on the victim's body and clothing and on samples of blood obtained from suspects Carter, Hicks, Harpster, and the victim. The results of this testing positively excluded Hicks and Harpster as sources of the semen found on the victim, but Carter could not be excluded as the source, because experts testified that his genetic markers were consistent with those obtained from the semen. The DNA testing determined six genetic markers. The frequency of any particular combination of these six genetic markers within the American population was determined by referencing established databases of genetic characteristics. It was concluded that the combination of markers common to both Carter and the semen found on the victim occurred in approximately 1 in 15,000 Caucasian-Americans, 1 in 1,200 African-Americans, and 1 in 5,500 Mexican-Americans. Defendant challenged the PCR technology and the conclusions reached here concerning his participation in the crime.[89]

Forensic Science Associates (FSA) analyzed the evidence submitted to it using the PCR method of DNA analysis. The PCR method, the expert explained, involves the copying or amplification of a short section of a strand of DNA, and it allows tests to be performed on very small quantities of genetic material. In this method, the DNA is extracted from a sample of cellular material such as blood or sperm cells. Then, depending on which genetic markers are being tested for, a particular location or set of locations on the strand of DNA is isolated and copied over and over until a sufficient quantity exists for testing.

FSA used two variations of this technique in this case. The first identifies the genetic marker known as DQ Alpha. The second, known as polymarker testing, identifies five genetic markers for any particular sample. The five genetic markers identified in polymarker testing are called LDLR, GYPA, HBGG, D7S8, and GC. Each of these markers consists of two alleles, one of which a person obtains from his or her father and the other from his or her mother. With the DQ Alpha marker, these alleles are identified as numbers separated by a comma. Thus, a person might have a DQ Alpha marker of 2,3 or 1.1,4. Polymarker traits are notated the same way but using letters, so a person might have an LDLR marker of A,B or a D7S8 marker of B,B.[90]

Performed in combination, these two tests identify six genetic markers. Each human being has these six markers, and the markers are the same in every cell that comes from a particular human. Thus, if any one of these markers identified from an unknown sample varies from the same marker identified from a known person, that person cannot be the source of the sample.

Looking only at the DQ Alpha markers, FSA experts testified that suspects Hicks and Harpster were positively excluded from being possible donors of the semen found on the body and clothing of the victim. Hicks' DQ Alpha type was 1.1,3, and Harpster's was 2,3. Carter's DQ Alpha type was 4.1,4.1, as was that of the semen recovered from the victim. Thus, the DQ Alpha test showed that Carter could have been the source of the semen, but that neither Harpster nor Hicks could have been. Similarly, the polymarker testing did not exclude Carter as the source of the semen.[91]

Expert Mihalovich testified in detail about the FSA laboratory protocols, stating that the FSA protocols were comparable with those of laboratories operated by Cellmark, the FBI, the California Department of Justice, and the Serological Research Institute. Mihalovich, as well as Chakraborty and Wisecarver, testified that any variations from the test kit protocols utilized were inconsequential and would in no way affect the reliability or accuracy of the testing.

Carter's argument that because the FSA protocols were not collected in one written instrument, the actual test procedures used could not be compared against that instrument to show compliance with the protocols was found to be without merit. The court noted that the actual steps taken by FSA in this case are known and all three experts testified that those steps were in substantial compliance with both the partially written protocols of FSA and the general protocol of the scientific community for DQ Alpha and polymarker PCR testing.[92] Based on that testimony, the court concluded that there was no error in the trial court finding that the FSA procedures produce reliable results if properly performed and that those procedures were followed in this case.

E. STR DNA

In *People v. Allen*,[93] the defendant was convicted of special circumstances murder and forcible rape. The state offered the results of laboratory DNA testing by short tandem repeats (STR) methods on a semen stain from the crime scene. The court ruled that this was competent evidence of general acceptance of testing in the scientific community.

Paul Colman, a senior criminalist for the Los Angeles County Sheriff's Crime Laboratory, conducted a DNA analysis on the semen stain. He typed six genetic loci by the RFLP testing process and found that two of those loci matched Allen's DNA sample. Colman concluded the DNA from the semen stain could have come from Allen, and calculated that the odds of a randomly selected African-American having the same two loci combination would be 6,200 to 1.[94]

Testimony on these same samples was also provided by Dr. Charlotte Word, a microbiologist and the deputy director of the prominent Cellmark Labs. Cellmark performed PCR testing, a method used when there is only a limited supply of DNA available for testing. Cellmark used three different kinds of PCR testing: DQ Alpha (which tests a single genetic marker), polymarker (which tests five genetic markers), and STR (which tests three genetic markers). The testing includes a total of nine genetic markers when the results of all three tests are combined. Dr. Word put the random match probability as determined by the DQ Alpha/polymarker testing at 1 in 1,700 African-Americans. She concluded from these results that the defendant could not be excluded as the source of the semen. Word specifically testified that the STR results had not excluded Allen as a source of the semen. Based on a combination of these results, Dr. Word testified she had concluded that Allen was the source of the semen stain "within a reasonable degree of scientific certainty."

Allen argued that the trial court erred (1) by finding that STR testing was generally accepted in the scientific community and (2) by admitting STR testing results while excluding the corresponding statistical probability evidence. The court rejected the defendant's arguments, noting that two out-of-state cases had approved STR testing.[95]

The court noted that in the 1997 case of *Commonwealth v. Rosier*,[96] the Supreme Court of Massachusetts had affirmed a trial court's finding that STR testing was scientifically reliable. The *Rosier* case was quoted as follows:

> The defendant's appellate counsel appears to suggest that STR testing is unreliable because it is too new. No specific scientific or forensic evidence or literature is offered to support that suggestion. The judge heard testimony that, in 1991, several years before the STR kit became commercially available, Cellmark, working under contract to the United States government, used STR testing to identify the remains of soldiers killed in Operation Desert Storm, and that, by the time of the hearing, Cellmark had performed STR analysis in approximately fifty cases and had been permitted to testify as to its test results in at least five cases. While we have not been directed to any decisional law approving STR testing, an authoritative scientific study, the 1996 report of the National Research Council entitled, The Evaluation of Forensic DNA Evidence (1996 NRC Report), has concluded that STR testing is "coming into wide use," that "STR loci appear to be particularly appropriate for forensic use," and that "STRs can take their place along with VNTRs as forensic tools." The latter comment appears to recognize that STR testing is similar in principle to the RFLP (or VNTR) method, which has been found to be reliable. Based on the evidence before him and his careful analysis of the subject, the judge properly concluded that the methodology underlying the PCR-based tests in this case, including the STR testing, was scientifically valid and relevant to a fact at trial.[97]

The *Allen* court also noted that in 1998, in *State v. Jackson*,[98] the Supreme Court of Nebraska affirmed a trial court's finding that the prosecution had shown STR testing was generally accepted by the relevant scientific community, emphasizing that a director of the University of Nebraska Medical Center Laboratory had testified that PCR STR testing was generally accepted in the scientific community. The expert had testified that this method had "been around several years now, and there is nothing unique about PCR STR versus any PCR."[99] The *Jackson* court concluded that based on this evidence, we can only conclude that the trial court was correct in determining that the PCR STR DNA test used in the instant case was generally accepted within the scientific community.

Finally, in response to Allen's argument that there was no evidence that STR testing had been validated by the time it was utilized in this case, the court stated that the issue was not *when* a new scientific technique is validated, but *whether* it is or is not valid, which was the reason the results generated by a scientific test once considered valid can be challenged by evidence the test has since been invalidated.[100]

Considerable effort is currently being expended to achieve uniform standards for PCR testing in the European Community. The major umbrella organization in coordinating this work is STADNAP (Standardization of DNA Profiling Techniques in the European Union). The organization states on its Web site that:

> Due to the rapid progress in the field during the past years, parallel developments of methods as well as typing systems have been made in the laboratories involved in forensic DNA profiling. This has resulted in heterogeneity of typing procedures as well as genetic systems used for forensic casework within the European Union. However, intercomparison of DNA typing results becomes not only desirable, but absolutely necessary within Europe as mobile serial offenders will not be detected by DNA profiling unless methods are standardized.[101]

STADNAP participants will work toward achieving six primary objectives:

1. To define criteria for the selection of forensic typing systems based on the PCR technique suitable for European standardization;
2. To evaluate PCR systems for forensic stain typing;
3. To exchange and compare methods for the harmonization of typing protocols;
4. To carry out exercises for intercomparison of forensic typing results;
5. To recommend reference PCR typing systems for European standardization; and
6. To exchange data for compilation of reference frequency databases for the European populations.[102]

It is hoped these goals will be achieved by the coordinated effort of 20 network partners as well as industrial consultants by organizing regular biannual meetings as well as practical collaborative exercises. Technology transfer will be carried out and exchange of personnel will be encouraged within the framework of the European Union fellowship programs.[103]

F. MtDNA

The most recent DNA testing methodology seeking court approval is mitochondrial DNA (mtDNA). The FBI is actively developing this technology and is currently publishing important preliminary papers about it on the excellent new FBI Web site.[104] A series of recent cases has been handed down establishing the general scientific acceptability and/or scientific reliability of identification opinions by forensic scientists based on mtDNA methodologies. States are beginning to pass legislation[105] that provides for automatic acceptance of the reliability of standard DNA methodologies, which will no doubt aid in the current efforts by the FBI to have a quick judicial acceptance of mtDNA.[106]

In *State v. Council*,[107] involving a hair found at the crime scene, the defendant was convicted of murder, kidnaping, administering poison, grand larceny of a vehicle, burglary, larceny, and two counts of criminal sexual conduct in the first degree, and was sentenced to death. The victim, a 72-year-old widow, was brutally sexually assaulted and asphyxiated by having her entire head covered with duct tape. The authorities found Mrs. Gatti's car near an apartment complex where the defendant sometimes stayed. The defendant, in two separate statements, admitted to being in Mrs. Gatti's house on the night she was killed; however, he asserted he had gone to her house with a man identified as "Frankie J.," later identified as being one Frank Douglas. The defendant denied any killing but admitted having sexual relations with the victim.

A body of forensic evidence was presented at trial: a shoeprint taken from a chair in Mrs. Gatti's house was identified as matching shoes taken from appellant; residue found on the chair positively matched debris found on appellant's shoes; fingerprints taken from Mrs. Gatti's car and from items in her car were identified as belonging to appellant; hair samples taken from appellant were consistent with hairs found in Mrs. Gatti's home; semen taken from a tissue in Mrs. Gatti's house was consistent with appellant's semen; several items identified as belonging to Mrs. Gatti were found in appellant's girlfriend's apartment.

During the guilt phase of appellant's trial, John Ortuno, a trace evidence examiner for the state, testified that the characteristics of pubic hairs found at the crime scene were consistent with the defendant's pubic hair. Ortuno further determined Frank Douglas could not have been the donor of the hair. To confirm those findings, the state sought to introduce testimony from Joseph Dizinno of the FBI laboratory regarding the results of mtDNA analysis performed on the hairs.

Dizinno's qualifications were deemed more than adequate to support any opinions on mtDNA in this case. Dizinno testified he had extensive training in both hair and fiber analysis and mtDNA analysis, and his mtDNA analysis research began in 1992. He testified mtDNA analysis has been used for research purposes since 1981 and over 600 papers have been written about mtDNA research. He stated that mtDNA analysis was a recognized methodology that had been used for many purposes, including the identification of bodies from the Vietnam and Gulf Wars. Dizinno opined that mtDNA analysis confirms, based on a scientific objective standard, the subjective microscopical comparison performed on the hairs.

The court noted the supportive testimony by Dr. Dizinno:

> Dizzino testified that Mitochondrial DNA is found in mitochondria, which are organelles contained within the cytoplasm of a cell and which serve as the cell's energy factories. Unlike nucleus DNA that contains genetic material inherited from both the mother and the father, mtDNA only contains genetic material inherited from the mother. Two advantages of mtDNA are that there are many more copies of mtDNA in the cell

than there are copies of nuclear DNA since each cell contains many mitochondria but only one nucleus and mtDNA is much more stable than nuclear DNA; therefore, the chances of extracting mtDNA from a degraded sample is increased. Further, unlike nuclear DNA which is only present in the living cells at the roots of a pulled hair, mtDNA is present in the shafts of hair.[108]

Continuing, the court noted Dizinno's explanation of the mtDNA laboratory procedure:

Dizinno explained that mtDNA analysis is performed by extracting the DNA from mitochondria. This DNA is then amplified and examined to determine its sequences of As, Gs, Ts, and Cs. This sequence is then compared to a sequence donated by a known person. If the sequence is different, the person donating the known sample can be eliminated as the donor of the unknown sample. If the sequence is the same, the examiner compares the sequence to the database of mtDNA sequences available to him to determine if he has ever seen that same sequence. Validation studies showed that about 62% of the hairs analyzed were sequenced on the first try. The other 38% could not be sequenced because the DNA could not be extracted. Of the 62% that could be sequenced, the reliability of getting a correct sequence was 100%.[109]

The database used by Dizinno contained 742 known sequences of which 319 were sequences obtained from African-Americans. Dizinno testified that while he had found a match between unrelated Caucasians, he had never found a match between unrelated African-Americans. According to Dizinno, the two regions analyzed are most variable in African-Americans.

Based upon the results of this analysis Dizinno excluded Frank Douglas as the person who deposited the hair found at the crime scene. Dizinno could not exclude appellant as the person who deposited the hair found at the crime scene. Based on the available database, Dizinno testified that most probably the hair that was recovered from the crime scene belonged to the defendant, while admitting that it was possible that the hair belonged to another individual. The court here concluded that the trial judge was well within his discretion in finding the results of the mtDNA analysis admissible.

Finally, the court rejected the defendant's claim that he was denied time to obtain his own mtDNA expert, a claim likely to be made many times in the near future. Defense counsel vigorously cross-examined Dizinno, revealing the minimal size of the mtDNA database and the fact that Dizinno had previously found matches between unrelated Caucasians.

In *State v. Underwood*,[110] a 1999 North Carolina case involving the hair of the victim, the defendant was convicted of first-degree murder and first-degree kidnaping of a man who dated his former girlfriend. Mitochondrial DNA evidence offered to show that a hair found in the trunk of the defendant's car could have been from the murder victim's hair.

Agent Hamlin, special agent with the North Carolina State Bureau of Investigation, testified as an expert in the field of hair examination and comparison. After conducting a microscopic examination and comparison of the known hair samples of victim Gunnarsson and the hairs found on defendant's trunk mat, Agent Hamlin testified that the hairs were microscopically consistent and could have originated from Gunnarsson.[111]

Dr. Dizinno, an employee of the FBI, was qualified as an expert in the field of hair examination and mtDNA analysis. Dr. Dizinno has training in microscopic hair examination and has performed mtDNA research and analysis. He is the chief of DNA Analysis Unit 2 where mtDNA tests are conducted. He performed a DNA sequencing from one of the hairs located on the defendant's trunk mat and compared it with the mtDNA sequence obtained from a known blood sample of victim Gunnarsson. Dr. Dizinno opined that the DNA sequence from the hair and the DNA sequence from the blood sample were identical. He concluded that Gunnarsson could not be excluded as a source of the hairs from the defendant's trunk mat.

The defendant argued that the court erred in admitting expert testimony concerning mtDNA evidence. Specifically, he argued that mtDNA testing was not scientifically reliable and its reasoning and methodology were not properly applied to the facts of this case. The court disagreed, noting that the admissibility of mtDNA evidence was an issue of first impression in North Carolina's appellate courts. The court began its analysis by examining the broad outlines of mtDNA analysis:

> In simplistic terms, mitochondria are microscopic particles found in the cell, but outside the nucleus. Mitochondrial DNA analysis is a method of DNA testing which was implemented for forensic purposes by the Federal Bureau of Investigation laboratory in June of 1996. It is based on the Polymerase Chain Reaction ("PCR") method of DNA analysis. The mtDNA is inherited solely from the mother and is the same for all maternal relatives. Mitochondrial DNA testing is performed by extracting the DNA from the mitochondria. The DNA is then amplified and examined to determine its sequences of A's, G's, T's, and C's. The sequence is then compared to another sequence donated by a known person. If the sequences are identical, the examiner compares the sequence to the available database of mtDNA sequences to determine if he has ever seen that same sequence. The statistic will be based upon the frequency of similar DNA patterns occurring within the database and within each group in the database. The final result simply either excludes the tested individual as the sample donor or confirms that such individual is within a certain percentage of the population which could have donated the sample.[112]

Here, the court noted, Dr. Dizinno testified as an expert in mtDNA analysis to establish whether the hairs found in the trunk of the defendant's car could have been those of victim Gunnarsson. The court found him to be eminently qualified to offer such testimony. Dr. Dizinno testified that he had served as the chief of the FBI DNA Analysis Unit 2, had earned a Bachelor of Science degree from the University of Notre Dame and a Doctor of Dental Surgery from Ohio State, was an expert hair examiner with 2 years experience in conducting mtDNA analysis, and had previously testified in court and given his opinion as an expert witness in mtDNA.

Regarding the testimony here, the court observed that the source of hair found in defendant's trunk was a crucial fact in this case and that mtDNA evidence was offered to show that the hair could have been Gunnarsson's. The court ruled that in light of evidence Rule 401, providing that evidence is relevant if it has a tendency to make a fact of consequence more probable or less probable than it would be without the evidence, even though the expert was unable to eliminate definitively the possibility that the hair came from someone else, the mtDNA was relevant to show that it was more probable that the hair belonged to Gunnarsson.[113]

The defendant's argument that mtDNA evidence was scientifically unreliable was rejected, the court noting that a new scientific method was admissible at trial if it is scientifically reliable. Here, the court ruled, Dr. Dizinno adequately spoke to the scientific reliability of mtDNA technology, testifying that there had been over 4 years of solid research, testing, and publications in peer-reviewed scientific journals on mtDNA analysis. The mtDNA analysis, Dr. Dizinno observed, provides results when genomic DNA analysis of hair shafts or any other biological specimen known to contain little or no DNA do not. Moreover, it had been widely accepted in evolutionary genetic studies and has been used in at least six other states.[114]

The court noted that Dr. Dizinno told the jury that mtDNA testing did not give proof of identification as conventional DNA testing did; however, the court ruled, while the scientific technique on which an expert bases a proffered opinion must be recognized as reliable, absolute certainty of result is not required. The court concluded that mtDNA testing was sufficiently reliable to warrant its admissibility into evidence.[115]

An important case involving pretrial discovery and mtDNA testing was recently decided by a Connecticut court. In *State v. Torres*,[116] a sexual assault case, the court considered a motion of the defendant to allow the presence of a defense expert during mtDNA testing of semen stains, and the state's motion to permit such testing to occur without defense observation. The state desired to have trace evidence of suspected blood and semen, seized during the investigation of the child victim's death, genetically tested by the FBI forensics laboratory to determine if the mitochondrial DNA detected, if any, matches that of the defendant as to the suspected semen and that of the victim as to the suspected blood.

The court noted that the specimens in question in this case were too meager for analysis by the more widely available nuclear DNA test, but that mtDNA evaluation could be performed even on quantities as minute as the specimens to be scrutinized here. Of great consequence here, the court recognized that the specimens would be consumed by the test procedures. The problem was that the FBI laboratory permitted no outside observers to monitor its examinations. The Bode laboratory, which can also perform such tests, likewise allows no observers. The LabCorp laboratory will permit restricted observation by a preapproved observer.

The state noted that contamination was of great concern with respect to the specialized testing to be done on these specimens. That concern, along with the added stress and inconvenience of conducting such monitored analysis, was the reason these laboratories refused to permit outside observers. LabCorp has indicated that it would allow the defense to use Dr. T. Melton as an observer but has not yet established a protocol or set limits for such observation.

The state also argued that the FBI laboratory should perform the testing because that laboratory had already received the specimens, had extracted the DNA from them, and was the first to engage in forensic mtDNA examinations and established the accepted protocol to utilize this methodology. In addition, the FBI technicians had previously testified in 10 other criminal trials regarding mtDNA analyses and findings. That laboratory has previously conducted such examination of seminal stains. There was also no fee charged to the state for this testing.

The defense contends that LabCorp offers a viable alternative to the FBI facility while permitting the possibility of defense observation. It should be noted that LabCorp has never conducted mtDNA tests on seminal stain evidence, nor have its personnel testified in a criminal trial.[117]

The court noted that Practice Book §40-9 established a general rule of discovery that, if scientific testing by one party will preclude further testing by the opponent, that opponent must be afforded the opportunity to observe or participate in the test. Section 40-9 also provides, however, that the court may dispense with this require-ment for good cause, meaning a "substantial reason amounting in law to a legal excuse" and a "legally sufficient ground or reason." The court found good cause under §40-9 to allow the mtDNA testing to be performed by the FBI laboratory:

> Evidence that mitochondrial DNA extracted from the suspected seminal fluid discov-ered on the victim's clothing matches that of the defendant and evidence that the victim's mitochondrial DNA matched that of the suspected blood on the defendant's clothing would be critically important to the state's case. Similarly, exclusion of either subject as the source of the stains would weigh significantly in the defendant's favor. Establishing the admissibility and credibility of any results flowing from such testing is, therefore, of utmost importance to the state.... The state legitimately wishes to present a strong case for the inclusion of and weight to be accorded to such analysis. The state anticipates the possibility of a Porter hearing with respect to this examination.... Prof-fering testimony from the leader in this field of analysis for criminal cases rather than from a less experienced laboratory is a reasonable and relevant preference by the state.[118]

The court concluded that any prejudice to the defendant by not having its expert attend the testing appeared less significant in this case than in others where the evidence will also be consumed by the test procedure. This was so because the FBI laboratory had already extracted the DNA from the specimens. Also, the extent to which LabCorp would permit observation was, as of yet, undetermined. For those reasons, the state's motion was granted, and the defendant's motion was denied.

G. Nonhuman DNA

At the present time there are no reported decisions addressing the acceptability of dog or cat DNA matches in a criminal case, although several trial court convictions have recently been reported and are working their way up the appeals process.[119] There is one decision concerning the admissibility of plant DNA testing to place a defendant at a crime scene.[120] It is simply a matter of time before mammal and plant DNA identification methodologies are also recognized as reliable,[121] especially since the amount of experience and solid scientific data in those areas is enormous and compelling.[122]

RESEARCH NOTE

The Journal of Forensic Sciences is the official publication of the American Academy of Forensic Sciences. By visiting the Academy's Web site at *http://www.aafs.org* and clicking on the "Journal of Forensic Sciences" link, one can get to a searchable index of the journal from 1981 to the present that uses common search terms. The site also provides tables of contents for more recent issues of the journal, and, for a modest fee, one can download individual articles from issues published after January 1, 1999. The index, content, and article availability site is maintained by the publisher, The American Society for Testing and Materials (ASTM). There are current plans to move toward Web-based publication of the journal, although the paper copy will still be available for some time. Individual subscriptions to this essential journal are also available from ASTM for those interested.

Visiting this important Web site on a regular basis and viewing the available abstracts are essential to the early stages of forensic science/forensic evidence research. Also see the recent bibliography prepared by D. J. Werrett, "DNA Evidence," *Proceedings of the 12th INTERPOL Forensic Science Symposium* (1998), at 57–77.

ENDNOTES

1. State v. Bowers, 1999 WL 1100472 (N.C.App. 1999).
2. *Id.* at *3.
3. See State v. Ledford, 315 N.C. 599, 607, 340 S.E.2d 309, 315 (1986).
4. See State v. Lyszaj, 314 N.C. 256, 266, 333 S.E.2d 288, 295 (1985).
5. Andrews v. Florida, 533 So. 2d 842 (Fla. Dist. Ct. App. 1988). See Gianelli and Imwinkelried: *Scientific Evidence* (2d ed. The Michie Company, Charlottesville, VA, 1993), Vol. 2, at 26, for a good discussion of the early days of judicial acceptance of DNA technology.
6. See, generally, Saferstein: *Criminalistics: An Introduction to Forensic Science* (6th ed. Prentice-Hall, Upper Saddle River, NJ, 1998) at 361 (Serology) and 403 (DNA); Robertson and Vignaux: *Interpreting Evidence: Evaluating Forensic Science in the Courtroom* (John Wiley & Sons, New York, 1995); Eckert (Ed.): *Introduction to Forensic Sciences* (2nd ed. CRC Press, 1997); Giannelli and Imwinkelried, supra, note 5, The DNS Genetic Marker, Vol. 2, at 1, and the 1998 Cumulative Supplement, at 1.
7. See, especially, Charles M. Strom: Genetic Justice: A Lawyer's Guide to the Science of DNA Testing, *Illinois Bar Journal,* Vol. 87, No.1 (January, 1999), at 18–26. Also see Giannelli and Imwinkelried, *supra,* note 5, The DNS Genetic Marker, Vol. 2, at 1, and the 1998 Cumulative Supplement, at 1. The supplement contains an extensive bibliography of DNA-related articles from the *Journal of Forensic Sciences* through 1997. Also see D. J. Werrett: "DNA Evidence," *Proceedings of the 12th INTERPOL Forensic Science Symposium* (1998), at 57–77, which contains an excellent bibliography of current references.

8. See the extensive testimony of DNA expert Dr. Robin Cotton in the O. J. Simpson criminal case regarding DNA testing and population projections. Dr. Cotton's testimony provides extensive information about both general and specialized aspects of DNA testing and use in the Cellmark Labs system. This is an excellent introduction to the subject as well as a model for laying a solid foundation for expert witness testimony. See People v. Simpson, Official Transcript, Examination of Robin Cotton, Docket Number BA097211, Superior Court, Los Angeles, Monday, May 15, 1995. Also see the DNA testimony of California DNA expert Gary Simms Tuesday May 23, 1995, in the O. J. Simpson collection on Westlaw.

9. See, e.g., *http://www.gene.com/AE/AB/WYW/index.html* (this Web site entitled "Winding Your Way through DNA," contains comprehensive information from the very beginnings of DNA research to updates on the latest DNA technology used; includes a resource book and copies of national lectures; an article to note is "From Corned Beef to Cloning" setting out an interesting evolution of DNA analysis); *http://www.ncjrs.org/txtfiles/dnaevid.txt* (this site contains a full version of the 1996 report titled "Exoneration by Science: Case Studies in the Use of DNA Evidence to Establish Innocence after Trial," which contains a message from Attorney General Janet Reno, and was completed for the U.S. Department of Justice for providing findings of the use of DNA in exoneration cases); *http://www.faseb.org/opa/bloodsupply/pcr.html* (this site provides both scientific and general background on DNA and the use of PCR) *http://www.ojp.usdoj.gov/nij/dna/welcome.html* (this is the home of the National Commission on the future of DNA evidence).

10. An interesting, broad overview and good graphics for beginners may be seen on the FBI site, under DNA Sequencing, located at *http://www.fbi.gov/kids/crimedet/dna/dnameth.htm.*

11. See, e.g., Bruce Budowle and Tamyra R. Moretti: "Genotype Profiles for Six Population Groups at the 13 CODIS Short Tandem Repeat Core Loci and Other PCR-Based Loci," located at *http://www.fbi.gov/* ; Alice R. Isenberg and Jodi M. Moore: "Mitochondrial DNA Analysis at the FBI Laboratory," Forensic Science Publications, located at *http://www.fbi.gov/programs/lab/fsc/current/dnslist.htm*; R. E. Gaensslen and J. L. Peterson: "Blind Proficiency Testing: The Experience with DNA Labs," located at *http://www.fbi.gov/programs/lab/fsc/current/abstractc.htm*. Also see U.S. Department of Justice, CODIS and NDIS press release, regarding computer systems update, located at *http://www.fbi.gov/pressrm/pressrel/98archives/dna.htm.*

12. See the Web page for the European Directory of DNA Laboratories (EDDNAL) listing contacts and addresses for 280 European DNA laboratories, located at *http://www.eddnal.com.*

13. See "Presentations at the International Symposium on Setting Quality Standards for the Forensic Community" (May 3–7, 1999), *Forensic Science Communications* Vol. I, No. 2 (July 1999) (back issues), located at *http://wwwfbi.gov/programs/lab/fsc/back-issu/july1999/sananton.htm*. This presentation summarizes important papers from the key working groups sponsored by the FBI, whose standards are certain to be either very influential or followed to the letter by American and European courts. Subjects include DNA Analysis Methods; Statistics; DNA Advisory Board Standards and Forensic Science Laboratory Accreditation Criteria; Blind Proficiency Testing in DNA Labs; and Accreditation Standards.

14. See "The Scientific Program—5th International DNA Fingerprint Conference," located at *http://www.webstudio.co.za/fingerprinting/scientificprogram.htm*. Papers

were scheduled for presentation in late January 1999. Topics include Ancient and Mitochondrial DNS; Medical and Forensic Applications of DNA Profiling; Animal Applications of DNA Fingerprinting; Plant Applications of DNA Fingerprinting; New Approaches to DNA Fingerprinting; DNA Fingerprinting of Microorganisms.

15. Charles M. Strom, *supra*, note 7. This is an excellent introduction to this most complex topic, written by the director of medical genetics and the DNA laboratory at Illinois Masonic Medical Center in Chicago. He is also qualified as an expert in Illinois courts on DNA testing.
16. In addition to Strom, *Id*., see D. H. Kaye: "DNA, NAS, NRC, DAB, RFLP, PCR, and More: An Introduction to the Symposium on the 1996 NRC Report on Forensic DNA Evidence," 37 *Jurimetrics J*. 395 (1997); Peter Donnelly and Richard D. Friedman: "DNA Database Searches and the Legal Consumption of Scientific Evidence," 97 *Mich. L. Rev.* 931 (1999) (excellent analysis of the National Research Council Reports I and III respecting the considerable statistical issues associated with population projections after a laboratory *match* opinion is proffered).
17. Strom, *supra,* at 19. The article also addresses the several modes of DNA contamination, so central to the O. J. Simpson case: natural contamination at the crime scene; contamination by evidence technologists; contamination in the crime laboratory; and contamination in the DNA laboratory. Dr. Strom also discusses the important subject of laboratory certification and proficiency testing conducted by the American Association of Blood Banks (AABB), which licenses laboratories performing paternity testing, and the College of American Pathology (CAP), which accredits DNA laboratories and has a proficiency testing program for paternity testing and forensic testing. However, no certificate or license can assure that the DNA testing performed in any case has been done properly and interpreted correctly.
18. See "Trace Evidence Recovery Guidelines," Scientific Working Group on Materials Analysis (SWGMAT), located at *http://www.fbi.gov/programs/lab/fs/current/trace.htm*.
19. See *http://www.fbi.gov/programs/lab/org/organiz.htm*.
20. The handbook may be seen at *http://www.fbi.gov/programs/lab/handbook/intro.htm*.
21. "Genetic Tests Highlight Errors in Justice," 12/28/99 *Kan. City Star* B6. These DNA tests were primarily fostered by volunteer lawyers and other support groups, such as Professor Barry Scheck and Peter Neufeld's Innocence Project at the Cardozo School of Law. See, Barry Scheck, Peter Neufeld, and Jim Dwyer: *Actual Innocence* (Doubleday, New York, 2000).
22. 725 ILCS 5/116-3 (Appv'd 07/14/99). New York, the only state with a similar law, limits the type of post-trial forensic testing to DNA.
23. G. O'Reilly: "A Second Chance for Justice: Illinois Post-Trial Forensic Testing Law" 81 *Judicature* 114 (1997).
24. *Id*. at 116.
25. Strom, *supra*, note 7, at 25.
26. See, Dissent, Dedge v. State, 723 So.2d 322, 324(Fla.Ct.App. 1998).
27. Strom, *Genetic Justice: A Lawyer's Guide to the Science of DNA Testing, supra*, note 7.
28. O'Reilly, *supra*, note 23, at 116.
29. People v. Dunn, 306 Ill.App.3d 75, 713 N.E.2d 568 (First Dist. 1999).
30. *Id*. at 571.
31. *Id*.
32. Pace v. State, 1999 WL 1087018 (Ga. 1999).

33. *Id.* at *2.
34. *Id.* at *3.
35. See Clarence Page: "When Innocence Isn't Good Enough," *Chicago Tribune*, Monday, January 3, 2000.
36. Thomas v. State, 1999 WL 1267801 (Ala.Crim.App. 1999).
37. *Id.* at *5.
38. Plain error is error that has or probably has adversely affected a substantial right of the appellant, or is so obvious that the failure to notice it would seriously affect the fairness or integrity of the judicial proceedings. *Id.* at *5. See Howard v. State, 108 Ala. 571, 18 So. 813 (1895).
39. *Supra*, note 36, at *26.
40. For cases characterizing DNA evidence as circumstantial, see, for example, People v. Groves, 854 P.2d 1310, 1315 (Colo.App.1992); Greenway v. State, 207 Ga.App. 511, 428 S.E.2d 415, 416 (1993); People v. Stremmel, 258 Ill.App.3d 93, 630 N.E.2d 1301, 1307, 197 Ill.Dec. 177 (1994); State v. Spaeth, 552 N.W.2d 187, 192–93 (Minn. 1996); Parker v. State, 606 So.2d 1132, 1140–41 (Miss. 1992). See also Edward J. Imwinkelried et al.: *Courtroom Criminal Evidence*, Vol.1, § 308 (3d ed., LEXIS Law Publishing, Charlottesville, VA, 1998) (noting that "many types of circumstantial evidence such as DNA tests are highly reliable"). Also see State v. Mosely, 338 N.C. 1, 449 S.E.2d 412, 433 (1994), cert. denied, 514 U.S. 1091, 115 S.Ct. 1815, 131 L.Ed.2d 738 (1995), for a case reference to a DNA match as direct evidence.
41. In specific regard to chain-of-custody requirements for critical DNA evidence, the National Research Council observed: "Even the strongest evidence will be worthless—or worse, might possibly lead to a false conviction—if the evidence sample did not originate in connection with the crime. Given the great individuating potential of DNA evidence and the relative ease with which it can be mishandled or manipulated by the careless or the unscrupulous, the integrity of the chain of custody is of paramount importance." National Research Council, The Evaluation of Forensic DNA Evidence 25 (1996) (hereinafter "1996 NRC Report.") Also see State v. Morel, 676 A.2d 1347, 1356 (R.I. 1996) ("[I]n the preservation and testing of DNA evidence, careful attention and proper handling of the crime sample by police and scientists are crucial in defending chain-of-custody issues and in ensuring that laboratory mislabeling and inadvertent contamination have not occurred." *Reference Manual on Scientific Evidence*, at 293 [Federal Judicial Center, 1994]); Sally E. Renskers: "Comment, Trial by Certainty: Implications of Genetic DNA Fingerprints," 39 *Em.L.J.* 309, 316–17 (1990).
42. See Imwinkelried et al., *supra*, note 40; Vol. 1, § 503, at 134–37.
43. State v. Armstead, 342 Md. 38, 673 A.2d 221 (1996).
44. People v. Miller, 173 Ill.2d 167, 670 N.E.2d 721 (1996).
45. *Id.* at 176.
46. *Id.* at 721, 730.
47. See State v. Anderson, 118 N.M. 284, 881 P.2d 29 (1994); Springfield v. State, 860 P.2d 435 (Wyo. 1993); or United States v. Jakobetz, 955 F.2d 786 (2d Cir. 1992), for a more extensive discussion of this topic.
48. *Supra*, note 44, at 185–186.
49. *Id.* at 187.
50. See People v. Stremmel, 258 Ill.App.3d 93, 197 Ill.Dec. 177, 630 N.E.2d 1301 (1994); People v. Watson, 257 Ill.App.3d 915, 196 Ill.Dec. 89, 629 N.E.2d 634 (1994); People v. Mehlberg, 249 Ill.App.3d 499, 188 Ill.Dec. 598, 618 N.E.2d 1168 (1993); People

v. Miles, 217 Ill.App.3d 393, 160 Ill.Dec. 347, 577 N.E.2d 477 (1991); People v. Lipscomb, 215 Ill.App.3d 413, 158 Ill.Dec. 952, 574 N.E.2d 1345 (1991). All of these cases agree that the theory underlying DNA profiling and the RFLP matching technique is generally accepted in the relevant scientific community.

51. See, e.g., Harmon v. State, 908 P.2d 434, 440 (Alaska App. 1995); Taylor v. State, 889 P.2d 319, 333 (Okla.Crim.App. 1995); State v. Cauthron, 120 Wash.2d 879, 896–97, 846 P.2d 502, 511 (1993) (citing 15 cases that support general acceptance of RFLP testing); United States v. Porter, 618 A.2d 629, 636 (D.C.App. 1992).

52. Ross v. State, 231 Ga.App. 793, 499 S.E.2d 642 (Ga.Ct.App. 1998).

53. *Id.* at 646.

54. *Id.* at 797. Also see Boone v. State, 224 Ga.App. 563, 564(3), 481 S.E.2d 569 (1997).

55. Chapel v. State, 270 Ga. 151, 510 S.E.2d 802 (1998).

56. *Id.* at 808. Also see State v. Cauthron, 120 Wash.2d 879, 846 P.2d 502, 511–512 (1993) (*en banc*); Fishback v. People, 851 P.2d 884, 887 n. 6, 893 (Colo. 1993); State v. Marcus, 294 N.J.Sup. 267, 683 A.2d 221, 233 (1996).

57. State v. Brown, 719 So.2d 146 (La.Ct.App. 1998).

58. *Id.* at 4.

59. *Id.* at 8.

60. *Id.* at 7.

61. People v. The Almighty Four Hundred, 287 Ill.App.3d 123, 677 N.E.2d 1332 (1997).

62. *Id.* at 127.

63. *Id.* at 128.

64. *Id.* at 129. Also see People v. Venegas, 18 Cal.4th 47, 954 P.2d 525 (1998) (there is scientific consensus that the National Research Council "modified ceiling" method used to calculate the statistical probabilities of DNA match is forensically reliable); Commonwealth v. Blasiol, 552 Pa. 149, 713 A.2d 1117 (1998) (statistical evidence based upon "product rule" method of analyzing DNA test results was admissible in courts of state); People v. Dalcollo, 282 Ill.App.3d 944, 669 N.E.2d 378 (Ill.Ct.App. 1996) (method used by FBI for calculating statistical probability of random match between DNA in crime scene sample and defendant's DNA, whereby FBI used product rule to estimate frequency of particular DNA test sample occurring in population unit by comparing DNA sample to previously constructed population database, was generally accepted in scientific community).

65. *Supra*, note 61.

66. *Id.* at 1312.

67. *Id.* at 132. The court stated in pertinent part: "For whatever it's worth, I will allow the witness to testify to that this [sic] is a common practice for validating the process and the database. So I will allow her to testify to that under it being basically a business records. This is the way this type of procedure is followed in order to do this and that these are the common procedures that people do it and go through it. I'll allow it in as a business practice more or less, and I will allow her to answer that question."

68. *Id.* at 132. See People v. Contreras, 246 Ill.App.3d 502, 511, 186 Ill.Dec. 204, 615 N.E.2d 1261 (1993); People v. Lipscomb, 215 Ill.App.3d 413, 435, 158 Ill.Dec. 952, 574 N.E.2d 1345 (1991).

69. Thomas v. State, 1999 WL 1267801 (Ala.Crim.App. 1999).

70. The National Research Council (NRC) has generated several primary sources cited almost universally in judicial decisions assessing DNA forensic analysis and the associated statistics. The NRC is a private, nonprofit society of distinguished scholars that is administered by the National Academy of Sciences, the National Academy of

Engineering, and the Institute of Medicine. The NRC formed the Committee on DNA
Technology in Forensic Science to study the use of DNA analysis for forensic
purposes, resulting in the issuance of a report in 1992. See Committee on DNA
Technology in Forensic Science, National Research Council: DNA Technology in
Forensic Science (1992); see, generally, State v. Marcus, 294 N.J.Sup. 267, 683 A.2d
221, 227 n. 6 (1996). A new committee was subsequently formed to study recent
developments in the field, which also issued a frequently cited report. See 1996 NRC
Report; see, generally, R. Stephen Kramer: "Comment, Admissibility of DNA Statistical Data: A Proliferation of Misconceptions," 30 *Cal.W.L.Rev.* 145, 147 and n.
17 (Fall, 1993) (noting that courts have traditionally deferred to pronouncements from
the National Academy of Sciences), citing Rorie Sherman: "DNA Unraveling,"
Natl L.J. 1, 30 (Feb. 1, 1993); Commonwealth v. Blasioli, 552 Pa. 149, 713 A.2d
1117, 1119–20 n. 3 (Pa. 1998).

71. *Supra*, note 69, at *46. The 1996 NCR Report states that "[i]n general, the calculation
    of a profile frequency should be made with the product rule." See also Giannelli and
    Imwinkelried, *supra*, note 5, Vol. 2, § 18-4, at 12 (Supp. 1998) ("With some modi-
    fications for special situations, the 1996 report endorses the use of the traditional
    product rule to compute the random match probability").

72. See Watts v. State, 733 So.2d 214, 226 (Miss. 1999) (citing court opinions from 14
    states for its observation that "courts which have considered the admissibility of
    statistical evidence based on the product rule have determined that the challenges to
    its use have been sufficiently resolved" and its finding that "the product rule has been
    accepted in the scientific community and found to be a reliable method of calculating
    population frequency data"); State v. Kinder, 942 S.W.2d 313, 327 (Mo. 1996), cert.
    denied, 522 U.S. 854, 118 S.Ct. 149, 139 L.Ed.2d 95 ("the overwhelming majority
    of recent cases in other jurisdictions ... approve the use of the product rule"); State
    v. Loftus, 573 N.W.2d 167, 174 (S.D. 1997) ("an overwhelming amount of scientific
    commentary and legal authority exist" resolving any earlier dispute concerning DNA
    statistical evidence, and the "product rule method ... is now generally accepted in the
    relevant scientific community"); People v. Chandler, 211 Mich.App. 604, 536 N.W.2d
    799, 803 (1995), cert. denied, 453 Mich. 883, 554 N.W.2d 12 (1996). See, for
    example, the following cases finding the product rule evidence admissible under the
    Daubert test: United States v. Chischilly, 30 F.3d 1144, 1153 (9th Cir. 1994), cert.
    denied, 513 U.S. 1132 (1995); State v. Loftus, 573 N.W.2d 167 (S.D. 1997). Also
    see the following cases relying, in part, on the 1996 NRC Report in upholding use
    of the product rule: State v. Marshall, 193 Ariz. 547, 975 P.2d 137, 141 (Ariz.App.
    1998), quoting State v. Johnson, 186 Ariz. 329, 922 P.2d 294, 299 (Ariz.1996)
    ("Endorsement by the NRC 'is strong evidence of general acceptance within the
    relevant scientific community' "); Clark v. State, 679 So.2d 321, 321 (Fla.App. 1996)
    ("product rule calculations are appropriate as a matter of scientific fact and law");
    State v. Kinder, 942 S.W.2d 313, 327 (Mo. 1996), cert. denied, 522 U.S. 854, 118
    S.Ct. 149, 139 L.Ed.2d 95 (1997); State v. Freeman, 253 Neb. 385, 571 N.W.2d 276,
    293 (Neb. 1997); State v. Copeland, 130 Wash.2d 244, 922 P.2d 1304, 1319–20 and
    n. 6 (Wash. 1996).

73. Thomas, *supra*, note 69, at *35.

74. 1996 NRC Report. See also State v. Morel, *supra*, note 41; Renskers, *supra,* note 41.

75. "Blood specimens ... should be handled with the greatest of care and all persons who
    handle the specimen should be ready to identify it and testify to its custody and
    unchanged condition," Imwinkelried et al., *supra*, note 40, Vol. 1, § 503, at 134–37.

Also see Ex parte Holton, 590 So.2d 918, 919–20 (Ala. 1991) for an extended discussion of the chain-of-custody question.

76. The PCR technique involves three basic phases: "First, a fragment of DNA is extracted from a sample of evidence. Second, during the amplification phase, millions of copies of the fragment are created by mixing the sample with enzymes, chemicals, and primers. Third, the finished product is tested for comparison with a known DNA sample from a victim or suspect." See United States v. Hicks, 103 F.3d 837 (9th Cir. 1996).

77. See Dedge v. State, *supra*, note 26.

78. *Modern Scientific Evidence*, C. Wecht (Ed.), Vol. 1, "Forensic Identification," § 16-3.0 at 679 (New York, 1997).

79. D. J. Werrett, *"DNA Evidence," supra*, note 7, at 61. See the excellent bibliography of current references associated with this paper.

80. People v. Davis, 185 Ill.2d 317, 706 N.E.2d 473 (1999).

81. *Id*. Dr. Violette Hnilica, the forensic pathologist who performed the autopsy, testified that the body was decomposing and swollen. Hnilica used dental records to make a positive identification of the body as Gwinn. She also identified injuries to the body including torn skin on the right side of the mouth and cheek; "broken back" fingernails; bruises on the upper abdomen, shoulders, and right side of the head; hemorrhages and tissue compression in the neck; a blunt-force injury to the scalp; and bruises in the vagina. Hnilica stated that the cause of death was strangulation and blunt-force injuries, and that the victim's injuries were consistent with sexual assault.

82. *Id*. at 477.

83. Miller v. State, 977 P.2d 1099 (Ct.App.Okla. 1998).

84. *Id*. The court ruled that when, as here, the state introduces only circumstantial evidence, that evidence is sufficient to prove guilt only if, when viewed in the light most favorable to the state, it rules out every reasonable hypothesis other than guilt. Also see Bryan v. State, 1997 OK CR 15, § 37, 935 P.2d 338, 358, cert. denied, 118 S.Ct. 383, 139 L.Ed.2d 299 (1997); Cheatham v. State, 1995 OK CR 32, § 26, 900 P.2d 414, 422.

85. People v. Buss, 187 Ill.2d 144, 718 N.E.2d 1 (1999).

86. Dr. Edward Pavlik, an expert in forensic odontology, testified that he was asked to assist in identifying the body recovered in Hunting Area 7. Based on the development of the teeth in the body and a comparison of these teeth to photographs of Christopher's teeth before his death, Pavlik determined that the body belonged to Christopher. Dr. Larry Blum, an expert in forensic pathology, testified that he performed the autopsy of Christopher's body. The body was unclothed and showed signs of decomposition. Blum found a contusion to Christopher's jaw and 52 stab wounds and cuts on the body, primarily to the chest, abdomen, and back. In Blum's opinion, the stab and slash wounds were made by a sharp, single-edged knife that was relatively long and narrow. This knife could have been a fillet knife. There was also evidence that this type of knife had been used to cut Christopher's genital area; his external genitalia were missing. None of Christopher's wounds, including one stab wound to his heart and 12 to his lungs, was sufficient to cause immediate death. Blum opined that the cause of death was multiple stab wounds. Haskell, a forensic entomologist, explained that certain insects are attracted to human remains, sometimes within seconds of death, and lay their eggs in these remains. Based on the stage of development of the insects found in a corpse, a precise estimation of the time of death may be obtained. Haskell analyzed the insects recovered from Christopher's body, as well as the

environmental conditions to which the body had been subjected. He concluded that the time of death was most likely sometime before sunset on August 7. *Id*. at 168–169.
87. *Id*. at 170–171.
88. State v. Carter, 255 Neb. 591, 586 N.W.2d 818 (1998).
89. *Id*. at 596.
90. *Id*. at 599.
91. *Id*. Both sources showed identical polymarker traits: LDLR type A,B; GYPA type A,B; HBGG type A,A; D7S8 type A,A; and GC type B,B. All three of the expert witnesses in this case testified that the DQ Alpha and polymarker testing used in this case, performed using the PCR process, is generally accepted in the relevant scientific community.
92. *Id*. at 600, 827.
93. People v. Allen, 72 Cal.App.4th 1093, 85 Cal.Rptr.2d 655 (Cal.Ct.App. 1999).
94. *Id*. at 1097.
95. "[O]nce a trial court has admitted evidence based upon a new scientific technique, and that decision is affirmed on appeal by a published appellate decision, the precedent so established may control subsequent trials, at least until new evidence is presented reflecting a change in the attitude of the scientific community." People v. Kelly, 17 Cal.3d at 32, 130 Cal.Rptr. 144, 549 P.2d 1240 (1976). Also see People v. Morganti, 43 Cal.App.4th at 666, 50 Cal.Rptr.2d 837 (1996) (pointing out that although PCR evidence had not been found admissible in any published California case, "courts in other jurisdictions have concluded that PCR analysis of DQ Alpha is generally accepted as reliable in the scientific community").
96. Commonwealth v. Rosier, 425 Mass. 807, 685 N.E.2d 739 (1997).
97. *Id*. at 743.
98. State v. Jackson, 255 Neb. 68, 582 N.W.2d 317 (1998).
99. *Id*. at 325.
100. Allen, *supra*, note 93, at 1101. See People v. Smith, 215 Cal.App.3d 19, 25, 263 Cal.Rptr. 678 (1989) (in determining whether a particular technique is generally accepted a defendant is not foreclosed from showing new information which may question the continuing reliability of the test in question or to show a change in the consensus within the scientific community concerning the scientific technique).
101. See "What Is STADNAP?" located at *http://www.STADNAP.uni-mainz.de/summary.htm*.
102. *Id*. The topics of the current exercises are (1) Pentameric STR systems, (2) efficiency of STR typing from artificially degraded DNA, (3) Y-chromosomal STR systems, and (4) mitochondrial DNA typing by enhanced mutation detection.
103. See L. A. Foreman, A. M. Smith, and I. W. Evett: "Bayesian Validation of a Quadruplex STR Profiling System for Identification Purposes," 44 *J. Forensic Sciences*, No. 3 (1999), at 478–486. Also see "Genotype Profiles for Six Population Groups at the 13 Codis Short Tandem Repeat Core Loci and Other PCR-Based Loci," *Forensic Communications*, Vol. I, No. 2, July, 1999, located at *http://www.fbi.gov/programs/lab/fsc/backissu/july*; The European DNA Profiling Group (EDNAP) located at *http://www.unimainz.de/FB/Medizin/Rechmedizin/ednap/group.htm* and the EDNAP Group's European Frequency Database Collection for Short Tandem Repeat (STR) Systems, located at *http://www.usc.es/~isfh/*. Also see the very useful European Directory of DNA Laboratories (EDDNAL, located at *http://www.EDDNAL.com*.
104. See Alice R. Isenberg and Jodi M. Moore: "Mitochondrial DNA Analysis at the FBI Laboratory," *Forensic Science Communications*, Vol. I, No. 2, July 1999, located at

http://www.fbi.gov/programs/lab/fsc/current/dnalist.htm., covering background, a six-step analysis procedure, interpretation guidelines, population database, and reporting statistics. This will undoubtedly be a major supportive document for the use of mtDNA identifications in criminal trials.

105. For example, Tennessee has a statute governing the admissibility of DNA, which provides, in part, as follows:

(a) As used in this section, unless the context otherwise requires, "DNA analysis" means the process through which deoxyribonucleic acid (DNA) in a human biological specimen is analyzed and compared with DNA from another biological specimen for identification purposes.

(b) (1) In any civil or criminal trial, hearing or proceeding, the results of DNA analysis, as defined in subsection (a), are admissible in evidence without antecedent expert testimony that DNA analysis provides a trustworthy and reliable method of identifying characteristics in an individual's genetic material upon a showing that the offered testimony meets the standards of admissibility set forth in the Tennessee Rules of Evidence.

(2) Nothing in this section shall be construed as prohibiting any party in a civil or criminal trial from offering proof that DNA analysis does not provide a trustworthy and reliable method of identifying characteristics in an individual's genetic material, nor shall it prohibit a party from cross-examining the other party's expert as to the lack of trustworthiness and reliability of such analysis.

Tenn.Code Ann. § 24-7-117

106. In State v. Scott, 1999 WL 547460 (Tenn.Crim.App.), involving mtDNA analysis of a hair identified as defendant's in a sexual assault case, defendant complained the terms of the statute authorized the admission of novel scientific evidence such as mtDNA without a showing that the evidence was reliable. Defendant argued that the mitochondrial technique was not even developed until June 1996, and that his case was only the fourth in the country in which this type of evidence had been admitted. The defendant unsuccessfully argued that the portion of the DNA statute which provided that the evidence was admissible "upon a showing that the ... testimony meets the standards of admissibility set forth in the Tennessee Rules of Evidence" requires that the state show the evidence is scientifically reliable.

107. State v. Council, 335 S.C. 1, 515 S.E.2d 508 (1999).

108. *Id.* at 516. Also see Brian Huseman: "Taylor v. State, Rule 706, and the DNA Database: Future Directions in DNA Evidence," 22 *Oklahoma City University L.Rev.* 397 (1997); Mark Curriden, "A New Evidence Tool: First Use of Mitochondrial DNA Test in a U.S. Criminal Trial," 82 Nov. *A.B.A. J.* 18 (1996).

109. *Supra,* note 107, at 517.

110. State v. Underwood, 518 S.E.2d 231 (Ct.App.N.C. 1999).

111. *Id.* After Gunnarsson disappeared, defendant had his car cleaned and trunk mat shampooed at a car wash. He later painted the trunk's interior to hide small scratch marks and a faint footprint. Despite the cleaning, several hairs were found embedded in the trunk mat. The hairs matched those of Gunnarsson when examined by mtDNA analysis. Any person in Gunnarsson's maternal blood line would have the same mtDNA sequence; however, Gunnarsson's family lives in Sweden.

112. *Id.* at 238. Also see 1996 NRC Report.

113. See N.C. Gen.Stat. § 8C-1, Rule 401 (1992). This is the basic relevancy definition followed in all state and federal courts.

114. *Supra*, note 110, at 239. Also see State v. Council, *supra*, note 107.
115. Also see State v. Ware, 1999 WL 233592 (Tenn.Crim.App.), also involving mtDNA analysis of hair in the rape murder of a 4-year-old female child. Also see 3 No. 11 Mealey's Daubert Report 12, for a reference to a very recent Pennsylvania pretrial ruling that mitochondrial mtDNA "has become generally accepted in the relevant scientific community." Commonwealth v. Rorrer, No. 3080 Philadelphia 1998, Pa. Super.
116. State v. Torres, 1999 WL 42326 (Conn.Super.).
117. *Id* at *1.
118. *Id*. at *2.
119. *The Toronto Globe and Mail* reports the matching of the blood of a dog, killed along with his owner in a 6-year-old murder case. Experts testified that blood on the defendant's shirt matched both that of the human victim but also that of his pet dog Chico. Experts testified to an 8 billion to 1 match with the dog's DNA. See 10/02/1999 *GlobeMail*, A10. A similar finding was testified to in the case of a double-murder in Seattle. Experts testified to a match of the victim's dog's blood, which had also been shot, to blood from the defendants' jackets. The DNA lab, PE AgGen, matched bloodstains on the two defendants' jackets and testified to a 1 in 350 million match. In New York, a man was convicted of murder based in part on the hair from defendant's cat, which had been found on a jacket discarded at the crime scene near the body of the homicide victim. Experts at the National Cancer Institute in Frederick, Maryland, who had been studying cat DNA for years, testified to a 1 in 45 million match between defendant's cat and the jacket he had thrown away at the crime scene dump site. See *Source News and Reports*, April 24, 1997. In Canon Lake, Texas, investigators have used DNA testing to identify a dog believed to have mauled a 77-year-old woman, available at *http://www.reporternews.com/texas/dogdna0515.html*.
120. See State v. Bogan, 183 Ariz. 506, 905 P.2d 515 (1995) (results of randomly amplified polymorphic DNA, RAPD, testing of seedpods from palo verde trees were admissible and expert testimony declaring "match" between palo verde seedpods found in defendant's truck and a palo verde tree growing at the crime scene was admissible).
121. See George Sensabaugh and D. H. Kaye: "Non-human DNA Evidence," 38 *Jurimetrics J*. 1 (1998) for an extensive discussion of this general issue.
122. See the following Web sites that address varying aspects of important animal DNA issues. These sites are important for obtaining nonhuman DNA in cases of mammals:
    Wildlife Forensic DNA Lab,
        trentu.ca/academic/forensic/labservices.html
    Breaking the Canine Genetic Code,
        http://www.canismajor.com/dog/gencode.html
    The Dog Genome Project,
        http://www.mendel.berkeley.edu/dog.html

11 Forensic Anthropology and Entomology

Full fathom five thy father lies,
Of his bones are coral made;
Those are pearls that were his eyes:
Nothing of him that doth fade
But doth suffer a sea change
Into something rich and strange.

—Shakespeare
The Tempest, Act I, Sc. 2.

I. ANTHROPOLOGY

This chapter briefly addresses the significant contributions made to the criminal justice system by the academic disciplines of anthropology and entomology. The theory and methods developed by scholars in these two fields have provided consistent and ongoing aid in the identification of the remains of homicide victims and in narrowing the range of time-of-death determinations. The analysis of human remains to reveal our cultural antecedents can also reveal much about the identity or general profiles of unidentified remains. The close study of the universe of insect species can be narrowed to species that consistently accompany the deterioration of the human body and provide investigative timelines of often decisive value to the state and defendant alike. The principles and practice of these two academic subjects are used in the fields of forensic anthropology and forensic entomology on a regular basis in the investigation and trial of criminal cases.

There are a number of discrete aspects of forensic anthropology with which the lawyer must be aware, as in the anticipated use of any other forensic discipline. The basic question of just what forensic anthropology can or cannot do as an aid to criminal investigation must be answered.[1] This is especially important with forensic disciplines such as forensic anthropology and forensic entomology, which are academic, university-based sciences where the forensic aspects are not the major focus or *raison d'etre* for their study. There is a lot to know in these two fields that has little to do with the identification of human remains or estimating a time of death.

How does a forensic anthropologist differ from a university anthropologist not associated with criminal investigations? Is the fact that prominent practitioners in this field are typically university professors of any importance? It is important to understand that here, as in all other forensic sciences or disciplines, opinion statements come in the same class or individualistic forms. There are a number of important investigative basic questions that may be readily answered by forensic anthropologists examining human skeletal remains.

Is it a bone at all, as opposed to plastics or tree roots? Is it a human as opposed to an animal bone? What bones are there from a total of 100% of the human skeletal structure and why those if less than total? Are missing bones the result of animal scavengers or human agency? Are the bones of more than one person present? If so is there any indication of the length of time all such bones have been there? What is the sex? What is the age range? What is the left- or right-handed status? What is the general type of build? What are the distinguishing dental traits? Does there appear to be a history of bone injuries? Are there any indications of disease processes? Finally, can experts pinpoint the racial characteristics of the person as claimed by forensic hair analysts?

A relatively new field utilized by investigators that is a staple of anthropological research is that of cranial/facial reconstruction techniques used to identify an individual from a skull.[2] Given the massive deaths in contemporary wars, forensic anthropology has once again been challenged to aid in the identification of war crimes.[3]

There are a number of excellent scholarly[4] and popular[5] books and articles devoted to the study of various levels and subdisciplines in the field of forensic anthropology, which will make for interesting or required examination for lawyers increasingly involved in the use of forensic anthropological techniques in the investigation and prosecution of a homicide. There are also a growing number of excellent and comprehensive Web sites devoted to anthropology proper and to the field of forensic anthropology.[6]

II. FORENSIC ANTHROPOLOGY CASES

The primary uses of anthropology in the investigation of crime have been in the identification of unidentified human remains and the analysis of skeletal parts to determine wounds indicating the basic nature of the death-dealing encounter. Given the prestigious pedigree of anthropology and the rigorous schooling and fieldwork associated with this discipline, there are few cases addressing any significant qualification issues in respect to academic anthropologists. However, as new techniques or theories emerge in the academy arena, foundational issues will follow the professors to the courtroom. Several of these areas will be touched upon in the discussion to follow.

The use of cranial reconstruction combined with photographic overlays was the key to a murder victim's identification in *State v. Nyhuis,*[7] a 1995 capital murder case. Photographs provided by the defendant and photographs obtained from his missing wife's immigration file were sent, along with photographs of two other missing females, to a forensic pathologist for overlay comparison with a skull. The pathologist determined that the skull was compatible only with the photographs of the wife.

A forensic anthropologist who specialized in identifying skeletal remains of unknown victims made a facial reconstruction from the skull. The anthropologist provided the Missouri State Highway Patrol with a photograph of the facial reconstruction. He also gave them an estimation of the victim's age, height, and weight, and informed them that the victim was an Asian female. After the Highway Patrol published the photograph, it received a phone call stating that the photograph resembled the defendant's wife, Bunchee Nyhuis.

The state offered the skeletal remains to illustrate the wounds and to demonstrate how the victim was identified. The cause of death, the nature of the victim's wound, and the identity of the victim were all at issue. The skull and bones helped to illuminate these issues and were thus probative. The appellate court ruled that the trial court did not abuse its discretion in admitting the skeletal remains.[8]

In *State v. Bondurant*,[9] the defendant was convicted of murder and arson. An excavation revealed burned human cranial fragments mixed with charcoal and burned soil. Dr. Bass, a forensic anthropologist, found seven cranial bone fragments that were large enough to make positive identifications. While the other bone fragments were too small to identify positively the area of the skull they came from, he was certain that they were human skull fragments. From studying the larger fragments, Dr. Bass testified that the bones appeared to have been broken before being burned, and that the irregular broken edges suggested that blunt trauma had occurred. He was more than 50% certain that some force had been applied to the skull before it was burned. Moreover, based on the thickness of six larger fragments that could be measured, Dr. Bass was 75% certain that the bones were from a human male, and he was 90% certain that the bones had been there 1 to 15 years.[10]

On occasion, human remains are subject to examination by forensic anthropologists long after death or burial has occurred, and nonetheless have yielded dispositive information about the existence of criminal agency. In *State v. Delgros*,[11] the defendant was convicted of a double murder. On January 3, 1978, a fire broke out at the residence of appellant and Donald D. Morris, her husband. They lived in a mobile home with Christopher Styles, John Styles, and Edward Bridge, appellant's children from two previous marriages. Donald Morris and Christopher Styles were found dead, and the other two children were seriously burned, but they ultimately recovered from their injuries. Appellant did not suffer any injuries. After the blaze, questions were raised concerning the cause of the fire, but the county coroner determined that, since both bodies had been severely burned as a result of the fire, the deaths were accidental. The file was reopened in 1993.

Another witness noted that when he had viewed the bodies in the morgue, Morris appeared to be missing an ear. Even though the body had been severely burned, he noted the charred remnants of one ear but not the other.

Edward Bridge, who had a lengthy criminal record and who was confined to prison in Pennsylvania stemming from a rape conviction, was contacted by police and stated that he had witnessed defendant strike Morris on the head, knocking him to the floor. According to Bridge, she then obtained a knife, stabbed Morris four or five times, poured some liquid by the furnace, and then set fire to the trailer.[12]

On the basis of this information, the bodies of the decedents were exhumed. The state contacted Summit County Coroner, Dr. Samuel Cox, and Dr. Douglas Owsley, a forensic anthropologist employed by the Smithsonian Institution, who conducted independent examinations of the remains. They both concluded that Morris had sustained multiple stab wounds to the back prior to the fire. Owsley examined the body and presented testimony using the actual bones during his presentation. However, at the conclusion of state's case, the prosecutor requested that the court admit the slides in evidence in place of the actual bones. After hearing the objection, and conducting an *in camera* inspection of the slides and the witness's proposed testimony, the court allowed the substitution. The court ruled that the substitution was appropriate, holding that the slides would be a better substitution than the actual bones themselves.[13]

On occasion, the use of statistics is combined with the tools of forensic anthropology to establish or assist in the identification of human remains. In *State v. Klindt*,[14] defendant was convicted of murdering his wife and using a chain saw to dismember the body. Joyce Klindt disappeared from her Davenport, Iowa, home on March 18, 1983 and on April 16, 1983, fishermen found a female torso lodged against a bank of the Mississippi River. The torso had been severed just above the navel and just below the hips. A pathologist testified that a mechanical saw, probably a chain saw, had been used to cut up the body. The state was faced with the task of identifying the torso as that of defendant's wife Joyce.

A statistician testified that the torso found in the river was more likely to be that of Joyce Klindt than any other person who had been reported missing in the area. Investigating officers had developed a list of all the white females who had been reported missing in a four-state area around Davenport as of April 16, 1983, the date the torso was discovered. This list, originally containing data on 17 women, was narrowed by eliminating those who had obvious identifying characteristics such as scars. Four missing women remained on the list, including Joyce Klindt.

Dr. Russell Lenth testified that, as a statistical analyst, he takes data or facts that are known and attempts to determine what is likely to be true by applying the mathematical laws of probability. He testified that he was furnished with data on the torso, including race, sex, age range, and blood type. He also considered the fact that the torso had borne a child, had had an episiotomy (a surgical procedure in connection with childbirth), and that it had not been surgically sterilized. Evidence showed Joyce Klindt fell within all of these categories. From other sources, Lenth obtained information concerning some of these conditions with respect to the other three missing women and determined the frequency of certain of these conditions among the general female population. Based upon the likelihood of the concurrence of those factors among the missing women, Lenth testified that the probabilities were over 99% that the torso was Joyce Klindt's rather than any of the other three. The court concluded that the statistical evidence utilized to identify the body was properly admitted.

Pinpointing the race of the individual's remains goes a long way toward aiding identification in certain cases, but is still a controversial subject. As noted by Pickering and Bachman in their recent treatise, *The Use of Forensic Anthropology:*

> It is important to recognize that of all the major biological variables, this one [determining race] is perhaps the most difficult and easiest to misidentify. For this reason, your consulting anthropologist may not always be able to determine the race.[15]

In *Pipkin v. State*,[16] the defendant was convicted of murder. The defendant argued that his trial counsel was ineffective for failing to challenge the qualifications of witness Emily Craig, proffered by the state to testify as an expert on the race of the human remains recovered from the river. Her preliminary testimony demonstrated that she was a doctoral student studying under Dr. William Bass at the University of Tennessee in forensic anthropology, had a master's degree from the Medical College of Georgia, and was slated to receive her doctoral degree in approximately 5 months. Her specialty in forensic anthropology was in the knee and shoulder, an area in which she had extensive training from working at the Houston Orthopaedic Clinic for 15 years.

Craig explained that she had spent the last 3 years researching a method to determine a person's race by measuring the end of the femur and the angle in the knee joint. In addition to being the topic of her dissertation, she had also written an article on that subject that had been accepted for publication. She stated that this area was not a new field of study, but rather a new method. Using this method, she testified that the human remains in this case were of a white or Caucasian person.[17] On cross-examination, Craig stated that she believed her methods had been generally accepted by the forensic science community. The conviction was affirmed.

In *Robedeaux v. State*,[18] the defendant was convicted of first-degree murder, and was sentenced to death in a case where a woman was beaten and dismembered. An examination of the skull and comparison to X-ray images of the decedent was performed by Dr. Larry Balding, of the medical examiner's office, and the famous anthropologist Dr. Clyde Snow. The conclusion reached was that the skull was that of the decedent. They also examined the leg found at Deep Fork River and were of the opinion that the leg was that of the decedent. Examining the arm and attached hand found at Coon Creek, the doctors opined that it too belonged to the decedent. Dr. Balding testified that there was no way, from the three body parts, to determine the cause of death, but because of the evidence of dismemberment of the body, he believed it to be a homicide.[19]

In *State v. Cross*,[20] the defendant was convicted of the murder of one Sharon Elise George. The trial court granted the defendant's motion to sever her case from that of her two co-defendants. In 1991 hunters found a human skull, later identified as that of the victim, who had disappeared in 1982. State witness Joseph Norman testified that he met the defendant, who lived next door to his mother, in 1981 at which time the defendant expressed jealousy of the victim, who was her ex-husband's girlfriend. She eventually solicited him to arrange for the murder of the victim, which was accomplished. The victim's ex-husband identified a picture of the victim, who had a chipped tooth and was wearing a brown belt with white lacing.

Dr. William Bass testified that he was a professor and director of the Forensic Anthropology Center at the University of Tennessee, where he worked as a member of the medical examiner's staff identifying skeletal remains. The Tennessee Bureau of Identification contacted him to identify remains of a teenage white female with chipped teeth. He said that the body was clothed when buried and that he found a black belt edged with white stitching around the waist. He stated that after taking a bitewing X-ray, he identified the remains as those of Sharon Elise George. He said that X-rays of the remains revealed a fracture to the back of the skull. He stated that this skull fracture could have resulted from the victim's being hit with a large, flat rock. He said that he found lead pieces, which were most likely shotgun pellets, in the vertebrae. He stated that the fragmented cervical bones in the upper body indicated that the victim had been shot with a shotgun.[21]

The use of forensic photography is a staple of crime scene investigation and most of the forensic sciences routinely used in criminal prosecutions. The use of such photography is normally limited to visual support for the laboratory or field examination opinion proffered at trial. However, on occasion forensic anthropologists are asked to examine photographs of a suspect's face or other body part to effect an identification of such person as the perpetrator of a crime.

In *United States v. Dorsey*,[22] the defendant was convicted of bank robbery arising out of two robberies of two institutions allegedly robbed by the defendant. In both cases surveillance photographs were available. A bank clerk was shown an array containing photographs of Dorsey and of five other black males by the FBI. Initially, she was unable to decide which of two of the six photographs portrayed the robber, at which point Special Agent Lane Betts asked her if viewing the bank surveillance photographs would refresh her recollection. After indicating that it would, Habersack identified Dorsey as the man who robbed her. On the same day, the photographic spread was also shown to Keeley, another eyewitness, who, after viewing the surveillance pictures, also identified Dorsey as the man who robbed the Signet Bank. At trial, both victim tellers made positive in-court identifications of Dorsey as the man who robbed them. The jury was shown both the photographic arrays shown to the tellers, and numerous surveillance photographs depicting each of the two robberies in progress.

At trial, Dorsey presented a defense of mistaken identity, and in support of that defense, Dorsey sought to introduce the testimony of two forensic anthropologists who would testify that Dorsey was not the individual depicted in the Bank of Baltimore surveillance photographs. He argued that the district court committed reversible error by excluding the testimony of these two defense witnesses. Spencer Jay Turkel and James Vandigriff Taylor, both forensic anthropologists, were hired to compare the surveillance photographs of the bank robberies with recent photographs of Dorsey and photographs of the boots which were seized from Dorsey's house. Their report concluded that the person depicted in the Bank of Baltimore surveillance videos was not Dorsey. The district court ruled to exclude the evidence, stating:

I am not so sure this is a recognized science such as a forensic chemist, or forensic scientist who does fingerprints, who does chemical analyses, who does handwriting, they are recognized. I think … what we are doing here is comparing, is comparing some photographs. What we are really asking this expert to do is to tell the jury not to believe the witnesses in this case, because the witnesses in this case have already made their identification of the same evidence. They have said I looked at the photographs at the bank and I have been able to I.D. these photographs that belong to Mr. Dorsey. And I think that becomes clearly a jury function as to whether they are or are not. They believe them, why should we need an expert to say that they are wrong? I don't believe an expert can usurp the jury function in that regard.... I don't believe that I would need it. He said he would conclude with a reasonable degree of scientific certainty. I don't even believe that is enough.[23]

The appeals court ruled that it was clear that the testimony to be presented by the two forensic anthropologists in the instant case did not plainly satisfy the first prong of *Daubert*—that is, that the evidence to be presented by the experts amounted to scientific knowledge.

However, the use of photographs by experts in forensic anthropology was accepted in the Supreme Court of Illinois 1988 decision in *People v. Hebel*,[24] where the defendant was convicted of aggravated criminal sexual assault and aggravated criminal sexual abuse. The defendant was accused of molesting and taking illicit nude photographs of overnight guests of his minor daughter. The defendant was arrested after a photograph development store called police.

The defendant contends that his conviction should be reversed because the only substantive evidence against him was a photograph. The photograph in question (People's Exhibit No. 15) was found in a search of defendant's home. It shows a hand spreading apart a minor female's sex organ. The victim's parents identified her as the female in the photograph, based on identifying marks.

The victim's father testified that to his knowledge his daughter spent the night at the Hebel residence only once in the summer of 1984. He stated that the victim has identifying moles, freckles, or brown spots on her right buttock and on her right thigh. He identified People's Exhibits Nos. 5 and 6 as photographs of his daughter asleep in a bed, People's Exhibits Nos. 12, 13, and 14, as photographs of her buttocks and vagina, and People's Exhibit No. 15 as a photograph showing a hand opening her "vaginal cavity." Number 17 was an enlargement of No. 15.[25]

Gerald Richards, an FBI agent specializing in forensic photography, testified as an expert witness in the area of forensic photography. Richards did a side-by-side comparison of People's Exhibit No. 15 with known photographs, looking for folds or creases of the hand, scars, marks, and general characteristics. He found a number of fairly unique characteristics in common; however, he was "not able to positively identify both hands to the exclusion of all other people in the world." Richards did find numerous characteristics that "strongly suggest" the hands in the photographs are the same hand. He did not observe any differences that would suggest they are not the same hand. He said the hands in the photographs appear to be those of a male.

Ellis Kerley, a professor of physical anthropology with the University of Maryland, testified that he specialized in forensic anthropology and, after questioning by the attorneys, he was declared an expert in that field. He compared the questioned photographs with the known photographs and photocopied one of the known photographs to mark for comparative purposes. People's Exhibit No. 26 is a marked photocopy of People's Exhibit No. 22K illustrating points of comparison in red ink. Kerley found no points indicating dissimilarity. He found 22 points of similarity. In his opinion, the hand in People's Exhibit No. 22K is the same hand depicted in People's Exhibit No. 17. Kerley admitted it was "possible" that the hands in the known and questioned photographs are not the same hand.[26]

The court accepted the expert testimony as a solid basis for the identification of the hand in the photograph as belonging to the defendant:

> Based upon the foregoing evidence, we believe defendant was clearly proved guilty beyond a reasonable doubt. Expert testimony that defendant's hand is depicted in the relevant photographs is convincing. We see the similarities noted by the experts. Moreover, when the strong circumstantial evidence is considered, proof that it is defendant's hand in the picture is overwhelming. The photograph was found hidden in defendant's house. Apparently, he was the only adult male that had access to the victim while she was asleep. He had taken photographs of the victim nude earlier in the day.[27]

Cultural anthropology, the study of religious and cultural beliefs, customs, and folkways in numerous cultures and world subcultures has recently been utilized in criminal cases as a guide to determining behavior or the outlines of certain cultural aspects tangential to a prosecution. Cultural and social anthropology are growing fields and there is much to learn about the cultures of recent immigrants or religious converts that is increasingly appearing in the criminal justice system.[28]

In *People v. Jones*,[29] the defendant was convicted of first-degree murder for the beating death of his wife. The court held that his trial counsel was not ineffective for failing to call an amir or sheik or other expert to testify regarding defendant's Islamic faith and its sanction of wife-beating.

> We seriously doubt that anyone knowledgeable on Islamic teachings would have proved helpful to this defense. Had such an expert been found, had he explained the righteousness of defendant's conduct, or merely explained how defendant may have believed that his actions conformed to religious teachings, the expert would not have changed the outcome. The sovereign State of Illinois has a longstanding rule of law that prohibits the engaged-in conduct. This society will not abide defendant's actions regardless of the religious beliefs that may have motivated them. If a religion sanctions conduct that can form the basis for murder, and a practitioner engages in such conduct and kills someone, that practitioner need be prepared to speak to God from prison.[30]

In *State v. Haque*,[31] the defendant was convicted of murder and assault with a dangerous weapon. The Maine Supreme Court ruled that a psychiatrist's testimony that the defendant was in a "blind rage" when he killed victim embraced an ultimate issue and was properly excluded, and that the testimony of a cultural anthropologist's was properly excluded as irrelevant.

In January 1991, Haque left his home in Raniganj, India, to attend college in Lewiston. Soon after his arrival, Haque was befriended by Lori Taylor, a fellow student, who was married and living with her husband and daughter. The two began a romantic relationship which led to an engagement. Problems between the two led to relationship counseling. Shortly after Taylor called the relationship off, Haque stabbed her to death with a kitchen knife.

At trial, the defense argued that Haque did not form the requisite *mens rea* to be guilty of murder and that he was guilty of manslaughter, rather than murder, because he acted while under the influence of extreme anger brought about by adequate provocation. The theory supporting the defense was that Haque's traditional Muslim Indian upbringing, immigrant experience, and psychological condition strongly influenced his perception of his relationship with Taylor and, eventually, the way he reacted to Taylor's termination of the relationship.

The court noted the testimony of Dr. Bloom, the defense medical expert, who stated that the defendant suffered from major depression and attention-deficit disorder. Bloom placed special emphasis on Haque's response to Taylor's statement that they were just too different, which, according to Bloom, Haque interpreted as meaning that she saw him as being racially inferior to her. Bloom testified that as a result of the statement, Haque was in "a state of blind rage and it was in that state of mind" that he acted. The trial the court excluded any testimony that Haque went into a rage.

The court also excluded all testimony by the defense expert, Dr. Caughey, a cultural anthropologist with an interest in psychological anthropology, who had conducted research into the experience of immigrants to the U.S. and how people manage multiple cultural traditions:

> During voir dire, Caughey discussed the various factors that affect an individual's transition between two different cultures and how those factors were relevant to Haque's experience in the United States. Caughey also discussed gender relationships in traditional Muslim India and how an understanding of that topic would help explain Haque's relationship with Taylor. According to Caughey, in traditional Muslim India there is no dating and relationships are expected to last for life. Caughey testified that given Haque's traditional Muslim upbringing, the "on again off again quality" of his relationship with Taylor "must have been ... extremely difficult to manage."[32]

Haque contended that the trial court erred in excluding Caughey's testimony on cultural transitions because the testimony would have assisted the jury in determining whether Haque had the requisite state of mind to be guilty of murder. The court recognized that a cultural anthropologist or other expert in cultural norms may very well possess specialized knowledge that can assist the trier of fact in settings requiring in-depth knowledge of foreign cultures and the impact of living in a new country.[33] However, the court stated, any such testimony must be relevant. Here, the expert's testimony had nothing to do with the important issue of the defendant's mental state:

> Dr. Caughey qualified as an expert in cultural anthropology, but was not qualified to, and did not, offer testimony as to Haque's state of mind. Although cultural differences may be relevant to a defendant's state of mind, Caughey's testimony was not relied on by Haque's psychiatric expert, Dr. Bloom. Moreover, Haque expressly disavowed any reliance on a cultural defense. Accordingly, the testimony of Dr. Caughey was irrelevant to any state of mind defense.[34]

The court concluded that the one area here where the testimony of the cultural anthropologist might be relevant would be the affirmative defense of adequate provocation, which might reduce murder to manslaughter, if the defendant demonstrates that he caused the death while under the influence of extreme anger or extreme fear brought about by adequate provocation.[35] Here, however, the court observed that the events which Haque contended provoked his extreme anger were Taylor's refusal to marry him, her desire to terminate their relationship, and her statement that "we [are] just too different." As mere words that ended a romantic relationship, they failed to so qualify.[36]

III. ENTOMOLOGY: CASES

Entomology is the study of insects, involving, among other topics, their biology, locations, mutations, and their control in relation to the world's environment. It is an extensive field with a worldwide network of university professors and commercial experts utilizing its findings in the areas of agriculture and other studies of natural phenomena. Entomologists are involved in studying the reduction of harmful species of insects that destroy food, housing, plants, and clothing, or cause sickness in humans, livestock, and pets. Other entomologists study new methods to increase the growth and spread of insects that provide food (honey), pollinate crops, assist in destroying harmful insects, or are eaten as food by birds and fish. There are a growing number of books[37] and Web sites[38] available to the neophyte in learning about this important subject.

Entomology is also a staple of the world of forensic sciences due to its significant contribution in resolving decisive questions regarding the time of death of victims of suicide or homicide. The arrival and departure of insects and their indicia have been proved to be accurate predictors of the relative time of death of a partially decomposed body. This is the primary use of this science, and its value and general acceptance is consistently recognized in reported decisions. Given the centrality of time-of-death estimations in homicide cases where an alibi is claimed, it is no wonder that this context is so often the basis for judicial scrutiny. However, given the very nature of forensic entomological testimony, claims are bound to arise in regard to the gruesome nature of the photographs used to support the forensic entomologist's testimony.

In *Seebeck v. State*,[39] the defendant was convicted of felony murder and second-degree larceny. Examination of the area in front of the victim's house revealed that a struggle apparently had taken place there, because the victim's hat, bow tie, and camera were strewn about. Near the front door, the police found an area of matted-down grass on which there was a bloodstained brick, and from that area, there were drag marks along the right side of the house to the rear corner where the body was found. An autopsy revealed that the victim had suffered extensive injuries to the head, a fractured skull, a broken right arm, a dislocated wrist, four stab wounds in the back, and six fractured ribs. The cause of death was a depressed skull fracture with laceration of the brain, caused by an object such as the corner of a brick. There was considerable maggot activity on the victim's head and body.

Stephen Adams, an assistant medical examiner, went to the scene to investigate the circumstances of the victim's death. On the basis of his observations of the victim's body, the yard, and surrounding locations, Adams concluded that the victim had died 2 to 4 days before his body was discovered on June 24. Catherine Galvin, the acting chief medical examiner, who had performed the autopsy, examined photographs of the victim's body taken at the scene, inspected temperature records, and viewed the actual scene. She concluded that within reasonable medical probability, the time span between the victim's death and the delivery of his body to the medical examiner's office on June 24 was between 2 and 4 days. Wayne Lord, a forensic entomologist who had been consulted by the office of the chief medical examiner, concluded that the victim's death occurred sometime between the late afternoon of June 19 and the early afternoon of June 21.[40]

The defendant claimed in the trial court that there was newly discovered evidence regarding, generally, developments in the field of forensic entomology, and specifically, alleged changes in the opinion of expert Lord, who had testified as a witness for the state in the original trial. As the present trial court, "[t]he focus of [the petitioner's] claim as newly discovered evidence is that Lord's testimony at the [criminal] trial was crucial in establishing the time of death of [the victim] to be late morning or early afternoon of Friday, June 20, 1980 [that is, before the petitioner had left the Waterford area], but, since that testimony in 1986, he has given [an] opinion in subsequent homicide cases which differs entomologically" from the opinion expressed in that testimony.[41]

In support of this assertion, the defendant offered in evidence two depositions of Lord, taken on September 7, 1990, and on June 9, 1992, as well as two scientific papers through the testimony of William Kriniski. One of the papers was entitled "Nocturnal Oviposition Behavior of Blow Flies" by Bernard Greenberg published in 1990,[42] wherein Greenberg reports observing nocturnal oviposition, or laying of eggs, by blow flies. The trial court stated:

> Kriniski, Greenberg and Lord, all entomologists, testified at the petitioner's criminal trial. Kriniski and Greenberg testified at the trial that in their opinion, from analysis of the stage of larvae on the [victim's] body, death could not have occurred before Saturday, June 21, 1980. Their opinions were based on their belief that nocturnal oviposition does occur. The [petitioner] did not offer [the testimony of Kriniski and the scientific papers introduced through him] simply to bolster Kriniski and Greenberg's opinion [expressed at the criminal trial] but [also] to show that in Lord's deposition of June 9, 1992, he did not dispute Greenberg's observation of such nocturnal oviposition.[43]

Thus, the petitioner claimed that Lord's deposition response, when asked about Greenberg's study, constituted new evidence that Lord had now adopted Greenberg's opinion. The trial court found, however, that the petitioner's evidence did not indicate any material change in Lord's opinion.

The trial court had apparently found that Lord still disagreed with Greenberg, noting that, when asked about Greenberg's study at his deposition, Lord had commented, "if Greenberg said he saw oviposition at night, he believed it," and that Lord further testified that no other scientist had been able to duplicate such observations and that another prominent entomologist had found to the contrary. On the basis of those findings, the trial court concluded that the petitioner had failed to offer any new entomological evidence. Rather, in the court's view, insofar as the evidence indicated that the opinions of Lord, Greenberg, and Kriniski had not changed, the evidence was essentially the same as, and cumulative to, the evidence offered at the criminal trial.

In addition, the appeals court noted that the trial court had ruled that Lord's opinion given in 1986 was not, as claimed, crucial in establishing the time of death. After carefully reviewing the record regarding this issue, the appellate tribunal found nothing in the record to suggest that the trial court's findings and conclusions were incorrect and concluded that the trial court did not abuse its discretion in denying certification to appeal with respect to this issue.[44]

In *State v. Thibodeaux*,[45] the defendant was convicted of first-degree murder. On Friday, July 19, 1996, the victim, 14-year-old Crystal Champagne, left her home at the Tanglewood Apartments in Westwego, Louisiana at about 5:15 P.M. to walk a short distance to a nearby supermarket. Defendant was related to the Champagnes through his mother's previous marriage to Dawn's brother. Crystal was defendant's step-cousin. After a search, Crystal's corpse was found on a concrete slab. She was naked, with her shirt and bra pulled up to her shoulders, revealing a red wire ligature wrapped around her neck. Her shorts and panties were pulled down around her ankles. Stacy recalled that she had washed the clothes Crystal had on the previous morning before she took her home. Maggots and ants had invaded her body. Stacy went and called the police, who arrived on the scene at 7:47 P.M.

Dr. Fraser MacKenzie of the Jefferson Parish Coroner's Office performed the autopsy on Crystal. He attributed the cause of death to asphyxiation by ligature strangulation.

Dr. Lamar Leek, professor of entomology at Louisiana State University, testified as an expert in the field of forensic entomology. He examined the insect samples taken from Crystal's body and testified that flies will lay eggs on a carcass within a couple of hours, but will not lay eggs after dark. Therefore, he determined that the eggs were laid before nightfall on July 19, 1996, and calculated the age of the fly larvae (maggots) to be between 24 and 28 hours old at discovery.[46]

In *Commonwealth v. Auker*,[47] the court focused on the possible prejudice to defendants by the exhibition of maggots and other insects on the body of the deceased in conjunction with the testimony of forensic entomologists. In *Auker*, the defendant was convicted of first-degree murder and kidnaping, and received a death sentence. Robert Donald Auker was convicted for the murder and kidnaping of his former wife, Lori Ann Auker. The body was discovered on a hot day, June 12, 1989, by a young woman who was walking down a dirt road near the home of her grandparents. She smelled an odor, investigated, and saw a badly decomposed body clad in a jacket, jeans, and sneakers. She rushed back home and her family contacted the police. The pathologist, Dr. Mihalakis, testified that the cause of death was homicide, most likely as the result of between 7 and 10 knife stab wounds in the back and chest area.

Dr. Mihalakis further confirmed the approximate date of death through the use of an entomological expert, Dr. K. C. Kim, whose specialty was the classification and identification of insects and parasites of humans and animals. The court summarized Dr. Kim's testimony:

Dr. Mihalakis collected samples of the various insects present on and within the corpse for analysis and Dr. Kim examined the insects. Dr. Kim testified that the presence and relative maturity of insects allowed him to estimate the approximate time of death. He testified that different decomposition stages attract different types of insects. He also explained that ambient air temperature and physical site (open field, shaded locale or aquatic area) also affect the rate of maturity of insects. In determining the approximate decomposition period, Dr. Kim utilized a climate report from the national weather service, description of the autopsy and description of the scene where the corpse was discovered.[48]

Dr. Kim identified samples of the insects found on the victim. He was also shown autopsy photographs depicting a mass of insects on the body and in the body bag. Dr. Kim concluded that accounting for the average mean temperature during the time the corpse had been missing, the maturity of the various insects present, and the stages of decomposition at which certain insects would be present, the body had been decaying 19 days to 25 days.[49]

The corpse was identified as Lori Auker through dental records. Lori had been missing since May 24, 1989, and was last seen wearing clothing like that found on the corpse. In all, 19 days had elapsed from the date of her disappearance until the discovery of her body on June 12, 1989. The defendant was connected to the crime by the May 24 film from an automated teller machine video camera and through strands of human and cat hair.[50]

The defendant alleged error in the exhibition to the jury of inflammatory photographs of the victim covered with insects. Both color and black-and-white photographs taken at the scene of discovery and at the autopsy were presented at trial. Seven black-and-white photographs of the body at the scene were presented to show the jury the unnatural position of the body in a secluded wooded area on a steep ravine and in a decomposing state. The autopsy photographs included color and black-and-white photographs. The 13 color photographs of the stained, knifed clothing and one small color photograph of the insects in the body bag without the body were presented. Two black-and-white photographs of the insects on the body were also presented. The first black-and-white photograph was of a totally jeans-clad lower body from below the knees down to the sneakers. The other was of the body from the position of the sneakers so that the decomposition of the upper body was not clearly visible.[51]

The court found no error in the presentation of such photographs since they were necessary to support the opinion of Dr. Kim on the implications of the presence and condition of the insects:

The photographs of the body with insects were all black-and-white. They were presented to assist the jury in understanding Dr. Kim's scientific testimony about the presence of various insects and the use of entomology in determining the relative date of death of the victim. As Dr. Kim testified, the approximate date of death could be determined by the presence of certain types of insects on the skeletal remains at that specific site and climate. Thus, the pictures helped the jury to understand and evaluate that testimony.[52]

In addition to the necessity of the photographs to bolster Dr. Kim's opinion, the court noted that the trial court, prior to the presentation of the black-and-white photographic evidence, warned the jury of the nature of the photographs and limited the period of time for viewing them.

However, in *State v. Hart*,[53] where defendant was convicted of aggravated murder and aggravated burglary, for purposely tying and leaving to starve to death a 90-year-old victim while committing or attempting to commit the offense of aggravated burglary, the case was reversed due to prosecutorial misconduct, in part, by displaying and focusing on disturbing evidence of the ravages of insect damage inflicted on victim Steffin's body over an extended period. Such evidence had only been admitted for limited purposes, and its significance was inappropriately distorted and reinforced by the use of photographs of the victim's corpse throughout the closing argument.

Although the time of death was an important fact in issue and was a proper subject of argument, the court ruled that the prosecutor's ploy, coming as it did immediately after urging the jury to contemplate a particularly horrid, lingering death, focused the jurors not on what the photographs proved, but on the feelings and emotions they evoked. The court ruled that while a prosecutor may use gruesome photographs to illustrate essential elements of the crime to be proved, he may not use them to appeal to the jurors' emotions. The prosecutor's use of the photographs, in this instance, the court concluded, further encouraged the jury to react emotionally and to convict on matters not before the court.

The defendant argued that the trial court erred in admitting seven photographs into evidence. Hart claims that the graphic photographic depictions of the decomposed and fly-ravaged body of Steffin were so gruesome, inflammatory, and repetitive that they influenced the jury unfairly. The court ruled that the trial court properly admitted a number of photographs of the victim's body. The court also excluded at least six photographs of the corpse. Only four of the photographs assigned as error were admitted over objection. The photographs that were admitted were relevant, not cumulative, and were used to illustrate the coroner's testimony and the testimony of expert witness Stein.[54]

ENDNOTES

1. See Pickering and Bachman: *The Use of Forensic Anthropology* (CRC Press, Boca Raton, FL, 1997), at Chapter 3 "What Forensic Anthropologist Can and Cannot Do, p. 15. Also see Geberth: *Practical Homicide Investigation* (3d ed., CRC Press, Boca Raton, FL, 1996) at 253; Fisher: *Techniques of Crime Scene Investigation* (5th ed., CRC Press, Boca Raton, FL, 1993) at 128.
2. See M. Y. Iscan and K.A. Kennedy: *Reconstruction of Life from the Skeleton* (Alan R. Liss, New York, 1989).
3. See Sebastian Younger: "The Forensics of War," Vanity Fair, October 1999, at 138. Also see DePaul University College of Law's Center for Law and Science Web site for forensic anthropology case summaries an a listing of international agreements supporting war crimes investigations, located at *http://www.law.depaul.edu/cls*.

4. Pickering and Bachman, *supra*, note 1. See their bibliography at pages 145–146; Mehmet Yasar Iscan and Susan R. Loth: "The Scope of Forensic Anthropology," Eckert (Ed.): *Introduction to Forensic Sciences* (2d ed. CRC Press, Boca Raton, FL, 1997); Geberth, *supra*, note 1, at 253; Reichs and Bass (Eds.): *Forensic Osteology: Advances in the Identification of Human Remains* (2d ed. Charles C. Thomas, Springfield, 1998); Burns: *The Forensic Anthropology Training Manual* (Prentice-Hall, Englewood Cliffs, NJ, 1999); Haas, Buikstra, and Ubelaker: *Standards for Data Collection from Human Skeletal Remains: Proceedings of a Seminar at the Field Museum of Natural History* (Chicago, 1994).

5. See, e.g., Smith: *Mostly Murder* (David McKay Company, New York, 1959) (The famous autobiography of Sir Sydney Smith, relating his work as a forensic specialist in numerous prominent cases in Egypt and England during the early years of the 20th century); Maples and Browning: *Dead Men Do Tell Tales* (Doubleday, New York, 1994); Jackson and Fellenbaum: *The Bone Detectives: How Forensic Anthropologists Solve Crimes and Uncover Mysteries of the Dead* (Little Brown & Co., Boston, 1996).

6. See, e.g., "Odontology and Anthropology Examinations," FBI Handbook of Forensic Services (1999), located at *http://www.fbi.gov/programs/lab/handbook/examodon.htm*; Osteo Interactive Web site, located at *http://www.medstat.med.utah.edu/osteo/forensics/for_frame.html* (good general introductory pages); American Board of Forensic Anthropology, located at *http://www.csuchico.edu/anth/ABFA* (AFBA Diplomate information and listing); Universia di Pavia Web site, located at *http://www.unipv.it/webbio/homepag1.htm* (excellent and very extensive links to world anthropology and related sites).

7. State v. Nyhuis, 906 S.W.2d 405 (Mo.Ct.App. 1995).

8. *Id*. at 408.

9. State v. Bondurant, 1998 WL 120291 (Tenn.Crim.App. 1998).

10. *Id*. at 7.

11. State v. Delgros, 104 Ohio App.3d 531,662 N.E.2d 858 (1995).

12. *Id*. at 533.

13. *Id*. at 536. Also see Armstrong v. State, 958 S.W.2d 278 (Ct. Appeals, Amarillo, Texas 1997), where there was extensive testimony by forensic anthropologists whether the victim was stabbed with a knife. Two of these witnesses, Drs. Harold Gill-King and Randall Frost, testified for the state. The other, Dr. Steven A. Symes, testified for the defense. Doctor Gill-King is an expert in anthropology and forensic pathology and director of the Laboratory for Human Identification and Forensic Anthropology at the University of North Texas Health Science Center. Doctor Frost is a forensic pathologist with the Lubbock County Medical Examiner's Office. Doctor Symes is a forensic anthropologist and is an instructor at the University of Tennessee Medical School and is an Assistant Director of the Regional Forensic Center in Memphis, Tennessee.

14. State v. Klindt, 389 N.W.2d 670 (Sp.Ct.Iowa 1986).

15. See Pickering and Bachman, *supra*, note 1, at 80.

16. Pipkin v. State, 1997 WL 749441 (Tenn.Crim.App. 1997) (not officially reported).

17. See Rebecca Tsosie: "Privileging Claims to the Past: Ancient Human Remains and Contemporary Cultural Values," 31 Arizona St. L. J. 583 (1999); C. Loring Brace: "Region Does Not Mean 'Race'—Reality Versus Convention in Forensic Anthropology," 40 *J. Forensic Sci*. 171 (1995).

18. Robedeaux v. State, 866 P.2d 417 (Ct.Crim. App.Ok. 1994).

19. *Id*. at 428–429.

20. State v. Cress, 1999 WL 1076958 (Tenn.Crim.App.).

21. *Id.* at *5.
22. United States v. Dorsey, 45 F.3d 809 (4th Cir.Ct.App. 1995).
23. *Id.* at 812.
24. People v. Habel, 174 Ill.App.3d 1, 527 N.E.2d 1362 (1988).
25. *Id.* at 1375.
26. *Id.* at 1376.
27. *Id.* at 31.
28. See Cultural Anthropology, the Web site for the *Journal for the Society for Cultural Anthropology*, located at *http://bernard.pitzer.edu/~cultanth*, and the Social/Cultural Anthropology Internet Guide, located at *http://www.ualberta.ca/~slis/guides/can- thro/anthro.htm*, for information on and links to this extensive field of anthropology.
29. People v. Jones, 297 Ill.App.3d 688, 697 N.E.2d 457 (1998).
30. *Id.* at 692–693.
31. State v. Haque, 726 A.2d 205 (ME, 1999).
32. *Id.* at 208.
33. See, e.g., Dang Vang v. Vang Xiong X. Toyed, 944 F.2d 476, 481 (9th Cir. 1991) (upholding decision in civil trial to allow epidemiologist to testify about women in the Hmong culture); People v. Aphaylath, 68 N.Y.2d 945, 510 N.Y.S.2d 83, 502 N.E.2d 998, 999 (1986) (reversing order excluding expert testimony on the stress encountered by Laotian refugees).
34. *Supra,* note 31, at 209. Also see State v. Girmay, 139 N.H. 292, 652 A.2d 150, 152 (1994) (testimony of expert in Ethiopian culture not relied on by defendant's psychi- atric expert in murder case involving Ethiopian defendant was irrelevant and properly excluded); People v. Poddar, 26 Cal.App.3d 438, 103 Cal.Rptr. 84, 88 (1972), rev'd on other grounds, 10 Cal.3d 750, 111 Cal.Rptr. 910, 518 P.2d 342 (1974) (testimony relating to defendant's culture properly excluded as to issue of diminished capacity).
35. In this context, it should be noted that states vary considerably regarding what categories of stress-producing incidents may be considered under the idea of "ade- quate provocation."
36. Also see State v. Tenerelli, 598 N.W.2d 668 (Minn.Sp.Ct. 1999), where defendant was convicted of assault, and ordered to pay restitution for the costs of a Hmong healing ceremony performed for his victim. The victim, Txawj Xiong, filed a victim impact statement and a request for restitution, including those relating to a traditional Hmong ceremony known as Hu Plig, which involves the sacrifice of live animals to heal the soul of someone who has been physically and emotionally harmed. After reviewing the testimony of the victim and a defense expert in Hmong religious ceremonies and the costs typically associated with them, the court concluded that the trial court was within its discretion in ordering restitution for the costs of Txawj Xiong's Hu Plig ceremony.
37. See, e.g., Haglund and Sorg (Eds.): *Forensic Taphonomu: The Postmortem Fate of Human Remains* (CRC Press, Boca Raton, FL, 1996); K. G. V., Smith, *A Manual of Forensic Entomology* (Comstock Publishing Associates, Cornell University Press, Ithaca, NY, 1986); Geberth, *supra*, note 1, (Chapter 9, "Estimating Time of Death"); Fisher, *supra*, note 1, at 439; Saferstein: *Criminalistics: An Introduction to Forensic Science* (6th ed. Prentice-Hall, Upper Saddle River, NJ, 1998) at 22.
38. Forensic Entomology Pages, International site, is an extensive site covering world entomology sites, bibliographies, basic texts, and much more. This important site is located at *http://www.uio.no/~mostarke/forens_ent/forensic_entomology.html*; XXI

International Congress of Entomology, located at *http://www.embrapa.br/ice/central.htm*; MSU Entomology on the WWW, containing a searchable database of over 700 articles and faculty publications and important links, is located at *http://www.ent.msu.edu/dept/*; Iowa State University's Entomology Index of Internet Resources, a very comprehensive link to virtually every entomological area of interest, located at *http://www.ent.iastate.edu/list;* Colorado State University Entomology Page, containing conference meeting schedules, recent literature cites, links, and a picture gallery, located at *http://www.colostate.edu/Depts/Entomology/ent.html;* American Board of Forensic Entomology, containing texts on general background, history, case studies, and useful references to professional standards and membership, located at *http://web.missouri.edu/cafnr/entomology/index.html.*

39. Seebeck v. State, 246 Conn. 514, 717 A.2d 1161 (1998).
40. *Id.* at 656–59, 557 A.2d 93.
41. *Id.*
42. B. Greenberg: "Nocturnal Oviposition Behavior of Blow Flies," 27 *J. Med. Entomol.* 797, 808 (1990).
43. *Supra*, note 39, at 1173.
44. Also see People v. Reynolds, 257 Ill.App.3d 792, 629 N.E.2d 559 (1994), where defendant, who claimed an alibi, was convicted of first-degree murder for the killing of his mother, Lealer Reynolds. Defendant's case consisted solely of the expert testimony of Dr. Bernard Greenberg, who was a consultant in the field of forensic entomology and had been studying maggots for 40 years. Based on his experience and a photograph of a maggot taken from the victim's body, Dr. Greenberg opined that the time of death was 1 P.M. on June 2, 1989, at which time defendant claimed an alibi.
45. State v. Thibodeaux, 1999 WL 694726 (La.).
46. Also see Commonwealth v. Copenhefer, 719 A.2d 242 (Pa. 1998), where a Commonwealth entomologist testified to the victim's time of death. The defendant's expert gave conflicting testimony. Trial counsel eventually agreed to the Commonwealth's estimate because the defendant had an alibi for that time; therefore, trial counsel was not unreasonable in basing the alibi argument on the Commonwealth's time of death.
47. Commonwealth v. Auker, 545 Pa. 521, 681 A.2d 1305 (1996).
48. *Id.* at 1311.
49. *Id.* at 533.
50. Human hairs later found in the Celebrity's upper door seal and from the door jamb were similar to those of Lori Auker. Hairs presumably on Lori's body from Lori's cats were found in the trunk and on appellant's Velcro splint.
51. *Id.* at 545.
52. *Id.* at 546.
53. State v. Hart, 94 Ohio App.3d 665, 641 N.E.2d 755 (1994).
54. *Id.* at 764. Also see Coe v. Bell, 161 F.3d 320 (6th Cir. 1998), where defendant was convicted of a rape and murder. The court ruled that the entomological evidence that defendant now marshaled (refuting the prosecution's asserted time of death based on the extent of insect infestation on Medlin's corpse) did not seem to have been such an obvious or common part of a defense in the time and place of Coe's trial that counsel was ineffective for neglecting it.

12 Epilogue

And indeed, most of the Law Books extant, if not all, (setting aside the Reports) are nothing else but Collections out of others. This I speak, not in Derogation of them, in the least; for as tis equally, if not more laborious, for tis full as glorious, judicially to cull Authentick Cases out of the Volumes of the Law (where so many are no Law) and rightfully place them in a particular Treatise, as tis to report the Judgements and resolutions from the Mouth of the Court.... Than which Benefit I know not whether any Man can ever imagine another, either to Lawyers more grateful, or to the Commonwealth more profitable, or for the Illustration of Divine Honor more fit. For with the least Labour, a small Price, and little Time, they present you with those Resolutions and Judgements which lie scattered in the Voluminous Books of the Law; which would otherwise cost much Time, Pains, and Charges to find out.

—Giles Duncombe
Trials Per Pais, or the Law of England Concerning
Juries by Nisi Prius (1725)

This book has attempted to set out the general framework of the ongoing use of forensic evidence in the criminal justice system. Forensic evidence, simply stated, is a body of factual material generated by a large body of forensic sciences to serve as evidence in criminal prosecutions. Due to the scientific bases of the processes used to generate any such testimony by forensic experts, each of the forensic sciences must continue to justify the basis for any class or individual characteristic linkage testimony proffered in a case. As evidenced by the recent rejection of ear print evidence and the ready acceptance of lip print testimony, discussed in Chapter 8, the challenge to the claims of the forensic sciences continues unabated.

The areas of forensic science addressed here at length—hair, fiber, ballistics, tool marks, soil, glass, and paint, footwear and tire impressions, fingerprints, blood spatter, DNA, and forensic anthropology and entomology—are staple fare of appellate tribunals in state and federal courts. For that reason, and because of the concomitant importance of them in the daily work of the players in the criminal justice system, they have been chosen for extended coverage.

The goal of this book has been to provide a comprehensive but not unwieldy, single volume, setting out the general lines of the judicial perspective on the use of forensic science in U.S. courts. The number of appellate decisions, not to mention statutory measures, addressing the forensic sciences analyzed here will yield an equal or increased volume of new decisions that will need to be found, analyzed, and classified.

The author recognizes that an equal amount of attention could be given to vast areas of highly specialized areas of forensic science such as forensic pathology, forensic toxicology, or forensic odontology. There is also room for lengthy studies of the development of laser technology, image digitalization processes, voice analysis technology, handwriting and computer-generated document analysis, and a host of subjects that will be the main concern of the future. Entire areas of what are often referred to as the "soft sciences" have also been omitted from coverage. Many of these essential disciplines, such as forensic psychiatry, forensic psychology, serial killer–profiling techniques, witness credibility assessment expertise, coerced confessions expertise, and a number of other mind science disciplines merit extended attention. Those chosen here are hard-science based, if grounded nonetheless in probability assessments in the final analysis.

The Appendix to follow will serve to acquaint readers with the major texts in the field and important Internet links to essential forensic science and evidence information sources. It is meant to serve as a sourcebook for detailed work in the extensive world of the forensic sciences and their progeny, forensic evidence. One hopes, with the utilization of the information provided in the individual chapters of this book, the reader will be equipped to begin efficient, practical work in the fascinating world of forensic science and forensic evidence.

APPENDIX

A Primer on Researching Forensic Science to Get to Forensic Evidence

The following is a lawyers guide to researching the forensic science cases: books, journals, databases, Web sites and other good ideas.

I. FORENSICS AND CRIME SCENE BIBLIOGRAPHY AND RESEARCH SOURCES

A. OVERVIEW AND HISTORY

- Thorvald: *The Century of the Detective* (Harcourt, Brace & World, 1965)
- Thorvald: *Crime and Science: The New Frontier in Criminology* (Harcourt, Brace & World, 1966)
- Wilson: *Clues: A History of Forensic Detection* (Warner Books, 1989)

B. STANDARD FORENSIC SCIENCE TEXTS

1. Bodziak: *Footwear Impression Evidence* (2nd ed., CRC Press, Boca Raton, FL, 1999)
2. Di Maio and Dominick: *Forensic Pathology* (CRC Press, Boca Raton, FL, 1993)
3. Di Maio and Vincent: *Gunshot Wounds: Practical Aspects of Firearms, Ballistics, and Forensic Techniques* (2nd ed., CRC Press, Boca Raton, FL, 1999)
4. Eckert: *Introduction to Forensic Sciences* (2d ed., CRC Press, Boca Raton, FL, 1995)
5. Eckert and James: *Interpretation of Bloodstain Evidence at Crime Scenes* (2nd ed., CRC Press, Boca Raton, FL, 1998)
6. Fisher: *Techniques of Crime Scene Investigation* (6th ed., CRC Press, Boca Raton, FL, 2000)
7. Geberth: *Practical Homicide Investigation: Tactics, Procedures, and Forensic Techniques* (3d ed., CRC Press, Boca Raton, FL, 1993)
8. Gerber and Saferstein (Eds.): *More Chemistry and Crime: From Marsh Arsenic Test to DNA Profile* (American Chemical Society, New York, 1997)

9. Gianelli and Imwinkelried, *Scientific Evidence,* Vol. I & II (2d ed., The Michie Co., Charlottesville, VA, 1993)
10. Hazelwood and Burgess: *Practical Aspects of Rape Investigation: A Multidisciplinary Approach* (2nd ed., CRC Press, Boca Raton, FL, 1999)
11. Hilton: *Scientific Examination of Questioned Documents* (CRC Press, Boca Raton, FL, 1982)
12. Houde: *Crime Lab: A Guide for Nonscientists* (Calico Press, Ventura, CA, 1998)
13. Lee and Gaensslen: *Advances in Fingerprint Technology* (CRC Press, Boca Raton, FL, 1994)
14. Maples: *Dead Men Do Tell Tales: The Strange and Fascinating Cases of a Forensic Anthropologist* (Doubleday, New York, 1994)
15. Moenssens, Starrs, Henderson, and Inbau: *Scientific Evidence in Civil and Criminal Cases* (4th ed., Foundation Press, Minneapolis, 1995)
16. Nickell and Fisher: *Crime Science: Methods of Forensic Detection* (University Press of Kentucky, 1998)
17. Ogle and Fox: *Atlas of Human Hair: Microscopic Characteristics* (CRC Press, Boca Raton, FL, 1999)
18. Pickering and Bachman: *The Use of Forensic Anthropology* (CRC Press, Boca Raton, FL, 1996)
19. Saferstein: *Criminalistics: An Introduction to Forensic Science* (6th ed., Prentice-Hall, Upper Saddle River, NJ, 1995)
20. U.S. Department of Justice, FBI, *Handbook of Forensic Science* (U.S. Government Printing Office, Washington, D.C., 1994)
21. Zonderman: *Beyond the Crime Lab* (John Wiley & Sons, New York, 1998)

C. RECOMMENDED PERIODICALS

The major authoritative periodicals for current and/or very specialized forensic research are the *Journal of Forensic Science* (U.S.) and *Science and Justice* (U.K.). These are where you find the important work by the international forensic science community. Look there first. These journals are available in most law school libraries. The index to the *Journal of Forensic Science* is available on InfoTrack in law libraries.

II. FORENSIC INFORMATION ON THE INTERNET

There are a growing number of Web sites that provide lists of information sources, journals, experts, professional associations, international forensics organizations, newsletters, university programs, international police organizations, and the like. A general search under any of the Internet search engines such as Yahoo will bring up most of them. The best is Zeno's Forensic Science Page, out of the Netherlands. It has updated links to all there is to get regarding forensics on the Web. It may be found at *http://forensic.to/forensic.html*. A new, superb resource is a site sponsored by the American Academy of Forensic Science (AAFS) and the American Society for Testing and Materials (ASTM), located at *http://www.aafs.org*, which allows searches of the index to the *Journal of Forensic Science*, the preeminent scholarly journal in this field, from 1980 to the present. The search result also allows for the viewing of the abstract associated with each citation located. Also see a comprehensive law and forensic science Web site, maintained by the Center for Law and Science of DePaul University College of Law, located at *http://www.law.depaul.edu/cls.*

A. DIALOG/WESTLAW SEARCHING

The Criminal Justice Periodical Index database CJ-PI will bring up a decent listing for a start on a literature search.

B. FORENSIC SCIENCE AND RELATED WEB SITES

1. Forensic Sciences

Alphonse Bertillon: Measuring the Head
 (*http://www.cimm.jcu.edu.au/hist/stats/bert/head2.htm*)
American Academy of Forensic Sciences (*http://www.aafs.org*)
California State Coroner's Association (*http://www.coroners.org/*)
Center for Law and Science (*http://www.law.depaul.edu/cls*)
China: FSER: Forensic Med in WCUMS (*http://members.xoom.com/legalmed*)
CRC Press LLC (*http://www.crcpress.com/*)
DNA — Gene Almanac Page (*http://vector.cshl.org/*)
The Dog Genome Project (*http://mendel.berkeley.edu/dog.html*)
Entomology: Insect Drawings
 (*http://www.life.uiuc.edu/Entomology/insectgifs.html*)
The FBI Laboratory's Combined DNA Index System (CODIS) Program
 (*http://www.euro.promega.com/geneticidentity/symposia/symproc6/
 niezgod.htm*)
Federal Bureau of Investigation — FBI Home Page (*http://www.fbi.gov*)
Forensic Anthropology: PoundLab
 (*http://web.anthro.ufl.edu/c.a.poundlab/poundlab.htm*)
Forensic Chemistry Network
 (*http://www.geocities.com/CapeCanaveral/4329/*)
Forensic Computing — Journal — Authoritative Comment
 (*http://www.forensic-computing.com/*)
Forensic Directories and Listings
 (*http://www.hypernet.on.ca/quincy/dirbib.htm*)
Forensic Entomology References
 (*http://www.uio.no/~mostarke/forens_ent/references.html*)
Forensic Firearms Identification, An Introduction
 (*http://www.geocities.com/~jsdoyle/*)
Forensic and Law Enforcement Web Sites
 (*http://www.shadow.net/~noslow/forensic.html*)
Forensic Pathology (*http://medic.med.uth.tmc.edu/publ/00000075.htm*)
International Association for Forensic Phonetics
 (*http://zeno.simplenet.com/iafp98/*)
International Association of Forensic Sciences 1999
 (*http://www.criminalistics.com/iafs-1999/*)

An Interview with DNA Forensics Authority Dr. Bruce Weir
   (*http://www.accessexcellence.org/WN/NM/interview_dr_bruce_weir.html*)
Jerry C. Lyell — Forensic DNA Home Page (*http://www.dnalwyr.com/*)
Medical Examiners Page (*http://www.thename.org/info/info.htm*)
MSU Forensic Science (*http://www.ssc.msu.edu/~forensic/*)
Northern Light Search (*http://www.globalindex.com/search.htm*)
Office of International Criminal Justice (*http://oicj.acsp.uic.edu/*)
Pathology and Forensic Medicine (*http://www.mic.ki.se/Pathol.html*)
Professor William Thompson's DNA Page
   (*http//www.scientific.org/web_admin/links.htm*)
Royal Canadian Mounted Police
   (*http://www.rcmp-grc.gc.ca/html/bugs.htm*)
Sciences of Soils — Home Page (*http://www.hintze-online.com/sos/*)
Shoe Print & Tire Track Exam. Resources
   (*http://members.aol.com/varfee/mastssite/home.html*)
Stranka Forensic Sciences-Fiber Imaging Process
   (*http://www.lim.cz/paa/text/forens_sci.html*)
Terminal Ballistics (*http://home.sprynet.com/sprynet/frfrog/terminal.htm*)
Trace Evidence Page (*http://www.adfs.com/trace.htm*)
U.S. Army Criminal Forensic Lab
   (*http://www.randomc.com/~german/usacil.html*)
Welcome to the World of Forensic Entomology
   (*http://www.missouri.edu/cafnr/entomology/index.html*)
Zeno's Forensic Page (*http://www.forensic.to/links/pages/*)

2. Law-Related Sites

ABA Net — Criminal Law (*http://www.abanet.org/crimjust/home.html*)
The Association of American Law Schools (*http://www.aals.org/*)
ATLA NET Public Homepage (*http://www.atlanet.org/*)
CataLaw: Metaindex of Law and Government (*http://www.catalaw.com/*)
Center for Law and Science (*http://www.law.depaul.edu/cls/*)
Cornell Legal Information Institute (*http://www.law.cornell.edu/*)
The Evidence Site, Main Page (*http://www.law.umich.edu/thayer/*)
The FBI Laboratory: An Investigation into Laboratory — Explosives
   (*http://www.tncrimlaw.com/fbi_indx.html*)
The Federal Judicial Center Home Page (*http://www.fjc.gov/*)
Fedstats: One Stop Shopping for Federal Statistics
   (*http://www.fedstats.gov/index.html*)
FindLaw: Internet Legal Resources (*http://www.findlaw.com/*)
Food and Drug Administration Home Page (*http://www.fda.gov/*)
Government Information Searches
   (*http://www.gpo.ucop.edu/search/default.html*)
Hieros Gamos—The Comprehensive Law and Government Site
   (*http://www.hg.org/hg.html*)
Illinois State Bar Association (*http://www.illinoisbar.org*)

Illinois Supreme Court Rules
  (*http://www.illinoisbar.org/CourtRules/Article2/home.html#e*)
ILRG's Legal Indices and Search Engines (*http://www.ilrg.com/indices.html*)
INREP Home Page — Artificial Intelligence and Evidence
  (*http://www.eurocongres.com/criminallaw/*)
International Commentary on Evidence (*http://www.law.qub.ac.uk/ice/*)
International Criminal Law Sites (*http://www.hg.org/crime.html*)
INTERPOL (*http://193.123.144.14/interpol-pr/Index.html*)
JURIST: The Law Professors' Network ... The Legal Education Portal
  (*http://jurist.law.pitt.edu/*)
Lexis-Nexis (*http://www.lexis.com/xchange/*)
Organization of International Criminal Justice Conferences
  (*http://www.acsp.uic.edu/oicj/confs.htm*)
The Police Officer's Internet Directory (*http://www.officer.com/*)
Search Government (*http://www.isleuth.com/gove.html*)
U.N. Crime and Justice Information Network
  (*http://www.ifs.univie.ac.at/~uncjin/uncjin.html*)
U.S. Court of Appeals, 7th Circuit (*http://www.kentlaw.edu/7circuit/*)
U.S. Department of Justice Home Page (*http://www.usdoj.gov/*)
U.S. District Court — Northern Illinois (*http://www.ilnd.uscourts.gov/*)
Welcome to Court TV Online (*http://www.courttv.com/*)
Welcome to Westlaw! (*http://www.westlaw.com/*)
The World Wide Web Virtual Library: Law: Criminal Law and Evidence
  (*http://www.law.indiana.edu/law/v-lib/criminal.html*)

3. Medicine-Related Sites

American Medical Association (*http://www.ama-assn.org/*)
Food and Drug Administration Home Page (*http://www.fda.gov/*)
HealthGate — EMBASE intro
  (*http://www.healthgate.com/embase/search-embase-pre.shtml*)
Internet Grateful Med (MEDLINE #2) (*http://igm.nlm.nih.gov/*)
JAMA — *The Journal of the American Medical Association*
  (*http://www.ama- assn.org/public/journals/jama/jamahome.htm*)
MEDLINE Journals Which Offer Full Text
  (*http://www.ncbi.nlm.nih.gov/PubMed/fulltext.html*)
MEDLINE Journals Which Offer Full Text [Name]
  (*http://www.ncbi.nlm.nih.gov/PubMed/fulltextpub.html*)
Monthly Catalog of Publications (MOCAT)
  (*http://www.access.gpo.gov/su_docs/dpos/adpos400.html*)
National Institutes of Health — Institutes, Centers, and Divisions
  (*http://www.nih.gov/icd/*)
National Institutes of Health (NIH) (*http://www.nih.gov/*)
National Institutes of Health — Online Journals
  (*http://www.nih.gov/science/journals/*)
National Institute of Standards (NIST) (*http://www.nist.gov/labs2.htm*)

The National Science Foundation (*http://www.nsf.gov/*)
Nature — International Weekly Journal of Science (*http://www.nature.com/*)
New England Journal of Medicine On-line — Home Page
    (*http://www.nejm.org/*)
The NIH Center for Scientific Review (CSR) Home Page
    (*http://www.drg.nih.gov/*)
NIST WWW Home Page (*http://www.nist.gov/*)
Pharmaceutical Information Network Home Page
    (*http://pharminfo.com/pin_hp.html*)
Welcome to PubMed (MEDLINE #1) (*http://www.ncbi.nlm.nih.gov/PubMed/*)
White House Office of Science and Technology Policy
    (*http://www.whitehouse.gov/OSTP.html*)
World Health Organization WWW Home Page (*http://www.who.ch/*)

4. Science Sites

Archaeology — ArchNet (*http://www.lib.uconn.edu/ArchNet/*)
The British Journal for the Philosophy of Science
    (*http://www.oup.co.uk/jnls/list/phisci/*)
Community of Science (MEDLINE #3) (*http://muscat.gdb.org/repos/medl/*)
Earth Sciences & Map Library Home Page (*http://library.berkeley.edu/EART/*)
Healthnet (MEDLINE #4)
    (*http://www.healthgate.com/HealthGate/MEDLINE/search.shtml*)
History of the Light Microscope
    (*http://fammed.utmem.edu/sf/hist/hist_mic.htm*)
Human Genome Project Information
    (*http://www.ornl.gov/TechResources/Human_Genome/home.html*)
IMSS — Institute and Museum of History of Science — Florence, Italy
    (*http://galileo.imss.firenze.it/*)
Library of Congress Home Page (*http://lcweb.loc.gov/homepage/lchp.html*)
Microscopes (*http://www.utmb.edu/mml/scopes/welcome.htm*)
MIT: Technology Review (*http://web.mit.edu/techreview/*)
National Academy of Sciences (*http://www.nas.edu/*)
National Museum of Science and Industry (*http://www.nmsi.ac.uk/*)
The National Science Foundation (*http://www.nsf.gov/*)
Scientific American (*http://www.sciam.com/*)
The World–Wide Web Virtual Library: Subject Catalog
    (*http://vlib.stanford.edu/Overview.html*)
WWWVL History of Science, Technology and Medicine — Overview
    (*http://www.asap.unimelb.edu.au/hstm/hstm_ove.htm*)

TABLE OF CASES

Dailey, People v., 15 Ill.App.3d 214, 304 N.E.2d 156 (1973)
Daubert v. Merrell Dow Pharmaceuticals, Inc., 509 U.S. 579, 113 S.Ct. 2786 (1993)
Davenport, People v., 11 Cal.4th 1171, 47 Cal.Rptr.2d 800 (1995)
Davenport, People v., 11 Cal.4th 1171, 906 P.2d 1068, 47 Cal.Rptr.2d 800 (1996)
Davis v. Mississippi, 394 U.S. 721, 724, 89 S.Ct. 1394, 22 L.Ed.2d 676 (1969)
Davis, People v., 217 Mich. 661, 187 N.W. 390 (1922)
Davis, People v., 185 Ill.2d 317, 706 N.E.2d 473 (1999)
Davis, People v., 304 Ill.App.3d 427, 710 N.E.2d 1251 (1999)
De La Cruz v. Johnson, 134 F.3d 299 (5th Cir. (Tex.) 1998)
Dedge, State v., 723 So.2d 322 (Fla.Ct.App. 1998)
Delucca, State v., 325 N.J. Super 376, 739 A.2d 455 (1999)
Diaz, People v., 169 Ill.App.3d 66, 522 N.E.2d 1386 (1988)
Digirolamo, People v., 179 Ill.2d 24, 688 N.E.2d 116 (1997)
Dunn, People v., 306 Ill.App.3d 75, 713 N.E.2d 568 (First Dist. 1999)
Eason v. United States, 687 A.2d 922(D.C. Ct. App. 1996)
East, State v., 481 S.E.2d 652 (N.C.Sp.Ct. 1997)
Eley v. State, 288 Md. 548, 419 A.2d 384 (1980)
Ex parte Freda S. Mowbray a/k/a Susie Mowbray, 943 S.W.2d 461 (Ct. Cr. App. Tex. 1997)
Fishback v. People, 851 P.2d 884, 887 n. 6, 893 (Colo.1993)
Fleming, State v., 350 N.C. 109, 512 S.E.2d 720 (1999)
Flores, State v., 595 N.W.2d 860 (Minn. 1999)
Floudiotis v. State, 726 A.2d 1196 (Del.Sup. Ct. 1999)
Frank, State v., 1999 WL 793677 (Neb.App.)
Fukusaku, State v., 85 Hawaii 462, 946 P.2d 32 (1997)
Fulminante, State v., 193 Ariz. 485, 975 P.2d 75 (1999)
Gattis, State v., 697 A.2d 1174 (Del.Sup.Ct. 1997)
Genrich, People v., 928 P.2d 799 (Colo.Ct.App. 1996)
Gomez, People v., 215 Ill.App.3d 208, 158 Ill.Dec. 709, 574 N.E.2d 822 (1991)
Goney, State v., 1999 WL 960585 (Ohio App. 2 Dist.)
Hanson, People v., 31 Ill.2d 31, 198 N.E.2d 815 (1964)
Haque, State v., 726 A.2d 205 (Me. 1999)
Harris, State v., 708 So.2d 1169 (La.App. 1998)
Hart, State v., 94 Ohio App.3d 665, 641 N.E.2d 755 (1994)
Hebel, People v., 174 Ill.App.3d 1, 527 N.E.2d 1362 (1988)
Henne, People v., 165 Ill.App.3d 315, 518 N.E.2d 1276 (1988)
Higgenbotham, State v., 264 Kan. 593, 957 P.2d 416 (Kan. 1998)
Hill, State v., 73 Ohio St.3d 433, 653 N.E.2d 271(1995)
Hinjosa v. State, 1999 WL 974918 (Tex.Crim.App.)
Hooker v. State, 716 So.2d 1104 (Miss.Sp.Ct. 1998)
Horinek v. State, 977 S.W.2d 696 (Tex.App.-Fort Worth 1998)
Howard, People v., 130 Ill.App.3d 967, 474 N.E.2d 1345 (1985)
In re Petition of Louis Vazquez v. Howard Safir, 673 N.Y.S.2d 12 (1998)

Noascono, People v., 80 Ill.App.3d 921, 400 N.E.2d 720 (1980)

Noel, State v., 157 N.J. 141, 723 A.2d 602 (1997)

Noel, State v., 157 N.J. 141, 723 A.2d 602 (1999)

Noel, State v., 303 N.J.Super. 435, 697 A.2d 157 (1997)

Nyhuis, State v., 906 S.W.2d 405 (Mo.Ct.App. 1995)

Ordway, State v., 261 Kan. 776, 934 P.2d 94 (1997)

Pace v. State, 1999 WL 1087018 (Ga. 1999)

Patterson, State v., 587 N.W.2d 45 (Minn.Sp.Ct. 1999)

Penman, State v., 964 P.2d 1157 (Utah App. 1998)

Perkins, State v., 1999 WL 334974 (Ohio App. 1 Dist.)

Pilot, State v., 595 N.W.2d 511 (Sp.Ct.Minn. 1999)

Pipkin v. State, 1997 WL 749441 (Tenn.Crim.App. 1997)

Planagan, People v., 65 Cal.App.2d 371, 150 P.2d 927 (1944)

Polite, State v., No. 84-525 (14th Judicial Circuit, Fla. Jun. 10, 1985)

Porter v. State, 519 So.2d 1230, 1232 (Miss.1988)

Profit, State v., 591 N.W.2d 451 (Minn.Sp.Ct. 1999)

Pruitt, People v., 16 Ill.App.3d 930, 307 N.E.2d 142 (1974)

Pruitt v. State, 270 Ga. 745, 514 S.E.2d 639 (1999)

Quince v. State, 721 So.2d 245 (Ala.Crim.App. 1998)

Regan v. State, 1999 WL 1980973 (Tex.Crim.App.)

Rhodes, People v., 85 Ill.2d 241, 249, 422 N.E.2d 605, 608 (1981)

Ricketts, People v., 109 Ill.App.3d 992, 441 N.E.2d 384 (1982)

Robbins, People v., 21 Ill.App.3d 317, 315 N.E.2d 198 (1974)

Robedeaux v. State, 866 P.2d 417 (Ct.Crim.App.Ok. 1994)

Robinson, People v., 157 Ill.2d 68, 623 N.E.2d 352(1993)

Ross v. State, 231 Ga.App. 793, 499 S.E.2d 642 (Ga. Ct. App. 1998)

Schoolcraft v. People, 117 Ill. 271, 7 N.E. 649 (1886)

Scott, State v., 1999 WL 547460 (Tenn.Crim.App.)

See, People v. Donahue, 50 Ill.App.3d 392, 394, 365 N.E.2d 710 (1977)

Sexton, State v., 311 N.J.Super. 70, 709 A.2d 288(1997)

Smallwood v. State, 907 P. 2d 217 (Ct.Crim.App.Okla. 1995)

Smith, State v., 909 P.2d 236 (Ut.Sp.Ct. 1995)

Smith v. State, 1998 WL 345353 (Tenn.Crim.App.)

Smoote v. State, 708 N.E.2d 1 (Ind.Sp.Ct. 1999)

Southern, State v., 980 P.2d 3 (Mont.Sp.Ct. 1999)

State v. Delgros, 104 Ohio App.3d 531, 662 N.E.2d 858 (1995)

State v. Montgomery, 341 N.C. 553, 461 S.E.2d 732 (1995)

State v., Parsons, 1995 WL 29526 (Ohio App. 6 Dist.)

Suggs v. State, 322 Ark. 40, 907 S.W.2d 124 (1995)

Sutherland, People v., 155 Ill.2d 1, 610 N.E.2d 1 (1992)

Taylor v. Hannigan, 1998 WL 239640 (D.Kan.)

Tenerelli, State v., 598 N.W.2d 668 (Minn.Sp.Ct. 1999)

Thames v. State, 221 Miss. 573, 73 So.2d 134 (Miss.1954)

The Almighty Four Hundred, People v., 287 Ill.App.3d 123, 677 N.E.2d 1332 (1997)

Index